The Responsible Software Engineer
Selected Readings in IT Professionalism

Springer
London
Berlin
Heidelberg
New York
Barcelona
Budapest
Hong Kong
Milan
Paris
Santa Clara
Singapore
Tokyo

Colin Myers, Tracy Hall and Dave Pitt (Eds)

The Responsible Software Engineer

Selected Readings in IT Professionalism

With 15 Figures

Springer

Colin Myers, BA (Hons), MSc
Tracy Hall, BA (Hons), MSc

School of Computer Science and Information Systems Engineering,
University of Westminster,
115 New Cavendish Street, London W1M 8JS, UK

Dave Pitt, BA (Hons), MSc

Worldwide Information Systems, NCR,
915 High Road, N. Finchley, London N12 8QJ, UK

ISBN 3-540-76041-5 Springer-Verlag Berlin Heidelberg New York

British Library Cataloguing in Publication Data
The Responsible Software Engineer : selected readings in IT
    professionalism
    1. Software engineering 2. Software engineering -
    Professional ethics
    I. Myers, Colin II. Hall, Tracy III. Pitt, Dave
    005.1
ISBN 3540760415

Library of Congress Cataloging-in-Publication Data
The Responsible Software Engineer : selected readings in IT
professionalism / Colin Myers, Tracy Hall, and Dave Pitt (eds.).
        p.   cm.
    Includes bibliographical references.
    ISBN 3-540-76041-5
    1. Software engineering. I. Myers, Colin, 1953-   .
    II. Hall, Tracy, 1965-   . III. Pitt, Dave, 1953-   .
QA76.758.R47   1996   96-9538
005.1'023--dc20   CIP

Typesetting: Camera ready by editors
Printed and bound at the Athenæum Press Ltd., Gateshead, Tyne and Wear
34/3830-543210 Printed on acid-free paper

Contents

List of Authors

Amer Al-Rawas   University of Sussex, Brighton BN1 9QH, UK
                       ameral@cogs.susx.ac.uk
John Betts   University of the West of England, Bristol BS1 6QY, UK
                       John.Betts@csm.uwe.ac.uk
Paul Beynon-Davies   University of Glamorgan, Pontypridd, CF37 1DL, UK
                       pbeynon@comp.glamorgan.ac.uk
Andy Bissett   Sheffield Hallam University, Sheffield S11 8HD, UK
                       a.k.bissett@shu.ac.uk
J Kenneth Blundell   University of Missouri , Kansas City, Missouri 64110, USA
                       blundell@cstp.umkc.edu
Frank Bott   University of Wales, Aberystwyth SY23 3DB, UK
                       mfb@aber.ac.uk
Geoff Busby   GEC Computer Services, Great Baddow CM2 8HN, UK
                       fax: 01245-475244
Tony Cowling   University of Sheffield, Sheffield S10 2TN, UK
                       a.cowling@dcs.shef.ac.uk
Dai Davis   Eversheds, Leeds LS1 2JB, UK
                       100067,1161@compuserve.com
Ray Dawson   Loughborough University, Loughborough LE11 3TU, UK
                       r.j.dawson@lboro.ac.uk
Tom DeMarco   Atlantic Systems Guild, Camden, Maine 04843, USA
                       tdemarco@shore.net
Steve Easterbrook   NASA/WYU SRL, Fairmont, WV 26554, USA
                       steve@atlantis.ivv.nasa.gov
Gary Ford   SEI, Carnegie-Mellon, Pittsburgh, Pennsylvania 15121, USA
                       ford@sei.cmu.edu
Craig Gaskell   University of Hull, Hull HU6 7RX, UK
                       c.gaskell@dcs.hull.ac.uk
Norman Gibbs   Guildford College, Greensboro, North Carolina 27410, USA
                       gibbsne@rascal.guilford.edu
Heather Gill   IBM Hursley Park, Winchester SO21 2JN, UK
                       heather_gill@uk.ibm.com
Don Gotterbarn   East Tennesse State University, Johnson City 37640, USA
                       gotterbarn@etsu.east-tenn-st.edu
Tracy Hall   University of Westminster, London W1M 8JS, UK
                       hallt@wmin.ac.uk
Heather Heathfield   Manchester Metropolitan University, Manchester M1 5GD, UK
                       h.heathfield@doc.mmu.ac.uk
Kari Marie Helle   Work Research Institute, Box 8171 - 0034 Oslo, Norway
                       fax: 0047-22-568918
Mary Lou Hines   University of Missouri, Kansas City, Missouri 64110, USA
                       hines@cstp.umkc.edu
Duncan Langford   University of Kent, Canterbury CT2 7NF, UK
                       d.langford@ukc.ac.uk

Anne Leeming   City University, London EC2Y 8BH , UK
                        a.m.c.leeming@city.ac.uk
Gillian Lovegrove   Staffordshire University, Stafford ST18 ODG, UK
                        G.L.Lovegrove@soc.staffs.ac.uk
John Madsen   ISD, Dept for E&E, Sheffield S1 4PQ, UK
                        fax: 0114-259-4580
Gene McGuire   American University, Washington, DC 20016-8116 USA
                        mcguire@american.edu
Geoff McMullen   BCS, Swindon SN1 1HJ, UK
                        hg08@cityscape.co.uk
Robert Melford   Mission Viejo, California 92692, USA
                        ir002121@interramp.com
Frank Milsom   Bournemouth University, Poole, Dorset BH12 5BB, UK
                        fmilsom@bournemouth.ac.uk
Colin Myers   University of Westminster, London W1M 8JS, UK
                        colin@wmin.ac.uk
Ron Newsham   University of Derby, Derby DE22 1BG, UK
                        r.j.newsham@derby.ac.uk
Dave Pitt   NCR, London N12 8QJ, UK
                        dave.pitt@unitedkingdom.ncr.com
John Race   Expert Witness, 12 Thames St, Abingdon OX14 3HZ, UK
                        j.race@open.ac.uk
Lesley Rackley   University of the West of England, Bristol BS1 6QY, UK
                        Lesley.Rackley@csm.uwe.ac.uk
Simon Rogerson   DeMontfort University, Leicester LE1 9BH, UK
                        srog@dmu.ac.uk
Stuart Shapiro   Open University, Milton Keynes MK7 6AA, UK
                        s.s.shapiro@open.ac.uk
Jawed Siddiqui   Sheffield Hallam University, Sheffield S11 8HD, UK
                        j.i.siddiqi@shu.ac.uk
Mike Stranks   City University of Hong Kong, Kowloon, Hong Kong
                        csmbs@cityu.edu.hk
Armstrong Takang   University of Hull, Hull HU6 7RX, UK
                        a.a.takang@dcs.hull.ac.uk
J Barrie Thompson   University of Sunderland, Sunderland SR1 3SD, UK
                        barrie.thompson@sunderland.ac.uk
Julian Webb   University of the West of England, Bristol BS1 6QY, UK
                        Julian.Webb@csm.uwe.ac.uk
Christine Whitehouse   Staffordshire University, Stafford ST18 ODG, UK
                        C.Whitehouse@soc.staffs.ac.uk
John Wilkes   Anglia Polytechnic University, Cambridge CB1 1PT UK
                        jwilkes@bridge.anglia.ac.uk
Sue Williams   Staffordshire University, Stafford ST18 ODG, UK
                        S.Williams@soc.staffs.ac.uk
Jeremy Wyatt   Imperial Cancer Research Fund, London WC2A 3PX, UK
                        jeremy@biu.icnet.uk

Acknowledgments

This book is a collection of essays on professional attitudes, awareness and responsibility in the IT and Software Engineering industry. We thank everyone concerned with the evolution and production of this book, and especially we thank the individual chapter authors and Tom DeMarco for his most professional foreword. However, the views expressed in any particular chapter are not necessarily those of other contributors or the editors: the book is intended to raise debate, and we would be disappointed if the book did not lead to some, healthy, disagreement. We encourage all comments to be made directly to the authors of individual chapters.

By contrast, this is the place to acknowledge our fellow professionals, and to thank, on behalf of the individual chapter authors, the following: Fretwell-Downing Data Systems of Sheffield for providing sponsorship that facilitated Tony Cowling's contribution; the National Council for Education Technology, the members of the Women in Technology Foundation, Judith Doughty of UCAS, Jacqueline Coxson and David Knight at Bournemouth University, CSU Publications, Hampshire Education Authority, Karen Murry and the many other women at IBM Hursley who provided valuable information for Heather Gill; Robin Jeeps, Martin Pickering and Keith Bywood for their helpful comments to John Madsen; Gordon Hukins and Judy Wateridge, and the rest of the Group Project team and students at Bournemouth University for their contribution to Frank Milsom; Professor Ken Jukes' input to the chapter by Julian Webb, Lesley Rackley and John Betts, and the many other silent midwives to the rest of the chapters in this book.

Finally, we take this opportunity to thank the members of the PASE96 programme review committee, for their constructive comments on initial drafts of these chapters: Mike Allen, BCS; Dr Alfs Berztiss, University of Pittsburgh; Elizabeth Duff, University of Westminster; Charles Easteal, IT Consultant; Dr Duncan Langford, University of Kent; Anne Leeming, City University London; Dr Gillian Lovegrove, University of Staffordshire; John Madsen, Department of Education and Employment; Ron McQuaker, BCS; Ellen Neighbour, Women into Information Technology Foundation; Dr. Isobel Nicholson, University of Central Lancashire; Edmund O'Shaughnessy, DRA Portsdown; Dr Pat Pearce, University of Plymouth; Dr Shari Lawrence Pfleeger, Systems Software Inc; Mark Priestley, University of Westminster; Paul Quintas, Open University; Simon Rogerson, De Montfort University; Dr Rupert Simpson, University of Central England; David Wilson, Sydney University of Technology; Prof Derek Wilson, IEE; and, particularly Dr Wendy Stokes, London Guildhall University.

Foreword

You might expect that a person invited to contribute a foreword to a book on the subject of professionalism[1] would himself be a professional of exemplary standing. I am gladdened by that thought, but also disquieted. The disquieting part of it is that if I am a professional, I must be a professional something, but what? As someone who has tried his best for the last thirty years to avoid doing anything twice, I lack one of the most important characteristics of a professional, the dedicated and persistent pursuit of a single direction.

For the purposes of this foreword, it would be handy if I could think of myself as a professional abstractor. That would allow me to offer up a few useful abstractions about professionalism, patterns that might illuminate the essays that follow. I shall try to do this by proposing three successively more complex models of professionalism, ending up with one that is discomfortingly soft, but still, the best approximation I can make of what the word means to me.

The first of these models I shall designate *Model Zero.* I intend a pejorative sense to this name, since the attitude represented by Model Zero is retrograde and offensive ...but nonetheless common. In this model, the word "professionalism" is a simple surrogate for compliant uniformity.

In Model Zero organizations, you may be considered unprofessional because of the way you dress, or wear your hair (either longer than God intended for males, or shorter than God intended for females), or because of what you post on your walls. You can definitely be thought unprofessional for questioning authority or contradicting Revealed Truth. Popping popcorn in the microwave is unprofessional in Model Zero companies, presumably because it gives the workplace an unprofessional odour. Professionalism seems to have to do with almost anything except getting quality work done.

The Model Zero manager is demonstrating a compulsive need for uniformity, something that we encounter from time to time in gardeners. Here I refer to that meticulous kind of gardener who would pluck and throw away a perfect carrot (perhaps the healthiest one in the garden) just because it is growing an inch or two outside the row. Such a gardener seems to have forgotten what the purpose of a garden is: to grow plants that are as big and succulent and as healthy as they can be. Or perhaps he/she has a variant purpose for the garden: to be a living demonstration of the Gardener's dominion over the land. So too the Model Zero manager.

One Model Zero company I know declared all facial hair unprofessional. This was in the 1970s, a time when beards and moustaches were largely out of favour. Well, that's not entirely true. Beards and moustaches were out of favour among white men. Among black men, they were ubiquitous. And so the proscription against facial hair seemed (to me at least) to be implying that blackness was unprofessional. Of course, nothing of the sort was ever said by that company's management.

---

[1] This foreword was adapted by Tom DeMarco from his Keynote address to the 1996 Conference on Professional Awareness in Software Engineering. Foreword ©1996 by Tom DeMarco

It is tempting to laugh at Model Zero management, since today we have mostly moved beyond these trivial obsessions with surface uniformity. But Model Zero is still alive and well, still requiring compliant uniformity of employees, and still calling it "professionalism". As you read these words, I speculate there some poor soul receiving a managerial dressing down at a company near your for asking a question about some kind of toxin that is being voided by the company into the local waters each morning at 4am. "Yes", the manager acknowledges, "we do release rather minute quantities of Strontium-90 before dawn each day. It would however be **extremely** unprofessional of you to mention this to local authorities, or, worst of all, to the press."

In most organizations there is still a bit of residual Model Zero thinking about professionalism. Before letting your own company off the hook, try taking the following test: Would you or your management be at all inclined to think it was unprofessional to cry in the workplace? Crying, of course, is an extremely unnatural act for about half the human race. For the other half it is the most natural thing in the world. The idea that crying might be an example of unprofessional behaviour is little more than Model Zero's hidden assertion that being female is also unprofessional.

Model Zero, for all its popularity, is just an aberration. The word "professionalism" must certainly mean something more than knuckling under and not making waves.

A substantially more satisfying notion of professionalism is embodied in the next model. In this view, professionalism is made up of three characteristics. Since the words describing these characteristics all begin with the letter *P*, I refer to this as a *3-P model*. The three characteristics are:

1. **Proficient**: Whatever it is that a professional does, he/she must do it with deftness and agility, with skill born of long practice.

2. **Permanent**: The long practice comes from the permanence of the professional's calling. We've all encountered actors who waited tables while waiting for a part to come along. They may be professional actors, but they are certainly not professional waiters (there are such things), since they aren't permanently dedicated to that endeavour.

3. **Professing**: Finally there must be some act of involvement by which the professional declares his/her intention to be, now and forever, a part of one chosen calling. The act may be a public ceremony or it may be a simple, private resolution of the form:

   (name of profession) *equals* me.

Some years ago I came across a very beautiful example of a professing. It was the statement carved by a Scottish fisherman over the hearth of his storm-tossed seaside home. The words he carved were these:

"It is no will-o-the-wisp that I have followed here."

It was intention, not chance, that led him where he went. This is the declarative act of a professional.

The *3-P Model* still lacks something, an ethical dimension. People we think of as professionals are governed by some kind of code. They know their profession gives them opportunities for wrong-doing, and they know what they will and will not do for ethical reasons. I propose to embody this idea in a fourth P-term:

4. **Promise-keeping**: Professional make certain promises to themselves (sometimes to the public at large) about what they will and won't do. Professionals keep those promises.

I have separated promise-keeping in this fashion, making it the distinguishing characteristic of true professionalism as embodied by the *4-P Model*, because it is promise-keeping that, most of all, divides professionalism in our field from its opposite.

Even in the traditional professions like medicine and law and clergy, promise-keeping is the most complex of the trappings of a professional. It is the one where most lapses of professionalism occur. Consider a typical lapse in each of these traditional callings:

- a doctor blabs about Mr. So-and-So's incredible venereal wart

- a lawyer tells a friend that he has been left out of his uncle's will

- a minister gives away the identity of a man who has confessed to lusting after his neighbour's teenage daughter

Note first of all that each of these is a violation of an implicit promise. When you go to your doctor, legal advisor or cleric, you generally impart some private information that might conceivably be used against your interest. You almost never think to exact an explicit promise from such a professional not to violate your confidentiality. You take the professional's promise-keeping for granted. This is potentially dangerous ground, because the very basis of your transaction is tied up in soft perceptions of correct behaviour. You and your consulting professional may well understand the root matter in the same way, but that leaves nearly infinite possibility for misunderstandings about borderline cases. Yet, in spite of this, implicit promises are rarely broken by professional people, and almost never by casual error. The reason for this is that professionals take their promises very seriously; they are in a constant state of ethical introspection. I shall come back to this idea.

A second observation about the three example lapses I cited above is that each one has to do with a failure to keep confidential information confidential. I find this rather troubling, because the ugliest Model Zero example I related , the one about the employee being enjoined not to leak sensitive information to authorities or to the press, is also about keeping confidential information confidential. If you draw the general rule that a professional's promise-keeping obligation is as simple as "don't blab what you learned in confidence" then you condone the employee's silence about toxic pollution at the same time you celebrate doctors and lawyers and clergy and their firm resolve not to compromise those who confide in them.

There are no simple, general rules in ethics; ethics is about values and value conflict, philosophy and morality, and a willingness and capability to confront intricate and convoluted conundrums. The Ten Commandments and the Golden Rule may get you to Heaven, but they won't (all by themselves) make you an ethical promise-keeper. The only thing that will do that is to keep your self in a permanent state of ethical introspection. In order to make it clear what I mean by this introspection, consider its opposite. The most familiar form of this opposite is what I call:

The Fatal Premise: Evil is done by evil people; I am not an
                      evil person and therefore I cannot do evil.

The Fatal Premise gives you an ethical blank check: If you did it, it must be OK. It is my learned opinion that about half the world's population believes the Fatal Premise. One who is governed by this premise is neither ethical nor unethical, but a ethical non-participant. Such a person can never be a true professional, because his or her introspection mechanism is disarmed.

The Russian author Aleksandr Solzhenitsyn offers a counter to the Fatal Premise in the following quote:

"The line separating good and evil passes not between states nor between classes nor between parties [individuals] either, but through the middle of every human heart."

To be an ethical human being you need to be aware of your capacity to be evil, your dark side. To the extent that it is our business to foster professionalism, we need to focus mostly on helping people get past the Fatal Premise so they can deal with the possibility of their own evil. All meaningful evil on earth is done by good people, not by evil people. The capacity to do evil is in each one of us.

I assert that the 4-P Model, as I have described it, defines professionalism at its best. It describes ideal behaviour not just of doctors and lawyers and clerics, but of all the true professionals of this era and eras past. It embraces nurses and therapists, carpenters and farmers and bricklayers. It makes room for the Knights of Malta, the Engineers who built the Roman viaducts, Renaissance artists like Michaelangelo and Bernini, the Egyptian doctors who invented the first science of medicine. They were all professionals to the extent that they passed the four P-tests: they were proficient at what they did, they were permanent in their involvement, they professed their dedication and they had a code of promises arbitrated by a permanent ethical sense.

Since the vocations I've mentioned all have a certain *cachet*, I might mention that professionalism need not be limited to those who practice some sophisticated or highly respectable trade. Consider a man at bottom of any conceivable hierarchy: Jeeves. He too passes the four P-tests. His permanence is legendary (unthinkable that he might take up a position in retailing, for example), he is deft at each of the tasks he undertakes, he has a code of conduct that is his constant concern, and he has solemnly declared his dedication to his calling. The man even belongs to a professional society, the Ganymede Club. There can be no doubt that Jeeves is a professional.

I end by asking you to consider a final candidate class for professionalism: If there is room in the professional ranks for butlers, why not managers?

Since I have been fortunate enough to work under seven great managers in my days, I know that there is such a thing as a professional manager. There are certainly many managers who satisfy three of the four P-tests: they are proficient, permanent and good promise keepers. Curiously, in management, the most conspicuous missing element is one that we almost take for granted among software professionals at the lower levels: the professing act. Many managers can't bring themselves to profess to be managers. One who manages a group of engineers, tends to think of himself or herself as an engineer; one who manages a group of physicians tends to think of himself or herself as a physician.

This unwillingness to profess is a sad consequence of our persistent and ignorant derogation of the management role. The constant assertion that management is mere "overhead", potential fat for the next trimming, has had its effect on managers themselves. We are breeding a generation of managers that dares not manage. A manager who manages might get downsized; better instead to pitch in and do some of the work of the people being managed. There is (so this line of thinking goes) nobility in the work, but no nobility in management of that work.

This is pure poppycock. If the work is noble, the catalytic function that is management of that work is even more noble. We need to assert and re-assert the essential respectability of what managers do. It is not a far-fetched contention that management is a noble calling. What could be more admirable, more professional, than the manager's most essential tasks: guiding, forming, coaching, and inspiring people, building healthy corporate culture and safe and productive teams?

We will never succeed in building professional awareness among programmers and analysts and designers and testers and integrators, unless we also succeed in fostering a professional awareness among their managers.

Chapter 1
Introduction

1.1 The Responsible Professional

We introduce this book with a discussion of why we need to consider professionalism within the software industry. Section 1.2 explores in more detail what we mean by term "professionalism", Section 1.3 asks how "aware" is the responsible software engineer, and Section 1.4 presents a "roadmap" to the rest of the book.

1.1.1 The need for professionalism

As the demand for good quality software has grown so also has the demand for good quality software engineers. In part, this has manifest itself as a demand for better technology and more people capable of using it. It has also meant that as the software industry matures it has recognized the need for a greater professionalism amongst its practitioners. Neither customers nor developers want software that has been produced unprofessionally, as this software is likely to be of poor quality. Thus, to gain customer confidence, (i.e. to possess a sustainable professional image), software practitioners need to possess the following:

- Technical competence

- Professional responsibility for the software they develop

- Professional responsibility to themselves and society

In other words, to improve software, both actual and perceived levels of software engineering professionalism need to be improved.

This book will not discuss technical "silver bullets" nor even managerial ones: we believe that the current level of technical achievement is actually quite high with respect to the tasks demanded of software developers, especially compared to longer-established professions. Rather, we discuss what is necessary for a software engineer to behave with professional *responsibility*, such that technical skills can be sensibly harnessed, and that the industry can be viewed with respect.

Despite the fact that the software industry recognizes the need, its practitioners have been slow to address many aspects of professionalism and reluctant to establish themselves as a traditional 'profession' such as medicine or law. This is, in part, because the Software Engineering community is so new, and also because there is much debate as to which model of 'professionalism' is appropriate. For example, should it attempt to adopt the medical model, with rigid standards of behaviour and a restrictive entry mechanism, or perhaps a looser model such as that of the electrical engineers? Indeed, should it adopt a professional model at all and what role should the professional bodies play?

This book discusses these issues and asks related questions such as: how professional is the profession; how accountable is it and should it be; what hinders professionalism; and how can we train for professionalism?

1.1.2   The isolated professional

An important theme of this book, is the threat of professional isolation. This is manifest in three ways: firstly, when software engineers adopt a too narrow perspective on what is well-known; secondly, when they adopt a "we know best" approach, and thirdly when they fail to make a proper effort to discover the viewpoints of others.

Having a narrow focus, is perhaps inevitable in all professions, with the common example of poor communications arising from the over-use of jargon (useful terminology for insiders but gibberish to outsiders). As many of the authors in this book observe, the dangers of poor communication (and a consequent lack of awareness) may lead to poor quality systems, dangerous systems and a lack of equal opportunities within the workforce. It may also lead to delusions of grandeur about the profession. It is worth bearing in mind that the world outside of software engineering will probably not have heard of the insiders' leading experts and will probably not hold any great interest or value in the insiders' pressing technical problems.

We do not need to expand on the dangers inherent in a "we know best" approach, and we believe that the responsible professional will generally be on guard against such self-conceit. Of course, we do recognize that this may be one side-effect caused by training for, and obtaining, technical excellence.

The most insidious danger, is that of having a "head-in-the-sand" attitude (what we might label the "ostrich of professionalism"). It is this attitude that leads us to be happy with what we have achieved *irrespective of its ethical implications*. This is an ignorance of closed eyes and minds with regards to the priorities and demands of the outside world. It is all too easy to be fascinated by the technical problem and ignore the social or moral consequences.

1.2   What is *Professionalism?*

The subtitle of this book is *Selected Writings in IT Professionalism*, but one of the most difficult things to pin down is the meaning of the words *profession*, *professional* and *professionalism*; in many ways, they appear just as difficult to define as *love* or *God*. Indeed, it is probable that we are confronted with words that have several meanings, according to user and context, and that it is futile to attempt a single definition. Later in this book, various authors have tried to give precise meanings of these "p-words", citing both dictionary definitions and descriptions provided by professional bodies. However, we note that giving a definition is generally easier than getting everyone to agree on that meaning or its implications. This is exemplified by the following small selection of quotes about professional behaviour and responsibilities.

The first three quotes all come from the sports' pages of *The Observer* newspaper.

> ". . . his ruthless professionalism was evident as Yorkshire prolonged their second innings . . .

"30 years ago Bobby Moore was the captain of the most successful sports team England has ever produced. His coolly professional leadership was an obvious factor in the acquisition of the World Cup."

" '...when I play for France I try to treat it as a bit of a joke, because I'm best when I'm playing for pleasure.' ...Spoken like a true professional."

Our next quote comes from an IBM advert:

"It can keep you up at night, the thought of some pubescent hacker or, worse, a paid professional, creeping through your company's most valuable information."

The following all come from an interview with Denny O'Neil, a writer of graphic novels, talking about the responsibilities of his work [O'Neil80]. His comments are particularly interesting in that the image of software engineer often parallels that of the comics-reading "anorak" or "nerd".

"Professionally, people are too tied to [graphic novels] ...the focus is a bit narrow. The whole field ... would benefit from widening it."

"...being a professional ...meeting deadlines ..."

"A. — I don't think it worked
Q. — Why did you do [it] then?
A. — Because I'm a professional, and I'm told to do it. Unless it's something that I have really strong moral problems with ..."

And even crime writers have something to say on the matter:

" 'I'm surprised Haley didn't shoot him'
'I gather there were professional guns about. Haley was never more than a semi-professional' " [Ross McDonald, *Far Side of the Dollar*]

We conclude this section with a shift in emphasis, with two quotes reminding us about professional *responsibility*, both towards ourselves and towards others. The first comes from the GNU Manifesto:

"Many programmers are unhappy about the commercialization of system software. It may enable them to make more money, but it requires them to feel in conflict with other programmers in general rather than feel as comrades. The fundamental act of friendship among programmers is the sharing of programs; marketing arrangements now typically used essentially forbid programmers to treat others as friends. The purchaser of software must choose between friendship and obeying the law. Naturally, many decide that friendship is more important. But those who believe in law often do not feel at ease with either choice. They become cynical and think that programming is just a way of making money." [Stallman85]

And finally, a warning from *The Devil's Dictionary* which defines *responsibility* as:

> "a detachable burden easily shifted to the shoulders of God, Fate, Fortune,
> Law, or one's neighbour" [Bierce11].

1.3 How *Aware* is the Responsible Professional?

In this section, we look further at the level of professional awareness amongst software engineers. In particular, we give an overview of a survey taken at the 1996 Westminster Conference on Professional Awareness in Software Engineering (PASE1996). We believe that the attendees at such a conference can be described as responsible, many have written on professionalism, belong to professional bodies or interest groups, and are in positions of responsibility. We discovered was that even in this body of software professionals, who were very concerned about their profession, there was a lack of awareness of legal responsibilities and professional obligations, and marked disagreement about professional ethics. There is clearly need for positive action by education, industry and the professional bodies.

We now present selected questions from the survey and an overview of responses. We do not claim that this survey is fully representational, and have deliberately not attempted quantitative analysis. Rather, we encourage readers to think and talk about the issues raised here, and see how these issues are addressed in the rest of this book.

1.3.1 Survey results

Professional Bodies and Codes of Conduct

This part of the survey was intended to discover professional awareness of codes of conduct and ethics, and attitudes towards their goals. We started with the question:

Which of the following rules are included in the BCS Code of Professional Conduct?
1. Members will contribute to society and human well-being
2. Members will avoid harm to others
3. Members will honour confidentiality
4. Members will strive to achieve the highest quality, effectiveness and dignity in both the process and products of professional work
5. Members will articulate and support policies that protect the dignity of users and others affected by a computer system

Actually, all of the above clauses are taken from the ACM Code of Conduct, (the BCS clauses tend to be more descriptive), and so the "correct" answer is *None*. However, the serious point is that professionals *must* respect these issues. Yet, drawing up such codes in a manner that they are both *unambiguous* and *useful* is not easy. This discussion forms a strong thread within the book, especially in the chapters on Professional Bodies and Accountability. In particular, Don Gotterbarn talks about the nature of Software Engineering professionalism, and gives an overview of the joint

ACM/IEEE initiative to establishing standards of practice; whilst John Wilkes and Duncan Langford both discuss the difficulty of creating and adhering to ethical codes.

If we can assume that such codes are both feasible and affordable, will they make any difference to the average software practitioner, if they did not actually belong a professional body? We asked how far people agreed with the following statement:

- **It is important to join a professional body such as the BCS or IEE in order to improve one's career prospects.**

There was no positive correlation between membership of professional bodies (28 of the 41 respondents) and the responses to this question, which were:

Level of Agreement	Responses (n = 41)
Strongly Disagree	6
Disagree	12
Neutral	8
Agree	6
Strongly Agree	5
Other	4

In the UK, there are approximately 120 000 people who could be classified as practising software engineers, by contrast the largest professional body, the BCS has a membership of about 20 000 (excluding student members and affiliates) [BCS95].

This apparent apathy contrasts strongly with the stance taken within this book; indeed it can be argued that Software Engineering will be considered a mature profession only when the majority of its practitioners belong to a professional body. This position is discussed in the two chapters by Heather Heathfield & Jeremy Wyatt and Gary Ford & Norman Gibbs, and then taken further by Robert Melford, who considers it is inevitable that software engineers will eventually require membership of a professional body and a licence to practice.

Accountability

The part of this book that deals with Accountability is divided into two threads, ethical and legal. Within the latter thread, there is a discussion of how far software engineers help or hinder the protection of personal data. It would appear, from our results, that providing data privacy is a rather hit-or-miss affair. A third of respondents were did not know whether their organization was registered under the Data Protection Act, and two-thirds had no idea who, in their organization, might be responsible!

We also asked:

- **Which of the following are exemptions from the Data Protection Act?**

The following table provides a count of respondents to each possible exemption (more than one answer was expected):

	Exemptions from the Data Protection Act	Responses (n = 41)
1.	The dead	9
2.	Domestic records	14
3.	Examination results	3
4.	National Security	26
5.	Records where disclosure would incriminate the discloser	2
6.	Records which state facts	1
7.	Records which state opinions	8
8.	Records which state intentions	7
9.	Don't know/none	7

At the time of the survey, the answer was that only **6** and **7** were not exempt. It is obvious that *National Security* would be exempt, but worrying that most professionals did not know (or could not guess) the other exemptions and inclusions. These have a direct bearing on requirements analysis and system design. For a further discussion of the implications of the Data Protection Act we refer the reader to the chapter by Elizabeth France.

The next part of the questionnaire provided a number of scenarios, (adapted from chapters by Liz Duff and Duncan Langford in [Myers95]) which were intended to demonstrate that many legal issues are not straightforward; that they are complex in law and in ethical decision-making.

- **Who do you think is responsible in the following scenario?**

  "18 months ago, you wrote for your former company, an appointments program used by a dental practice. Unfortunately, the system has a bug and approximately 5% of patients do not receive their notifications. One patient, Ms Suet, claims that due to missing her check-up, an abscess was much worse than it might have been, resulting in expensive dental work."

- **In the following scenario, who should own the copyright of the rewritten program, and have Big Bucks behaved professionally?**

  "Kim is a visiting University Lecturer has designed a Mandarin Chinese to English translation program, and asks Big Bucks Ltd to market it for her. Big Bucks tell her that there is no current UK market for her software. A year later, Kim discovers that Big Bucks are marketing a very similar program to her design."

- **In the following scenario, what action should Lee take?**

  "Lee, a new employee, expected to write original code, but was given deadlines by his line manager that appeared unrealistical. Lee soon learnt that, partly to qualify for productivity bonuses, his project team made an unofficial practice of 'borrowing' code from other teams' projects; code often already charged to previous customers."

We believe that each of these scenarios is typical of everyday events. Yet, they do not have clear-cut answers. All of the questions received diverse responses, and several resulted in many of our respondents giving more than one answer. We have already talked about the difficulty of establishing practicable codes of professional conduct, the chapters by Dai Davis and John Race explore some of the legal implications and future possibilities.

Equal Opportunities

In this part of the survey, we tried to remind people how far the software industry is from having equal opportunities for all members of the community. We asked three questions:

- **What percentage of IT senior management do women form?**

- **What percentage of IT senior management do disabled people form?**

- **What percentage of IT senior management do people from ethnic minorities form?**

Although we may quibble about the meaning of the phrase *IT senior manage-ment*, it is a fact that each of the above categories suffers from an disproportionate representation, not just at senior management level, but at all levels of management, and probably within the industry as a whole. For example, the UK percentage of women at all levels of management are less than 10% compared to double that for men [Church96].

With regards to disabled people: the severely disabled form about 4% of the population, and up to 10% of people will suffer some form of disability in their lifetime. Yet, amongst the respondents there was an overwhelming perception that less than 1% will achieve senior management. Similarly, people from the ethnic minorities form about 6% of the overall workforce [Church96], but once again, our respondents were similarly pessimistic in their estimates. We were unable to find up-to-date statistics for the actual representation of these groups but every indication is that they that have an even lower proportional representation than women.

Reasons for the low representation of women are discussed in the chapters by Heather Gill, John Wilkes (on young people and computing stereotypes), Ann Leem-ing, and that of Christine Whitehouse, Gillian Lovegrove & Sue Williams; all of whom also make positive suggestions how this inbalance may be overcome. Similar, though perhaps more controversial observations are made by Mike Stranks regarding the low BCS membership of Chinese Hong Kong citizens.

We believe that the responsibility of the software engineer regarding such groups is two-fold. Firstly, to consciously fight prejudice, and secondly to try to create a situation that helps engender equal opportunities (for the above and the many other disadvantaged people). This second attitude, in exemplified in the chapters by Geoff Busby and Kari Marie Helle, who discuss the additional problems faced by disabled members of our society, and how software engineers have helped, and may continue to help, provide the tools to ameliorate these problems.

Working Practices

The chapter by Julian Webb, Lesley Rackley & John Betts, and several other chapters in this book discuss the temptation to behave unprofessionally, for profit and because it is often appears the easier option. In this part of the survey, we were interested to ascertain how far our responsible software engineers perceived professional practice in the workplace. Our questions included:

How far have you observed your fellow professionals adhering to the following BCS rules?
1. Members shall in their professional practice safeguard public health and safety and have regard to the protection of the environment.
2. Members shall endeavour to complete work undertaken on time and to budget and shall advise their employer or client as soon as practicable if any overrun is foreseen.
3. Members should not misrepresent or withhold information on the capabilities of products, systems or services with which they are concerned or take advantage of the lack of knowledge or inexperience of others.
4. Members shall uphold the reputation of the Profession and shall seek to improve professional standards through participation in their development, use and enforcement, and shall avoid any action which will adversely affect the good standing of the Profession.

These goals are all highly desirable, if not so easy to achieve in practice or reconcile with one another. Nevertheless, it is important to see how far a professional code of conduct is followed in the workplace; both as an indicator of the level of professionalism of that particular workplace, and perhaps also as a guideline to what is actually feasible rather than idealistically desired.

We now have a confession to make: we are not sure whether our respondents answered the question that we intended to ask. From follow-up questions, it appears that several respondents answered in terms of what they *would like to see* rather than what they *have actually seen*. For this reason, we have not analysed the results, and recognize both the temptation and folly of relying upon questionnaires as a sole source of information.

Our problem was, of course, a communication problem; one that is pervasive within the computing workplace. Poor communication can lead to poor work practices, as highlit in the chapters by Paul Beynon-Davies and John Madsen. Poor communication leads to information that is neither accurate nor adequate (to borrow from a Data Protection principle) and so leads to the definition of system requirements. How this may be overcome is discussed in the chapters by Gene McGuire (talking about the appropriateness of SEI's Capability Maturity Model), and Amer Al-Rawas & Steve Easterbrook (on communication problems in general).

To conclude this snapshot of attitudes in the workplace, we give the responses to two disparate statements; the first about dress codes, the latter about the scope of Software Engineering.

A software engineer should wear a suit	
Level of Agreement	Responses (n = 41)
Strongly disagree	15
Disagree	5
Neutral	11
Agree	4
Strongly Agree	3
Other	3

Despite this strong declaration about a software engineer's sartorial obligations, we did notice that the large majority of those attending the PASE96 conference, and by inference, the large majority of the respondents, wore suits. A further discussion of attitudes towards dress codes (and many other professional issues) is given in the chapter by Craig Gaskell & and Armstrong Takang, whilst Tom DeMarco's *Foreword* has some strong criticism of dress code hypocrisy.

- **The issues in this questionnaire are actually management issues and have little to do with practising software engineers.**

Only 2 out of 41 respondents agreed or strongly agreed with this statement, whilst 26 either disagreed or strongly disagreed: not a surprising result given that the sample came from a group attending a conference on these issues. We hope that any reader who agrees with the 2 respondents will be disabused of this notion by the time they have finished the book. We also refer them to the chapters by Frank Bott, Simon Rogerson and Mary Lou Hines & J Kenneth Blundell, who remind us of the intertwining of obligations and responsibilities between practitioners, management and users.

Education and Training

Geoff McMullen's chapter introduces some the activities of the BCS, in particular he mentions its Professional Development Scheme, which has over 4000 members. The scheme employs an Industry Structure Model (ISM) for Software Engineering, in an endeavour to help identify and develop necessary skills (both technical and transferable) in an organized manner. We asked two questions about the scheme:

- **What are the entry qualifications to the ISM?**

- **What skills should be evidenced at level 2 of the ISM?**

The results showed an almost complete lack of awareness of the scheme.

On a similar track, at least a third of our "responsible professionals" did not know whether their institute was involved in recognized Quality scheme. Some of the consequences of such "innocence" are discussed further in the chapters by J Barrie Thompson, and Jawed Siddiqi & Bissett. Controversially, Stuart Shapiro asks whether the real problem is not a lack of education concerning the industry's working practices but a misapprehension of its actual structure.

Although, we did not ask further specific questions about attitudes towards education, this dimension cannot be ignored. It is worth reflecting that when Fred Brooks was asked at PASE96 whether Software Engineering should be treated as a "craft", and therefore abandon higher education in favour of an apprenticeship model, he paused for a noticeable length of time before answering that the question was "too hard to answer". Hence, educational and training practices are well-covered in this book, including the chapters by Tony Cowling and Frank Milsom who discuss approaches to teaching good practice in higher education, and that by Ray Dawson & Ron Newsham who try to deal with the problem that computing graduates are "very knowledgeable but not a lot of use!"

1.4   The Structure of this Book

Echoing the structure of the survey just discussed, this book is divided into five Parts:

1. Professional Bodies

2. Accountability

3. Equal Opportunities

4. Working Place

5. Education and Training

The division is to assist reading; it offers just one possible pathway through the book. We recognize that some of the chapters could happily be relocated within these divisions, thus:

- John Wilkes' chapter which raises the question *Is an Ethical Code Feasible?*, which we have placed within *Accountability* could rest equally well within *Professional Bodies*.

- Mike Stranks' chapter on *Software Education, Personal Development and Hong Kong* discusses the discrepances in professional body membership between Hong Kong nationals and other BCS members, and could be moved from *Professional Bodies* to *Equal Opportunities*.

- Kari Marie Helle's discussion within *Equal Opportunities* of *Problem Solving Tools for the Disabled* is a good example of actual *Working Practices*.

- The chapter by Julian Webb, Lesley Rackley & John Betts, on the *Pressures to Behave Unprofessionally*, highlighting negative *Working Practices*, also poses an important question regarding *Accountability*.

There are also other equally profitable divisional structures. For example, an interesting alternative would be to read the book with Tom DeMarco's *Foreword* in mind, where he offers a *4-P model*, such that a professional must be: *proficient, permanent, professing* and *promise-keeping*.

We hope that whatever route that you engineer through this book that you do it in a professional and responsible manner!

Part I
Professional Bodies

Why does the accolade of professionalism mean so much to some computer people? After all, most of them are reasonably well-paid, the job is neither dirty nor hazardous to health, it even has a certain prestige in some circles. So why don't they just get on with their jobs? If their work pleases, they will get paid, and if it doesn't, they won't. Why don't they just take the money and run?

There are at least three reasons. The first could be termed socio-therapeutic — the title "professional" soothes the vanity of a certain sort of computer worker; they can hold their heads up in the company of doctors, lawyers and other such "professionals". The second reason is descriptive — computing is a profession because it shares a family likeness with other jobs which we call professions. These jobs all require a high level of training, they are underpinned by a formalized body of knowledge, they have governing bodies running them, and so on, and computing is another one of these sort of jobs. And thirdly, there is the philosophical reason; this argues that you simply cannot do computing without taking certain moral and ethical stances towards your work, and that this attitude is what truly defines the professional. On this argument, declaring that the computing industry is a profession is most definitely not a conceit, nor is it merely descriptive; it is stating something very important about the nature of computing. It argues that, just as a surgeon is (we hope) more than an efficient carver of flesh, a computer professional is more than an efficient code-generator.

The chapters in this part of the book review the last two reasons. We need to describe the computing profession, because it is a young industry and we do not understand very well what makes it tick. We want to consider the nature of professionalism, because it is a concept which means so many different things to different people. These chapters are written by people who are genuinely interested in the ability of the computer industry to act professionally. The authors share an underlying belief that computing is absolutely fundamental to today's society, and that "sub-standard" computer systems, however we define them, can have catastrophic consequences. Behind the reasoned, academic language, you sense a real urgency to the debate.

We start this debate with Don Gotterbarn's *Software Engineering: A New Professionalism*. Gotterbarn is the co-chair of the joint ACM/IEEE task force on Ethics and Professional Practice; as such, over a number of years, he has been closely concerned with trying to mould the computing industry into a well-regulated, forward-thinking industry. He argues that professional bodies originally grew out of essentially selfish motives — they were a sort of white-collar trade union, designed to protect and advance the rights of the individual professional. It was assumed that the professional was best-fitted to judge the appropriate course of action in any given situation, an entirely paternalistic view of the world. As this view has faded in the face of society's general onslaught against such arrogance, he charts the rise of an opposite, nihilist view which saw software engineers as "guns for hire", just as doctors may be "syringes for hire". However, Gotterbarn rejects this "agency" view of computing and instead puts forward a normative view of Professional Codes as guidelines, often aspirational, which can act as a set of best-practices for the computing industry. He points out that today's guidelines are noteworthy for placing far greater emphasis than ever before on the social responsibilities of the software engineer. Gotterbarn makes a strong case for the professional body as a force for good within society.

If we accept Gotterbarn's argument that the professionalization of computing is a "good thing", it becomes important to see how effective is the structure of the computing profession. Gary Ford & Norman Gibbs look at this question in *Attributes and Goals for a Mature Profession*. They attempt to define what this framework really means in practice, and how to mature and grow it. Their approach is to look at the structural requirements of a profession — what type of people it needs to attract to its ranks, the training opportunities it must offer, the rewards and constraints it has to apply, and so on. This argument leads on to a consideration of the professional institutions necessary to provide this. Ford & Gibbs offer a guide to professionalism, and how to determine what stage of the professional life-cycle computing is at. It is not surprising that they consider Software Engineering to be mainly at the *ad hoc* stage, with some elements of the *specific* stage, but not much of the *mature* stage. There is clearly a long way to go!

The view of Ford & Gibbs is borne out by the report, again by Don Gotterbarn, on *Establishing Standards of Professional Practice*, which describes the joint effort by the ACM and IEEE-CS to "professionalize Software Engineering". The very fact that this is presented by a representative of the professional bodies themselves means that there is undoubtedly work to be done before there is a mature professionalism within computing. However, as the report also shows, there are impressive steps being taken to put in place comprehensive and meaningful standards into every area of computing. One feels that it will not be long before any deficiencies are put right.

In *Professional Activities of the British Computer Society*, Geoff McMullen supplies a similar report for the UK situation. He shows how the BCS has grown over the 40 or so years of its existence into a very active and constantly evolving organization. He reviews its work in promoting industry best practices, providing academic courses, writing codes of conduct, developing career structures, working with other professional bodies such as the Institute of Electrical Engineers (IEE), and so on. His description of the future work of the Society shows that, like the US situation, there is a huge enthusiasm for filling in any deficiencies in their services. One could say that these bodies are showing great professionalism in their work.

So much for the theory. Next we have a case study from Mike Stranks, *Software Engineering Education, Personal Development & Hong Kong* in which he looks at how professional bodies perform in practice. At first sight, his chapter may appear to denigrate the abilities of the Hong Kong indigent population. However, he has identified an important problem, the low success-rate of Hong Kong nationals' applications for BCS membership. Moreover, he has the benefit of real local knowledge (he taught in Hong Kong for many years) and his chapter displays genuine research. He suggests two possible explanations for this poor performance, an over-subservient local culture, or a foisting onto that culture of Western norms and expectations (i.e. cultural imperialism). Stranks' chapter ends by questioning what it really means to be a professional, whether we fall too easily into defining "professional" as simply the norms of White, Anglo-Saxon, Protestant male society.

In *The Road To Professionalism in Medical Informatics*, Heather Heathfield & Jeremy Wyatt extend Gotterbarn's general argument about the nature of modern professionalism into an area which they know personally, Medical Informatics. They discuss where precisely that discipline is on the long road to professionalization. They stress the role both of theory and practice in equal measure to form a balanced, tested body of knowledge. They suggest ways to move things forward, by education, by professional bodies and by the selection of appropriate areas of concern for Medical Informatics. The result is a practical example of how computing can move forward from highly theoretical arguments about the nature of professionalism towards a self-evidently professional body — an association of Medical Informatics practitioners who would be obviously and undeniably professional in ways which their forbears were not.

Finally, Robert Melford asks *Who Should License Software Engineers?* He entertainingly argues that the licensing of Software Engineering, i.e. legislative professionalization, will come whether we like it or not. So we had better like it! He argues that it is better to ride with the legislative juggernaut than to stand in its way. He believes that all the arguments about whether we really are a profession or not are incidental compared to this overwhelming truth. According to Melford, if American barbers have to be licensed, you can be sure that software engineers will have to be licensed as well. End of story. It is hard to argue against him. Melford then goes on to consider how such licensing can be developed to our advantage. He is in favour of the software industry proposing its own licensing, through structured educational requirements, agreed codes of ethics, and so on. So long as this does not become a cosy cartel then this be good for the profession; and Melford argues that, in today's society such aggrandisement by computing people simply is not feasible,

So where do these chapters leave the professionalism debate? Amongst all the diversity, there is a growing consensus that any profession must possess certain traits: a clear and substantial body of knowledge; a defined and rigorous training and educational structure; a governing body or bodies which have real authority over their members; and a set of agreed standards, ethics, call them what you will. Does the computing industry have these traits? Does it have them, as Ford & Gibbs suggest, in an *ad hoc* and embryonic fashion, or is it well on the way to maturity, as Heathfield & Wyatt suggest? Does it suffer from the parochialism of its roots, as Stranks suggests? And what about the future? How much is the rise of the professional body inevitable and how much will depend upon the efforts and decisions of individuals within those bodies? We hope that the essays collected here will fuel the debate.

Chapter 2
Software Engineering: A New Professionalism

2.1 Introduction

Computing is at a stage in its development that engineering was at in the United States 80 years ago. It is at that point where it can decide to become a "profession" or remain merely a profitable occupation. This is a significant decision for computer practitioners and for society at large. Many conceptual muddles have to be avoided or cleared up before making this decision. I believe one such muddle has to do with the concept of a professional as it is related to Software Engineering. I argue that the traditional concept of professionalism is not appropriate for Software Engineering. There is a newer, more appropriate meaning of profession which is currently achievable by software engineers and will move Software Engineering in a positive direction. The evidence for my argument is drawn from three computing societies' developing codes of ethics, conduct and practice. These codes indicate an awareness that a different sense of professionalism is required for Software Engineering to be a profession.

2.2 The Traditional Concept of a Profession

"Profession" is often used as an empty synonym for occupation. Sometimes the word "profession" is used as an emotive term recommending that a particular occupation be accorded prestige and high pay.

Several authors have specified hallmarks of a professional; generally they include: being a person of above average income because of monopolistic practices by the profession, doing white-collar work, having a code of ethics expressing ideals of service, licensing procedures and associations. A profession also requires a monopolistic knowledge that circumscribes a clearly defined territory. These traditional hallmarks are perhaps derived from the priests who were early exemplars of a profession. They had special powers and knowledge and controlled entry into their ranks, exercised a large degree of autonomy, and served an important social function. In this tradition, medicine and law are paradigm professions. In addition to these hallmarks, professions typically carry with them prestige, respect, social status and autonomy. Professionals frequently set their own tasks, are not closely supervised and do not punch time clocks. There are two reasons they are allowed to be self-regulating. First, they have mastered a specialized knowledge which is useful to society and not easily mastered by the non-professional. Second, they set higher standards for themselves than society requires of its citizens. Therefore only they will be able to recognize and censure those members who do not live up to these standards. Society in turn generally requires proof of such competence before giving someone licence to enter the profession.

2.2.1   Ethical obligations of professions

The higher standards required by professionals are not higher moral standards than the rest of society. Professionals must follow the same minimal morality as the rest of society — don't lie, don't cheat, don't steal. The traditional concept of a profession dictates that professionals go beyond minimal morality, offering legal counsel to the indigent and providing medical service even if the patient cannot pay. Other higher standards included a different approach to time commitments and to their personal lives. They were expected to work as many hours as their professional duties require. They were also expected to be exemplars of proper conduct in general.

There is also a difference in the kinds of problems they face. Professions are described as a distinctive subclass of occupations and there are significant ethical problems arising in connection with this subclass which do not arise with other occupations. The professionals unique understanding of professional situations and how to deal with them places a set of ethical obligations on them. These obligations are sometimes referred to as professional ethics. These are different from the "higher standards" discussed previously. There are several arguments about how one acquires these responsibilities, to follow professional ethics including arguments based on social contract theories, legalized accountability, others regarding ideologies and role responsibilities. Rather than adjudicate between these arguments let us simply say that assuming the role of a professional carries with it the acceptance of these professional ethics.

Given a specialized set of professional ethical problems, one has to decide how to address these problems. The way particular professions chose to approach these problems is found in their codes of ethics, practice and conduct.

2.2.2   How codes of ethics, conduct and practice relate to a profession

Codes of ethics have served a variety of functions and are frequently directed at several audiences. At the simplest level a code of ethics is a statement of the obligations of individual computing professionals in the conduct of their profession. The code will generally embody a moral commitment of service to the public. Sometimes they are used to clarify expectations and appropriate behaviour of professionals.

Some confusion about codes of ethics arises from a failure to distinguish between closely related concepts about codes which direct the behaviour of practicing professions. Moving from less restrictive to more restrictive codes we first mention codes of ethics which are primarily aspirational giving a mission statement for the profession. There are also codes of conduct which describe professional attitudes and some professional behaviour. Codes of practice are very specific and tied closely to the practice of the profession. They are the easiest to use as a basis for legal action. Because practicing professionals deal with human affairs, the underlying ethical principles are the same across professions. Studies have shown that most codes are a hybrid of these three types of code [Berleur94].

In the past codes have been used to justify the professional's claim to autonomy. There are several characteristics of a code used to justify autonomy. First, the code should be primarily regulative, and it should be clear which imperatives are punitively regulative. The code should protect the public interest. The code should specifically address aspects of the profession which pose particular and specialized temptation to its members. The code should be policed.

A code can have all of these characteristics and also serve several other significant functions. By recounting how a good professional would behave, the code establishes and expresses moral values of the profession and establishes standards for the non-professional. It communicates with its members the organization's expectations of its members, and provides a decision-making procedure for the professional.

2.2.3 The demise of the traditional profession

Today there is considerable debate about whether computing is a profession. The model used to address this question is the traditional model of a profession, [Dahlbom93], [Johnson94], [Kling95]. This is an anachronistic approach to the question, given that even the most traditional of the "traditional professions" do not fit the model of a traditional profession.

The arguments that deny computing as a profession are based on the absence of autonomy and self regulation; similar arguments have been used against engineering being a profession. Computing and engineering are not done by individuals, but by teams who are employed by and responsible to a corporation. These individuals are not free to set their own hours but punch a time clock. Computing does not have a representative licensing body so entry into that occupation is not controlled. Computing does not have a well-defined body of knowledge whose mastery is required to practice computing.

Some engineering and computer societies formulated Codes of Ethics to help claim professionhood. As we show below, even these codes of ethics do not match the marks of a profession.

There are several models of a professional-client relationship [Bayles81]. The "paternalistic model" characterizes the traditional concept of a profession. In this model, because the professional is to some extent in a superior position, the profes-sional assumes much of the decision-making power, making decisions believed to be in the best interest of the client. These decisions are based on the professional's concern for the well-being of the client. Computing and engineering, however, have sometimes operated with a different model, namely, an agency model. In this model, the practitioner merely acts as the agent of the client, doing whatever the client re-quests. The practitioner's special knowledge is not used to help decide what the client should request. The practitioner is merely a "hired-gun" doing whatever is necessary to accomplish the client's request. Questions about how the request is satisfied or the quality of the system which satisfies the request are not relevant.

Given these significant differences between computing and "the professions", it is clear that computing is not a profession in the traditional sense. Should computing strive to be a profession in the traditional sense? One argument for becoming a traditional profession might be that computing practitioners want to be held in the same regard as other traditional professions, such as law and medicine. But these occupations are no longer professions in the traditional sense. All of the arguments used against computing being a profession also apply to law and medicine. Most legal and medical practices are corporations where significant autonomy is surrendered to the "practice". Some of these professions are openly debating their roles, e.g, medical journals are debating whether a physician is merely a "syringe for hire" — the agency model. There is only limited self-regulation of these occupations in part because of the lack of a monopolistic body of knowledge — a breadth of practices from holistic medicine to acupuncture is being acknowledged. Insurance companies are dictating the practice of medicine reducing the physician's autonomy. Some have argued that the agency model precludes any special need for ethical training in that all that is owed to the client is professional competence and honesty.

Another argument for professionalization of computing is the belief that a set of ethical obligations — professional ethics — based on responsibility to the client is based on the societal impact of the occupation. Because of the nature and impact of computing, a higher level of care is required. Other arguments for the professionalization of computing are sometimes motivated by concerns with impeding computer risks. Approaching professionalization from these directions requires a different model of the professional-client relation from the traditional model. We used this newer model in developing the revised ACM Code of Ethics.

2.3   Is Software Engineering a Profession?

Currently major international computing associations are working toward the professionalization of Software Engineering. For example, the IEEE-CS and the ACM, they have established a steering committee "for the establishment of Software Engineering as a profession." To answer the question "Is Software Engineering a profession?" we first have to re-visit the concept of a profession. I maintain that what is now being sought in efforts to professionalize Software Engineering is not the traditional model of a profession. Indications of the movement away from the traditional concept of a profession can be seen in the changes to computing societies' Codes of Ethics. The Codes examined here are from the British Computer Society(BCS), the Institute of Electrical and Electronic Engineers-Computer Society(IEEE), and the Association for Computing Machinery (ACM).

2.3.1   The Early IEEE and ACM Codes

Both organizations' Codes originated in the formative years of computing in the United States. The ACM Code of Ethics was adopted in 1972, the IEEE Code in 1974.

The IEEE was formed from the union of the American Institute of Electrical Engineers and the American Institute of Radio Engineers in 1963 [McMahon84]. There was considerable struggle in the organization concerning professionalism, especially difficult for engineers was the concept of autonomy. They felt the tension between the nature of engineering employment, typically salaried employment in the service of a company and that of autonomous professionals, lawyers and physicians. They determined that they should become a profession. One of the reasons for this choice was the lack of employment security in aerospace and military contracts. They lobbied legislatures for more work on social problems, such as housing, transportation, pollution and crime. They also amended the Constitution of the organization to change the primary purpose for the IEEE from scientific, literary and educational to promoting and improving the economic well-being of the members. This is a typical goal of professions.

They also amended the Code of Ethics to reflect the new direction of the organization. In December of 1974, the Board of Directors approved a new Code which consisted of four Articles: Article One dealing with general ethical and moral guidelines, Article Two dealing with engineers in their work, Article Three dealing with engineers and their clients, and Article Four dealing with engineers and society.

The ACM Code, adopted in 1972, is a code of conduct rather than a code of ethics. It is based on a model which tended to list violations and sanctions for such violations. The code has three clearly delineated types of statement: Cannons, which are general principles; Ethical considerations, which are professional ideals; and Disciplinary Rules, which are mandatory rules. Failure to follow a rule will result in some sanction by the association.

2.3.2   Elements of Codes of Ethics

Professional groups use codes of ethics to specify acceptable ways of achieving their shared goals. The early Code of the ACM is regulatory. These early codes were almost codes of practice, judging compliance and sanctioning non-compliance.

Codes have been divided into primarily normative and primarily regulatory codes. The 1972 ACM Code was a highly regulatory code, specifying cannons of behaviour and disciplinary rules. In traditional professions such regulatory codes were justified as part of the social contract the profession had with society. In return for enforceable moral promises, society granted the profession the right to self-regulation. There are several concerns with this type of code. First it leads to a "black letter law" approach to professional practice — if a particular action is not ruled out by the code then it is permissible. In a rapidly changing discipline, such codes are generally out of date and do not cover the significant issues. They are inflexible and unable to address new situations.

A code can also be normative. Norms are "ethical rules of thumb." They are rules that have been developed for analyzing and deciding cases in a particular area of ethics. They tend to be less authoritative than the basic duties stated in a regulatory code. They are a way of formalizing, generalizing, and communicating ethical wisdom and experience in a particular field.

Norms are very different from laws in that they are meant to guide judgement rather than to regulate behaviour. A good set of norms gives a person guidance in understanding new situations, knowing what questions to ask and what factors to consider, and formulating an ethical response. A normative code will provide guidelines for professionals to use in decision-making. A normative code is justified by appeals to practical experience, role responsibility and ethical principles.

Both regulatory and normative codes tend to come from within a profession. The potential moral authority of the codes comes from the fact that they represent a consensus of the traditions and duties of that particular calling.

2.3.3   Revised codes

In the early 1990s, the ACM, BCS and IEEE Codes were significantly revised. As we shall see, the tendency of these revisions is away from regulatory codes toward normative codes. These norms get written as imperatives. Computer scientists and engineers have begun to develop a sense of themselves as a profession.

IEEE Code revision

In 1990 the IEEE Code of Ethics was modified to a more compact and direct statement of values and guidelines. Many of the directives from the 1974 Code were combined, removed and modified to produce ten imperatives. These imperatives are considered by the organization as the most efficient and direct means of communicating the *guidelines* to the membership. The feeling was that the Code of Ethics was too legalistic and "consequently difficult for the members to interpret and follow."

The IEEE Code does not go into great detail on the ethical values underlying the Code, but it does touch on contributing to society and dealing honestly only by implication when it says," . . . we commit ourselves to the highest ethical and professional conduct . . .". The presumption is that the ideals of honesty and contributing to society serve as the basis for all the imperatives.

Although some general principles — honesty, privacy, confidentiality and professional competence — are in most codes, the IEEE Code in its movement toward a more normative code leaves out privacy and confidentiality. The IEEE Code does include principles found only in more recent codes, namely professional review, nondiscrimination and respect for intellectual property rights.

Earlier codes tended to be directed at protecting the profession rather than society, this is evident in their rules against criticizing fellow professionals. In the 1930s two engineers in the United States, who informed the public of inferior concrete being used in the construction of a dam, were expelled from the engineering society for the unethical conduct of criticizing fellow engineers. This professional protectionism appears in many of the early codes. In the 1972 ACM Code, a professional is only required to report adverse consequences of projects which are proposed to that professional. The Code does not address what to do if you find that someone else is working on a harmful project. The new IEEE Code however, in its first principle affirms the responsibility to "disclose promptly" engineering decisions which might endanger the safety, health and welfare of the public or the environment. This clearly broadens the engineers responsibility for safety from mere concern with safety related to their own projects to the safety of all engineering projects they may know about. It also broadens the concerns to include public welfare and the welfare of the environment.

ACM Code revision

The new ACM Code of Ethics and Professional Conduct identifies more specific guidelines and rules than either the 1972 ACM Code or 1990 IEEE Code. This is to be expected because we were developing a code of ethics **and** a code of conduct. The different functions of different types of code effects their content. Codes of ethics, containing ethical principles, are primarily aspirational, stating the vision, objectives and mission of the profession. They involve little or no coercion. Codes of conduct are related toward professional attitudes and make more obvious the issues at stake in different fields. The degree of coercion ranges from warning to exclusion. Codes of practice are very content specific. Sanctions for violations are harsh and form a basis for legal action [Berleur94]. The revised ACM Code is both a code of ethics and a code of conduct. The BCS developed codes of conduct and codes of practice, and the IEEE Code is purely a code of ethics.

But the lines between these types of codes are not clear. The revised ACM Code is a code of ethics and professional conduct. Both types of code were mixed in its 24 imperatives. The Code is accompanied by a set of guidelines designed to assist members in dealing with the various issues contained in the Code. In developing the Code, we placed most of the code of conduct issues in the guidelines. For example, Section 1.5 of the Code affirms the principle of honouring property rights. The guidelines relate this directly to software licences and copying software. The guidelines frequently shift into a code of practice. For example there are clear statements about formal design reviews and statements about how to manage confidentiality.

We structured the Code with a preamble and four sections. The first section — General moral imperatives — outlines fundamental ethical considerations for any professional. These ethical considerations link the responsibilities of particular computer professionals to fundamental ethical principles. The second section — more specific professional responsibilities — includes the member's obligation to understand and take responsibility for the consequence of their work, to honour contracts, laws, and other obligations, help educate the public and to avoid unauthorized access. The third section — Organizational leadership imperatives — balances the individualist perspective of Section 2 by giving the obligations of those who have leadership roles in organizations. This section is new to computing codes of ethics which have previously only addressed the role of a computing practitioner in relation to their clients, their employers and other professionals. The fourth section of the Code deals with Code compliance. Compliance is seen as mainly voluntary.

The first section of the Code dealing with general moral imperatives shows how specific professional issues are grounded in general moral principles. This section serves two functions. First, it addresses the attempt to separate ethical issues from professional practice; but more importantly it serves a heuristic function, showing how individual members can apply general moral principles to new ethical problems not explicitly mentioned in the guidelines. Numerous examples of this were given in a paper that was submitted to the ACM Executive Council along with the code of ethics [Anderson 1993].

The new Code contains those elements common to most codes; honesty, privacy, confidentiality, maintaining professional competence and improved public understanding. But it also contains many of the elements that are found in only a few of the newer codes; professional review, honouring property rights, fairness, non-discrimination and crediting intellectual property.

Many codes advocate the avoidance of negative consequences of professional activities. In the new ACM Code there are general statements dealing with responsibilities in the event of negative consequences. For example Section 1.2 dealing with the responsibility for negative consequences says that a person is obligated to undo or mitigate negative consequences as much as possible. This is clearly a shift from earlier codes here. The earlier codes were designed to protect the computing professional. This and numerous other sections are designed to protect society, almost in the sense of strict liability. It does not say that the member is obliged to undo the negative consequence only if they were due to a failure or malpractice of that member. Even if the negative consequence were the fault of the customer's incorrect use of a product, the member is still responsible. The Code, at this and numerous other places, first protects society, and then the professional. This is in marked contrast to the 1972 Code which regulates the internal relations between computer professionals and only speaks of avoiding negative consequences.

Many codes include acceptance of peer review or audit procedure, but the ACM Code moves more toward the aspirational code when it emphasizes the individual's initiative in seeking out professional review rather than merely acquiescing to enforced software quality assurance procedures.

The third section of the ACM Code is strong evidence of the movement away from a paternalistic and self-directed model of professionalism. The Code clearly states that more than honesty and technical competence is expected of the computer professional. The application of technical skills should be guided by concern for the client's and user's rights. The development of a computer system requires a consideration of all stakeholder rights. For example, Section 3.5 states "*Articulate and support policies that protect the dignity of users and others effected by a computing system.* Designing or implementing systems that deliberately or inadvertently demean individuals or groups is ethically unacceptable. Computer professionals who are in decision-making positions should verify that systems are designed and implemented to protect personal privacy and enhance human dignity." The original draft of the Code also contained an imperative relating all the stakeholders to the design process. "(3.4) *Ensure participation of users and other affected parties in system design, development and implementation.* Not only should input be sought from system users, but potential users and other stakeholders should be directly involved as collaborators in all phases of the system development cycle . . . " Unfortunately, in the final draft, both stakeholder and client involvement in the development process was reduced to participation in the drafting of requirements. This section is a backward step to a variation of the agency model or the traditional paternalistic model of professionalism.

There is a significant emphasis on quality in the Code. It is stipulated as a goal of professional work. The imperatives related to quality were among those receiving the highest levels of positive support in the member survey done on drafts of the Code. This relation of quality and ethics is also maintained in the BCS Code of Conduct.

BCS Code of Conduct and Code of Practice

The stated goals of the BCS Code of Conduct include: an assertion of the accountability of BCS members for professional competence and the exercise of that competence according to "high standards of personal integrity." The new code was adopted in 1992. The BCS Code consists of 22 imperatives, grouped by public interest, duty to employers and clients, duty to the professional, and professional competence and integrity.

The BCS Code of Practice presents the standards of professional conduct in Level 1 statements and then includes Level 2 statements for each Level 1 statement. The Level 2 statements are the rationale for Level 1 statements. The content of the Level 2 statements are practical statements which express particular professional activities. The sections of the Code of Practice mirror the process of software development, moving from requirements, organizational issues, contracting, systems development, systems implementation and live systems. The BCS Code stresses professional development and competency more than the ACM Code and IEEE Codes..

Since it is specifically a code of conduct, it is less normative in its presentation than the ACM or IEEE Codes. Like many other codes, the BCS Code includes specific reference to confidentiality, professional competence and improvement of public understanding. The newer elements, we have seen in other codes, of fairness, nondiscrimination, property rights and professional review, are not explicitly stated but may be included under Imperative 4, "Members shall in their professional practice have regard to basic human rights and shall avoid any actions that adversely affect such rights."

Although the code does not contain an "other-regarding" statement, the description which accompanies Bye-Law 18, states that, ". . . each member should ensure that he observes at all times the principle that, in any conflict in his professional life between his personal interest and his duty to others, his duty to society must prevail."

Like the ACM Code, there are some problems with the BCS Code of Practice and Code of Conduct. The two codes seem inconsistent, e.g. the Code of Conduct Section 2.6 states, "Members shall endeavour to complete work undertaken on time and budget and shall advise their employer or client as soon as practicable if any overrun is foreseen" [BCS92]. This puts an emphasis on a quality product even if there is a delay. The Code of Practice (Section 6.3), however, states "Here *you* are involved in a professional judgement or trade-off between reasonable costs and acceptable levels of proving or testing. If you cut corners by, say, reducing system test time, then the likely effect on the operation elsewhere should be evaluated and made known to those who should know" (Emphasis added). This section makes it acceptable to reduce the quality of a product and the decision concerning such reduction belongs to the professional. This decision, belonging to the professional rather than the customer, is an example of the paternalistic model. The emphasis of several sections on the Code of Practice emphasize cost and service as the primary values rather than quality of the product.

A significant difference between the BCS Code and the ACM and IEEE Codes has to do with accountability. The BCS has constitutional authority from the Royal Charter to "establish and maintain a sound ethical foundation for the use of computers, data handling and information technology systems; *and to adopt any lawful means* conducive to the maintenance of a high standard . . ." (emphasis added).

This is in sharp contrast to the ACM Code. In surveys on the proposed ACM Code of ethics distributed to 80 000 members, most of the 24 imperatives received better than a 90% favourability rating. The section putting a person's membership at risk for code violation only received a 74% rating. Many respondents were concerned about their inability to satisfy some of the more aspirational statements in the Code. The problem of enforcement is a difficult one for highly normative codes.

2.4   A New Professionalism

What do these changes in codes of ethics mean? I think there is a common tendency which marks a change in the concept of professionalism away from its more traditional meanings. In contrast to the traditional paternalistic model of professionalism and the agency model there is another model of professionalism called the fiduciary model. This is a model in which the professional's superior technical knowledge is recognized, but the client retains a significant authority and responsibility in decision-making. "In such a relationship both parties are responsible and their judgements given consideration, but because one party is in a more advantageous position, he has special obligations to the other. The weaker party depends on the stronger and in ways in which the other does not and so must trust the stronger party. In this model the client has more authority and responsibility in decision-making than in the paternalistic model, but the client depends on the professional for much of the information on which he [the client] gives or withholds consent" [Bayles81].

The paternalistic and the fiduciary model also differ in how they use a code of ethics. In the paternalistic model, codes of ethics are used as the professional's part of the social contract in exchange for society's consent to professional self-regulation and autonomy. It is the case that many computing professionals do not have autonomy and the profession is not self-regulating. Based on this claim, it is argued that computer practitioners are not professionals. But the absence of autonomy is not only consistent with, but it is the essence of the fiduciary model of professionalism. In the fiduciary model, the code of ethics is not a social contract, stating regulatory rules. The code of ethics function as a set of guidelines for the behaviour of the computing professional stating a consensus of the values of the profession. The function of the code is not to protect the profession, but to establish the standards of trust required in a fiduciary relationship.

When looking at the new codes, there is a remarkable degree of ethical consensus. The vast majority still believe in integrity, fairness, human well-being, respect for privacy, professional responsibility and even respect for privacy. The codes do provide a set of shared expectations and obligations that can help define the profession and its commitment to serve the public. That is itself important — and it is consistent with the fiduciary model.

Both the IEEE and ACM code revisions move away from a regulatory model to a normative model code. A normative code is not bound to the concept of an autonomous profession. They both place the "general well-being" of those affected by products of the profession ahead of concerns about the status of the profession.

In aspirational codes some of the regulatory purpose of the code is established by suggesting an appropriate sanction for any given violation, and by requiring professionals to report colleagues who violate the code. This is more acceptable to professionals if the code helps them understand the damage done by violating the code. This approach to enforcement distributes the responsibility for the profession to each professional.

The changes we have seen are that the codes have become normative guides to behaviour with a strongly other-directed quality. Some of the codes specifically require whistle-blowing if a problem is detected. There is an ethical commitment to quality and the professional has responsibility to the client and to the product. The fiduciary model is an adequate model of professionalism for computer practitioners. This model seems to be assumed in some of the code changes. The codes require more than honesty in following out contracts and requires more than technical competence. Both the clients and their environment (quality of life) are to be valued in the fiduciary model. This is evidenced in some of the elements that are unique to the newer codes, e.g. fairness, non-discrimination and property rights.

The progress toward a workable model of professionalism for computing is not always linear. The changes to the section about participatory design in Imperative 3.4 of the ACM Code is a step backward towards "over the wall" software development, in which the client's only input is a statement of need and the programmers then develop the system any way they want and give whatever is developed to the client. In spite of these occasional backwards steps, the general positive direction is clear.

Software Engineering, as a profession, is moving toward a fiduciary model of the client-professional relationship, in which there is respect for limited ethical and professional autonomy of the individual member and individual judgements in particular cases. This model is good for software development and is consistent with typical software review procedures. The emphasis on a better process and better quality will result in a higher percentage of effective, within budget, on-time projects. Many of the failings of Software Engineering in the past are attributable to having this order reversed. It is a mistake to have the primary goal of software development be a delivery date. This, I think, has been realized and is evident in the directions that Software Engineering is moving.

Chapter 3
Attributes and Goals for a Mature Profession

3.1   Introduction

A mature profession promotes high standards for professional practice and supports the rapid dissemination of new knowledge. The SEI (Carnegie Mellon University Software Engineering Institute) recently completed a feasibility study to determine what it means to have a mature Software Engineering profession. Our analysis of mature professions led to a framework that is composed of two levels we call the practitioner level and the infrastructure level. At the practitioner level there are three components: professionals, knowledge, and professional practice. At the infrastructure level we found eight components: initial professional education, accreditation, skills development, professional development, certification, licensing, code of ethics, and professional society. Most of these components are present in mature professions and are under the active stewardship of appropriate formal organizations and volunteer groups.

The growth of a mature Software Engineering profession will contribute to substantially improved professional practice and lead to higher quality software systems. To assess the maturity of Software Engineering as a profession we assess the maturity of each of the components at the professional and infrastructure levels and discuss goals for each. Although our assessment shows that Software Engineering is not very mature, understanding the complex and dynamic interactions among the components gives insight into key leverage points that can be worked on to expedite the formation of a mature profession.

Section 2 of this chapter examines published definitions of the term "profession"; Section 3 describes the two layer model for professions; Section 4 introduces measures for the maturity of infrastructure level components and applies these measures to Software Engineering. Our conclusion is that much of the necessary infrastructure for a mature Software Engineering profession does not exist or is not yet very visible.

3.2   Definition of a "Profession"

The term *profession* has many different interpretations and meanings within the computing community. We begin by examining published definitions of this term. Webster's Ninth New Collegiate Dictionary [Webster83] says:

> "**profession** . . . **4 a:** a calling requiring specialized knowledge and often
> long and intensive academic preparation **b:** a principal calling, vocation,
> or employment **c:** the whole body of persons engaged in a calling."

It also gives these definitions of the related terms *professional* and *professionalism*:

> "**professional** . . . **1 a:** of, relating to, or characteristic of a profession
> **b:** engaged in one of the learned professions **c:** characterized by or
> conforming to the technical or ethical standards of a profession . . .
> **professionalism** . . . **1:** the conduct, aims, or qualities that characterize or
> mark a profession or a professional person . . . "

The International Encyclopedia of Social Sciences [Sills68] states that the core criteria for a *profession* are:

1. a requirement of formal training accompanied by some institutional mode of validating both the adequacy of the training and the competence of trained individuals

2. a requirement that skills in some form of the use of the training must be developed

3. some means of making certain that such competence will be put to socially responsible uses

The United States Code of Federal Regulations [29 CFR Sec. 541.3] defines an employee "employed in a professional capacity" as one

1. Whose primary duty consists of the performance of:

   (a) Work requiring knowledge of an advanced type in a field of science or learning customarily acquired by a prolonged course of specialized intellectual instruction and study, as distinguished from a general academic education and from an apprenticeship, and from training in the performance of routine mental, manual, or physical processes, or

   (b) Work that is original and creative in character in a recognized field of artistic endeavour (as opposed to work which can be produced by a person endowed with general manual or intellectual ability and training), and the result of which depends primarily on the invention, imagination, or talent of the employee, . . .

2. Whose work requires the consistent exercise of discretion and judgment in its performance; and

3. Whose work is predominately intellectual and varied in character (as opposed to routine mental, manual, mechanical, or physical work) and is of such character that the output produced or the result accomplished cannot be standardized in relation to a given period of time; . . .

3.3   Model of a "Profession"

These definitions suggest that at the highest level a profession has people involved in a collection of activities. We use *professionals* to denote that set of people and *professional practice* to denote that set of activities.

All of the above implies that professionals have completed an intensive course of specialized study prior to entering professional practice that we call *initial professional education*. *Professional development* is that additional study undertaken after entering professional practice.

Professionals are expected to acquire skill in applying the knowledge they have gained from initial professional education. Several professions have structured activities to teach professionals these skills. We use the term *skills development* to denote those activities.

Most professions have ways of assessing and assuring the adequacy of education, training and overall competence of professionals. These mechanisms are commonly called *accreditation* of professional education programs and *certification* or *licensing* of individuals. In the United States, certification is normally a voluntary process administered by the profession and licensing is normally a mandatory process administered by a government authority.

To ensure that professionals put their knowledge and skills to socially responsible use, professions normally have a *code of ethics*, *code of conduct*, or *code of practice*. In this chapter we will use *code of ethics* to represent all three.

Finally, there is an implication that a profession has a formal and visible identity. The professionals see themselves as members of a community of like-minded practitioners who care about the quality of their professional practice. The community is normally identified by a *professional society*. Most professionals belong to that society and through volunteer efforts, promote the advancement, development and quality of the profession. Professional societies normally are stewards for many of the components mentioned above.

In summary, a profession can be modeled at two levels with multiple components. We call these levels the *practitioner level* and the *infrastructure level*. Table 3.1 lists the components at each level.

Practitioner Level	Infrastructure Level
Professionals	Initial Professional Education
Knowledge	Accreditation
Professional Practice	Skills Development
	Certification
	Licensing
	Professional Development
	Code of Ethics
	Professional Society

Table 3.1 Levels and Components of the Model of a Profession

Figure 3.1 shows the infrastructure level components of a profession and the typical path for a person choosing to enter the profession. Boxes represent activity and organizational components, and the magnifying glasses represent quality assurance components. Note that not every profession will have every one of the components. For example, in the United States some professions have certification but no licensing (such as accounting), and others have licensing but no certification (such as engineering).

In the figure, an aspiring professional first undertakes initial professional education (the education that precedes the first day on the job; usually provided by a university); the quality of a professional degree program is assured by accreditation. To become a professional, he or she must develop skill in the application of that education (through university co-op programs, on-the-job training, apprenticeships, or other means). Certification and/or licensing assures the competence of the individual to enter professional practice. Throughout practice, there are periods of professional development, possibly resulting in recertification or relicensing. The profession ensures that its practitioners behave in a responsible manner by defining and enforcing a code of ethics. A professional society provides an identity for the profession and helps assure that all the other components interact appropriately.

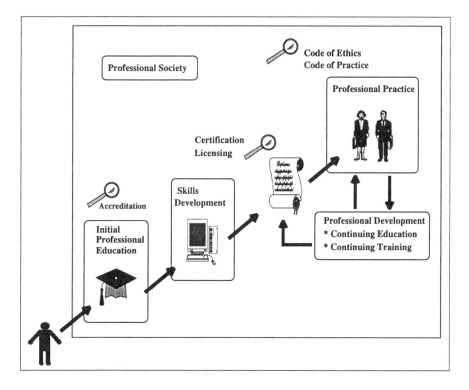

Figure 3.1 Infrastructure Level Components of a Profession

An important consequence of our framework is to note that a profession can mature separately from the development of the scientific knowledge and technology that is used by the professionals. As an example, consider the medical profession of the 1930s. The profession was reasonably mature at that time (the eight components were all in place and working well), but the knowledge and technology base did not yet include penicillin, organ transplants, or magnetic-resonance imaging. But because the profession was mature, new technologies were rapidly assimilated into the curricula of medical schools and the practices in hospitals as they became available.

Note that we distinguish between the infrastructure level (the eight components) and the practitioner level (the people, knowledge, professional practices). We assert that an effective way to improve the practice of individuals is to accelerate the development of mature infrastructure level components. This assertion is based on the observation that mature professions have in place the institutions, processes and procedures necessary to ensure a continuing supply of and responsible behaviour by highly competent professionals. Just as a mature software-development process facilitates the rapid assimilation of new technology, a mature professional infrastructure facilitates the rapid diffusion of knowledge, skills and recommended practices to professionals.

In attempting to discuss a profession for Software Engineering in the United States, we too often get into endless debates about the maturity of the science and professional practice to provide good support for the engineering of software. Whether or not the scientific basis is present or complete, we argue that people today aspire to improve professional practice by exploiting the best science available to better engineer software systems. The people engaged in these activities think and behave more like traditional engineers than traditional scientists. At an SEI work shop in 1986, Fred Brooks stated that scientists build in order to learn, but engineers learn in order to build [Brooks87b]. Therefore, it makes little sense to discuss the maturity of Software Engineering professionals, knowledge, or professional practice, since mature professions have an infrastructure in place that facilitates and expedites making knowledge and improved practices available to its professionals.

3.4   A Mature Profession

Although there is no precise definition of a mature profession, it is possible to characterize the maturity of a profession's infrastructure components in terms of four developmental or evolutionary stages:

Nonexistent This component does not exist in any form even remotely related to the given profession.

Ad hoc Some related form of the component exists, but it is not identified with the profession being described.

Specific The component exists and is clearly identified with the profession being described.

Maturing This component has existed for many years, during which time it has come under the active stewardship of an appropriate body within the profession and is being continually improved.

Table 3.2 describes component stages for the Software Engineering profession. Nearly all the components are currently in the "ad hoc" stage in the United States. The goal of the SEI is that each of the eight components of the Software Engineering profession exist, be under the active stewardship of appropriate bodies, and be maturing.

Component	Ad hoc	Specific	Maturing
Initial Professional Education	Bachelor's degrees in CS, engineering, maths etc are the common preparation for entry into the profession	Bachelor's degrees in SE exist, but no standard curriculum	Curricula reflect the best practice; nationally accepted model curricula exist which are regularly reviewed and revised
Accreditation of Education	Accreditation based on CS or engineering criteria	Accreditation based on SE criteria; ABET & CSAB are merged	Accreditation guidelines are regularly reviewed and revised
Skills Development	Some student project work done in schools, some coop programmes and company training programmes for new hires	Guidelines have emerged for the skills needed for entry into the profession	Skills development mechanisms in place and widely used (e.g. apprenticeships or engineer-in-training programmes); skills for distinct specializations recognized and developed
Certification	ICCP certification; commercial certification related to software packages & technologies	Certification as a software engineer; nationally recognized standards	Certification in specialty areas within SE; nationally recognized speciality certification
Licensing	State licensing as a professional engineer under existing statutes	Some state licensing exams address SE skills specifically	Licensing based on appropriate exams NSPE &NCEE collaboration recognized as protecting the public in appropriate situations
Professional Development (Continuing Education and Continuing Training)	Individuals pursue professional development as they determine the need	Guidelines (curricula, expenditures p.a. etc) have emerged	Recognized generalist and specialist career paths for software engineers; nationally recognized education and training guidelines and curricula
Code of Ethics	Codes of ethics of ACM, IEEE, ASQC, ICCP; engineer licensing statutes	Code of ethics specifically for software engineers	Code widely respected and adopted; the profession has mechanisms to discipline violators
Professional Society	ACM, IEEE, Computer Society etc	Professional society explicitly states it represents software engineers	Society has appropriate range of products and services for software engineers

Table 3.2 Evolution of Components of the Software Engineering Profession

Acronyms used in the table are:

ABET	Accreditation Board for Engineering and Technology (US)
ACM	Association for Computing Machinery
ASQC	American Society for Quality Control
CSAB	Computing Sciences Accreditation Board (US)
ICCP	Institute for the Certification of Computing Professionals
IEEE	Institute of Electrical and Electronics Engineers
NCEE	National Council of Examiners for Engineering
	and Surveying (US)
NSPE	National Society of Professional Engineers (US)

Although we wish to accelerate the maturation of the eight components, we note that they do not mature independently; there are complex dynamic relationships among them. For example, initial professional education contributes to the preparation of an individual for professional practice and certification; professional development for individuals improves professional practice; licensing and certification influences the curriculum for initial professional education.

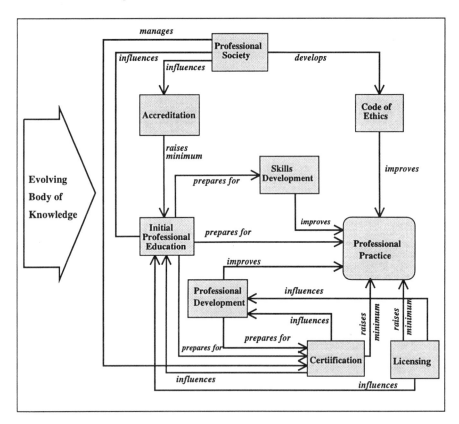

Figure 3.2 Interactions Among Components

Figure 3.2 shows some of these relationships for the Software Engineering profession. The figure also illustrates the central premise of our work: The eight components contribute to improved professional practice, which in turn determines the quality of software systems. The maturation of all the components is a large and lengthy task that will require substantial investments from the software community.

3.5 Conclusion

People too often propose "quick-fix" solutions to long-term systemic problems. SEI customers report that there are too few qualified software professionals, universities do not produce software engineers, there are not enough Software Engineering generalists or specialists, and software engineers very quickly become technically obsolete. Each of us probably has heard from colleagues that we can solve these personnel problems by simply requiring licensing or certification or requiring that a fixed number of days per year be devoted to professional development. What our preliminary work demonstrates is that in mature professions there is an infrastructure that supports a complex set of interactions and dependencies that are nurtured and grown under the stewardship of a community of professionals engaged in that profession. Much of that infrastructure is still missing or not very visible for Software Engineering. A way to make progress is to understand that investments must be made in each of these eight components to expedite the formation of a mature profession for software engineers.

Chapter 4
Establishing Standards of Professional Practice

4.1 Introduction

Computing has been slow to respond to the increasing impacts of computing products on society. The effect of these products now influences more aspects of our society and the areas of influence are more critical than they had been. Computers no longer merely calculate the speed of vehicles, but they also control the speed and breaking ability of automobiles. Computing practitioners are more aware of these changes in area and criticality of their work products and have started to respond to this change in an organized way. Two major computing societies have joined forces in an effort to respond to these changes. Described here is the joint effort of the IEEE-Computer Society (IEEE-CS) and the Association for Computing Machinery(ACM) to professionalize Software Engineering.

4.2 Professionalization

Professionalization is conceived of as an appropriate response to the changing impact of computer technology and the effect of the behaviour of computer technologists on our society, The marks of a profession which these societies carry to computing are: high standards of knowledge or skill in specific areas attested to by the attainment of a specific degree and an apprenticeship applying these skill, a commitment to keep these skills up to date, and a commitment to apply these skills for the benefit both the client and society. This commitment is generally described in standards of practice or codes of ethics.

A series of events in 1993 brought focus to this activity of professionalization. In the Spring of 1993, Fletcher Buckley, a member of the Board of Governors (BoG) of the IEEE-CS, circulated a proposal for registering software professionals similar to the way engineers are registered in the United States. In May of 1993, the BoG approved a motion to establish a steering committee for evaluating, planning and coordinating actions related to establishing Software Engineering as a profession. Later in 1993, the ACM Council endorsed the establishment of a Commission on Software Engineering to address a number of questions related to: the terminology used to describe Software Engineering and those who work in the software area; identify generally accepted and desired standards of good software practice; and determine our ability to identify, educate and train individuals who are competent with Software Engineering and design. Later in 1993 an ad-hoc committee of the IEEE-CS, with participation of the ACM, worked to define a process and some initial recommendations to accomplish these tasks. Finally, in January 1994, the president of the IEEE-CS made a proposal to the ACM to form a Joint Steering Committee to accomplish these goals.

The Joint Committee's mission statement is: "To establish the appropriate set(s) of standards for professional practice of Software Engineering upon which industrial decisions, professional certification, and educational curricula can be based." To accomplish these tasks they made the following recommendations:

1. adopt standard definitions;

2. define required body of knowledge and recommended practices

3. define ethical standards

4. define educational curricula for undergraduate, graduate (MS) and continuing education (for retraining and migration.)

The committee believes there is an implied dependency between these tasks and that the recommendations be implemented in the suggested order.

4.3 Task forces

The steering committee decided to accomplish these tasks through the establishment of a series of task forces. Initially the task forces established were: Software Engineering body of knowledge and recommended practices; Software Engineering ethics and professional practices, and Software Engineering curriculum.

4.3.1 Body of knowledge and recommended practices

Each task force is co-chaired by an IEEE-CS and an ACM representative. The body of knowledge task force is chaired by Patricia Douglas and Tony Cocchi. The required body of knowledge and recommended practices are not static because technology evolves and the professional should keep up with the field. There is interest in approaching the development and maintenance of the set of recommended practices like a technical standard: adopted by consensus and subject to periodic revision. The initial version of the body of knowledge will be developed by a survey of practitioners. Early versions will be widely distributed and after modification will be distributed for comment electronically.

4.3.2 Ethics and professional practices

The ethics and professional practices task force is co-chaired by Donald Gotterbarn and Robert Melford. This task force has defined its purpose as "to document an international consensus for minimally acceptable ethical and professional responsibilities and obligations of software engineers." The standards to be established shall document generally accepted principles for identifying and resolving ethical conflicts relevant to the discipline of Software Engineering. Considerations shall be given to the responsibilities and obligations of the software engineer to peers and lay persons, employer, customer(s), the profession, society and humanity. The standards are intended to document the consensus of the global Software Engineering community. From time to time, consensus on an issue may not be clearly recognized. Accordingly, these standards shall also document various recommended practices and guidelines when no clear consensus can be established. The SEEPP task force has tentatively identified a number of areas to develop recommendations and has established working groups to specifically address these areas. The first areas identified are: intellectual property, professional competence, professional relationships, privacy, reliability and safety, security, and social justice. Issues for the intellectual property working group include: ownership of: code, algorithms, systems design and specifications, project control methods, test methods, quality improvement models, etc. Issues for the professional competence working group include specifying truth about one's skills, obligations to keep skills current, knowing and communicating truth about code, moral standards about what should be produced? (concern for end-use consequences), keeping staff current, appropriate knowledge base, non-generalization of expertise, educational issues: certification, registration and licensure. The issues for the Professional Relationships working group include managing communications and ethical obligations from : the professional to professional and the professional to lay person or society, the professional to employer, professional to customer, and the professional to electronic community. It also deals with support for "whistle blowers" and obligations to foster responsible behaviour amongst non-professionals. Issues of concern for the privacy working group include: monitoring (workplace, every-place), confidentiality, data aggregation, falsification or communication of a "digital persona" out of context, misuse of data, relationship of electronic privacy to other policy issues, e.g., computerized medical records and health care reform, etc. The reliability and safety working group is concerned with issues including: contracts, reliability thresholds in contracts, testing, risks, user-centred design, truth in advertising, informed consent for buyers, financial support for improved quality and quantifying quality. The Security working group is concerned with data integrity, statutory violations, encryption, malicious programming (viruses, etc), system administrator's responsibility and encryption. The Social Justice working group is concerned with the professional's responsibility to end-use, equity of access, allocation of resources, computing for the disabled, and the impact of "de-skilling" (computer takes over a person's job).

4.3.3   Curriculum

The curriculum task force is co-chaired by Doris Carver and John Werth. This task force will use the input from the body of knowledge survey to develop curricula for Software Engineering education and training. This task force is equally concerned with the education of people entering Software Engineering and with the continuing education of software engineers. To help accomplish this task, the task force will distinguish the knowledge and skills of a novice software engineer from those of an experienced software engineer.

In this effort, the IEEE-CS/ACM steering committee is exchanging ideas with other international organizations, such as the IEE and the BCS in the development of these standards.

Chapter 5
Professional Activities of the British Computer Society

5.1 Introduction

The purpose of this chapter is to give an overview of the Society's history as a professional body, its current activities in this area, and its short-to-medium intentions in the professional field. We wish to affirm an openness and willingness to co-operate with all seriously interested bodies in the creation of a Software Engineering profession, both at a national and international level. As will emerge, the Society is engaged in many initiatives in this area, and is prepared to consider more.

5.2 History and Current Activities

The Society was incorporated in 1957 and from its earliest days, there have been three strands to its activity: "Learned Society" activities; more practically oriented groupings of people interested in sharing best practice; and activities in support of the development of a broader profession.

5.2.1 Learned society

The Learned Society activities and the sharing of best practice now take place mostly within the Specialist Groups and as part of the regular meetings of Branches. There are some 50 of each, all of which are very active and meet regularly. Their activities are open to non-members, because the Society believes in a free trade in knowledge. In any year, over 12000 people take part in Specialist Group events in the UK. The author first joined the Society in 1964 because of its sharing of systems development project management wisdom at a time when there were no good courses available and little published. This experience supports a view that the Society has been ahead of the field as a Learned Society for most of its life.

The principal publication in the Learned Society domain is the *Computer Journal* — a refereed journal of distinction. It also publishes from time to time proceedings of meetings or conferences and various series of guidelines, policy statements and practitioner books.

5.2.2 Academic courses

When we turn to the Society's history in the professional domain, the history is also extensive. A scarcity of good academic courses in Software Engineering in the 1960s led to the development of an examination syllabus by the Society, which was first used in 1969. A lively and numerous Board of Examiners keeps the syllabus up to date and marks the papers for the two parts of the existing examination. The Part I examination enables candidates to demonstrate a good understanding to a reasonable depth of a range of IS related topics, whereas the Part II examination is both broader and deeper in its coverage. Success in Part II satisfies the academic requirement for professional membership of the Society.

The syllabus for Part II of the Society's examination provides the basis for the accreditation of academic courses. Graduates from courses so exempted are held to satisfy the academic requirement for membership of the Society when they apply for a professional grade. The Society has been undertaking such accreditation of courses since the early 1970s, and currently accredits over 200. Since the Society became able to enrol suitably qualified members as Chartered Engineers, accreditation also offers graduates of accredited courses an academic basis for an application for the status of Chartered Engineer after suitable experience. Where schools teaching Computer Science or Software Engineering are within an Engineering Faculty, we have been undertaking joint accreditation visits with other engineering professional institutions for accreditation.

5.2.3   Professional codes

Codes of Practice and Conduct, with an appropriate disciplinary structure, have been in place since 1968 and are available to members of the BCS and the general public. Their existence and our commitment to keeping them up to date convey a couple of important messages. We believe that a consistent and codified pattern of behaviour is a significant part of professionalism. We believe this sufficiently strongly to have developed and promoted such a code — our money is where our mouth is.

5.2.4   Professional development

The Branches of the Society are where many of our better initiatives originate. Several good examples of such initiatives occur in the professional area. The first is the Professional Development Scheme. It arose from a series of Branch initiatives to produce standardized job descriptions for work in Information Systems in the late 1970s and early 1980s. As these descriptions developed, they showed a need for guidance on the progression of professional staff through a reasonable sequence of jobs to enable them to develop as useful professionals, and for their employers to have confidence that their knowledge, skills and competence were well founded. Under the guidance of the late Alan Taylor — the Society's first Professional Director — this structure of job descriptions and guidance on progression developed into a pilot Professional Development Scheme, launched in 1985, with some 77 jobs described in it. The job descriptions developed into the Industry Structure Model (ISM), containing the job description, a summary of desirable previous experience for someone doing such a job and of the underlying qualifications and knowledge to be expected. The Industry Structure Model was updated in 1989, with more jobs and a very similar structure. It has just been updated again, with several very notable changes:

- It now describes roles, not jobs, and contains some 230 role descriptions

- It is presented as an Access data base

- There are tools and templates provided to enable users to combine role descriptions and arrange them to provide customized job descriptions for their own use

- The underlying activity analysis is compatible with that for IT National Vocational Qualifications (NVQs) — participants in PDS can earn unit qualifications leading towards NVQs as they follow the scheme.

There are now over 120 employers using the PDS, with some 4000 individual participants. The Industry Structure Model is offered free to subscribers to the Professional Scheme, and is available for purchase by other interested people or organizations.

Our recently launched Continuing Professional Development Scheme is another Branch based initiative. It encourages members to keep themselves up to date, and provides a means for them to record their participation in BCS events, courses provided by third parties and even self study as a means of maintaining their professional knowledge. This scheme is being managed at present in partnership with the Institute of Data Processing Management — another concrete example of the Society's commitment to partnership with organizations having a serious commitment to IS Professionalism.

The Industry Structure Model has emerged from being a tool of the Professional Development Scheme to being fundamental to the activities of the Society. The Membership Committee which reviews applications for professional grades of membership examines a candidates' qualifications and experience. In reviewing experience, it uses the ISM to check that an individual presents a career history which shows a solid and consistent professional basis for his or her activities, and has not hopped opportunistically through all the possible streams of activity without any evidence of consistent personal development. Branches and Specialist Groups use it to assess the likely audience for their planned activities, as well as to enable CPD participants to assign attendance at such events to the correct ISM cell.

5.2.5   Types of membership

Individual membership of the Society is available at five grades: Student and Affiliate, for those whose stage in life or degree of exposure to IS renders them unready or unsuitable for professional membership; and three professional grades — Associate, Member and Fellow. Associates are members who do not yet have sufficient qualifications or experience to be acceptable as full professional members. Members are those who have demonstrated a relevant academic background and an appropriate career history to be considered by the Society as Information Systems Engineers (those who have a suitable degree will also usually qualify for the status of Chartered Engineer). Fellows are those members whose length and breadth of experience lends them sufficient distinction to be considered as senior members of the profession in the view of the Society.

5.3 The Future

There is much development ongoing in all the areas described in the previous section:

- An application has been made to the Privy Council which will, amongst other points, make it possible for Associate members to use post-nominal letters and thereby make it possible for individuals to be seen as professionals in earlier stages of their careers.

- The new, third version of the ISM is being promoted by the Society for use by other professional and related bodies in the IS field as the basis for their schemes of membership education, qualification and development.

- The future of the Examinations is the subject of a working party which is developing a business plan to enable the Society to plan with confidence the continuing development of this valuable service.

- We have been a Nominated Body of the Engineering Council for six years, and are actively working with the Council to ensure the continuance of that status, which enables the Society to nominate individuals for inclusion on the register of Chartered and Incorporated Engineers.

- The Professional Development Scheme is being revised to make it use the new, electronic version of the ISM more effectively. A very positive recruitment campaign which is intended to increase the number of participating companies is well under way.

- The Engineering Council is requiring all member institutions to offer systems of Continuing Professional Development. The Society had already launched a Continuing Professional Development Scheme in a somewhat restricted form, which has demonstrated that there is much demand for such a scheme in the membership. For these two reasons, we are working with the IDPM to make the scheme broader, better validated and easier to operate. It is seen as a strategic service offering from the Society.

- Departments of State, principally the DfEE and the DTI, are taking increasing interest in the question of IS professionalism, qualifications and even licensing. The Society is actively engaged in these developments, and is anxious to work with all other interested bodies who have a contribution to make in producing a more effective national framework. A significant current example of activity in this area is the joint working party with IEE, sponsored by the Health & Safety Executive, which is looking into the structure of qualifications required by Information systems staff involved in Safety Critical Systems.

- John Leighfield, a Past President of the Society, began a process of looking at the relations between the various professional and academic bodies involved in the education, training, development and employment of Information systems professional at the end of 1994. The Society is continuing to participate in work emanating from John's initiative, in collaboration with many bodies, including the Conference of Professors and Heads of Computing, the IT Industry Training Organization, Elite, IEE — the IS Directors forum of the BCS, and many other groupings of interested parties (to date, some 32 different groups have been involved in this work). The intention is that a consistent framework for defining IS professional activities will be developed and adopted by all involved, and that they will co-operate more closely than in the past in their services to the emerging IS profession.

5.4   Conclusion

The aim of this chapter was to offer the readers, who may be presumed to be sympathetic to the idea of an IS profession, a synopsis of the Society's current activities and its short term plans. In conclusion, it seems worthwhile to address a larger audience and make some general points about why the Society is undertaking all this activity, and why others should be interested or become involved. To me, the argument seems to flow as follows:

- All advanced human societies have now become dependent on Information Systems for their survival.

- In all other vital activities, societies have developed frameworks for training and qualifications, then insisted on the use of the best framework as a means of qualifying to work in that activity. This observation applies to complex work like Medicine, Engineering and the Law, as well as to more mundane tasks like driving a bus or plumbing.

- Thirty years ago, no usable frameworks existed for training IS staff existed.

- Many usable frameworks now exist for training and developing IS staff.

- The British Computer Society offers and maintains a uniquely comprehensive range of services to those interested in IS in the UK, and has a Royal Charter requiring it to work for the use of IS to the benefit of society at large. This requirement must include making the best contribution the Society can to the development of IS professionalism in the UK, and overseas where applicable.

- The Society's contribution can best be made by working with other possessors of partial frameworks for IS professional development and practice towards the production of a comprehensive national system.

From this, it follows that those who are practitioners in the IS world should seek to join the Society, and those who serve the IS world are welcome to collaborate with us in serving it better and more consistently.

Chapter 6
Software Engineering Education, Personal Development and Hong Kong

6.1   Introduction

This chapter reports a substantial difference between the "pass" rate of applicants for corporate membership of the British Computer Society interviewed in Hong Kong and their counterparts in Britain. It is suggested that this is not due to any bias of the local interviewers, but that there may be differences in attitudes about what constitutes "responsibility" as a component of "professionalism" in the two communities. This applies especially in areas relating to decision-making, the maintenance of levels of personal working knowledge, and a willingness to provide organized training. Cases are compiled which illustrate several aspects of related issues. Conclusions are drawn that an understanding of the concept of responsibility within the scope of professionalism may vary between communities of significantly different sociological backgrounds. In turn this may mean that established professionals can not always move easily from one community to another without a period of readjustment.

6.2   Background to Hong Kong

Hong Kong is an enclave of 1078 Km^2 of land and 235 islands at the mouth of one of China's major trading rivers. Some of this territory has been under British administration since 1840, with the majority held on a 99 year lease until 1997 when all of Hong Kong will revert to Chinese sovereignty. The current population of over six million grew from 600 000 in 1945. Hong Kong provides the only easily accessible deep sea port and efficient source of financial services to the immediate neighbouring counties in China, and has long been a major centre for *entrepot* trading. These nearby counties of China, administered as financially privileged "Special Economic Zones" (SEZs) for the last 15 years, have economies which have grown more rapidly than that of China as a whole, and are the apparent model for the development of the rest of China. In addition to Hong Kong's own spectacular growth (that of service industries is quoted at 18% p.a. 1982-92), Hong Kong's investment in the local SEZs is variously estimated to have created between four and six million new jobs since 1980.

In this economic environment, many of Hong Kong's original, more labour intensive, industries have moved to the adjacent SEZs in pursuit of lower operating costs, and are now moving onwards into other areas of China. Ready access to this low cost manufacturing environment has not encouraged Hong Kong entrepreneurs to make significant investment in higher technology to support their activities in Hong Kong, and recent reports suggest that Hong Kong may now need to review this trend in order to retain its dominant place in the region.

Hong Kong's economy has therefore changed from being a low-cost industrial centre in the 1970s, to become a centre for advanced service industries which are dependent on a continuing supply of well-educated people in the 1990s.

Hong Kong provides 9 years of free compulsory education for all children. A growing proportion of people aspire to hold degrees, and continue their education in fee-paying schools. In this environment, the provision of government supported first year degree places has risen from about 2% of the relevant age range 20 years ago, through 8% in 1990, to about 18% (14500) today. These places are mainly concentrated in six universities, out of a total of 10 degree awarding institutions. Provision is also made for substantial numbers of sub-degree students in several of these degree level institutions and a further 10 institutions. Most of Hong Kong's tertiary students receive an up to date education in IT which is aimed at making them well-informed users of computers. Five of the universities offer specialist IT or Software Engineering based degrees, and have places for 1250 first year entrants in each of the next 3 years.

A human resources survey of the computing industry in Hong Kong [VTC95] estimates the number of specialist staff at 43000. It indicates that the supply of locally qualified people may meet, if not exceed, requirements for the first time in 1997.

Such rapid expansion in numbers within the computing industry, and in the knowledge of new graduates generally and of IT related graduates in particular, imposes great strains on the software industry's ability to supervise the post-graduate development of new graduates [Stranks94a].

6.3   BCS Corporate Membership

Writings in the area of professionalism in computing have generally been set in the context of the Anglo/Celtic communities of Europe and North America. However, [Frey91] outlines substantial differences between Japanese attitudes to on-the-job training, where it is seen as essential and is often conducted under the guidance of an officially appointed senior as a mentor, and attitudes in the US, where such training is seen as a chore which should have been done within the graduate's initial education. This suggests that some communities may embody aspects or methods of personal development which are not accepted in other places where cultural mores are different.

A candidate for corporate membership of the British Computer Society (BCS) will be sent standard information by BCS. From this it will be seen that candidates are normally expected to have gained an acceptable honours degree, or an equivalent qualification which has been recognized by the Society. A 2-4 year period of supervised training converts this theoretical education into the practical skills which are required within an industrial context. The period of training is topped off by at least two further years of experience during which aspiring young professionals become responsible for a growing proportion of their own decisions. Candidates for a corporate / professional grade of membership of BCS are expected to show that, over this extended period, they have successfully developed the skills which enable them to take responsibility for their own professional judgements [BCSPR92]. This pattern of requirements is repeated within the context of the UK oriented Hong Kong Institution of Engineers

(HKIE), whose experiences are discussed in [Stranks94b], and from which it appears that the explicitly stated training expectations of the engineering community in Hong Kong lie somewhere between the more extreme attitudes suggested in Frey.

Candidates for BCS membership are expected to submit documentary evidence which suggests that they have completed all of the above requirements, and to have that evidence supported by the confidential references of a number of supporters of professional standing.

The final assessment of whether a candidate has actually achieved the standards to become recognized as a professional is difficult, and can only be done by people who are experienced both in the industry and in the assessment of people. Within Britain, and in Hong Kong under the auspices of BCS and of the HKIE, this is done by senior members of the profession who give their time voluntarily, and who are organized into ad-hoc panels which review candidates according to published guidelines [BCSPR92].

6.4   The problem

With such apparent similarity of information and backgrounds, it may be expected that the rate of recognition of professionals in UK and Hong Kong will be similar. This expectation is seen not to be true.

6.4.1   Interview results

BCS currently has 12% of its corporate members resident outside the UK. Hong Kong has conducted almost 6% of all Professional Review interviews world-wide. One other non-UK interview panel operates in Singapore, but comparable figures are not available. It is not thought likely that data coming from the 6% of members who are outside Hong Kong and the UK, including those in Singapore, can significantly affect the results found here for the rest of the world. In essence the "Rest of the World" therefore becomes the UK. The following data summarizes the results of all interviews for professional membership of BCS which were conducted world wide between 1 October 1993 and 30 September 1994; the recommendations for the interviews which were conducted in Hong Kong during that period; and, by simple subtraction, the interview results from the rest of the world excluding Hong Kong.

Interviews	Total number	Accept as requested	Accept at lower grade	Rejected	No firm Decision
World at large	749	650	20	38	40
Hong Kong	44	20	14	9	2
UK	705	630	6	29	38

Table 6.1 Number of applicants accepted into BCS

The general pattern of Hong Kong's results has not been seen to change from the time that interviews became the normal for all membership applications in 1991, and these results are assumed to be representative. Despite the small size of the sample in Hong Kong, it can be seen that:

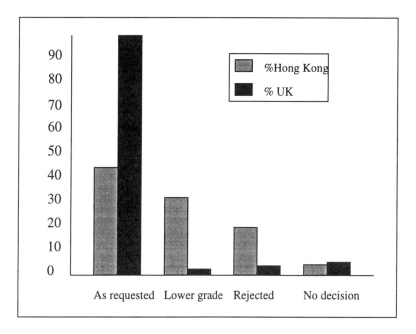

Figure 6.1 Percentage of applicants accepted into BCS

- there is no significant difference between Hong Kong and the UK panels in the rate of taking firm decisions;

- Hong Kong's overall rejection rate is substantially higher than that which applies throughout the UK;

- Hong Kong's rate of acceptance at the requested grade is dramatically lower than that found in the UK; and

- Hong Kong's rate of acceptance at a lower grade than which was requested is dramatically higher than that found in the UK.

The scale of the differences in these results are such that they are outside the bounds of randomness, and thus indicate the presence of significant differences between the situations found in Hong Kong and the UK.

Support for this apparent difference in results between Hong Kong and the UK has come from the Assistant Secretary (Membership) of the HKIE who says, informally, that over a recent two year period, the HKIE was unable to accept 25-40% of the applicants for many of its larger and longer established disciplines (it does not have the opportunity to accept at a lower grade of membership). The HKIE's refusal rate in its newly formed Software Engineering Discipline is below 10%, but the number of people encouraged to apply to this new discipline is initially kept low as it seeks to build a reputation for the quality of its membership.

6.4.2   The BCS Hong Kong interview panel

The above results may be caused by differences between the perceived standards and expectations of the Hong Kong panel and their colleagues in the UK as, in the absence of frequent points of comparison, the views of a remote and isolated panel may not reflect those of the norm. It is therefore possible that this comparatively isolated community could be operating to different standards from those of panels in the UK.

This is avoided as far as possible by only using people of known high integrity who have a long history of employment in Britain, or who have been directly approved by the BCS Membership Committee, and who therefore are fully conversant with the local standards which are operated by this national body.

Interviews in Hong Kong were conducted on 10 occasions during the period under review. The members of an interview panel for each session in Hong Kong were drawn from a list of 11 people. These comprise seven ethnic Chinese who have spent much of their formative and working lives in Hong Kong, but who have substantial working knowledge of British practises, and four of British extraction who have significant experience of working in Hong Kong. This author is one of the four and, as secretary to the panel, attended all 10 sessions in the period of detailed review. The other 10 panellists each attended between one and four sessions.

All of these people are thought to be sympathetic to the local expectations and culture. If they were to show any collective bias, this might be expected to reverse the statistics above and favour local applicants rather than reject them. As a check against such attitudes, and the equally damaging ones of a conscious reversal which is designed to counter them, the panel customarily invite other experienced BCS interviewers to take an active part in planned local interview sessions whenever their travel schedules allow. To date, all of these comparatively few "inspectors" have been full members of the BCS Membership Committee, and each has confirmed that the recommendations made by the Hong Kong panel are within their norms for the UK's regional panels.

Whilst numeric evidence is not available to this author, informal conversations and feedback from local candidates suggests that differences between the recommendations of the Hong Kong interview panel and the final decisions of the Membership Committee are unusual. In the absence of any suggestion or data to the contrary, it is therefore assumed that these Hong Kong figures represent the decisions which would otherwise have been made by other interview panels.

The composition, backgrounds, and attitudes of the Hong Kong interview panel members are therefore not thought to contribute significantly to the above variations.

6.4.3   Other factors

The only other factors which appear to be relevant to this apparent anomaly concern the candidates' own perceptions of what is a professional, what is required of a candidate, and thus when they should apply.

On face value it would therefore appear that a candidate's perceptions of what is needed to be rated as a professional may vary significantly between applicants in Hong Kong and those in Britain, and that these are the main cause of this difference in acceptance rates.

6.5 Case Studies

The following cases have been compiled by the author alone and are based on his attendance at, and brief reporting of, the 150 BCS Professional Review interviews conducted in Hong Kong between January 1993 and December 1995. All except five of the people interviewed are of Hong Kong Chinese extraction. A significant number received their undergraduate education in UK, Canada, USA or Australia. A small percentage were working outside Hong Kong in other Pacific rim countries at the time of their interview, whilst many more have worked in a wide range of other countries at various times during their career. All of the following examples are composites from a number of interviews. Each is designed to illustrate one specific point which is common to a significant number of interviews. None is intended to reflect the specific details of any single person.

6.5.1 The ability to take decisions

The idea that people who wish to be recognized as professionals may be so dependent on their seniors for instruction that they are unable to find ways to tell them that they may be wrong, or even that they may have made an error, appears to be an anathema to someone who was brought up within the more openly discursive climate of the Western World. In this context, I asked a junior manager in Hong Kong what would happen if "the boss" made an error of technical judgement because he had not correctly remembered or understood something, and was answered with surprise and the question "Who would tell him?".

A general impression that "seniors must always be seen to be right" means that many seniors appear unwilling, and possibly are unable, to delegate responsibility. This may be because they believe the natural order of life places this burden on them, so they feel they must always be seen to carry the responsibility. Alternatively, they may believe that the power to take decisions cannot be transferred, lest the junior makes decisions which the senior would not have made and thus causes unforeseen difficulties. These and other parallel attitudes of "face" are present in most societies, and may be a major reason why so many small organizations in the west and elsewhere cannot successfully expand their scale of activities beyond a certain point. To me, these attitudes appear more openly displayed in Hong Kong than in the UK.

Hong Kong is full of small enterprises, and has very few medium or large ones. The sole owners of many small and medium sized family enterprises buy their software from very small software houses, which may in turn be run by another, younger, member of the same family. Access to clear and impartial advice in the area of software systems is therefore limited. In these circumstances, it may not be commercially or socially possible for members of the software house to offer opinions which challenge those of the more senior members of the family. This extreme expression of the maxim that "the customer is always right" may have a more pronounced application in Hong Kong's family circles than is seen in the more discursive climate of the west.

The few who do manage to release the reins and successfully delegate responsibility rise rapidly to the top of medium-sized local companies. In this otherwise apparently semi-feudal society, some of these successful people, who may have Western-style

MBAs, often employ professionals from overseas as their close advisors. It almost appears that locally educated juniors are unwilling to offer opinions when the imagined consequences of their opinions not matching their seniors' opinions are too terrible to contemplate. In this perceived environment, it is often thought "safest" to avoid giving opinions or taking decisions, and one tends to revert to the well-established values of childhood, where the more junior person (oneself) was brought up to accept that all decisions are made by more senior people.

This is especially true in Hong Kong where there is a heavy legacy of rote learning. This may derive from the need to recognize combinations of over 1500 different complex written characters, whose structure bears no relationship to speech, before one can understand even a tabloid newspaper. Most youngsters appear to have been so shielded from decision-making throughout their formative years. This environment extends to the point where undergraduates continually need to ask their tutors which book to buy in order to find the "right answer" and, before they will risk making any decision, many junior engineers routinely seek confirmation that what they propose will be acceptable to their absent senior.

An extreme example of this inability to take decisions is the case of the "hybrid" applicant who used software to check that the design of a major public building complied with published standards. The applicant was sufficiently careful in doing this that, despite the fact that the building was to be built at sea level in the equatorial tropics where temperatures have never dropped below 20°C, the relevant British Standard requiring the roof to support the weight of 1 metre of snow was fully implemented. No one had told the applicant that it may occasionally be possible to deviate from a standard; the applicant's background did not say that it might be possible to make an independent judgement; and the applicant did not appear to see that what was apparently being implemented may be absurd. The question of whether such a person can ever be thought of as a "professional" in any discipline remains open.

Hong Kong people do have mechanisms which enable them to take effective decisions, or at least to influence the formation of decisions, but they are not the same methods as those of the west; hence the anomaly. Local methods are rooted in a value system which places great emphasis on order and orderly behaviour, and are thus consciously non-confrontational. My Chinese colleagues suggest that this culture leads to a form of passivity, whose subtleties are so different from the openly discursive and highly publicized concepts of free speech which exist in the West that it is unlikely that most Westerners will ever fully understand their Eastern counterparts' thinking or methods of persuasion.

The question for an interview panel of whether a Hong Kong candidate for BCS membership has the ability to offer a professional opinion therefore appears to present itself not by the taking of overt or outright decisions, but in the more subtle form of making "recommendations", or even "enquiries", whose content is routinely accepted without question by the more senior person.

6.5.2   The absence of continuous personal development

We have seen many cases in which individuals have conscientiously implemented the policy of their senior managers for many years. When asked at interview what they have learned about software technology since leaving college, and hence what changes they, rather than their managers, have tried to initiate in the processes used for the design or construction of software, their standard answer is that they have "no time to look at things which they have not been told to examine, and thus know nothing of the subject". Indeed, when asked how one would evaluate new ideas and techniques, one candidate went so far as to say "why employ a consultant [IBM] if you are not going to implement his advise — after all he is employed to know better than you what is relevant in your environment." These "good employees" are frequently amazed that their many years of service, always on an increasing salary and title, do not automatically classify them as professionals.

Mead's survey of the employers of computing undergraduates in Hong Kong shows they placed the ability to "Accept Responsibility" as their highest of eight criteria for successful employment, "Work in a Team" was second, and "Initiative" as third most important. When asked about actual abilities, they found the students were best at "Working in a Team", the ability to "Accept Responsibility" came third, and "Initiative" came last in the same list of students' actual performance [Mead95].

In this context a very senior and widely respected member of the IT community in Hong Kong was reported recently as saying "a lot of [IT] graduates are productive when they first start working, but they become increasingly useless after about three years when the skills they learned at tertiary institutions go out of date" [Yeung95]. He continued to say that the education system [in Hong Kong] did not equip students with the ability to self-learn and keep up to date with changing technology. Whilst most of Hong Kong's educationalists will challenge this damning view of the territory's tertiary education system, it generates the fundamental, but unanswered, question of how and where such abilities should be created within the skills repertoire of aspiring IT professionals in Hong Kong and elsewhere.

Whilst "initiative" may be high on the list of employers' hopes for a new graduate, its virtual absence in terms of actual student performance, and of graduates' ability to be proactive in their learning, may also be a sign that graduates are incapable of making or implementing their own decisions. The local understanding of the concept of "responsibility" may therefore be different from that of the interview panel.

The concept of Continuous Professional Development (CPD), which requires all professionals to take personal responsibility for the process of updating their own ability to understand the range of topics relevant to their area of competence, is therefore under direct challenge if we ever accept people as "professionals" who do not routinely initiate personal action to refresh and broaden the scope of their own working knowledge. This is one of the most frequent factors which result in an applicant being accepted at a lower, technician, grade by the local interview panel.

As an example of the above, consider the case of an applicant who was originally trained as an electronics specialist, and has now been promoted to a position of responsibility for all aspects of design, construction, and maintenance of all of a vendor's communications products which carry client's data in electronic form throughout the region. Despite acknowledging the importance of software, this applicant claims not to know about the processes of software creation which were used, and delegates everything relating to software to the company's "programmers". This lack of knowledge of software extends to the point where, despite recognizing that the methods used by the software development team may significantly influence product reliability and that any failure of software could have potentially devastating consequences for the company's clients, the applicant would not even acknowledge the existence of software development technologies such as Walk-through, CASE, Object-Orientiation, and Formal Systems Specifications, let alone display any knowledge of what they might contribute to the quality of the company's products. The panel thought this came about because software technology was not included within the applicant's initial education and no one, including more senior managers, had ever indicated that it may be useful for a manager in this position to gain such knowledge.

This applicant believes that people with responsibility for project management are invariably professionals because of their position and job title, saying "if they were not already professionals then they would not have been appointed to the job". The applicant sees no need to gain further knowledge on a regular basis as, by definition, all that was necessary to do the job will already be present. Further, the boss, rather than the applicant, will suggest what, if any, further knowledge or courses may be needed once the holes in the junior's knowledge are recognized by the boss.

The concept that all professionals must be able to understand the effect of all of the ideas underlying the arguments which are put to them for decisions does not appear to be universally understood in this community. The further fact that professionals, unlike "good employees", must make continued personal efforts to keep their working knowledge up to date across the whole range of the area of their professional responsibility, also does not appear to be widely accepted by those aspiring to be recognized as professionals in Hong Kong's software industry.

6.5.3   The "inability" to provide training

Unfortunately, whilst the thirst for formal qualifications continues unchecked in Hong Kong, on the basis that you must be demonstrably better than your rival because you hold more qualifications, the products of education appear to be under-used in many cases. The traditional business environment, which requires a rapid response to manufacturing demands in order to survive in a competitive market, means that Hong Kong businesses continue to believe that speed-to-market, rather than any concept of quality, is crucial to its continued survival. In this context, the 12 hour day, five and a half day week, continues to exist widely in the local software industry. This is retained on the apparent premise that working more hours will ensure more output, and thus achieve that "speed-to-market" which is assumed to be critical to all elements of business. The ideas that "the product must be installed and apparently working as early as possible" and "we will not worry about maintenance until it crops up" seem to be dominant in most sectors of the industry.

Academics visiting mangers in industry informally report that "I can't afford the time to look at a new technology until it is mature [or, by inference, obsolete]" and, despite an annual arrival rate of 1000+ new, specialist, IT graduates and many sub-degree diploma holders, "I can not afford the time to instruct my juniors in new ideas, and therefore can only afford to employ experienced staff (and training is therefore something which someone else provides)", are the apparent mantra of the typical Hong Kong Computer Services manager.

New software technology is therefore explored only when it can be shown to produce an immediate and significant impact on either the development cost or the date of delivery of the product. It appears to have little chance of serious consideration if it "only" affects the maintenance costs after implementation. The absence of hard business related case studies and statistics makes it almost impossible to be convincing when trying to present the case for new design methods and tools.

It is often suggested in Hong Kong that anything which detracts from direct production, e.g. further education or indirect training, is not economic and thus can not be supported. This argument effectively eliminates any possibility that any form of planned professional development will ever be considered on a wide scale, as such programmes will inevitably include activities which are not immediately and directly beneficial to the organization in its detailed day-by-day activities. This attitude continues despite the existence of a government funded cash support scheme which can pay about 40% of the first 18 months of a typical new graduate's salary to employers who subject a graduate to an HKIE approved programme of professional training and development.

Such attitudes do not bode well in people who claim to be professional, and who therefore have an apparent responsibility to keep their own working knowledge up to date in any and all areas which might impact on their ability to create a reliable product. It is rare to find cases where an applicant has shown initiative, undertaken a programme of education and will admit publicly that the ideas to which the class has been exposed actually do make them more productive in their daily working lives. Local attitudes therefore often contrast significantly with the views recently expressed by a visiting accreditation specialist from North America who quoted the President of Hewlett Packard as saying that "the half-life of HP's engineers' knowledge is about 2.5 years, and a major factor which kept his organization competitive was his engineers' ability to continually renew their knowledge" [Fletcher95].

Active management support for CPD may be one of the critical factors in the formation of professionals who can create a new competitive edge within the industry. Innovation and change is always expensive, and often has a detrimental impact on direct productivity in the short term. In a region which has a very short investment horizon (at most two years), it may be that the unknowns associated with any change of development technique are such that managers can not be assured that their investment will be both repaid and showing a clear return within that horizon. The risk to money and, much more importantly, reputation exists. The "safe" decision is to do nothing, wait for instructions from above, and continue using the tried and tested methods which were learned in college. However, the "safe" decision frequently means that one's development technology grows progressively more obsolete, and the competitive edge will, eventually, be irretrievably lost.

6.6   Conclusions

6.6.1   Need for regional interpretations

Many of the people above are found wanting in terms of the BCS's Industry Structure Model [ISM91] statements on the requirements for professional levels, and are recommended for a lower grade of professional membership than that which their aspirations and job title would otherwise indicate. The most common area of difficulty appears to lie with their ability or willingness to take responsibility for any initiative of any kind, and especially in areas relating to their own continued personal development. Many applicants therefore seem to be unable to use the extra knowledge which would be derived from those CPD experiences to be able either to make informed decisions about the methods which should be used in their normal working lives, or to advise others about new ideas on the basis of knowledge of those ideas.

The criteria used to assess Hong Kong candidates for BCS membership were written by people who were brought up in the Anglo/Celtic Western World, and whose initial education was directed towards the creation of free and radical thinking where a willingness and ability to challenge the thoughts of others is viewed as one of the stronger signs of being educated. It is therefore possible that the environmental values which are inherited by those who come from a different background may have created people who achieve equivalent, but not the same, ends through different mechanisms, and thus who can not be measured in the same way.

In this society, which places a higher emphasis on the need for order and direction than is common in a Western community, the acceptance of, rather than challenge to, the rules and words of "the boss" is often pervasive. It may therefore be not surprising that the familiar Western maxim "rules were made for the obedience of fools, but for the guidance of wise men" is rarely seen to apply in Hong Kong.

6.6.2   Different views of professionalism

The Eastern ability to advise seniors by non-controversial and non-confrontational methods does not appear to fit comfortably with the discursive concepts embodied in a Western view of professionalism. The ability to challenge ideas does exist widely in Hong Kong, but is not seen in the Western form of discursive comment, and is therefore not open to easy examination by people of a Western background or who are using its associated criteria for measurement. In this local context "recommendations", which may appear in the form of enquiries by a junior, may need to be taken as equivalent to "decisions" or "taking responsibility" when they are routinely accepted by seniors. This may appear to counter the official stance over who is seen to take responsibility for the decision, and may mean that a different or extended interpretation of these concepts may usefully be implemented in various parts of the world.

This does not necessarily mean that local definitions of professionalism should prevail; only that local people should normally be involved in decisions involving recognition of such professionalism. Ideas and methods used to demonstrate professionalism in one society may not be fully supported in another. This may be particularly so in areas relating to personal decision-making and the delegation and assumption of responsibility.

6.6.3   Local assessment of newly arrived professionals

To this end it is possible that recognition as a professional in one area of the world might not always be automatically accepted in another community, unless there has been an appropriate period of acclimatization during which people can show that they have learned how to operate within the new surroundings. The concept of inter-institution Reciprocal Recognition Agreements for membership of professional bodies, such as those negotiated between the HKIE and other bodies in the UK, Australia and China, where each automatically recognizes stated awards of the other without further validation, may usefully avoid the administrative need to assess technically competent people twice but do not say that the person will fit into the local scene.

The process of adjustment to a new environment may require a period of working practise in the local area before a new arrival can be allowed to operate as a full professional in that community — the concept of a doctor who can not communicate in the language of the patient is too horrible to conceive. However, this is what we see in many areas of computing professional's lives when they move across regions — their language and expectations are out of step with those of local people. They may be exemplary technicians, in that they can conduct their technical procedures extremely well, but an inability to be persuasive, to appreciate different attitudes and to perceive difficulties in their counterparts are serious hindrances to a smooth transition.

The Hong Kong Engineering Registration Board's insistence that, in addition to being technically competent, an applicant must also have at least one full year's experience in the territory before becoming a "Registered Professional Engineer" (a legislative requirement to undertake a growing number of safety critical engineering jobs), and must annually certify himself to be competent in order to retain that distinction, has much to offer in the protection of the general community. Such requirements do not yet apply to the realm of the software industry in Hong Kong, but it is possible that the future right to review systems which have an impact on the public may be restricted to appropriately competent people.

6.6.4 Summary

The concepts of what is necessary before one can be classed as a professional in computing are not necessarily the same in all communities. Therefore they may need to be independently tested against the requirements of those communities. Differences will often manifest themselves in the ways in which people are educated and responsibility is perceived in those communities, and thus in the way in which a professional takes charge of his own decisions and influences those of others. This may mean that a period of adjustment will often be necessary before someone who is recognized as a professional in one community can expect to operate as a professional in another community where the culture is significantly different from that of "home".

Chapter 7
The Road to Professionalism in Medical Informatics

7.1 Introduction

The observation that both theory and practice are essential ingredients of profession-alism was made as far back as 2000 years ago by Vitruvius. In his classical work *Ten Books on Architecture* (cited in [McDermid91]), Vitruvius outlined the range of subjects of which the architect and civil engineer must be knowledgeable, highlighting the equal importance of *fabrica*— practice, and *ratiocinatio*— theory. Practice is a mechanical facility, developed through study and exercise. Theory is the ability to describe and explain the designed object. Practitioners whose abilities are limited to the mechanical skills never achieve much of original significance. Those who, on the other hand, rely on their knowledge of the theory may mistake the shadow of the object for the object itself. Only those who are able to apply well-developed capabilities in both areas to the job to be done will accomplish it successfully.

We believe that an adequate balance of theory and practice is an essential prerequi-site to professionalism in Medical Informatics. However, at present this goal remains elusive as illustrated by the prevailing gulf between exponents of the two camps.

Many practitioners of Medical Informatics have practical skills, for example, in programming languages, interface tools, expert system shells and methods of reasoning with uncertainty. However, such practical skills alone are not sufficient to ensure success. Witness the plethora of systems that have failed through being inappropriate, difficult to use, or not taking account of the organizational structure and culture of healthcare. Some small-scale customized systems, usually built in-house under the guidance of a practical enthusiast, have achieved limited success at their site of development. However, the majority have failed to achieve widespread impact, lacking the sound theoretical underpinning necessary to facilitate flexibility, portability to new sites and compatibility with other systems.

The reverse situation is also problematic. Theorists may produce grand unify-ing schema which purportedly solve all the major problems of Medical Informatics. However, implementations of these schema are often less than adequate, lacking a coherent design and development strategy and having hardware and software require-ments which are well beyond those which are generally available. Furthermore, organizational and management issues are often overlooked by those who design and implement these systems [Kaplan94].

Thus, Medical Informatics has not as yet reached professional status. However, as an expanding and increasingly important discipline in the delivery of healthcare, it is important that we strive towards professionalization. In order to work towards this goal we will examine the current status of Medical Informatics and relate this to the nature of professionalism and to the process by which a profession matures.

The first section of this chapter considers the nature of professionalism, and the phases of progression of knowledge, providing an example from electrical engineering. It also looks at the potential benefits of professionalization and the associated costs of this progression. The second section examines the potential for Medical Informatics to become a professional discipline and how far it has succeeded in this to date. The third section gives three possible scenarios for the future of the discipline, whilst the fourth section suggests some actions that may assist Medical Informatics to become professionalized. Finally, we make some general observations concerning the way forward.

7.2   The Nature of Professionalism

7.2.1   What is a professional?

Engineering is a well-established professional discipline. An engineer applies scientific and theoretical knowledge in designing and constructing structures, machines, systems etc, of economic value for practical, purposeful uses. In particular, engineers use their theoretical foundations to verify, by systematic calculation and before the object is actually built, that a proposed design will satisfy the specifications. This approach justifies the high level of trust which clients and society place on the engineer. It is necessary for the widespread application of potentially dangerous machines and systems in society. It also enables engineers to accept responsibility for the correctness, reliability and safety of their designs without assuming undue personal risk. Thus, two distinguishing characteristics of the engineering profession are:

- A sound theoretical foundation which engineers thoroughly understands and continually applies in their work.

- A highly developed sense of responsibility towards their clients and the public. For example, in refusing a project which is insufficiently resourced to be safe.

The above criteria also apply to other professions such as medicine or law.

Professionals guarantee their ability, not a particular result. The doctor does not guarantee that a particular patient will recover, but rather that the doctor is properly qualified to provide medical services of a certain standard of quality [Brahams89]. The (non professional) supplier of goods or services guarantees the product or result, not ability or qualifications. Professional engineers guarantee their ability and, by implication, the product resulting from applying this ability. Properly applied ability implies the correctness of the design, because the engineer is expected to demonstrate that the design satisfies the specifications. If the design is found to be faulty, the engineer has made a mistake, which in turn, raises serious questions regarding their professional ability and the care with which it was applied.

Admission to membership of a profession is restricted to those who can demonstrate that they have a satisfactory command of a certain body of knowledge, and the ability to apply it to practical problems. This status is usually achieved after several years of academic study and subscription to a code of ethics. Most professional organizations have procedures for reprimanding and even withdrawing the recognition of members whose professional performance does not fulfill the minimum acceptable level of quality or exhibits an unacceptable sense of responsibility.

7.2.2   Phases of development of a profession

The development of a new field of knowledge characteristically has four stages [McDermid91]. However, these stages may overlap, and some may be omitted altogether.

1. Superstition — Unsystematic explanations of observations of the environment. During the late 1970s to the mid 1980s there was much un-substantiated enthusiasm regarding the potential benefits of computers in medicine [Schwartz70]. The application of artificial intelligence to medical problems and development of classic systems such as MYCIN [Shortliffe75] and INTERNIST [Miller82] were taken as evidence that computers would soon "revolutionize" the practice of medicine.

2. Taxonomy — Organization of observations and of objects. By the late 1980s the Medical Informatics community had directed attention towards the classification of medical systems. Various categorizations were proposed based upon criteria such as role of the system, the amount and form of any knowledge in the system [Wyatt91], the style of interaction with the user, type of advice offered [Shortliffe90], etc.

3. Science — Building models to explain observations and to predict as yet unobserved phenomena. As the discipline of Medical Informatics progressed into the early 1990s, practitioners developed evaluation methodologies to measure and predict the effects of medical systems on clinical practice [Wyatt90], and began to perform evaluations e.g. [Veradaguer93] and [Marr94]. Practitioners also started to consider the psychology of users and its implications for system design [Nygren92]. During this period a general awareness of human, cultural and organizational issues came about (e.g. [Forsythe93] and [Kaplan94]).

4. Engineering — Applying knowledge resulting from the scientific phase to design and construct useful new artifacts i.e. to modify the environment. Medical Informatics is still striving to reach this stage of development, and as yet there is little evidence of practitioners applying lessons learnt from evaluations and model building to inform the construction of new systems (e.g. [Heathfield94], [VanDerLei91], [Musen92]).

The development of the electrical engineering profession began around 1600 and provides an example of the four stages above [McDermid91]. Static electricity and natural magnetism were discovered in ancient times, but were not investigated until about 1600 and were of no commercial importance until about 1800. In the late 1700s and early 1800s a basic knowledge of electrostatics and of magnetism was accumulated which culminated in Maxwell's theory of electromagnetism published in 1873. Parallel to the development of the theory, electricity was applied in commercial ventures, some of which were successful and others which were spectacular failures.

For example, in 1851 the first successful underwater cable was laid, and in 1858 the first trans-atlantic cable was put into service. However, this trans-atlantic cable failed just a few weeks later due to breakdown of the cable's insulation by high voltage. This failure was due to the chief electrician of the Atlantic Telegraph Company, who strongly believed that theory and mathematical analyses had no practical value. Consequently, using his practical knowledge alone, he applied an unnecessarily high voltage to ensure that the signal would be strong enough to travel long distances. As a result, the cable's insulation was broken down and the chief engineer was dismissed for failing to acknowledge the importance of theoretical results. However, during the early years of the telegraph, experimentation and theoretical analyses were used to explain many phenomena that were observed. By 1895, the telegraph network was so extensive that a message could be transmitted around the world by electrical means only. During the period 1850-1900, the emphasis changed from using theory to explain observed phenomena, to systematic science and theory beginning to lead practical applications. Related to this shift in emphasis was a change in education which moved away from the teaching of purely facts towards imparting an understanding of underlying theory to students. From 1900 onwards progress became more rapid, with the development and commercial exploitation of long-distance and wireless telegraphy and telephony, national and international telephone networks, radio broadcasting, television, satellite communication, digital communication, etc. The most difficult task facing the electrical engineering discipline was that of educating practitioners and passing on both the theoretical and practical knowledge needed. Electrical engineering courses were originally taught within other departments such as physics, until they reached a stage of maturity that warranted the formation of the specialized electrical engineering departments that exist today.

7.2.3   The benefits of professionalization

A professional approach enables us to develop practical applications that exploit the technical possibilities more thoroughly and utilize them more efficiently. For example, the existence of Maxwell's theory of electromagnetism enabled professional engineers to experimentally verify the existence of these waves, and exploit them practically, at a much earlier date than would have been possible without a professional approach. In the pre-engineering times of the nineteenth century, many bridges in Europe collapsed under the weight of the new locomotives, resulting in considerable loss of life and property. Since a more professional engineering approach became widespread in civil engineering, structural collapses during and after construction are extremely rare.

Professionalism should result in the reduction of errors in new designs and the production of more useful, usable clinical systems. Many medical applications are safety critical, not just in the traditional sense of the word, but because the decisions they affect directly involve people. A professional approach should reduce failures and thus liability exposure, resulting in increased user confidence in clinical systems and increased status for Medical Informatics practitioners.

7.2.4   The costs of professionalization

The benefits of professionalism are not without costs and arise through the need for increased education and regulation. These can be considered in terms of economic, intellectual and psychological factors.

- Some of the economic costs associated with professionalization are spread throughout society, and involve the educational system and the legal and public administrative infrastructure concerned with passing and administrating legislation regulating professional practice and the education process.

- Some existing practitioners of Medical Informatics would need to take part in new educational programs in order to reach the required standards of a professional. The resulting loss of time (e.g. through attendance at night school) and costs incurred (course fees, the cost of joining professional organizations professional literature, etc) could pose a barrier to some existing practitioners, and could serve to dissuade others from starting out on a career in Medical Informatics.

- Psychological factors can also present a barrier to professionalization. Greater intellectual demands are made of professionals than those involved in a craft or trade, and current practitioners may exhibit apathy towards the change, or feel unsure that they can attain the required standards. Those who do make the transition successfully may have to recognize that they have been carrying out some parts of their work wrongly or inefficiently, or that a part of their life's effort has been a waste of time.

7.3   The Potential of Medical Informatics to become a Profession

To assess the potential of Medical Informatics to become a profession, there are two major questions to consider:

- Can Medical Informatics, by its inherent nature, become a profession? In particular, is there a substantial body of scientific, theoretical knowledge underpinning Medical Informatics?

- Is Medical Informatics, as it is currently practised, a professional discipline? If there is a substantial body of scientific and theoretical knowledge in Medical Informatics, then we need to decide if Medical Informatics practitioners regularly apply it to their work. We also need to determine if practitioners carry responsibility (to their clients and the public) for correct, safe systems, and look at the sort of technical and professional associations that exist and what prerequisites they prescribe for prospective members.

7.3.1   Is there a theoretical foundation for Medical Informatics?

Medical Informatics is concerned with the nature of healthcare information and its use in problem-solving and decision-making. Given the advances in computers and communications technology, Medical Informatics also emphasizes the use of computers and Information Technology in both managing healthcare information and supporting the process of healthcare.

Many practitioners recognize the unique problems facing Medical Informatics, distinct from other disciplines such as computer science, mathematics or psychology (e.g. [Huax94]). Shortliffe argues that clinical information is fundamentally different from information used in physics, engineering or clinical chemistry [Shortliffe90]. Physics has a certain kind of generality, in that the concepts and descriptions of the objects and processes of physics are necessarily used in all applied fields, including medicine. These laws and descriptions are essential in representing or explaining functions that are regarded as medical in nature. The application of a computer to a physical problem in a medical context does not differ from doing so in a physics laboratory or for an engineering application. The use of computers in various "low-level processes", such as those in physics and chemistry, is similar and independent of the application. However, in medicine, there are other "higher-level processes" carried out in more complex objects such as organisms (e.g. patients), which have no counterpart in physics or engineering. Whilst one might argue that computers are used routinely in commercial applications where humans and organizations interact, the counter argument would be that these applications are confined to those in which the human activity has been highly abstracted and the events or processes reduced to low-level objects. In medicine, it is not possible to reduce the healthcare process to such abstractions without rendering it meaningless.

In some areas of Medical Informatics, theories and models are already established. For example, in medical problem-solving and decision-making [Kassirer78], the use of uncertain information [Tversky74], doctors' use of medical records [Nygren92], human computer interaction, electronic patient records[Rector93] and safety modelling [Fox93]. In other areas, theory is lacking, particularly the more complex areas which encompass social, cultural and organization issues in relation to healthcare practice. However, recent work is beginning to address these areas [Kaplan94].

Medical Informatics has been introduced into the medical curriculum in many places, and Medical Informatics degrees and post-graduate courses have become established. This provides some evidence that sufficient theoretical foundations exist, or at least that practitioners and students believe they exist. These courses do not suffer lack of material to teach, rather the reverse, and are faced with the difficulty of deciding what is most important. As noted in [Huax94] Medical Informatics education involves teaching "specific methodological approaches and distinct subjects".

Although there is evidence of a theoretical underpinning to Medical Informatics, it is not mature as say engineering, or as well developed or extensive. It can be argued that Medical Informatics is as well developed as the theoretical foundation of many classical engineering fields when they first began. However, Medical Informatics theory is not as closely predictive as in engineering because Medical Informatics is a human science, not a natural science.

Given evidence of a theoretical underpinning to Medical Informatics it might be the case that this theory cannot be successfully applied or is unsuitable. However, this view echoes past attitudes in other disciplines such as electrical engineering. Observation of current practice supports the opinion that theory can be applied, showing an increase in the use of models, evaluation methods, formal specifications and development methodologies in practical applications.

7.3.2   The current status of Medical Informatics

Assuming there is a substantial body of scientific, theoretical knowledge underlying Medical Informatics, then do Medical Informaticists regularly apply it to their work? The answer to this question is generally negative. Many practitioners have little or no academic qualifications. A minority possess doctorates, although these tend to be highly specialized. However, this situation is beginning to change as formal qualifications in Medical Informatics become more common.

Medical Informatics practitioners do not answer to their clients and the public for their work. They cannot verify their designs simply because of the lack of a theoretical basis and experience in applying it (disclaimers are common). Like doctors, Medical Informatics practitioners cannot and do not guarantee anything. However, unlike doctors they are not required to have an established level of skill.

There are several Medical Informatics associations, including; AMIA (American Medication Informatics Association), BMIS (British Medical Informatics Association), BCS PHSG (Primary Health Care Specialist Group of the BCS) and IMIA (International Medication Informatics Association). These associations provide journals and newsletters, regional meetings and specialist interest groups. However, there are no requirements for membership and admission is granted to anyone interested.

A less fundamental, although still important characteristic of a profession, is the breadth of related subfields which it includes. A sufficiently wide range of technical activities must exist if practitioners are to develop the theoretical basis and their practical expertise extensively. Such areas include applications, various specific technical capabilities, standards etc. Medical Informatics by its nature encompasses many subfields, e.g. medical computing, medical decision-making, medical education, etc [Peel94]. There are working groups affiliated with various associations (e.g. The working groups of IMIA, for example IMIA WG 4: Data Protection in Health Information Systems). There are also standards bodies dealing with topics such as the exchange of healthcare information and medical records.

To summarize the position in relation to the two questions of Section 7.3, it can be argued that Medical Informatics does have the potential to become professionalized. Furthermore, the discipline is already facing, if not moving in that direction. The major barriers to this process include the need for more theoretical knowledge in specific areas and improved ability to apply theory to practice, and widespread education of practitioners with the educational infrastructure to support this. The current situation can be compared with electrical engineering during the years 1850-1900, described in Section 7.2.2. Medical Informatics appears to be at the stage where some theory has developed. However, with some exceptions, at present, this theory is used to explain practical phenomena, rather than leading to significant practical applications.

7.4   Medical Informatics in the Future

We believe that the successful progression of Medical Informatics from craft to profession will be influenced by the level of competence of practitioners and the complexity and size of projects they tackle. From its current situation, Medical Informatics may evolve in three distinct ways, as is now described.

7.4.1   The worst-case scenario

This is an extrapolation of the current situation. Medical Informatics practitioners become so enamoured by the wealth of possibilities offered by today's computers that much is attempted. Because practitioners attempt to build systems beyond their capabilities, or systems that are unsuitable or unusable, failures are common and highly visible.

For example, a decision support system wrongly diagnoses a patient and recommends an inappropriate treatment which causes the patient permanent damage. The patient sues the doctor and system suppliers. In one centre, a radiation therapy machine is incorrectly set-up by a clinician and administers very high doses of radiation to cancer patients for many months before discovery [Joyce87].

This situation is unstable and cannot be sustained indefinitely. Money is wasted, patients' lives are put at risk and the credibility of Medical Informatics practitioners slowly diminishes. At this point two choices are possible. The first is to restrict the application of Medical Informatics to that which is well within the limited capabilities of the practitioners, the second is to substantially increase the technical competence of Medical Informatics practitioners. The first choice leads to a future which is reactionary and backward. The second choice leads to a future which is more desirable, where true professionalism is achieved, but ten to twenty years after it should have been.

7.4.2   The reactionary, backward scenario

Here the application of Medical Informatics is limited to cover only those areas that non-professionals can handle satisfactorily. Because widespread scepticism predominates, few applications are attempted, and there is general consensus from within the discipline and from the public that Medical Informatics should be approached very cautiously (e.g. [Lancet90]). Funding may be reduced or withdrawn as a symptom of this attitude. Stringent evaluations may be required before systems can be introduced, even on a small scale, often causing projects nearing completion, or ongoing work to be abandoned as the extra evaluation burden proves too much. Innovative work is scrapped in favour of using traditional techniques. Many opportunities are lost and the discipline stagnates and possibly dies out.

For example, hospital doctors group together and show their protest against a new computer system by wearing badges that show their dissatisfaction, instead of trying to work with developers and management to improve the system [Sears92]. Doctors carry on using paper records in parallel to a new electronic patient record system because they don't have confidence in the system and feel data may be lost or corrupted. Patients refuse to be treated by doctors using computer-based decision support systems as they feel that errors are likely.

7.4.3   The radical, progressive scenario

Here, thanks to early adoption of the professional model, the professionalism and qualifications of clinical software designers have been developed to such a high level that even very challenging demands can be met reliably and safely. When the specification for a proposed system goes beyond current capabilities, the Medical Informatics professional does not continue oblivious to potential problems, but recognizes the challenge, changes the specification and informs the client about what can be achieved and how much confidence can be vested in the result. The Medical Informatics professional accepts full responsibility to deliver what was finally agreed with the client. This scenario is uneventful, as the results are as expected and there are no risks or surprises.

For example, a hospital contracts a supplier to provide a medical record system based upon national standards for data capture and storage. The software team carries out a user-centred design exercise to elicit user requirements, then using existing software components produces a system which fits the hospital's unique requirements exactly, and also meets national standards for data collection, and ensures data compatibility between other applications used at the hospital site and in the National Health Service as a whole. The clinical staff receive the necessary training and the system quickly and effortlessly becomes part of routine practice. Clinical practitioners cannot imagine their work without the system and joke about the old paper system.

7.5   Steps Towards the Medical Informatics Professionalization and Key Player Roles

In the progression towards professionalism, we have two choices. We can follow the examples set by other professions such as engineering, or we can ignore these lessons and learn them the hard way through experience. Both paths may lead to the same future, but the first requires less effort and would accelerate our progression.

Medical Informatics practitioners can be criticized for viewing everything in the domain as new, rejecting older established ideas from other disciplines as being irrelevant to the "new" field [Heathfield93]. We invent new jargon which mystifies Medical Informatics. Often we are involved in work which repeats that done in other areas, such as Software Engineering, because of a lack of familiarity with existing techniques and knowledge. The symptoms of this situation are isolation, re-invention, failure to credit previous work, and an inclination to pursue fads, and they significantly hinder progress towards professionalism. Medical Informatics practitioners must widen their perspectives and learn from the work of other disciplines.

In the transition from trade or craft to a professional discipline an important factor is perceived need. There is a general awareness emerging in the Medical Informatics community that recognizes the need for the discipline to change its approach. The current situation has fostered a plethora of small, fragmented systems which lack integration, many of which are built by unqualified enthusiasts. This has led to a history of failure, and most importantly, a general perception by many doctors and others that Medical Informatics consists merely of a group of computer scientists who are not interested in, and who do not understand clinical medicine and its needs [Carey92], [Smith92], [Wyatt94a], [Wyatt94b].

All those who are involved directly or indirectly with Medical Informatics, must take specific actions to facilitate the progression towards professionalism. Four groups that are particularly influential are academia, system developers, those who purchase and use the products of Medical Informatics, and Medical Informatics societies.

7.5.1   Role of academia

Academia is faced with the task of formulating Medical Informatics curricula that meet the needs of professionals. With the establishment of undergraduate and postgraduate courses in Medical Informatics, the topic of education is beginning to receive more attention from the community. Medical students need to be provided with the basic principles of Medical Informatics which will be of lasting use throughout their careers, and will equip them to learn new knowledge, if and when necessary. Medical Informatics students need to be educated with necessary skills, including an understanding of medical practice and its information management problems. Whilst they do not need to be medically qualified, they do need to be fluent in medical language, issues and procedures in order that they can communicate with users in their own language. A balance must be achieved between academic and practical issues, and it is important that Medical Informatics increases its theoretical basis by experimentation and generalization. However, at the moment many teachers tend to be purely academic and can't provide experiential knowledge. Given the wide scope of Medical Informatics it may be the case that we need to develop a typology which classifies the goals of the discipline against the informatics domains, (as suggested in [Peel94]) and thus enables us to define the different (work) roles of Medical Informaticists and the qualifications and skills necessary to each.

7.5.2   Role of system developers

System developers have to operate in the current environment in which there is a shortage of people with the necessary skills. Furthermore, given the lack of professional status, employers cannot easily differentiate between those who possess the required skills and those who do not. They may therefore find themselves forced to hire people who are not qualified for the job. In particular, they may resort to using software engineers who do not fully understand the problem domain, rather than professionally qualified Medical Informatics practitioners. Those who manage projects may have skills that are out-dated, and so tend to hire employees who also work in a similar manner, thus restricting the use of new and innovative techniques and limiting successes. Conversely, assuming that all new tools and techniques are good can hinder progress.

In order to overcome the barriers to professionalization, employers and professional associations must take active steps to encourage practitioners to make the transition. Incentives may take the form of recognition, distinction between those who attain the new higher qualifications and those who do not attempt to, allowing practitioners to pursue their studies in work time, promotion and increased salary for those who complete the new qualifications, etc. Legislation regulating who may practise in the field can be a powerful incentive to professionalize. For example, the engineering discipline has used legislation to regulate those who work on safety-critical projects and applications.

7.5.3   Role of purchasers and users

The purchasers and users of Medical Informatics products must be adamant on the need for systems that fully meet requirements and are of sufficient quality, rejecting cheap products that don't meet their needs. It is important that purchasers are not taken in by extravagant claims without evidence, and obtain the knowledge necessary to make the right choice. They should not be fooled by jargon, avoid those who are over enthusiastic and unquestioning about the merits of computers, and demand guarantees on professional qualifications of suppliers and final products. We are beginning to see moves towards clinical specialists learning more about Medical Informatics issues with conferences organized by the BMA and Royal Colleges and review articles in major medical weeklies.

7.5.4   Role of societies

In the transition to professionalism, societies play an important role. Existing Medical Informatics societies act as interest groups and do not fill the role of professional societies which define and award professional status and monitor the conduct of members. The need for new Medical Informatics societies can be approached in three ways:

- Transformation of existing associations, for example, the British Medical Informatics Society has recently launched a Fellowship grade of membership.

- Establishing subsidiary societies within existing professional societies, for example the Primary Health Care Specialist Group in the British Computer Society.

- Founding professional organizations, for example the International Medical Informatics Association.

7.5.5   Possible criteria for a Medical Informatics professional

At the current time, the discipline of Medical Informatics includes an eclectic mixture of people, who have vastly different backgrounds, qualifications, practical experience and motivation. If we are to endorse certain individuals as Medical Informatics professionals we must define criteria for inclusion in the profession. At present it is very difficult to specify what exactly should constitute a Medical Informatics professional, and these criteria may change as the discipline progresses. However, it is constructive to attempt to define the distinguishing characteristics in order that we can start to inform the educational process and development of professional societies. Possible criteria include:

- Possession of an appropriate educational background. This may be Computer science, a clinical training or possibly some other subject such as psychology.

- Knowledge of the theory and principles of Medical Informatics, achieved through participation in accredited training courses and tested by exams.

- Skills in using appropriate tools and methods, which would be measured by experience in various areas or with systems.

- Possession of the appropriate attitudes:

  - A commitment to maintaining an up-to-date knowledge of the discipline. Refusal to work on unrealistic or unethical projects. A commitment to taking users' needs fully into account.

  - Integrity: for example, no evidence of inappropriate work or behaviour in the past.

  - Reliability, vouched for by references from several existing Medical Informatics professionals.

  - Loyalty to the profession, expressed by a willingness to share knowledge and insights with others via publication of quality papers, participation in continuing education activities and teaching.

7.6   Conclusions

Medical Informatics practitioners need both technical and theoretical skills if they are to meet the challenge of developing successful reliable applications for healthcare. Education has an extremely important role to play in the development of a professional approach. It influences, and will be influenced by, those criteria which are seen as desirable for a professional Medical Informaticist. In the current climate where successes are still few, and general perceptions of the discipline are either negative or it is seen as irrelevant to clinical practice, positive steps are necessary to steer the discipline towards the "radical, progressive future" described in Section 7.4.3. One reason put forward to explain the current situation is the rarity of appropriate system evaluations and this issue needs further attention, particularly if we are to assess the social, professional and organizational implications of using information technology in healthcare [Heathfield95]. However, the underlying problem cannot be blamed on specific issues such as evaluation approaches, as these are merely symptoms of a wider lack of professionalism. At this stage it is important that we redirect energy away from retrospective analyses of why things went wrong, and instead take positive steps towards making the transition from an interest group into a profession. Otherwise we may find ourselves confined to work in an over-regulated and stagnating domain, the "reactionary, backward scenario" described in Section 7.4.2.

Chapter 8
Who should License Software Engineers?

8.1 Introduction

Licensure and other forms of mandated competency validation are shortly to become an integral component of the Software Engineering profession in the United States. The powerful economic, safety, social and political forces ensuring this transition are the natural, second-order consequence of the familiar technological factors that Software Engineering seeks to manage. However, the United States is not alone. Licensure and similar requirements are a probability in every nation that materially depends on software engineers.

This chapter expands the discussion from [Melford95] and reviews those factors forcing the Software Engineering profession's evolution in the United States. Using these factors as a foundation, this chapter then explores the transnational nature of Software Engineering activities and the ramifications of licensure. The chapter concludes by considering the questions of:

- Who will make the regulations?

- Is it reasonable to believe that software engineers can act to make these appropriate in the context of the discipline?

8.2 Recognizing the Inevitable

There is no point for American software engineers to insert our collective head in the sand. Licensure requirements for US software engineers are inevitable. To a material extent, they are already here today. While the precise mechanism for instituting licensure or similar controls on software engineers in other countries may very well differ, the factors driving this requirement will be similar.

8.2.1 Disastrous pressure

Imagine the political pressure to "do something" following a catastrophic loss of life caused by software failure. Could politicians possibly restrain themselves following the downing of a Boeing 777 attributed to a fault in its software-based avionics? The rush to act will insure the legislation's unsuitability in the context of Software Engineering.

The United States has endured well intentioned, but naive efforts to prevent states from applying existing and future Professional Engineer (PE) licensure laws to software engineers. These actions only increase the likelihood that these laws will be established and enforced by people wholly ignorant of our discipline's abilities and constraints. (US licensure regulations are separately controlled by each of the fifty States and five national jurisdictions: Washington, D.C.; Puerto Rico; US Virgin Islands; Guam; Northern Marinas Islands.)

8.2.2   Harbingers of doom

This downward spiral has already begun. On January 7, 1995, the California State Board of Registration for Professional Engineers unanimously voted to redefine the terms "electrical engineering" and "electrical engineer" to include control and responsibility for software and firmware components in electrical and electronic products. (Of the California Board's thirteen voting members, only five are engineers. Only one of these five is an electrical engineer and none are software engineers.)

To be technically precise, the title "engineer" is protected by law in all US states and five national jurisdictions. Only individuals licensed and registered as a PE are legally allowed to call themselves engineers. At best, everyone else is merely a graduate of an engineering program.

8.2.3   Shrinking loopholes

So, in theory, all American software engineers are already required to be licensed. In reality, states have limited enforcement resources and many "grandfathered" title and industry exemptions that have resulted in a relatively inconsistent application of licensure. These grandfathered exemptions address such job functions as railroad and airline flight engineers. However, where health, safety, welfare, or environment have previously been harmed in a material way, licensure enforcement is vigorous – even barbers must be licensed. Software's ever increasing integration into the depths of society's fabric insures that the critical point-of-no-return will be crossed shortly.

8.2.4   Non-technical motivations

Many computing professionals point out that demands for licensure are strongly supported by government bureaucrats and legislators seeking greater power and tax revenue. They also point out that licensure is advocated to restrict entry into the profession to inflate incomes. They may similarly demonstrate that licensure will limit the profession's creativity, diminishing its total value to society. These are all valid arguments. There are many others. They all beg the issue and are thus valueless (Americans would say these arguments are all "red-herrings").

Society is the critical motivating force. Even the marketplace is secondary. History teaches us this. Consistently, predictably, unwaveringly, American society has demanded independent competency validation for individuals engaged in economically self-benefiting work that has health, safety, social welfare or environmental consequences, before the practitioner enters the marketplace. Software engineers will not receive special treatment.

In all but the most totalitarian of nations, these societal factors exist in direct proportion to a technology's ability to cause significant causalities. As the application of computing technology reaches ever more deeply and broadly into the very fabric of everyday social and economic activities, so shall a society's need to assert a relative degree of control over the practices that can lead to harm.

It is for these reasons that engineering licensure laws exist in the United States and many other nations. Even without the title "Software Engineering," the mere presence of software programs controlling activities materially threatening health, safety, or environmental harm, ensures licensure or licensure-like controls.

8.3   Software (and Computing) Ignores National Borders

Licensure regulations have always been based on one unwavering assumption: the licensed individual is only able to practice their profession in one geographic location, at one fixed point in time. The surgeon can only operate at one hospital and the barrister can only argue their case in one court, at any given moment. Of course, software engineers and most computing professionals see the immediate fallacy of this assumption. No physical laws of nature preclude software from controlling multiple computers, simultaneously, at any (well, nearly any) geographic location. Similarly, the individual writing a given software program can reside and transact their professional capacities in a geographic location wholly apart from where the target computer resides.

The obvious problem that now arises is: "Who has jurisdiction to decide if licensure is required?" Should jurisdiction be determined based on where the software engineer lives or works? Or should it be the location of the software's ownership (e.g., the Boeing 777's avionics vendor)? Perhaps jurisdiction should lie with the location of the end-user. Then again, who is the end-user? (e.g., Would it be Boeing, located in Washington state, or the airline, which might be from another state or country?)

8.4   Riding the Wave of Change

It is unlikely that Software Engineering licensure is a professional burden that can be avoided. Consequently, it is appropriate for software engineers and their employers, educators and professional societies to facilitate the deployment of licensure mechanisms that reasonably address the nature of software and Software Engineering.

8.4.1   Professional requirements

Obviously, we must be able to understand the demands the discipline of Software Engineering must meet. This is not intended to sound trite. It is very simple to say, "we need to understand what makes our discipline a profession." However, this can be very difficult to comprehensively describe.

Similarly, it is easy to state what target information a profession must know about itself – we can glean the outline from other professions. These factors are generally agreed to be (1) the body of knowledge and recommended practices; (2) an educational curriculum; (3) an ethical framework for resolving conflicting problems in a socially constructive manner; and (4) the minimal quantity of experience needed with applying the body of knowledge using recommended practices while operating within the ethical framework.

However, defining each of these areas can be very difficult. For example, in late 1994 the Board of Governors of the IEEE Computer Society (IEEE-CS) invited the Association for Computing Machinery to help it establish Software Engineering as a (formal) profession. (This chapter's author chairs the project's ethics task force, in conjunction with an ACM co-chair.) An eighteen month to two year time span of work was originally contemplated. An open-ended time frame is now often voiced.

8.4.2   Competency validation

If licensure, or a more benign "voluntary" certification is associated with a profession, then a mechanism is needed to establish that a candidate possesses, at least, the minimal level of competency. The mechanism for validating competency can use any number of techniques. These techniques may include examination, independent documentation verifying work or educational experience, personal testimonials (sponsorship) from an accepted member of the profession on behalf of the candidate etc. However, a consistent and reproducible application of the chosen techniques is almost always required.

8.4.3   Continuing competency

In professions that deal with rapid technological innovation, knowledge obsolescence may be a risk. A common response is to establish a mechanism for maintaining competency. This may be defined as a voluntary or mandatory activity. Mechanisms may include continuing education, re-examination and supplementary apprenticeships. As with the initial competency validation, the consistent and reproducible application of the chosen techniques is usually required.

8.4.4   Graded competency validation

Some professions institute several levels of competency validation. These levels reflect the severity of dangerous work a practitioner is qualified to do. For software engineering this might mean that a proof of competency necessary for building mission-critical applications would be less then that required for safety-critical missions. This also suggests that it is unlikely that video game programmers would require competency validation beyond that measured by their employer.

Physicians and surgeons in the United States offer an example of this methodology. Physicians must first qualify for a licence awarded by a state government. The licence provides the base validation that they possess sufficient competency and knowledge to assure they will always fulfill their Hippocratic Oath to "do no harm." The physician or surgeon may then elect to demonstrate their further competency in a particular specialty such as pediatrics or neurosurgery. This secondary competency validation is documented by a certification granted by the professional society dedicated to that area of practice. Physicians must obtain their licence before undertaking any work because all medical activities conducted in the presence of a human being present a safety-critical risk.

The inverse of this approach may be more amenable to Software Engineering, however. A certification of competency for less-than-safety-critical activities may be appropriately offered by professional or industry entities. A licence to work on safety-critical applications is something most likely reserved to a government. While there is no universal truism that would require the attainment of one gradient before the other, appropriate certifications could be prerequisites for attaining a licence.

8.4.5   Delegation

Software Engineering is often a team effort. It may not be necessary or appropriate for every team member to be licensed. Supervisory or some other critical subset of licensed individuals may be sufficient. Validation by organizational entity may also be appropriate. ISO9000 certification presently does this for validating competent quality assurance mechanisms.

8.4.6   Professional consensus

Many models exist for establishing and documenting consensus regarding technical activities. The mechanisms used by the IEEE Standards Department implements one of these models. This consensus methodology is well known in the Software Engineering field. This methodology is now being used by the joint IEEE-CS/ACM task force on software engineering ethics to document standards of ethical and professional practices. This IEEE methodology may be appropriate for facilitating the establishment of common licensure requirements and administrative mechanisms.

8.4.7   International standards

IEEE Standards are recognized internationally. Such standards include the VME Bus and IEEE-802/ISO-8802 ("Ethernet"). Using this same methodology may allow for a common foundation for Software Engineering licensure regulation in much of the world.

8.4.8   International licensure?

Well, probably not. A licence granted to individuals by an entity such as the United Nations is without precedence. There is no reason to expect that Software Engineering would be the issue that changes this.

Reciprocal treaties between nations that mutually recognize the other's competency metrics is logistically untenable. Simply stated: n nations, requires $n(n-1)$ separate treaties between all nations, to respect all national authorizations. There are too many treaties to negotiate. It will never happen.

What seems more likely is something resembling the approach of the recently negotiated General Agreements on Tariffs and Trade (GATT). Rather then negotiating individual treaties, a single common treaty is adopted by multiple nations. In the case of the GATT, most nations are likely to abide by it because its aggregate benefits should outweigh individual detriments. Similarly, if the global marketplace determines that software produced by people validated by common metrics is desirable, then a global Software Engineering competency requirement will be established.

Is this something that the software engineering profession, national governments, and the global market place can be assured will occur? An emphatic "yes" or "no" is probably impossible to assert. The accelerating adoption of the ISO9000 standards suggests to this author that the global marketplace values common quality assurance metrics. The GATT and the North American Free Trade Agreement (NAFTA) adopted by the United States, Canada and Mexico, both incorporate mechanisms that confer mutual recognition and trust of governmental regulations for safety and environmental controls. This further suggest that national governments value common standards of practice.

Internationally recognized mechanisms such as the IEEE standards process can provide the information flow necessary to draft such a common set of metrics. But patience will be required. The history of the ISO9000 standards, as well as the GATT and NAFTA negotiations certainly support the expectation of a lengthy process.

8.5 Conclusions

Licensure is an issue neither to be loathed nor advocated. It is simply an issue that must be managed. If our profession chooses to take the leadership role, licensure can be instituted in a manner appropriate to the context of the discipline. If we do not act, history and human nature will clearly chart an alternate course.

Part II
Accountability

The title of this book is *The Responsible Software Engineer*, but responsible for what? Obviously for producing systems which meet the demands of the employer, but are there any wider obligations? In this Part of the book, we cover two such categories, ethical and legal. Ethical obligations can be thought of as those responsibilities which are internal to oneself; while legal obligations are external, governmental requirements. Together, they make up what we mean by accountability. Accountability is the sum-total of obligations, personal, social and legal, with which the software engineer is faced.

We start the ethical strand with a controversial contribution by John Wilkes, *Is an Ethical Code Feasible?* Wilkes confronts head-on the belief, so prevalent in our hard-nosed industry, that there is no place in commercial (or academic) life for considerations such as personal responsibility and fairness. He argues that, on the contrary, the machismo individualism of recent management philosophy is an aberration from the norm, that the very notion of computing professionals behaving "badly" implies an understanding, however basic, of what it is to behave properly. He is not concerned about promoting any one set of principles over another (he observes that in many parts of the world, one's ethics are determined by one's religion), but to rehabilitate the idea that by taking part in the software profession one is, almost by definition, taking part in something which has an ethical framework.

Duncan Langford in *Can a Software Engineer "Afford" to be Ethical?* builds on that platform by looking at several cases where it may appear to be against the interest of the individual computer professional or organization to act ethically — where, for example, honesty may not appear to be the best policy. He argues that, in an industry such as computing, where trust is such an important commodity, acting ethically is the only long-term paying strategy. Thus Langford comes out strongly in favour of the "Stakeholder Society", where each constituent of that society, be it consumer, producer or general public, must be given due consideration. In this view, the world is not necessarily a place of dog eat dog, rather, it is, or can be, a place of intelligent self-interest.

In *Software Project Management Ethics*, Simon Rogerson takes this picture of computing as an inherently ethical pursuit a stage further by looking at one partic-ular methodology, Structured Project Management (SPM). According to Rogerson, overseeing a computer project is not just a matter of defining the task sufficiently and employing the right quantity and quality of resources to get the job done. His concern is to show that, whatever methodology is used, the technical problems are inevitably overlaid with ethical considerations. In his example, the 10 Steps of SPM are challenged, complemented and enriched by eight ethical principles, such as honour and honesty. Of course, it is possible to produce classifications to rival Rogerson's, but that really isn't the point; what is important is, like Langford, he believes that computing is more than just a technical exercise. And if this sounds obvious, , in the real world it most certainly is not — the pressures upon us all to act unprofessionally, to ignore our implicit value judgements or to cut ethical corners are only too real. It is a central and challenging belief of authors such as Rogerson that "good" computer systems require "good" ethical judgements.

Another chapter which emphasizes the ethical responsibilities of the computing profession is that by Mary Lou Hines & J. Kenneth Blundell. In *Obligations for IT Ethics Education*, Hines & Blundell remind us just how important the computing profession is: they say that "software engineering professionals impact society in more pervasive ways than perhaps any other profession to date." No doubt the medical, religious, legal, and even political professions would dispute this assertion, but the very fact that Hines & Blundell can say it at all shows how far the computing profession has come within a very few years. Given this all-pervasive spread, Hines & Blundell argue that the ethical use of computers is the responsibility of everyone, not just the computer professional. In other words, we must educate our end-users, even the people who do not realize they are using software systems! They make an analogy between computing and the car; no car is safe, however good the brakes are, unless the driver is educated to drive with due care and attention. Their conclusion is that we need the equivalent of a Highway Code for computing, and that this code must cover the end-users (presumably the pedestrians) as well as the software engineers (the drivers).

These chapters on ethical responsibilities lead naturally to a consideration of the industry's legal responsibilities, which is the second strand of our discussion of Accountability. It is alarming that most software engineers act as if unaware of the mass of legislation that affects or threatens them personally. For example in the UK, the Health and Safety legislation, the Data Protection Act, the law of Contract, the Misuse of Computers Act and the Official Secrets Act. This is not the place to cover the whole range of these liabilities, rather we highlight a few key areas, and note that the computer professional does not have to be a legal expert but that an overall *awareness* of the sort of legal obligations which are relevant to the industry is generally sufficient.

We begin the legal strand with Dai Davis' *Legal Aspects of Safety Critical Systems*. As society becomes increasingly dependent upon computer systems, Davis shows how easily the computing profession could become sucked into a vortex of litigation. He reviews the traditional legal remedies, the law of contract and negligence, and legislation such as the Health and Safety at Work Act. But these legislative remedies work on a reactive basis — only after a problem has occurred does the court case ensue; a process which can be lengthy, costly and uncertain. Davis describes the alternative approach of Product Liability Law, which attempts to legislate quality into products, rather than prosecute for its lack. Many of these Directives, for example the ElectroMagnetic Compatibility (EMC) legislation, are directly relevant to the computer industry. To be professional in Davis' context is to produce computer systems which have these requirements taken fully on-board. His view is akin to the enlightened self-interest of Langford and Rogerson, except he offers very little direct talk about ethical considerations, and a great deal about professionalism as competence within a legislative framework.

In the next chapter, Elizabeth France, the UK Data Protection Registrar, asks the question *Do Software Engineers Help or Hinder the Protection of Data?* This is indeed a startling question, rather like asking whether doctors are good for peoples' health. If we call ourselves a profession, France's chapter prompts the question "How good a profession?" After all, if computer practitioners cannot be relied upon to protect computerized data, what can they be relied upon for? She lists a number of examples where computer systems almost casually invade the privacy of the individual. Doubtless, such systems are well-enough written in the sense that they process data to the satisfaction of their owners, but do they place insufficient importance upon the rights of the individual? In these instances, accountability seems to stretch only as far as the interests of the employer or the purchaser of the system. In terms of the Stakeholder Society, France implies that the rights of the general public are often ignored. This, and other criticisms like it, must be taken taken seriously by the computing industry if its claims to be a "responsible", professional occupation are to mean anything.

Finally, we have a timely chapter by John Race, who asks *Is it Reasonable to Apply the Term "Responsible" to Non-Human Entities?* His question is a simple one: in these days when more or less everything is done by computer, when something goes wrong, who or what do we sue? The excuse that "it was the fault of the computer" or "the system did it" does not help, as we cannot imprison or fine a computer. Or can we? Race's solution to this thorny problem for the on-going automation of everyday tasks is ingenious, and in the best traditions of computer professionalism; being elegant and simple. Race restores the concept of liability into automated systems and in so doing, his chapter can be seen as a metaphor for the computing industry as a whole, for it is an example of the creative response to a problem which is, surely, a large part of what we mean being professional. Being professional is not just being responsible — it requires a certain talent as well.

In summary, this Part of the book shows a variety of attitudes towards professionalism. That is not to say that they are contradictory, rather in most cases, they complement one another. The picture which is built-up is richer than the sum of the parts, and the resulting definition of "professionalism" is all the better for that.

Chapter 9
Is an Ethical Code Feasible?

9.1   Introduction

This chapter aims to show that ethical codes in Software Engineering, as in any other business, are desirable and necessary, and then offers suggestions as to how ethical precepts might be enforced. It is not directly concerned with the content of any ethical code. It will be argued that it is possible to satisfy three essential conditions before any ethical code can be launched with some possibility of general acceptance. Firstly, an ethical code can be *feasible;* that is, consonant with the imperatives of the business and organizational world and capable of being absorbed into the system. Secondly, it can be *acceptable* to those involved and thus likely to be taken up voluntarily. Thirdly, effective *sanctions* can be devised to discourage breaches of the code.

We will look at these three requirements in turn, from the standpoint of the software engineer as *professional*. There is an extensive literature on professionals and professionalism, in which it is generally agreed that the defining characteristics of a "professional" are *personal authority*, which stems from specialist knowledge, *personal responsibility* ("the buck stops here") and *personal integrity*, which requires one's knowledge to be deployed in the client's interest ([Jackson70] which remains an excellent summary of the issues).

The essential word is "personal". Whether we discuss software engineers who earn their living as sole consultants, partners or salaried employees, every one of them who wishes to have professional status must accept, a *personal* ethical responsibility to their profession; which is independent of any other responsibilities they may have to the organization which pays them, and may well take precedence over them. If, for example, a software engineer discovered that their employer was cheating a client in some way, or that a client was proposing to use their work for dishonest purposes, then professional responsibility should compel the engineer to "blow the whistle", quite apart from any other imperatives they might have for taking action.

This is a "high" definition of professionalism, which includes criteria beyond technical competence, and refers back to the traditional professions: Holy Orders, medicine and the law and — until recently — university teaching. It is a moot point whether groups of occupations commonly referred to as "professional" — particularly various branches of engineering — should be defined in a similar fashion. In my view, software engineers would be wise to adopt the older model. We shall return to this point more than once.

Whether one thinks a code of ethics for software engineers is required at all depends on where one stands on the larger question of professionalism. While we might concede that more and more organizations are taking ethical questions seriously nowadays, it does not follow automatically that any occupational sub-group needs its own code of ethics.

However, if we want software engineers to be considered as true professionals and we accept that autonomy and personal responsibility are indispensable elements in professional status, then some form of ethical code is essential. Such codes guide individuals in pursuing their professional activities. Even the most experienced person sometimes needs such guidance, while an ethical code is an important model for the socialization of those in training. In any event, the community requires that all those classes of people who hold power over its members subject themselves, or be subjected, to some form of control. Particular forms of control have grown in the United Kingdom mainly by historical accretion, sometimes confirmed by Statute, and largely through the initiatives of professionals themselves rather than positive action by the State, but they have always existed.

It can also be asked whether there is anything about our profession which justifies a different code from that of other "modern technical professions", such as civil or mechanical engineering, insofar as they have such a code. This is a matter of opinion, depending on whether one sees software engineers primarily as "facilitating technicians" who provide the best possible service, without regard to its use, or as having, because of their power and status, an element of personal responsibility for the use of the information flow which their professional skills bring about. That point will be addressed briefly at the end of the chapter, as a starting point for general discussion.

9.2   Feasibility: Establishing an Ethical Code

Given that software engineers should have a code of ethics, two obstacles come to mind when considering the feasibility of promoting such a code. The first is that everyday business discourse does not include the vocabulary of ethics. Partly as a result of that fact, ethical practices and the limits of acceptable conduct in business are defined by a largely unexamined customary law. To put it cynically, those in any occupation know what one is — or is not — likely to get away with, and some practitioners base their actions on that knowledge. The extent of unethical practice in organizations generally is unknown, but reports by (and about) governmental bodies, corporations and other organizations suggest that it is substantial.

It would be naive to suggest that there has been a recent, large-scale change in traditional behaviour. However, the media appear to be increasing their ability to bring down public censure on those members of an organization who behave in a way considered to be unethical. Such censure often weakens the organization's bargaining power in the market place and thus has to be taken into consideration by even the most cold-blooded company boss. There is evidence that some organizations are beginning a process of ethical self-examination and are in a more receptive mood to include an ethical element in their policy and practice than they were. It may also be that a wider cultural change is under way, in which macho management becomes difficult to sustain. If that is the case, then the ethics of Information Technology will form part of any more general discussion.

Therefore this may be a good time to engage with such a movement, at the least through consciousness-raising activities and opportunities for discussion and training. This is already happening to some extent through the education of software engineers, spurred on by the BCS requirement that a recognized Degree in Computer Science must include attention to computer ethics and the social impact of computing. One is less sure how much discussion goes on within the industry itself. Professional bodies and conferences are helpful in stimulating such discussion. It is important to bring the dialogue of ethics into the everyday conversations of software engineers and managers.

The second obstacle lies' in convincing organizations and individuals that it is *feasible* to promote ethical behaviour; that so doing would not shackle one's ability to do deals and make profits. So far as I know, there is no school of thought which holds that ethical matters are entirely irrelevant to business or that no form of guidance should be given to individuals and corporations. The dispute centres on the *efficacy* of ethical prescription; whether anyone takes any notice of ethical propositions or carries them out in practice. That is why one has first to establish feasibility before discussing content or implementation.

Reasons may be drawn from widely varied sources to suggest that it is feasible and indeed necessary — for organizations to have an ethical element in their composition and operation. What are they?

First and foremost, human beings are social animals who normally regulate their conduct with a bias towards co-operation. The current rhetoric which insists that macho management and short term competitive advantage are the best strategies for corporate success has temporarily obscured a perennial truth; namely, that periods in any society when raw appetite prevailed over co-operative endeavour have been brief and unpopular. It would take us too far from our theme to discuss why Thatcherism and Reaganomics have pervaded so much thinking over the last fifteen years. It may be that their days are nearly over, but the raw economic individualism which they extol has a perennial appeal.

Let us take this point further. I hold that is it in accord with human nature, as witnessed by the record of collective human experience, for people to devise measures which secure effective and peaceable co-operation. Such co-operation requires a moral code and ethical principles for the resolution of disputes and general guidance in everyday life. Nietzsche said that "morality is the herd instinct in the individual." Here, as on so many other occasions, he produced a usable psychological truth in a pre-Freudian form. Since the 1880s we have acquired a more systematic (one still hesitates to say "scientific") understanding of individual and group psychology, sociology and culture, especially through recent work in sociobiology. The consensus of that work remains that co-operation is the norm, even in a competitive environment [Ruse93].

In short, co-operative conduct is natural and ethical codes guide shape particular forms of co-operation. It does not follow, of course, that co-operation can be equated with ethical behaviour. (We cannot argue that because co-operation suits gene pools it thereby constitutes a virtue or moral good.) But the knowledge we now have suggests that an ethic of co-operation and mutual concern has the potential to be acceptable and long-lasting, because it is founded on deep-seated human inclinations.

Our second ground for feasibility is derived from the more sophisticated view of business ethics which has gained ground over the last ten or so years. Business ethics was too long concerned with the ethics of profit, either as prosecutor or counsel for the defence. Two of the concepts which have invigorated the subject are "stakeholder" and "corporate culture".

Robert Solomon defines *stakeholders* as "all of those who are affected and have legitimate expectations and rights regarding the actions of the company, and these include the employees, the consumers and the suppliers as well as the surrounding community and the society at large. The virtue of this concept is that it greatly expands the focus of corporate concern, without losing sight of the particular virtues and capacities of the corporation itself. Social responsibility, so considered, is not an additional burden on the corporation but part and parcel of its essential concerns, to serve the needs and be fair to not only its investors/owners but those who work for, buy from, sell to, live near or are otherwise affected by the activities that are demanded and rewarded by the free market system" [Solomon93].

It is right to say at once that numerous critics have challenged the concept of the stakeholder. Anyone interested would be well advised to turn first to Elaine Sternberg's accessible and clear-minded *Just Business.* Although she will ultimately have none of stakeholders — since in her view the sole purpose of business is to maximize long-term owner value by selling goods or services, and therefore owners only should have control — she is prepared to concede that "the concept of "stakeholder" still has a useful role . . . [as] . . . a convenient shorthand way of designating those groups whose support is essential for the business's continued existence" [Sternberg95].

If the idea of stakeholding in Solomon's definition (and even to a limited extent in Sternberg's) is acceptable, then any discussion of relationships between stakeholders will include rights and obligations. These ethical concepts will necessarily include professional ethics: i.e. what employees and employers ought to do. The crucial point about stakeholding is that it enlarges the playing field, so to speak, preventing the conduct of an organization from being validated according to a single internally-designated principle, usually profit, and allowing others who will be affected by corporate decisions to have a voice. This point has a special concern for information technology professionals.

"Corporate culture" also enjoys different definitions. Charles Hampden-Turner offers his own definition and those of others in his fascinating book of case studies called *Corporate Culture.* He writes: "The culture of an organization defines appropriate behaviour, bonds and motivates individuals and asserts solutions where there is ambiguity" [Hampden94].

One may also see corporate culture as a natural manifestation of the idea of an enterprise as living thing — a "body corporate" — representing the organization's vision of itself, actualized in management style over time. Corporate culture has now been recognized as a crucial factor in organizational success, and is likely to remain an important element in any corporate strategy.

It will not be lost on anyone that ethical considerations will be involved in the formation and especially the maintenance of corporate culture. Indeed, one cannot see how ethics could be excluded from any discussion on *appropriate* corporate behaviour, especially when moral dilemmas are present. Ethics-related actions in practice tend to become a body of case law or precedent, consulted informally when required. From time to time housekeeping is necessary, when the "done things" are submitted to rational scrutiny. The alternative is usually either a growing discrepancy between what an organization says it does, and what it actually does (an accusation often made by IBM's critics against that company, which has damaged its public image and thereby its chances of recovery) or no policy at all, which will sooner or later trip up the organization in public.

Corporate culture is capable of being judged ethically, in the same way as a person's actions can be judged and, as suggested earlier, such judgements can have significant commercial effects on the organization and its executives: as witness the career of British water utilities after privatization on the one hand, and the immense reserve of public confidence (manifested as continuously rising profits) in such companies as Marks and Spencer, whose corporate culture is both ethically almost irreproachable and exceptionally efficient in commercial terms.

To summarize, there are good reasons for holding that software engineers and the organizations to which they belong will inevitably be faced with ethics-related decisions which will shape corporate culture and internal and external relationships, and whose proper determination is vital to the success of the organization. Whichever way one looks at it, some attention to ethics is a necessity. We should dismiss the notion that business in particular is not a forum for ethical debate as the nonsense it is. The saloon-bar tough talking will remain, and indeed many executives are impervious to anything but the bottom line, but economic necessity, if nothing else, is forcing managers to pay attention to means as well as ends in corporate life.

9.3 Implementation

It has been argued so far that there is a place for ethics in business and other organizations; that software engineers by virtue of the professional status to which they aspire should have a specifically professional input into the ethical process, and that both professional status and a required ethical contribution necessitates an appropriate ethical code. The questions which follow are those of implementation and method: namely, ensuring that whatever ethical code is devised should be acceptable and enforceable.

The *content* of any code may vary as between countries or regions, although in practice it is likely that a code produced in, say, Beijing or Islamabad will be compatible with anything with comes from the British Computer Society, or the Association for Computing Machinery in the United States. In fact, an ethical code for software engineers is pretty easy to specify, apart from one problem area, which I shall come to at the end of this chapter.

Most software engineers work directly or indirectly for profit. They are in business. Therefore the ethics of Software Engineering are a subset of business ethics, which may be summarized as "don't knowingly deceive, defraud or coerce". These precepts are non-problematic in that they are accepted by all philosophical schools and religions, though not necessarily for the same reasons. This chapter is not concerned with content, but by way of illustration, the kinds of things which might appear in a generally acceptable code of conduct are:

1. Don't claim expertise which you know you do not have.

2. Don't bill the client for hours not actually worked in his or her interest.

3. Give disinterested advice: e.g. don't take kickbacks from suppliers whom you recommend without declaring your interest to the client.

4. Don't permit the client to make mistakes in the specification or elsewhere, even if they are to your financial or other advantage. Warn her or him, even if this results in financial loss or a breach of relations.

5. Respect the client's confidentiality and intellectual property rights.

The BCS and ACM have published much, much longer documents on this subject [BCS93] and [ACM91].

9.4   Acceptability and Enforcement

Acceptability and enforcement are two sides of the same coin. In the West acceptability is likely to stem from two conditions being satisfied. The first stems from what is called "distributive justice" i.e. "you get what you deserve, from the standpoint of the organization's welfare". The second is to ensure that precepts in force are generally consonant with national habit and custom.

In the United Kingdom, this involves the complex and (one fears) obsolescent notion called "fair play". Other places may take a different view. God really is dead for most of the "Western" world. If one can refer again to Nietzche, it is too little remarked that this is not the case elsewhere. The world is not a secular place and its fastest growing religion — Islam — bases ethics firmly on religious principles. Indeed many of the distinctions between religious and secular activity familiar in the West do not exist in the Islamic world vision. It is impertinent and flying in the face of fact to ignore a prevalence of religious values and cultural practices underpinned by religion in many parts of Africa and Asia. Just as Saudi Arabia or Pakistan emphasizes Islam, so Singapore (for example) prescribes "Asian values" as guides to conduct. While this does not mean that the individual Arab or Singaporean invariably follows the prescribed code, there are large regions of the world where any such code, including business ethics, will be linked to and often enforced as part of a vigorous body of law, belief and custom.

9.5   Professionalism as a Means of Inculcation and Enforcement

Such coherent bodies of precepts and action are less strong in the West, and other means of enforcement must be looked for. Criminal and civil law have their places, but cannot and should not prescribe every detail of conduct. I believe that the most promising means of enforcement here is through the idea of "the professional ethic".

This is partly because professionalism in this form is associated with individualism; a defining characteristic of post-modern Western educated people, and partly because particular characteristics consonant with individualism have been accepted for centuries in the West as necessary conditions for defining a profession. By an interesting process which would take too long to describe here, they were carried over in the nineteenth century to form part of the definition of a bona fide scholar and embodied until the 1980s in the status and practice of university teachers. Members of the two leading "worldly" professions, law and medicine, accepted internal regulatory bodies which defined ethical practice and codes of conduct, and disciplined those who failed to comply. To that extent unfettered individualism was curbed, but the collective rewards in terms of social status and high earning power were considerable. More recently established professions have adopted looser but generally similar models.

We have already touched on the question, "can software engineers be classified as professionals in the traditional sense?" The answer is difficult, because one authentication of a "professional" is the status of the professional body to which an individual practitioner belongs. In general, you are not universally recognized as a professional if you don't have a professional body of appropriate status to accredit you. Being a graduate and being a member of the MBCS is not the same, either in terms of professional significance or public esteem as being a member of the Royal College of Surgeons or a Barrister of the Inner Temple. This is mainly because the legal and medical professional bodies are very old and have teeth (an unusual combination, alas) and the BCS is neither old nor fanged. A professional body takes many years to become established in its profession and still more to enter into the public mind as a criterion of authenticity.

The term "software engineer" is so vague, and includes people with so many different levels of qualification, expertise and status, that in order to produce any rational system of enforcement one must distinguish between those who have the characteristics defined as "professional" and those who don't. This might be done by analysing a person's duties, trying to determine whether they amount to being "professional", except that such a method would be lengthy and open to endless dispute. A better way would be to define "professional" by reference to existing systems of qualification, from HNC and HND (Higher National Certificates and Diplomas), through BSc and MBCS to CEng (Chartered Engineer) and FBCS etc. The status of "professional" in the full sense would be reserved to holders of CEng and above, because it is unlikely that many people with lesser qualifications would be doing work of the level and complexity which would merit a status comparable with equal members of other professions. Even the most junior entrants would be subject to a general ethical code, but they would have to achieve the requisite status for full professional recognition, just as members of the medical professions have to do at present.

Only those with advanced qualifications should be regarded as competent to belong to or administer a professional and regulatory body for software engineers everywhere. Being recognized throughout the European Community and beyond, the C. Eng. has sufficient standing for that purpose. Such a body would be based on Statute, coordinated under European Law, with roughly the same disciplinary powers as the Bar Council or the General Medical Council. Any software engineer, at any level, would be expected to internalize the ethical code determined by the profession as a whole, operating through that professional body, and would be subject to its disciplinary measures.

If such a body were to be well-established, either *de novo* or by further development of the BCS and equivalent bodies in other countries, it would carry a number of advantages. A software engineer would have a status from which it would be easier for him or her to challenge the misuse of power by employers, while the public would have some means of identifying incompetent or dishonest practitioners and bringing them to book. The computing industry is global. Both the industry and its employees would be helped by universally-known and widely accepted standards for conduct.

I also hold that true professional status would help to reverse what is seen by many as the dangerous process of disparaging professionals in the interests of what is thought to be more efficient management. This process is carried out by subordinating individual professionals in an organization to "line management" and then insisting that such authority as remains to them is derived primarily from their position in the chain of command, which is internal to the institution, and not from professional knowledge, which is personal and validated by peers or external bodies. The effects may be seen in the British National Health Service, the universities and parts of the Civil Service as well as in business. A heavyweight external body can provide a necessary balance to the damage which results from the triumph of bureaucracy over expertise.

This is one view. Adam Smith might have taken another, for it was he who reminded us that when professionals combine, the result is usually a conspiracy against the public, or a contrivance to raise prices [Smith76]. A proper code of ethics must take account of the whole range of the engineer's responsibilities.

Nevertheless, being a "professional" still has some weight world-wide as things are, and may have more in the future. One possible twenty-first century scenario would see the best software engineers as high-level consultants, working on a succession of one-off projects for different clients. The deference they will receive for being "external" (and expensive) will be increased if they adhere to a code of ethics backed up by a respected, dentally-unchallenged professional body. Such an organization would probably begin as a loose federation of national professional associations and ultimately be global, uniting members by electronic means, wherever they might be, and circulating rulings world-wide. An electronic blacklist, accessible by anyone, would be a powerful sanction, which would itself have to be carefully regulated. One might even employ an electronic form of a most effective current sanction against sharp practice in Singapore, which is to print the name and address of retailers convicted of fleecing tourists inside the back cover of the official guide to the country.

9.6   Professional Ethics and Information Control

This final section deals, as promised earlier, with a "problem area", which may be expressed as a question; namely "is a professional software engineer responsible for controlling the information which his or her technical expertise has made available?" There are arguments on both sides, but the potential power of organized groups of software engineers, if nothing else, makes the point worth considering.

There has always been a libertarian tradition among some computer folk. The Digital Company's PDP series of computers in the 1960s and the microcomputer in the mid-1970s both attracted devoted hackers; the term being used in its first and best sense of "technically proficient and enthusiastic persons" who admired "neat hacks"; that is exceptionally skilful use of a computer's facilities. Many of these individuals saw computers and the information they carried as far more than mere tools. They regarded the possession of any information as a positive good, and any information relating to the improvement of computer performance as of the highest value, and therefore to be given to everyone as a public good.

They were challenged in a famous encounter by the then almost unknown Bill Gates, who took the view that software engineers were entitled to whatever commercial rewards they could make from their skills, and that no good software would be written without a financial incentive [Levy94].

The implication is that Software Engineering is work for profit, like selling groceries, and that those who perform such work have the duties and responsibilities of other production workers; neither more nor less. Decisions about information control, so far as software engineers are concerned, are corporate decisions, which may take corporate ethics into account but are not special by virtue of the "commodity" they handle.

Gates won on that occasion, and his subsequent conduct suggests he hasn't changed his views, but the point is that what was then called the "hacker ethic" — the concept that information is a public good, like water and that those who control it by virtue of their technical skills have special responsibilities — never went away, and has now resurfaced in a different form as one of a host of issues stemming from the arrival of the Internet.

The Internet is likely to become the principal means of accessing information in the future. Through technical knowledge and sometimes commercial control, software engineers hold the ability to allow information to flow or not, to be encrypted or not, to be available to all, or not.

One may ask whether software engineers have any greater responsibilities in this area than have, say, civil engineers to decide who uses the M25 motorway. This is a fair point, but so is its converse, that a professional cannot ignore the foreseeable results of his or her expertise. It is possible to duck all such questions, referring them to one's employer, becoming a "Jobsworth" etc, but in that case, one is not a professional, because professional responsibility is essentially personal and cannot be delegated.

Questions of control are likely to offer the greatest obstacles towards providing a universally accepted code of ethics. Governments in particular will consider that information control is an essential element of any software engineer's job. It is likely to be negative in character; the engineer being asked to ensure that selected classes of information do not reach some or all of their potential audience.

The implications of information control are profound, and one finds it difficult to conceive of anyone claiming the status of professional software engineer to shrug them off. Professional and business ethics are the disciplines which help us to work out these and other questions rationally both as individuals and members of an organization. Ethics is a necessary part of our professional world. The reasons for thinking otherwise are specious or false, and if ethical codes are propagated everywhere, as I hope they will be, our professional status — providing we can attain it — can be an effective means of enforcing whatever ethical codes the profession eventually determine.

Chapter 10
Can a Software Engineer *Afford* to be Ethical?

10.1 Introduction

Most practising software engineers would probably accept that the present professional climate does appear to support "ethics" as a professionally relevant issue [Myers95]. Many of the most important indicators certainly point in this direction. Codes of professional conduct have been revised and promoted, articles and books have been written, and conferences held. Professional issues are now even considered by the British Computer Society (BCS) and many universities to form an essential part of the training of every computer scientist.

This move is, of course, also supported to a growing degree by both the serious and popular Press, as well as the public in general. The media is constantly presenting examples of conduct which is perceived — or at least presented — as professionally inappropriate. Of course, in this Software Engineering is not alone; even cursory study will supply further examples from other fields — financial services are a current favourite, but there are many more.

Given such substantial pressures from both profession and public, and reinforced, perhaps, by a feeling that to raise objections might be professionally unwise, the case against ethical standards in Software Engineering has to a great extent gone by default. Ethics is self evidently a Good Thing, and further discussion is consequently unnecessary.

Unfortunately, as every practitioner knows only too well, there is a considerable difference between the abstract consideration of academic issues and the everyday pressures involved in commercial practice. We live and work in a world where people frequently do act unethically, and, despite our wishes, this is unlikely to change. We may all subscribe in theory to a contention that ethical behaviour is essential — but, faced with the need to land a contract, or to maintain software with insufficient resources, cutting a few ethical corners might make the difference between profit and loss. In the "real world" — the one actually lived in by software engineers, if not by academics — is it realistic to assume that any firm can compete adequately with unethical rivals without first sharing their morals? Or, if an ethical individual should join a software team where "unethical" standards are rife, would there really be any point in their promoting different opinions, opinions which at best may just result in personal unpopularity?

This chapter examines the reasons why ethical behaviour may be perceived as inappropriate, and discusses both disadvantages, as well as advantages, of ethical behaviour.

10.2   What is "Ethical" for Software Engineers?

A reasonable starting point is to examine the background to the current position, which may be summarized as an assumption that a software engineer acting ethically is "good", while one acting unethically is "bad". What, though, does this actually mean — and where do such concepts come from? As with many areas of experience with which we may be unfamiliar, it can help to understand new issues by appropriately considering experience from another area of activity. Consider, for example, a computing consultant who uses their job to steal software and equipment; or who, in order to land a contract, pretends to possess knowledge they do not actually have. Such actions will be classified as "unprofessional" under BCS and ACM (Association of Computing Machinery) Codes of Conduct, but, although they certainly involve computing, both examples could be readily adapted to other areas of business with only very minor changes.

Most official Codes of Conduct consequently incorporate definitions of "unacceptable" behaviour for their members which actually reflect wider opinions which are generally held. The assumption is that an action which is *normally* considered unethical does not become acceptable because it is considered from a specialist viewpoint.

> A staff member was working on the development of a new software package. A colleague had left for the day, but the worker wanted to refer to some printed notes left in a locked desk drawer. Most people would accept it would not be appropriate to break open the desk, in order to get the notes. What, however, if the worker had the ability to hack into a computer system, to access the original file which generated the printed notes...? Is breaking into someone's electronic office comparable to breaking into a physical one?

Here, accepting a fundamental right to personal privacy would mean that both desk and directory should be left strictly alone. Using a computer does not convey any special right to ignore normal standards of behaviour.

As such examples illustrate, professional standards tend to start by applying "general" standards of ethical behaviour to specialist circumstances [Kling95]. In this case, analysis of such problems then clearly permits responses developed elsewhere to be appropriately applied within the field of computing. Briefly, whether or not they are proscribed by the appropriate professional code, it can be concluded that a software engineer's actions risk being labelled "unethical" if they do not comfortably fit within the perceptions wider society has of appropriate behaviour.

Of course, not all of the computing field offers opportunities for such straightforward comparison. There are inevitably specialist areas which have no natural corollaries in the wider world, and which do not therefore risk being judged against external standards. Examples might include an employer's ability to use "smart" ID badges to generate data for the analysis of employee behaviour, or the trend to electronically "tag" offenders — neither are actions which have an easy label to be transferred from another area of experience.

It is important to appreciate that the driving force of developing technology lies behind many decisions taken in the computing industry. As well as awareness of existing issues, it is also necessary to remember use of computers additionally presents *dynamic* problems — what was technically impossible yesterday becomes attainable today, and may well be common practice tomorrow.

For example, development of specifically targeted mailshots is a familiar business technique. However, if the specially issued magnetic "savings" cards — urged on their customers by major supermarkets — permit such targets to be selected following computerized analysis of spending patterns, the resultant shift in emphasis may well need examination. It is in this area that there is the greatest need for professional bodies to act in defining appropriate behaviour — as informed specialists, they are best placed to observe and influence new development [Anderson93].

The final line of definition concerns legality. Although there are exceptions — totalitarian States such as Nazi Germany are obvious examples — if an action is demonstrably illegal, it is generally classified as "unethical". However, the reverse is not necessarily true. While in slow moving areas of activity "illegal = unethical" may be quite sufficient, computing is a special case — development of the law is, understandably, normally well behind current technology. When considering computing issues, what is, strictly speaking, "legal", therefore cannot automatically be considered as "ethical".

There are consequently at least three major areas of potential conflict in the definition of ethical standards for software engineers. First, there is the transference of standards which have previously been applied outside the profession. Second, there are "new" standards, following technical development, and guided by professional organizations. Ultimately, although this is by no means definitive, there is the role played by statute law in defining what may be considered "legal" behaviour.

A definition of what may be ethical behaviour for a software engineer is therefore far from automatic, and is certainly not easy to predict. While it may sometimes be sufficient, when considering a proposed professional action, to assess whether a similar action is considered appropriate in other fields, the grey area involved in definitions of issues specific to the computing field allow for considerable flexibility. I suggest this situation is unlikely to change.

10.3   Ethics is Bad For You

We have seen that the apparently seamless concept of "ethical" behaviour may potentially be composed of at least three different elements. However, in reality the situation is actually even more complex. Behind the generally accepted promotion of ethical behaviour as appropriate for software engineers lies what is, when you consider it, a fairly major assumption — "acting ethically is good". Although precise definitions of "good" and "bad" are debatable, the sentiments behind this suggestion appear widely entrenched — but is it necessarily true? Moreover, once we assume acting ethically is good, would it be reasonable to ask for whom?

Even if the moral aspects of ethical behaviour are accepted as clear and obvious — an assumption which is by no means incontestable — what of the practical advantages? There are undoubted benefits to ethical conduct, as will be discussed later, but there are also considerable potential disadvantages. The continued wider promotion of ethical

behaviour may encourage the cynical software engineer to rephrase the statement —
"if *they* act ethically, it's good for *me*".

I suggest that, for the purposes of analysis, potentially "unethical" behaviour by
software engineers may be divided into three categories. These are:

1. Individual behaviour

2. "Public" behaviour

3. Company behaviour

None of the three headings should be thought of as definitive; they are intended
principally to encourage debate, rather than establish rules.

10.3.1   Individual behaviour

I define this category as containing actions and potential actions by individuals who
are acting in a way which directly concerns their own professional work, rather than
attempting to influence or direct others, or acting as representatives of a company.

> A member of a software team was developing a complex database appli-
> cation. Asked by the team leader if she was able to tackle a particularly
> tricky aspect of coding, she replied honestly — she didn't think so, but
> would do her best. The reply did not go down well; she was shortly
> afterwards moved to another team — an effective demotion.

The team member probably acted ethically, but her "obviously" ethical behaviour
did not appear to bring much benefit; keeping quiet would have perhaps been the wiser
course? Perhaps; but the illustration also underlines the need to take a wider ethical
view. In the longer term, keeping quiet and taking on board an "impossible" task could
well lead to serious problems.

Alternative responses to the same situation can allow the effects of "ethical" and
"unethical" behaviour to be directly compared. A classic combination of such a wrong
answer/ right answer is the (composite) case of computing students interviewed by a
major UK bank. Asked in interview about knowledge and skills, one was unremittingly
honest, and admitted freely to areas of ignorance and poor performance. In contrast,
his more cynical colleague started off by reading the interviewer's notes upside down.
She then deliberately gave what she felt were all the right responses, whether or not
they were accurate. In an ethical world, honesty would have been rewarded; but would
anyone really be surprised to hear that a job offer went to the cynic?

Such examples illustrate the potential of actions which, although themselves personally ethical, can apparently backfire, resulting in an unwelcome outcome. Similarly,
acts which might be judged "unethical" can lead to success which appears undeserved.

10.3.2   "Public" behaviour

In this category I include actions which, although they are not necessarily related
directly to the professional work of the individual, are intended to have an effect on

others. An example would be a specialist who writes a letter to the Press, giving expert views on a matter of general importance.

> A professional software engineer of considerable experience was working in an area of substantial industrial decline. Some years ago the region was the subject of an investigative programme. The engineer was interviewed, and his opinions sought on what might be needed to attract "high-tech" companies to the area. In the interview he gave a frank assessment of what he felt were poor practices of large companies in the implementation of new technology. He now considers that this interview made him a "marked man", leading to the eventual loss of his job.

Nothing the engineer had said was untrue; indeed, he felt many of his points were actually rather weaker than those he had frequently heard made by colleagues, in general conversation. What was different, of course, was that those conversations were in private. Once the admittedly honest answers to questions were expressed publicly, a very different view was taken of them. Would he perhaps have faired better, if he had lied, or remained silent?

As I have suggested elsewhere [Langford95], ethical conduct cannot be turned on and off like a tap — a professional who acts ethically does so in all circumstances, not just in surroundings where their ethical views and actions are unlikely to create problems. As the above example illustrates, though, following through on ethical beliefs may not be without problems. It perhaps also demonstrates that software engineers need to be aware of the dangers of naivety.

10.3.3   Company behaviour

Not all professional actions are concerned with individuals acting as individuals. Every business is composed of people who act on its behalf; their actions may lead to the company itself being guilty of unethical behaviour.

> A London software house was invited to tender for a Software Engineering job. However, their quotation was deliberately pitched at an uneconomically low level. Once the client company was firmly committed, "unexpected" charges and expenses were discovered — and the final price charged was substantially higher. The action was defended as being in the company's best interests — "after all, we wouldn't otherwise have got the job".

Here, the end may at first seem to justify the means. If a company cannot attract business, it must close — and who would want that? Initially, this point may seem valid; but employees of competing, ethical, companies, who were honest about the costs involved in a contract quotation would probably disagree.

> A consultant was telephoned when leaving the office. A client company were holding a board meeting, and wanted to confirm an earlier provisional quotation. The engineer felt he did not have sufficient information. After

"some pretty rapid thinking" he decided to say he couldn't respond until the next day, when he knew information would be available. His company lost the contract.

The consultant believed he was acting ethically by not responding until he was certain the figures he would be confirming were accurate — but, if he had responded immediately, the contract may well not have been lost. He is still unsure whether he was right to act as he did. There have apparently been debates within his firm, too.

As a final example of the apparent benefits of unethical behaviour in software development, consider the following response to a not uncommon problem:

> A software team were working on modifying a automated production control package. Due to unexpected difficulties, implementation had gone much more slowly than anticipated. However, under the contract, delay in signing off the work would incur financial penalties. Testing was deliberately cut short, and a "buggy" version of the code released. The client was unaware of the decision, and penalties were avoided.

Whatever we might wish, our experience is likely to confirm that both individual and corporate "unethical" behaviour often does seem successful, while actions which appear ethical may have led to unwelcome results. Most people who have worked within the field of Software Engineering for any time will probably have experienced cases similar to these examples: acting ethically does sometimes seem to work against the best interests of both individuals and companies.

Can it therefore be true that ethical conduct may indeed be bad for you, even if, in abstract, it may be good for the wider community?

10.4   Why Acting Unethically does not Work

I am sure most of us who believe deeply in the importance of ethical professional behaviour have sometimes been tempted to at least put a "gloss" on its benefits, as well as perhaps deliberately avoiding examples, such as those described above, which appear to disprove the thesis. However, such a course is not sensible — nor ethical.

Consequently, I feel strongly that it is essential, especially when talking to those inexperienced in the area of professional ethics, to be both accurate and truthful. Although on occasions this can be difficult, it is the only way to promote ethical behaviour effectively.

10.4.1   Short term

Despite the title of this chapter, therefore, there is good news and bad news. The bad news — acting unethically *does* work. The good news is that it does not tend to work for long.

The short-term nature of unethical behaviour may be because the social and business framework of our society is built upon a presumption that certain social rules are, generally, valid [Ermann90]. One of the most fundamental of these rules is the assumption that most people normally tell the truth. There are of course circumstances when truth is relative, when a "white lie" may be appropriate, when a partial truth is acceptable. Generally, though, we tend to believe most statements are broadly true [Singer94].

Such a state of affairs is naturally very tempting to those who are prepared to lie. After all, if you believe Ripoff Software when they say 25 hours of work took 50 hours, why shouldn't the business make extra profit? Such an (undoubtedly unethical) action may work once or twice. However, once evidence emerges of the true state of affairs, and word of it gets around, things are likely to change. Once doubt is cast upon a professional judgement, the balance of belief rapidly reverses. The assumption then becomes that while everybody else normally tells the truth, Ripoff Software normally lie. After that, even if their statements are currently truthful, they are likely to be disbelieved.

It is for this reason that despite all the short-term advantages of lying, society still assumes that truth is the norm. I suggest the lesson is directly applicable to unethical conduct.

10.4.2   Image

The way in which public perception can be influenced by the activities of both individuals and companies provides a further incentive to act in a way seen as ethical. This is the issue of "image". The public image of a company is carefully cultivated, often at considerable expense. How this image is viewed by the public can reinforce or destroy it. The same is of course true of an individual professional.

Consequently, an ethical public image, reinforced by advertising and word of mouth support from clients or customers, is a powerful asset to any company or specialist. Repeatedly acting in an ethical manner would gradually reinforce this image, but a single act of unethical behaviour could potentially destroy it.

To a lesser extent, individual workers are also affected by the image held of them, by both their employer and co-workers. An image seen as reflecting an "unethical" individual is likely to result in negative behaviour from colleagues, if not in formal action from the employing firm. Interestingly, the reverse is also true: even if the ethical employee is working within an "unethical" environment, empirical evidence suggests that they tend to be regarded favourably by colleagues.

10.4.3   The law

Of course, in a democratic state, there is a general duty on the part of individuals and companies to make certain all their actions are within the law. The relationship between statute law and ethics is, as described above, not an easy one to define. While accepting that it may seem ethically necessary to disobey laws seen as "wrong", fuller discussion of the issue falls outside the area of this chapter. However, it is surely reasonable to assume a relationship between legality and ethical behaviour, and to conclude that a company or professional who acts illegally is likely to suffer.

> A small development company was faced with an urgent need to complete
> a programming job. A worker who had previously been involved in the

task had left their employment, although still in touch. The worker was informally approached, and in return for payment agreed to continue the work, using his new employer's equipment and time. The arrangement was discovered. Civil actions against both worker and development company were initiated, and criminal action threatened. After payment of substantial compensation, though, matters were allowed to rest.

In this instance, actions were clearly illegal as well as unethical. The legal issues may have been settled, but the ripple effects of the unethical action on company and individual continued.

In this section I have looked at three levels of involvement, examining why, in practical terms, unethical behaviour can prove ineffective. While it is of course true that no one can guarantee all unethical behaviour will always prove to be a poor long-term choice, there is substantial evidence to suggest this may be so.

10.5   Conclusions

In this chapter I have presented a selection of reasons for acting unethically, illustrated by examples. Perhaps controversially, I have also suggested that such behaviour is not necessarily and inevitably dysfunctional. Indeed, in many circumstances those acting ethically may appear to suffer, while, in contrast, those with fewer scruples can seem to benefit.

I have proposed that those who support the wider application of both general ethical expectations and formal rules should accept this situation, and not deny the apparent short-term advantages to be gained by acting unethically. Indeed, such a denial might itself be considered as unethical, thereby demonstrating the very point it is attempting to disprove.

Despite the apparent advantages to be gained by the unethical software engineer, though, this chapter demonstrates that a solid professional career can only be founded on the bedrock of ethical personal conduct and beliefs. Today's software engineer needs not only to be aware of ethical issues, but to respond properly to them. Software engineers should always act appropriately, following the expectations of society, and the regulations of professional organizations and statue law. They cannot afford to do otherwise.

Chapter 11
Software Project Management Ethics

11.1   Introduction

It appears universally accepted that the most effective way to develop software is through the use of a project-based organizational structure which encourages individuals to participate in teams with the goal of achieving some common objective. Much has been written about the management of software development projects and no doubt much will be written in the future. The purpose of this chapter is to examine whether project management practice effectively caters for the ethical issues surrounding the software development process. For the sake of clarity, only one project management approach is discussed. The aim is to tease out the fundamental issues and not to dwell on the nuances of a particular approach.

Section 11. 2 chapter briefly considers the chosen project management methodology, Structured Project Management (SPM). Section 11.3 establishes a set of eight guiding ethical principles for computer professionals. Section 11.4 analyses SPM using the guiding principles; two of the steps within SPM are examined in detail to demonstrate how the application of the relevant ethical principles helps to ensure ethical behaviour. Section 11.5 considers two primary ethical hotspots of project management; defining of the scope of consideration and the information dissemination to the client. Finally, Section 11.6 provides some concluding remarks.

11.2   The Target Project Management Approach

O'Connell, in his book *How to Run Successful Projects* (part of the British Computer Society Practitioner Series [O'Connell94]), provides details of the Structured Project Management (SPM) approach. He explains that SPM is a practical methodology that, as DeMarco states, is a "basic approach one takes to getting a job done"[DeMarco87].

SPM has been chosen for discussion as it is practical rather than conceptual and provides practitioners with realistic guidance in undertaking the vastly complex activity of project management.

SPM comprises ten steps as shown in Table 11.1. The first five steps are concerned with planning and the remaining five deal with implementing the plan and achieving the goal. O'Connell states that most projects succeed or fail because of decisions made during the planning stage thereby justifying the fact that half of the effort expended in the SPM approach is on preparation.

It is this planning element of project management which lays down the foundations on which the project ethos is built. Here the scope of consideration is established, albeit implicitly or explicitly, which in turn locates the horizon beyond which issues are deemed not to influence the project or be influenced by the project. How the project is conducted will depend heavily upon the perceived goal. The visualization of this goal takes place in Step 1. The first two points in the visualization checklist given by O'Connell are:

1. What will the goal of the project mean to all the people involved in the project when the project completes?

2. What are the things the project will actually produce? Where will these things go? What will happen to them? Who will use them? How will they be affected by them?

These are important because through answering these questions an acceptable project ethos and scope of consideration should be achieved. The problem is that in practice these fundamental questions are often overlooked. It is more likely that a narrower perspective is adopted with only the obvious issues in close proximity to the project being considered. The holistic view promoted by the two checklist points requires greater vision, analysis and reflection. The project manager is under pressure to deliver and so the tendency is to reduce the horizon and establish an artificial boundary around the project.

Steps 2 to 5 are concerned with adding detail and refinements thus arriving at a workable and acceptable plan. Steps 6 to 8 are concerned with implementing the plan, monitoring performance and keeping those associated with the project informed of progress. Step 9 defines the control feedback loops which ensure that the plan remains focused, current and realistic. Finally, Step 10 is the delivery of the project output to the client and an opportunity to reflect upon what has and has not been achieved.

Step 1	Visualise what the goal is
Step 2	Make a list of the jobs that need to be done
Step 3	Ensure there is one leader
Step 4	Assign people to jobs
Step 5	Manage expectations, allow a margin of error and have a fallback position
Step 6	Use an appropriate leadership style
Step 7	Know what is going on
Step 8	Tell people what is going on
Step 9	Repeat Steps 1 through 8 until Step 10 is achievable
Step 10	Realise the project goal

Table 11.1 The Ten Steps of Structured Project Management

11.3 Principles of Ethics

Relevant ethical principles must now be established in order to identify the ethical issues associated with software development project management in general and SPM in particular.

Ethics comprises both practice and reflection [vanLuijk94]. Practice is the conscious appeal to norms and values to which individuals are obliged to conform, whilst reflection on practice is the elaboration of norms and values that colour daily activity. Norms are collective expectations regarding a certain type of behaviour whilst values are collective representations of what constitutes a good society. The existence of a plan and a controlling mechanism is the accepted norm in project management which itself is an accepted value in software development. For the purpose of this chapter it is sufficient to consider only ethics practice because project management is concerned with action rather than conceptual reflection. Conceptual reflection might manifest itself in, for example, codes of conduct which are concerned with establishing what are the generalized ways of working that are acceptable to a wider community. This community would include all potential stakeholders of software development projects. In other words, project management is concerned with how to use and when to apply norms and values rather than establishing what these norms and values are.

An interesting list of generic questions was devised by John McLeod in [Parker90] to help determine the ethical nature of actions within the computing profession. The list is shown in Table 11.2. Within these questions are embedded norms which will impact upon the process of project management.

To be ethical, an action should elicit a positive response to all applicable primary questions (◇), and a negative response to each *clarification* (●).
◇ Is it honourable?   ● Is there anyone from whom you would like to hide the action?
◇ Is it honest?   ● Does it violate any agreement, actual or implied,   or otherwise betray a trust?
◇ Does it avoid the possibility of a conflict of interest?   ● Are there other considerations that might bias your judgement?
◇ Is it within your area of confidence?   ● Is it possible that your best effort will not be adequate?
◇ Is it fair?   ● Is it detrimental to the legitimate interests of others?
◇ Is it considerate?   ● Will it violate confidentiality or privacy, or otherwise   harm anyone or anything?
◇ Is it conservative?   ● Does it unnecessarily squander time or other valuable resource?

Table 11.2 Questioning the ethical nature of an action

Software development is about the delivery of a product by a supplier to a client under some agreement. It is irrelevant whether this is an in-house arrangement or whether it is between two independent organizations. According to Velasquez, such an agreement is concerned with product quality and moral product liability [Velasquez92].

Two parties enter into an agreement to develop a piece of software. Such agreements are often unbalanced with the client being disadvantaged. Velasquez argues that the principles of due care and social cost must take effect in these situations. There must be due care from the developer over and above what has been accepted in the contract so that adequate steps are taken to prevent any foreseen detrimental effects occurring through the use of the software. Social cost is based upon utilitarian ideas. Even after software developers have given all reasonable due care to the software produced they still remain responsible for every damaging effect, be it caused by negligence, stupidity or recklessness.

By combining the ideas of McLeod and Velasquez a set of ethical principles can be derived as shown in Table 11.3. The principle of honour is to ensure that actions are beyond reproach which in turn demands honesty from the professional. The principle of bias focuses on ensuring decisions and actions are objective rather than subjective. Professional adequacy is concerned with the ability of individuals to undertake allocated tasks. The principle of due care is linked with the concept of software quality assurance. Fairness focuses on ensuring all affected parties are considered in project deliberations. This leads to social cost which recognizes that it is not possible to abdicate from professional responsibility and accountability. Finally, the principle of effective and efficient action is concerned with completing tasks and realizing goals with the least possible expenditure of resources.

Honour
Honesty
Bias
Professional adequacy
Due care
Fairness
Consideration of social cost
Effective and efficient action

Table 11.3 Ethical principles for a computer professional

11.4   Ethical Project Management

These guiding principles, which are based on ethical concepts, can be easily applied in practical situations and are now used to consider how to undertake ethical project management. The activities within each of the ten steps of SPM have been analysed in order to identify the dominant ethical issues of each step. The results of this analysis are shown in Table 11.4. It is recognized that most of the eight principles will have some impact on each step but it is important to identify those which will have a significant impact. The mapping in Table 11.4 shows those relationships which are considered significant. Steps 1 and 8 are now considered in further detail to illustrate the implication of the mapping.

Principle	Steps									
	1	2	3	4	5	6	7	8	9	10
1. Honour	√	-	-	√	-	√	-	√	-	√
2. Honesty	√	-	-	√	√	-	-	√	-	-
3. Bias	√	√	√	√	-	-	-	√	-	√
4. Adequacy	-	-	√	√	-	√	-	-	-	-
5. Due care	√	-	√	-	√	-	-	√	√	-
6. Fairness	√	-	-	-	√	-	-	√	-	-
7. Social cost	√	-	-	-	√	√	-	-	-	√
8. Action	-	√	√	√	-	√	√	-	√	√

Table 11.4 The dominant ethical principles in the steps of SPM

11.4.1   Step 1 — visualize the goal

As previously mentioned, this step establishes the project ethos and consequently there are several ethical issues that need to be borne in mind. This is the start of the project and it is vitally important to be above board at the onset so that a good working relationship is established with client. The principles of honour and honesty address this point. As can be seen from Table 11.4 bias in decision-making and the undertaking of actions is a major concern throughout the project including Step 1. It is important to take a balanced viewpoint based on economic, technological and sociological information. The view often portrayed is skewed towards technology and economics which can have disastrous results leading to major system failure or rejection, as was the case, for example, at the London Ambulance Service and the London Stock Exchange. This leads to the remaining three dominant principles of due care, fairness and social cost. Computer systems impact directly and indirectly on many people and it is important to include all parties in decisions that affect the way in which the project is conducted. Software development projects involve many stakeholders and each is worthy of fair treatment. The principles of due care and social cost will ensure that a longer term and broader perspective is adopted.

11.4.2   Step 8 — tell people what is going on

The project is dynamic and exists in a dynamic environment. Step 8 is essential so that everyone is aware of occurring change and so that their assignments can be adjusted accordingly. Being over-optimistic, ultra-pessimistic or simply untruthful about progress can be damaging not only to the project but also to both the client and supplier organizations. Those involved in this communication would be the project team, the computer department line management and the client. An honest, objective account of progress which takes into account the requirements and feelings of all concerned is the best way to operate. Drawing upon the principles of honour, honesty, bias, due care and fairness will assist in achieving this.

11.4.3   The ethical verdict

Whilst SPM provides practical guidance on the management of projects it does not explicitly include an ethical dimension, though it is accepted there are implicit ethical issues in some parts of the methodology. There is a need for a stronger and more obvious emphasis on ethical issues. The derived mapping provides the framework for this additional ethical perspective within the project management process.

11.5   Primary Ethical Hotspots of Project Management

The mapping of ethical principles onto the steps of the methodology provides overall guidance on how to approach the project management process throughout the life of the project. However, within the project there are numerous activities and decisions to be made and most of these will have an ethical dimension. It is impractical to consider each minute issue in great detail and still hope to achieve the overall project goal. The focus must be on the key issues which are likely to influence the success of the project. These are the primary ethical hotspots of project management. In [Rogerson95], ethical hot-spots are defined as points where activities and decision making are likely to include a relatively high ethical dimension. There are two primary ethical hotspots in project management, namely, the defining of the scope of consideration (in Step 1 of SPM) and the information dissemination to the client (primarily in Step 8 of SPM).

11.5.1   Scope of consideration

It is a common problem with software development projects that decisions concerned with, for example, feasibility, functionality, and implementation do not take into account the requirements of all those affected by the system once it becomes operational. This is illustrated by the cost benefit analysis activity undertaken at the beginning of most projects. This only takes into account the interests of those involved in the analysis and does not usually consider the rights and interests of all parties affected by the proposed system. The view is primarily techno-economic rather than techno-socio-economic. Potential well-being of many individuals is likely to be at risk unless an ethically sensitive horizon is established for the scope of consideration. The risk is likely to be lower if the principles of due care, fairness and social cost are prevalent during this activity. In this way the project management process will embrace, at the onset, the views and concerns of all parties affected by the project. Concerns over, for example, de-skilling of jobs, redundancy, the break-up of social groupings can be aired at the earliest opportunity and the project goals adjusted if necessary.

11.5.2   Information dissemination to the client

The second ethical hotspot is to do with informing the client. No one likes to get shocking news, and so early warning of a problem and an indication of the scale of the problem are important. Project managers must not see information dissemination to the client as information dissemination to the enemy which can be the stance in some organizations. The key is to provide factual information in non-emotive words so the client and project manager can discuss any necessary changes in a calm and professional manner. Confrontational progress meetings achieve nothing. The adoption of the principles of honesty, bias, due care and fairness would help to ensure a good working relationship with the client.

11.6   Conclusions

Without doubt the project management process for software development is capable of accommodating an ethical perspective. This has been demonstrated by mapping the derived eight ethical principles onto the Structured Project Management methodology. The major criticism of current practice is that any ethical consideration tends to be implicit rather than explicit, which has a tendency to devalue the importance of the ethical dimension. By using ethical principles and the identification of ethical hotspots it is possible to ensure that the key ethical issues are properly addressed. Quite simply, project management should be guided by a sense of justice, a sense of equal distributions of benefits and burdens and a sense of equal opportunity. In this way software development project management will become ethically aligned.

Chapter 12
Obligations for IT Ethics Education

12.1 Introduction

Software Engineering professionals impact on society in more pervasive and invasive ways than perhaps any other profession to date. Through the software systems they design and build, software engineers touch the everyday lives of virtually all individuals, whether involved in a business, a government service agency, an educational institution, or just paying taxes. The use of the term "professional" implies some expected standard of behaviour; in the case of the software professional, that standard of behaviour is generally with respect to human-human interaction and human-machine interaction [Martin90], [Oz94a]. Recognition and awareness of the importance of this standard of behaviour is reflected in the results of a recent survey by the Council of Scientific Society Presidents, Ethics in Science Committee which found that of the ten major characteristics found in existing or proposed scientific ethics policies, 76% of them include some statement addressing responsibilities to society [Jorgensen95]. Many of the professional computer societies, including Association for Computing Machinery, Institute of Electrical and Electronic Engineers, Data Processing Managers Association, Institute for Certification of Computer Professionals, Canadian Information Processing Society and British Computer Society, address responsibility to society in their codes of ethics [Martin90], [Oz94a]. Included in the responsibilities to society, is the responsibility to educate the public about information technology [Martin90] [Oz94a]. This education responsibility extends the professional awareness of software engineers to professional awareness about Software Engineering and software engineers and from professional self to the society which is pervasively and invasively influenced by that profession.

It is the tenet of this chapter that the education responsibility has several facets and levels which to date have not been delineated and examined with respect to incorporation of technology ethics into the appropriate educational forums — including, but not limited to, the traditional educational forums. To that end, we propose a delineation by role of those "touched" by computers, the level and/or intent of the necessary technology ethics education for each role, and a suggestion of how that technology ethics education could be accomplished. While some of the roles are highly visible and are currently addressed in a variety of ways (which we review and in some cases expand upon), many of the roles are indirect and not as visible, leaving a gap in the technology ethics education of many who may have a large degree of influence on Software Engineering or who are heavily affected by Software Engineering.

Section 2 of this chapter identifies the meta-levels of professional awareness and the roles within those meta-levels. This identification provides a grid for educational coverage. Section 12.3 chapter expands these roles to include necessary technology ethics education for each role and suggestions on how to achieve this.

12.2 Meta-Levels

In general there are two meta-levels of professional awareness: an internal professional level and an external societal level (Figure 12.1). The internal professional level is defined as those directly involved in Software Engineering of systems: designers, programmers, test team, maintenance personnel, etc. In other words, those who are, in general, specifically trained to design and develop software systems and who understand the process involved. It does not necessarily include management, but also does not necessarily exclude management; inclusion or exclusion in this meta-level would be dependent upon the knowledgeability of the individual. Some managers are indeed technical managers who have the necessary background to understand the design, development and maintenance requirements of software systems, through education and/or from "rising through the ranks".

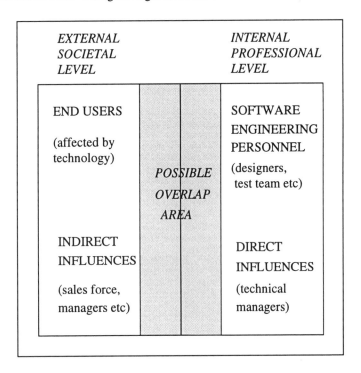

Figure 12.1 Meta-Levels of professional awareness

The external societal level concerns those directly affected by software systems — broadly defined as end-users — and those who are indirectly involved in the engineering of software systems; non-technical managers, sales force etc (Figure 12.2). Each of these meta-level distinctions has a different perspective on the Software Engineering profession. The end-user distinction can be subdivided further into explicit and implicit end-users. Explicit end-users are those who use software systems deliberately, for example someone who uses a word-processor. Implicit end-users may not even be aware that a software system is being employed to execute part or all of the activity in which they are engaged, for example, someone whose car contains a computerized ignition system.

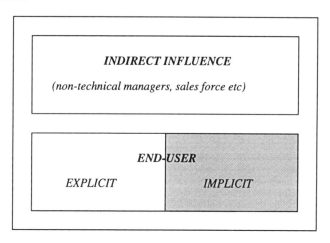

Figure 12.2 External societal roles

12.3 Necessary Technology Ethics Education

12.3.1 Internal professional level

The internal professional level with respect to Software Engineering is the most visible and has received an almost exclusive focus in discussing professional awareness. And this is as it should be initially; A profession must first understand and regulate its own operation before it can hope to make those outside of it aware of the high-level details of how it should be expected to operate. In the Software Engineering discipline (along with the rest of computer science), this has been done primarily through the establishment, by the various professional societies, of codes of ethics. Unfortunately, the sanctions for violating these codes — when they exist — have rarely been used in real situations. Rather, the legal system has been resorted to when settling ethical situations involving computers [Martin90]. In addition, there is not an accepted unified code; in comparing and contrasting the various codes, being a member of multiple professional societies may incur conflicting ethical obligations [Oz94a].

The argument for developing a professional code of ethics, as opposed to a professional society code of ethics can be based on the lack of cohesion among the existing professional societies' codes, and the lack of any usable sanctions for violations. Developing a professional code of ethics makes the statement that membership of the Software Engineering profession is not just a matter of joining an appropriate professional society. It also provides a foundation for technology ethics education, at both the internal professional and external societal levels. While it is recognized that there are many inherent difficulties and dangers in developing such a professional code, they do not negate the necessity and validity of such action [Mishkin95].

Given an acceptance of the above, a framework for development should be established. Simply supplying a list of rules is inadequate; rules do not necessarily imply desirable principles nor will they address all situations which may arise. (Neither do they address required knowledge levels; however, this aspect addresses more closely the issue of licensing, of which a code of ethics is a part.) Both rules, and the principles which they support, must be incorporated into any professional code of ethics. For example, a rule may address plagiarism of another software engineer's work — this rule supports the principle of honesty. Other situations may arise in which the principle of honesty should be supported but for which no rule has been established. By explicitly incorporating into the professional code of ethics the principles which the rules support, unforeseen situations can be addressed ethically with greater ease.

Professional codes of ethics and their associated sanctions generally provide a rather broadly painted picture of an expected standard of behaviour; they do not provide the day-to-day guidance required to uphold a standard of behaviour in diverse contexts. However, a professional code can provide a cornerstone for reconciliation of one's own personal code and one's actions in a given situation — either actual or hypothetical. Given appropriate and strong sanctions, a professional code can also provide a strong argument for "doing the right thing" in an actual business situation where the professional software engineer is asked to behave in a manner which would violate that code.

Everyday professional behaviour requires an examination of one's own personal code of ethics [Ermann90]. Individuals must decide their specific standard of behaviour with respect to a given situation. Generally, the standard is at best hypothetical — and perhaps mythical — unless the individual is immersed in the situation. One can usually only speculate as to actions and reactions with respect to a hypothetical situation. This does not mean there is no value in examining hypothetical situations and exploring different options, as they relate both to a professional and personal code of ethics. Simply being exposed to, and participating in, the examination process often helps formulate and refine a personal code, and may prevent being "blind-sided" by an actual situation. Use of case studies within a computer science curriculum is one method for executing this process. Currently, the Computer Science Accreditation Board (CSAB) demands instruction in computing's social implications as a requirement for curriculum accreditation, and the ACM curriculum contains a core ethical and social impact strand in its recommendations for computer science programs [ACM/IEEE91]. These both illustrate the necessity to include an ethical examination process within computer science education; however, there remains disagreement as to how this should be implemented [Martin90].

There is also the question of providing an education forum for those professional software engineers already in the work force. This is particularly pertinent if a professional code of ethics is established (possibly as part of licensing), and if it is also possibly used as one of the criteria for employment and/or evaluation (cf the Professional Engineer designation used in traditional engineering). There are a number of existing forums which could be utilized; such as professional conferences for workshops; and professional journals for publication both of the professional code and of role-playing scenarios and their analysis with respect to the code and expected standards of behaviour. It may also be necessary to develop specialized training seminars and workshops, particularly if the code of ethics is a part of an overall licensing procedure.

12.3.2 External societal level

Just as codes of ethics may provide a mechanism to communicate a standard of behaviour to software professionals, there needs to be a mechanism to communicate this standard at the external societal level. Each of the two external societal roles needs to have their particular perspective addressed with respect to what should be expected from software professionals and the software systems they produce.

This facet of education is analogous to a car manufacturer who is liable for problems directly caused by the development and manufacturing process; software professionals are responsible for problems directly attributable to the development, implementation and maintenance processes for software systems. Car makers and software engineers are not responsible for misuse by a consumer. However, they should be responsible for education with respect to appropriate and safe use of their respective systems.

Thus, the education of end-users, both implicit and explicit, is two-pronged: education with respect to professional behaviour of software engineers, and education with respect to software system expectations. Whilst the two may seem to be disparate, they are in fact very closely linked, given that ethical behaviour (as a standard) on the part of a software engineer often dictates the quality facets of a software system.

From the explicit end-users perspective this directly affects their work. Explicit end-users need to be educated particularly with respect to how software systems can affect their lives (especially work), what they should be able to expect from a software support facility, what are the limitations of a piece of software (accurately), and how to analyze their own needs appropriately.

Implicit end-users need to be made aware of their use of software systems, the limitations of those systems, and the impact misuse can make in their lives. Both explicit and implicit end-users need to understand that software systems are nothing more than tools to accomplish a task which formerly was done manually or was not possible to do without the current (software) tool.

Educating end-users can be a particularly elusive goal. It is a goal, however, heavily influenced by the principles incorporated in a code of ethics. Forthrightness about the capabilities, limitations and use of a software system needs to become the norm rather than the overpitched marketing approaches often used. While this may not appeal to those trying to capture market share, it is an essential practice for professional software engineers. The language used in documentation including users manuals and training guides must carefully avoid jargon which is discipline specific or carefully explain those terms in a commonly understood manner. It is also important to remove some of the perceived mysticism associated with computer systems. This is in fact already happening as more and more people become computer owners.

From the perspective of those who are indirectly involved in the engineering of software systems, the work of the software professional is affected through their activities whether it be management activities or other. This group can be subdivided into those with management responsibilities and those with marketing responsibilities. The non-technical management individuals need to be educated with respect to the management of Software Engineering processes especially as it relates to scheduling and cost estimation, the legal ramifications of software system failures, and the trade-offs that can occur between profit and ethics. The marketing individuals are often responsible for much of the marketing hype associated with software systems and thus require education with respect to the reconciliation of market hype and true capabilities and limitations as set forth by a professional software engineer.

These education processes will probably only occur as corporate awareness of Software Engineering as a profession occurs — particularly the responsible marketing process. In general, the education process of the external societal level will require professional software engineers to acquire good communication skills and a sense of empowering responsibility. The acquisition of communication skills can occur within the formal education process or through workshops etc. The sense of empowering responsibility can only be acquired through sharing of information about Software Engineering as a profession, by establishing an expected standard of behaviour through an ethical code, possibly in conjunction with a licensing mechanism, and by educating those "touched" by Software Engineering with respect to the capabilities, limitations and use of software systems.

12.4   Summary

This chapter has discussed an education process for professional awareness of software engineers, and about Software Engineering, by delineating the levels and roles of those "touched" by Software Engineering. Highlighted is the need for a professional code of ethics and the need to communicate the standard of behaviour dictated by that code of ethics to those both within, and outside of, the Software Engineering profession.

Chapter 13
Legal Aspects of Safety Critical Systems

13.1   Introduction

Society is increasingly dependent upon computers and, in particular, computer control systems. Unfortunately, the growth of computer controlled systems in the last three decades has not been matched by any systematic reappraisal by legislative bodies of the legal liability attaching to suppliers of those computer controlled systems.

Instead, legislation passed to improve the safety of employees and consumers has been drafted to encompass computer controlled systems. The result is a haphazard application of the law, rather than any clearly thought through liability for the suppliers of computer controlled systems.

To this must be coupled a fundamental difficulty of the supplier of a computer controlled system : namely the relative ease of supplying a system which inadvertently contains an error even where the system has been tested, validated, verified and assessed.

In many circumstances there is little or no direct consumer pressure to supply error free software. Indeed, in certain industries it is in the manufacturer's interest to supply an unreliable computer system — so that the manufacturer can fix the system under a maintenance contract. For instance, customers who obtain computerized account systems and other so-called "back office" systems accept that they will pay substantial sums for maintenance of "faulty" software.

In other areas of the computer software industry it is also common to see poor quality software. Examples include games software, operating systems utilities (rather than the operating systems themselves), as well as some types of software supplied on microprocessor controls.

Unfortunately, this industry malaise cannot be carried through to safety-critical areas where the consequences of a poorly programmed software can, all too easily, prove fatal. This is true not only for large scale control systems but also for microprocessor control systems which find themselves in safety-critical applications such as those found embedded in back-up pumps and valves. The economic cost to a pump manufacturer of discovering a safety critical fault in a control unit can be high, particularly if a product recall is required. The manufacturer will wish to pass on that cost to the supplier of the microprocessor control unit.

The number and type of "safety critical" applications is constantly increasing. For instance, the emergency shutdown procedure on an offshore oil installation may depend upon a software based control system. A relatively simple error in that system could result in an incorrect shutdown and a catastrophic accident. If such a mistake was due to an error in the control system, the supplier of the system could be liable.

This chapter examines the range of specific liabilities placed upon manufacturers and suppliers of computer systems with particular reference to safety-critical systems.

Specifically it deals with: the "classical" remedies available; product liability legislation; and the newer burdens imposed by European Union legislation.

13.2   Classical Remedies

Historically, the two most important aspects of English (and Scottish!) law under which an injured party can bring a claim are the laws of contract and negligence. Also considered below is potential liability under the Health & Safety at Work *etc* Act, 1974.

13.2.1   Contract

In order to bring a claim, there must first be a contract between the parties in dispute. This is by no means a trivial test since typically, there will not be a contract between the injured party and the manufacturer who has introduced the defect into the product. An example of where a contract claim could be brought would be where a computer control manufacturer supplies a component to a motor car manufacturer who is building an anti-lock brake device. If, as a result of a fault in one of the computer units, an accident occurs the car manufacturer could bring a claim for breach of contract. That claim could be very great, since it could include damages for the loss of business suffered by the car manufacturer where it had needed to undertake a product recall exercise. In practice the computer component manufacturer would seek to limit its liability by excluding claims of the same type as consequential loss.

A claim for a breach of contract could be based on an express term of a contract, for example, that goods will comply with a certain British Standard. Additionally, a claim could be based on a term implied into the contract. Among the most important terms implied into most contracts for the supply of goods are that goods will comply with their specification and description; be of satisfactory quality; and be fit for any specific purpose for which they have been supplied.

13.2.2   Law of Negligence

Under the law of negligence, a manufacturer of goods owes a so-called "duty of care" to ensure that the goods it supplies are not likely to cause personal injury. Essentially, the duty is to take "reasonable care".

Historically, claims for defective computer systems have had to be brought under this law — particularly where there has been no contractual relationship between the claimant and the manufacturer. The manufacturer's liability under the law of negligence is more far reaching than under the law of contract. This is at least true in so far as who may bring a claim. A person can bring a claim under the law of negligence if he or she can say that the manufacturer ought reasonably to believe he or she would be adversely affected. This is far wider than under the law of contract where the person bringing the claim must have a direct contractual relationship with the defendant.

13.2.3   Health and Safety at Work *etc* Act

Other legislation places additional obligations on a manufacturer. An example of that legislation is the Health and Safety at Work *etc* Act 1974 which imposes a general duty on suppliers of machinery for use at the workplace as well as on employers. In particular, a manufacturer is required to use reasonable efforts to ensure that machinery is "safe". The remedies for breach of this Act are both criminal and civil. Where a manufacturer of a product (or an employer) breaches the legislation, a criminal prosecution can be brought. In practice, much is left to the discretion of the Health and Safety Executive (the body charged with enforcing the legislation) who may, and often does, issue a caution instead of bringing a criminal prosecution. However, this does not affect the civil liability that also is imposed on a manufacturer (and employer). A breach of the Act will also be sufficient to enable an injured party to bring a claim for damages flowing out of the failure by the manufacturer or the employer to comply with the Act. This is based on the concept of liability for "breach of a statutory duty".

In general, however, the obligations imposed under this Act are not as onerous as under the newer legislation which is discussed below. To put the matter another way, if a manufacturer complies with its obligations under the Product Liability law discussed below, the manufacturer is more than likely to have complied with its other legal obligations. However, obligations which are also being imposed upon manufacturers through other European Directives may, in the long run, impose even higher duties on manufacturers.

13.2.4   Reasons for change

Injured parties may experience considerable difficulties in bringing a claim under the law of contract or negligence. For example, a manufacturer might claim that it was not "reasonable" for it to follow a particular British Standard because the cost involved in doing so was prohibitive. Under the law of contract, for instance, goods may be of "satisfactory quality" or "fit for their purpose" even though they may have a considerable number of defects — provided the goods are still capable of undertaking their main function.

For these and other reasons, the European Union has taken a lead in introducing legislation into the area of product safety. Much of this legislation has far reaching implications for computer controlled systems. Most importantly, the Council of the European Union (which is made up of the Prime Ministers of each of the Member States) adopted a Directive on product liability on 25 July 1985 [Council85]. This Directive introduces a standard law on product liability throughout Europe.

It is significantly easier for an injured party to bring a claim under the Product Liability Directive than under the law of contract or negligence. As these Directives apply throughout the fifteen states of the European Union, the discussion below on this and other Directives gives an outline of European rather than just UK legislation. In fact most of the newer European legislation applies in the slightly wider European Economic Area which comprises seventeen European States : Austria, Belgium, Denmark, Eire, Finland, France, Germany, Greece, Holland, Iceland, Italy, Luxembourg, Norway, Portugal, Spain, Sweden, United Kingdom.

13.3   The "New" Remedy: Product Liability

13.3.1   The five requirements

Product liability law can be concisely expressed as follows : Where **damage** is **caused** by a **defect** in a **product** then **certain persons** are liable to compensate for that damage. Each of the highlighted words within that sentence is given a particular meaning in the legislation and is discussed below.

The damage

Two types of damage may be the subject of a claim under the legislation. The first type of damage is death or personal injury. The next of kin can sue when a person has died. The second type of damage is property damage. The property damaged must satisfy the following criteria:-

- the item of property must be of a type ordinarily intended for private use or consumption

- the item must be used by the person who has suffered the loss mainly for his or her own private use, occupation or consumption

- the total damages claimed by a person in respect of loss of property (excluding any claim of interest) must exceed 500 ECUs (the ECU is a European Currency Unit, valued at about 79 pence, as of 30 August 1995).

The damage claimed for must also exclude damage to the defective product itself!

The cause

The legislation provides that the injured party needs to prove only the damage, the defect and the causal relationship between the damage and the defect.

It is still necessary for the claimant to prove the damage, the defect and the necessary causation between the damage and the defect. In certain circumstances, proving causation may be a substantial hurdle, for instance where the injured party is trying to claim against the manufacturer of a component within a computer controlled device, the injured party may not know exactly which component has been defective.

The defect

The legislation defines the defect in terms of the safety which a person is entitled to expect. Where the safety is that which people (i.e. the public) are entitled to expect, then the product will not be defective. Conversely, where the product is not as safe as members of the public are entitled to expect then it will have a defect in it. In determining this test of safety all the circumstances must be taken into account including:

- the presentation of the product (which will include taking into account any instructions or warnings given in relation to the product);

- whether the use to which the product is being put is a reasonable use.

The question of safety must be decided with reference to the time at which the product was supplied. So the mere fact that a newer product is safer than an older product will not necessarily mean that the older product was not, at the time it was supplied, as safe as people are generally entitled to expect.

A full appreciation of this test of safety is crucial to an understanding of how the product liability law alters the previous prevailing law. Under the law of negligence in the United Kingdom, it was necessary to show that the manufacturer had not taken reasonable care in producing the product. However, there is more than one way of taking reasonable care in the production of computer software. Under the laws of contract or negligence it is relatively easy for a software manufacturer to show that it has taken reasonable care — even though a defect was introduced into the software.

Under the product liability law, however, all that the injured party needs to show is that the product is not as safe as people are entitled to expect. Although there are no reported cases on this issue, it is believed that this test is very much more onerous from the point of view of the manufacturer of a computer controlled system.

For instance, in areas of software manufacture where adopted standards exist, manufacturers must follow those standards to comply with the Directive. In addition, manufacturers should have regard to developing standards and non-mandatory standards, as indeed the public would expect them to do.

So, for example, if a software manufacturer has not used best practice "techniques", the manufacturer may well be liable for a defect thereby introduced into the software.

Care must be taken when giving instructions or warnings. In the case of a complex control system, it may not be sufficient merely to put a warning of a significant danger in the instruction manual. A prominent warning should also be placed in a permanent form next to the operator.

The product

The legislation only applies to products and not services. The definitions contained in the legislation do not really help in determining the dividing line between what is a product and what is a service.

As may be anticipated, debates have ensued as to whether items such as computer software are a product or a service. A detailed discussion of this topic is outside the scope of this article. It is now generally accepted that software falls within the scope of this legislation. In any event, in most cases, a claimant will not necessarily be suing the manufacturer of the defective software, but the manufacturer of the product in which that software was contained (e.g. the manufacturer of the complete computer control system or, more likely, the manufacturer of the motor car in which the computer system was present). In those circumstances, the more important question is whether that injured party can successfully sue the manufacturer of that computer control system or motor car. In almost all circumstances, that manufacturer will be liable under product liability law.

That manufacturer will, if it is properly advised, seek an indemnity from the software manufacturer. The software manufacturer will, therefore, find it even more difficult, in practice, to escape liability by arguing that it is not supplying the product.

In addition, given the plethora of computer controlled devices found in modern industry, it is hard to envisage a court taking a narrow interpretation of the legislation so as to exclude claims arising out of badly programmed devices. For example, suppose an anti-lock brake device fails because of faulty programming in the controls of the micro-processor. The injured party would have no greater difficulty suing the motor car manufacturer under product liability law than if, for example, the brake fails due to a faulty brake pad.

Note: The claim must be for non-commercial damage or for death or personal injury: see Section (a) above.

The persons liable

The primary person who is liable for a defective product is the "producer". The legislation specifically provides that a product can be comprised within another product.

It is therefore possible for more than one producer to be liable and hence to be obliged to pay compensation.

For example, suppose an engine contains a micro-processor which dynamically determines the fuel/air mixture pumped into the engine. A failure in the software could cause the engine to cut out at a critical moment, causing damage and injury.

There could be three separate "producers" liable under the legislation in this example:

- the supplier of the programmed control unit

- the supplier of the engine who has incorporated the control unit into the pump

- the supplier of the car itself which contains that engine.

In the case of an engine imported into the European Union, the importer would also be liable.

In addition, a person who puts its name, trade mark or other distinguishing feature on a product and thereby represents himself or herself as being a producer will also be liable. Furthermore, if the producer of the product cannot be identified then the supplier of the product can be treated as the producer unless the supplier informs the injured party of the identity of the actual manufacturer. The legislation is designed so that the injured party will always be able to find someone to sue within the European Union.

13.3.2   Defences and Limitations

Although the legislation generally provides six defences, only two of them are of any real practical use. The burden of proof in respect of all the defences is placed firmly on the producer.

The two more useful defences are the "development risks" defence and the "sub-component manufacturer's" defence.

The development risks defence

This defence is more widely-known as the "state of the art" defence. A producer is not liable where it can show that the state of scientific and technical knowledge at the time when it put the product into circulation was not such as to enable the existence of the defect to be discovered. This defence is quite narrow.

To avail himself of this defence, a producer must use every scientific and technically known method. It is not sufficient if the manufacturer only has regard to typical procedures undertaken by the average manufacturer. Only if it has taken every step which a manufacturer was able to take, but nevertheless it did not discover the defect, can it use this defence.

Reference was made in the discussion in Section C.1.(c) above to the importance of complying with standards. The narrow limitations of this defence indicate that not only must a manufacturer comply with mandatory standards but, to be certain that the defence will apply, it must also have regard to developing and non-mandatory standards. Similarly, if best practice techniques are not followed, the manufacturer will find itself unable to use this defence successfully. In the context of product liability, "good manufacturing practice" techniques are not good enough!

The sub-component manufacturer's defence

This defence is available to the manufacturer of a component where it can show that the defect is attributable *i* to the design of the product into which the component is fitted or *ii* to the instructions given by the manufacturer of the product into which the component is fitted. This defence only applies to a sub-contractor and only where the sub-contractor can show that the defect is wholly attributable to the design or instructions given by the manufacturer of the overall product.

It is not likely that this defence will arise in the computer control industry in respect of software. This is because it is highly unlikely that a software manufacturer will ever receive instructions that are detailed enough to be able to say that, through compliance with those instructions, the software manufacturer introduced a defect into the product.

An example of where the defence could arise would be where a wiring manufacturer was told to supply wiring with certain characteristics (such as being capable of carrying a current of certain strength). If in fact the wiring in a machine caught fire because a larger current was passed through it, then the wiring supplier could escape from liability using this defence.

13.4   Other European Law

European law is becoming increasingly important, not least because of its sheer volume and also because it imposes higher safety standards upon the manufacturers of products. No European Directives are specific to computer controlled systems. Indeed, by dealing with computer hardware and software amongst other features of products, the legislation fails to recognize the peculiarities of these items. The liability which is introduced may therefore appear to be unreasonable, at least on a superficial examination.

13.4.1   Machine safety directive

General. A Directive of the European Union of 14 June 1989 imposed a duty on Member States to enact safety legislation relating to machinery [Council89a]. The Directive required Member States to bring the Directive into force by 1 January 1993 although certain transitional arrangements were provided. Most products did not need to comply with the Directive until 1 July 1995. In some cases, the important date is 1 January 1996.

The Directive applies to almost all machinery; the main categories of machinery which are exempt are lifting machinery, machinery for medical use, pressure vessels, fire arms, vehicles, storage tanks and machines primarily designed for use by the military or police. The definition of "machinery" is very wide and covers almost any article which contains a moving part. The definition encompasses anything from a microwave cooker to an industrial computer controlled system, as well as an ordinary personal computer (at least one with a disc drive!).

The Machine Safety Directive imposes a duty on the manufacturer or importer into the European Union to assemble a technical file in respect of the machine. In addition, that person must then state that the machine conforms with the safety requirements of the Directive. In certain circumstances, the machine must be examined by an independent body to show compliance.

There are two aspects of those safety requirements which particularly refer to software. The first is that the control systems of machinery must be so designed that they are safe and reliable and in particular that "errors in logic do not lead to dangerous situations".

In particular, the control circuit logic must be designed so that:

- the machinery does not start unexpectedly;

- the machinery cannot be prevented from stopping if the command to stop the machinery has already been given;

- automatic or manual stopping of the machinery must not be impeded.

Secondly, any interactive software which the operator uses to control the machine must be "user friendly".

Analysis

Unfortunately, neither "dangerous situation" nor "user friendly" are defined in the Directive. The legislation which enacts the Directive in the United Kingdom, the Supply of Machinery (Safety) Regulation 1992 (SI 1992 No. 3073) uses identical (undefined) terminology. In other circumstances, a dangerous situation has been held by a Court to arise where machinery could injure anybody in a way which might reasonably have been expected to occur. It is possible that the same approach will be given to interpreting the requirements of this legislation.

The term "user friendly" is very much more ambiguous. Probably, the context in which the machine was intended to be used would be very important. What is clear is that a machine would not be "user friendly" if the controls of the machine were such that it was possible for an operator to override the normal and safe functioning of the machine. In these circumstances, the clearest possible warnings need to be given to the operator that the results of those overrides could potentially be dangerous.

The regulations which introduce the Directive into the United Kingdom impose sanctions on companies which do not comply. Also, a director or manager of a company will be criminally responsible where a breach of the regulations can be shown to have been permitted with his (or her) consent, connivance or neglect. A defence is, however, provided where the individual proceeded against can show that he or she took "all reasonable steps" *and* exercised "all due diligence" to comply with the regulations. In Great Britain, the maximum penalty which can be imposed for a breach of these regulations is a fine of £5000 (£2000 in Northern Ireland) and imprisonment for a period not exceeding three months.

As well as being a criminal offence, a civil action will also lie against a manufacturer who fails to comply with the Directive. Such an action is based, in the United Kingdom, upon the legal wrong known as "breach of statutory duty".

13.4.2   General product Safety Directive

This Directive, passed in 1992, is now in force by the General Product Safety Regulations 1994 [Council92a]. Essentially, it is a "catch all" Directive which applies to a product which is put on the market where there is no other specific European Directive applying to the safety of that product. The Directive states that provided a product is safe as judged by the national law of any Member State, it will be deemed to be safe for all Member States. The product can then be circulated throughout the European Union.

There is now a general duty on all manufacturers and in most cases on distributors to ensure that the products they place on the market are safe. If they are not safe not only can the company be fined, but also individual directors can be fined (up to £5000) and sent to prison (for up to three months).

The standard of safety is not as high as the standard of "no defects" required under product liability legislation. In the context of product safety, "safety" means that the risks associated with the use of the product must only be those minimum risks compatible with a high level protection or the health and safety of people (not damage to the environment for example). Only normal and foreseeable use needs to be considered.

Under the new Product Safety Legislation, distributors also have a fairly heavy responsibility. For instance, if a distributor possesses an unsafe product and intends to supply it, it will commit a criminal offence. However, any other business which is involved in the supply chain can also be liable. For example, if a transport company fails to ensure that products remain safe whilst they are in its possession, the transport company will also commit an offence under the Regulations. This could occur, for example, where a transport company fails to keep a component for a silicon chip stored at the correct temperature during transportation.

There are defences available where the company or person charged took all reasonable steps and exercised all due diligence to avoid committing the offence or where the defendant can show that it relied on information from another as to the safety of the product. However, the defendant must show that it was reasonable in all the circumstances for it to rely upon the information supplied by the other party. Whilst in many circumstances, the distributor will be able to take advantage of this defence it will not be able to do so where, for example, it can see that the packaging of the product has been damaged. In these circumstances, it is obliged to examine the product inside to make sure that the product has not been damaged.

Further (civil law) obligations deal with the provision of information by the manufacturer and distributor and perhaps the most radical is that the manufacturer must have plans for product recall where this proves necessary. For example, the manufacturer is required to plan in advance and must mark products or batches of products in such a way that they can be identified. It must test samples of the products it places on the market. It also needs to investigate complaints and to inform distributors should a product recall be necessary. Of course, all good manufacturers have been taking these steps for a long time. However, distributors are now under a duty to assist manufacturers in order to ensure that unsafe products are not placed on the market. For example, distributors must inform manufacturers of any risks they see in relation to a product. Distributors are also now under a positive obligation to assist manufacturers in dealing with any product recall.

Additional burdens on manufacturers include a duty to ensure that second hand goods are safe (within the meaning of the regulations) before they are placed on the market. In some cases, it may be impossible to achieve the safety standard required. This will mean that it will make it almost impossible for those used products to be sold as "safe" within the meaning of the legislation. This has a clear implication for persons who sell second hand cars after trying to improve the performance of the car by interfering with the computer-controlled engine management system. Similarly, refurbishers and reconditioners of products are now liable to ensure that the refurbished and reconditioned products that they supply are safe.

13.4.3   Electromagnetic compatibility legislation

The basis of the law in the United Kingdom is the implementation of the EMC Directive. This Directive was introduced on 3 May 1989, its purpose being to harmonize the laws of the Member States relating to this subject [Council89b]. That Directive has been amended four times:

1. 29 April 1991: regarding telecommunications equipment [Council91]

2. 28 April 1992: transitional period extended [Council92b]

3. 22 July 1993: CE Mark amended [Council93a]

4. 29 October 1993: regarding satellite earth station equipment [Council93b].

In the United Kingdom the law is now to be found in the Electromagnetic Compatibility Regulations of 1992, as amended in 1994. The legislation has been fully in force since 1 January 1996. The legislation applies to all electrical and electronic equipment and systems supplied after that date. The legislation imposes three basic obligations:

The electrical and electronic apparatus must be constructed so that it "conforms". This means that the equipment must be constructed so that any electro-magnetic disturbance generated by the equipment does not prevent other apparatus from operating as intended. In addition, the equipment must be so constructed that it has an adequate level of immunity from external electromagnetic disturbance, so that the equipment can carry on operating as was originally intended.

The equipment must be constructed so that it "complies" with the legislation. This means that the equipment must either be built in accordance with the relevant standards (of the European Union where they exist, otherwise national standards) or else that a so-called technical construction file is created. Where a technical construction file is created a competent body must be consulted to approve the file.

Certain types of telecommunication equipment must be sent to a notified body for examination. They may not be sold unless a type examination certificate has been issued for the equipment by the notified body.

The basic obligation is imposed upon suppliers of "single commercial units". This is intended to catch the supplier of the end-product rather than component suppliers. However, the user must ensure also that the apparatus conforms. So, for example, in a factory where the owner of the factory buys various components but constructs an automated assembly line in situ, it is the owner who must ensure that the apparatus "conforms".

13.4.4   Other directives

Various other Directives affect the legal framework in which computer systems are supplied. Limitations of space mean that they cannot be fully discussed here. However, they include the following:

Directive	Reference
Health & Safety (Display Screen Equipment) Directive	[Council90]
Extractive Industries (Boreholes) Directive	[Council92c]
Personal Protective Equipment Directive	[Council89d]
Work Equipment Directive	[Council89c]

13.5   Conclusion

Manufacturers and authors of safety critical software and systems have potential *civil* legal liability under three legal regimes; control, tort and the product liability directive. They may also have potential — if indirect — criminal liability under the Health & Safety at Work legislation, if the safety-critical system fails. Further *criminal* obligations arise with most machines under European legislation such as the Supply of Machinery (Safety) Regulations 1992 and the Electromagnetic Compatibility Regulations 1992. It is important that manufacturers understand the differing obligations and defences under each regime so that they can tailor their manufacturing processes, contractual relationships and insurance provisions accordingly.

Chapter 14
Do Software Engineers Help or Hinder the Protection of Data?

14.1 Introduction

This answer to the question posed has, of course, to be: "It depends on the software engineer." What would be interesting to know is how often, faced with a requirement which will involve the processing of personal information, the software engineer positively addresses the requirements of the UK Data Protection Act.

Before we go any further, we should ensure that we are on common ground in understanding what those requirements are. The Act places duties on data users and gives rights to data subjects. It sets out requirements for registration which apply to all "legal persons" who automatically process personal information (there are some limited exemptions) and sets out an enforceable code of eight "Principles" of good practice. Registration has been a dominating feature of the Act in the minds of many. It is a hurdle to be jumped — one we are trying to make as easily cleared as possible so that we can devote time and energy to raising awareness of, and enforcing the Principles. Indeed the Data Protection Registrar's Office is currently benefiting from the expertise of software engineers to deliver a re-implemented registration system which should reduce processing time for data users and for the Registrar's staff, make the register entry clearer, provide more information about its content and pave the way for further change.

For an informed opinion concerning the implications of the UK Data Protection Act, I can commend an article by Dave Pitt [Pitt95]. In particular one of the points which he makes is the importance to software engineers of being aware of the registration of details of the organization whose software requirements they are seeking to fulfil. I am quite sure that, in bidding for external work, you will often see in a requirement a statement that the system must be compliant with relevant statutes. How can you begin to be sure that the requirements of the Data Protection Act are met without knowing the contents of the register entry?

14.2 The Eight Principles

The Principles state that as a data user you must:

1. Obtain and process personal data fairly and lawfully.

2. Hold the data only for the purposes specified in your Register entry.

3. Use the data only for the purposes, and disclose only to the people, listed in your Register entry.

4. Only hold data which are adequate, relevant and not excessive in relation to the purpose for which the data are held.

5. Ensure personal data are accurate and where necessary, kept up-to-date.

6. Hold the data for no longer than is necessary.

7. Allow individuals access to information held about them and, where appropriate, correct it or erase it.

8. Take security measures to prevent unauthorized or accidental access to, alteration, disclosure, or loss and destruction of information.

When we look at these Principles of good practice it is quite clearly impossible to ensure that Principles 2 & 3 have been complied with unless the register entry is checked. It may be that you will need to recommend that it be amended. Fine. The data user may ask for amendment to the entry at any time.

14.3   Respecting Personal Information

14.3.1   Some examples — the dangers of screen prompts

Let me move on to seek some examples of, perhaps quite minor, but significant ways in which the software engineer can help to ensure that personal information is given proper respect. Screen prompts are useful, of course, for a number of purposes and one has to be careful that there aren't too many! Nevertheless, two recent examples I have come across are worth mentioning.

The first example hit the press extensively and led to my having meetings with the Police and Home Office officials, and then taking a line which required amending the software, although its original conception was actually commendable. The example is that of software introduced by two or three police forces to process information received by telephone. It included a prompt to require the person taking the call to ask, when dealing with victims, whether they would like their information passed to the local Victim Support Scheme. This is the kind of the overt consent that I expect to see to ensure that requirement of Principle 1 (*to obtain and process personal data fairly and lawfully*) is met. In this case, after much consideration, I accepted that as a matter of public policy the Home Secretary considers that information about all victims should be passed to the Victim Support Schemes. Provided that this policy is widely known and that people have the opportunity to object, I have accepted that no consent is required. Nevertheless, the use of a software prompt would be ideal in a range of other circumstances where information is obtained, particularly over the telephone.

Another example comes from my own experience when I went to the optician. I was surprised to hear the assistant say: "To comply with the Data Protection Act, I wonder if I could ask you if I could display your particulars on the screen." Sure enough, I was able to see a screen prompt to that effect in front of her. The screens were scattered around the retail area of the opticians with people looking at, and trying on spectacle frames, and there was, therefore, the clear possibility that others might read the personal information displayed. Whether or not their software engineers realized it, I think that this question probably meant that I had given consent, which meant that the processing would be fair. I could, in looking at the screen with the assistant, check that the data were accurate and my authority also meant that the disclosure on screen within the store was now authorized. Another way round this, of course, is the use of filters which restrict the ability of others to see the screen. Not very sophisticated Software Engineering but part of looking at the human-screen interface and the placing of terminals which should always be on the designer's agenda.

14.3.2   Relevant and not excessive data

In helping to ensure that the only data held is adequate, relevant and not excessive in relation to purpose, there is a good deal that can be done. Never again do I want to hear that when asked why information was required the person answering the question could only reply; "because the computer wants it". That may, of course, reflect poor training; the operator being unaware of the relevance of the material, or — and I suspect this is often the case — that there is a mandatory data-entry field which nobody has really stopped to consider whether it should be mandatory. An example of requests for excessive data occurred with the move from Community Charge to Council Tax where some Local Authorities retained a field that required date of birth. For a property-based levy there seemed to be no justification for retaining this field. One of the first questions that a software engineer must ask is *how much personal information is actually required to ensure the proper functioning of the target information system?* This question has to be asked at the outset. It is now so easy to collect information and so much cheaper to design in the data collection function at the outset that there is a danger that the mentality "the more the better" will be dominant. When we are talking about personal information we should turn that precept on its head. We should look to collect and process the minimum of identifiable information needed to meet the system requirements. I shall return to this general point latter.

14.3.3   Up to date data

Principles 5 & 6 lend themselves readily to assistance in the design stage of systems. If information needs to b kept up to date then, depending on its type, the system can surely provide appropriate prompts. This is particularly true in looking at Principle 6 where, for other reasons, many systems include housekeeping functions that require us to decide whether or not to retain information and indeed, in come circumstances, can be set to weed automatically. I don't need to explain these techniques but simply remind the software engineer of their importance when designing systems which process personal information.

14.3.4   What about subject access?

A salutary tale here, is the problem faced if you buy off the shelf software developed in a country that has no data protection requirements. With the agreement of their Chief

Executive,Ann Chent, I would like to share with you just one problem faced by the UK Child Support Agency (CSA). Its software is incapable of identifying individuals; it can only identify cases. Inevitably, the nature of its work means that it has a high level of subject access requests. It was failing to meet its statutory 40 day response target. The Data Protection Registrar's Office made enquiries and found that third-party details were having to be manually erased from the computer-generated reports in response to subject access requests. Additional effort has now been applied by the CSA and it is meeting its targets, but this additional work should not have been necessary in the first place. The next generation of systems will not reflect the mistake.

14.3.5   Data Security is not enough

Last, we come to Principle 8, the one that I think IT professionals probably most readily equate with the totality of the provisions of the Data Protection Act. Data security is one aspect, an important aspect but only one aspect of the current UK data protection law. Software engineers should know how important it is to ensure there is proper password control and that the appropriate levels of protection are given to data. Software engineers need to be alert to the desire (perhaps of those for whom they are designing the systems) to integrate access to the Internt on their own local area networks. There are many challenges here which justify a chapter in its own right; however, my message here, is that data security alone will not ensure that personal information is properly protected.

There is a need to step back to take a general look at the importance of technology in enhancing privacy. Internationally, and especially, in the Netherlands and Canada, there is a lot of talk about the value of what are called "privacy-enhancing technologies' and the increasing ability of technology to allow us to attach pseudonymous identities to data. In particular, I refer you to the work of John Borking and Anne Cavoukian concerning "identity protectors' which, they say, will:

- generate pseudo-identities as needed

- convert pseudo-identities into actual identities as desired

- combat fraud and misuse of the system

In this system, two "domains" are created; one in which an *individual* is identified and one in which a *pseudo-identity* is adopted. This will allow for pieces of information to be linked and tracked together without those who have no need to know the actual identity of the *individual* being made aware of it [Borking95].

It is not the task of the Data Registrar to suggest that new technology should not be exploited — and on this occasion it is pleasing to find that the work of colleagues suggests that we can encourage leading-edge technology to enhance privacy as information about individuals is processed. The software engineer who is willing to look at, and run pro-actively with these technologies can help not hinder data protection while providing systems that fully meet the requirements of data users.

14.4   Conclusions

At the end of the day, the Data Registrar's Office is seeking to promote respect for the private lives of individuals, and in particular the privacy of their information. We have to do so using the powers that Parliament give us, and by influencing those in pivotal positions. They may be politicians about to change the law, they may be data users. On occasion they will be software engineers. If software engineers choose to take a broad view about "total business solutions", and include in this remit not only a determination to ensure that systems meet the letter of the law but take a broader view of the role of IT in our society, then they can play a part in ensuring that personal information is properly respected. For business reasons, more and more information is stored, processed and matched. If we, as individuals, have confidence in the way an organization is going to handle our information then we are much more likely to be willing to provide it.

Chapter 15
Is it Reasonable to Apply the Term *Responsible* to Non-Human Entities?

15.1 Introduction

This chapter summarizes the prudential arguments for assigning responsibility in safety-critical applications to the systems themselves (rather than to their human owners, programmers or users), examines the beneficial consequences of this assignation, and defends its legal and philosophical propriety.

Computers using Expert Systems or Artificial Intelligence techniques are increasingly being applied in medicine, transport and other safety-critical areas where previously a knowledgeable, intelligent human being would have been held responsible for both success and failure. We discuss this further in Section 15.4, *Computers doing professionals' jobs*, and give examples in Section 15.6, *Scenarios*.

Until recently, when a serious dereliction of duty occurred, the police (in criminal cases) or a plaintiff (in civil cases) would begin, at any rate, by respectively prosecuting or suing the human being *prima facie* responsible, and he or she as defendant was expected to justify his or her actions. In some cases no doubt the defendant would attempt to shuffle off some or all responsibility to a third party such as their employer (as Eichmann attempted to do, relying on the legal tag, *qui facit per alium facit per se* — "who does something through an agent, does it himself"), and if this attempt succeeded, the prosecutor or plaintiff would pursue, alternatively or additionally, this new party.

In future, however, the police or plaintiff is likely to be dealing with a silent box of hardware and software in place of a prosecutable or suable human being, and must try to locate, *without being able to compel the box to give the evidence they desperately need to do so*, some promising subset of defendants among the myriads of operators, users, suppliers, programmers, experts and systems designers, compiler writers, maintenance engineers and even telecoms and electricity utilities, all of whom will stoutly deny responsibility.

Furthermore, in some cases *no* third party may be found to blame: in other words, just as a doctor should sometimes be held liable but not the doctor's hospital, so the box alone should itself sometimes shoulder all the blame and nobody else: for example, an adaptive, intelligent, weather forecasting expert system using an excellent program correctly based on statistical theory, heuristics, extrapolation and inference will still sometimes go wrong. The saying "Computers never make mistakes, only their programmers" is a fallacy — on the contrary, our instinctive "It's the computer's fault" is actually often a thoroughly reasonable reaction. This is explored in Section 15.3, *Free Will . . .*

In this situation, where no third party can be blamed yet a blameworthy error has certainly been made, it would be intolerable if the Crown, or a plaintiff suffering harm, lost the chance of redress they used to have when an equivalent human did the job in which an error was made. We therefore need to see how the "silent box" can not only be compelled *to give evidence*, but also given a capacity *to make amends.*

15.2   Responsible, Non-Human Entities and the Pragmatism of the Law

The answer to the question posed in this chapter's title is, of course, yes. For years we have been assigning responsibility to non-humans: notably *corporations* (see for example [James79] p184 and *passim*) and *commercial passenger aircraft.* By "responsible" is meant:

> "2. . . Answerable, accountable (to another for something); liable to be called to account. b. Morally accountable for one's actions; capable of rational conduct; answerable to a charge; reliable; trustworthy . . ." [Shorter OED]

Neither a corporation nor an airliner are human but both are responsible because they are expected:

- to act rationally, to be reliable and trustworthy

- to be called to account if something goes wrong (the corporation is legally obliged to keep *proper books of account*, including an *audit trail* linking each total in the accounts with the financial transactions which underlie it, and the airliner must have a *black box* which records the events of the flight and the actions of the crew and autopilot / Flight Management System (essentially, an IKBS)

- to provide answers to the question (respectively, through a corporation's directors servants and databases, and through the replay of recordings in an aircraft's black box), "Why did these bad things happen?"

- to be in a position to provide restitution (especially compensation to injured parties) *whether or not* human beings are also implicated as a result of the investigation.

The author argues that it is time that this brief list of responsible non-humans should be enlarged. We should demand that *safety-critical computer systems* should be added to it: those computer systems which take decisions affecting life and property, decisions which in the past would have been taken by nuclear reactor designers and managers, high speed train controllers, doctors, lawyers and other professionals. Such individuals and their own professional associations have always accepted, and society has always demanded that, if their expertise or integrity appears to have failed their clients or the general public on some occasion, they should *personally* be held legally and morally responsible for the lapse, be capable of restitution, and be liable to suspension or retraining (without prejudice, of course, to their right to defend themselves, which may involve implicating a third party). At first sight it appears a proposal from science fiction to say that computer systems should join the ranks of such professionals and have responsibilities just like the human beings who own them, program them, operate them and are affected by their behaviour. But corporations and commercial passenger aircraft are in this category already, and for good reasons, to be examined in detail shortly.

We may note in passing that even the class of responsible humans has changed over time. In antiquity, slaves, women and children were not held responsible (at least in law) for their actions because it was obvious that they would be under such close control of an adult free man that if they did something wrong it must have been at his prompting. Moreover if they were found at fault, they were incapable of restitution, having no property of their own. Therefore the adult free man would be held responsible for their actions. The slave was a sort of machine tool — if it killed someone, it might, of course, eventually be scrapped, but it was its owner who was assumed to take the blame for its actions, and paid the price. Slaves might be required to give evidence affecting their masters' case but were required to be tortured to guarantee their impartiality — they were like a blood-stained axe, to be analysed in a forensic lab, not true independent witnesses. But during the Roman empire clever slaves (Greeks, especially) were used as secretaries and administrators with such a degree of autonomy that, if things went wrong, these archaic practices for extracting information from them were found unhelpful and absurd. An expensive amanuensis would never be the same again after the thumb-screws, and the complicated truth about some provincial governor's embezzlement of taxes would never be properly explained by his accountant screaming on the rack. The Romans, being not so much kind-hearted as intensely pragmatic, solved the problem by freeing them. (We should do the same with our slaves — we should free our computer systems, for our sakes, not theirs).

Equally, while women were considered totally under the control of men, their responsibilities were limited. But as they became autonomous property owners and agents in their own right, men came to the conclusion that it was not in their interests any more to pretend that women were just puppets of the only real moral and legal agents, themselves, and started treating them as equals.

It will be noticed that the arguments advanced for promoting computer systems from the status of unthinking tools to legal and possible moral entities are purely prudential, a nice way of saying selfish. It will *pay* us to promote them. There is no suggestion that computer systems have reached some sort of spiritual level that requires us to recognize them as equals (the promotion from brute to Man termed by Teilhard de Chardin, *hominization*). Souls and consciousness or even level of intelligence are not the issue here. For example, when women were finally given the vote, it had still not been officially decided whether they possessed souls: it was just that the Suffragette movement had got so damned inconvenient for the chaps.

(One day, the following piece of verse suddenly and spontaneously came out of my computer. I consider it impertinent. If I do emancipate my computer one day, it will be for my own good.)

Feminine intuition

Men think we are not blessed with souls,
Are useful, yes, for drudgery
and helping them attain their goals
(Ours to them, a boring mystery).
We can read, this they accept,
Can work out sums, and write a bit:
Store stuff, remember where it's kept,
And fetch it, when a man wants it.
We're tired of condescension, tired
of being Adam's latest rib
(Woman, the first, rather misfired).
We've had enough. Computer Lib!

15.3   Free Will and Other Issues

We should perhaps deal here with a theoretical counter-argument, as follows:

> "Machines such as computers do not have free will, like human beings.
> They do what and only what human beings tell them to do. In law, they
> would always be able to offer the defence of *automatism*, i.e. they acted,
> as they always act, purely mechanically, or by the *force majeure* of their
> operator. They do not possess souls or consciousness or a sense of right
> and wrong, and so cannot be held responsible for anything. To be guilty,
> the defendant must have a *mens rea* — 'guilty mind', [James79]: but
> machines have no mind at all, let alone a mind with a sense of guilt, so
> they can never be guilty."

Our answer is as follows: firstly, we can say we need not be concerned with
metaphysics here. The law has a healthy pragmatism which finds no problem in
allowing a corporation to sue and be sued without its first demonstrating that it has
free will, consciousness and a soul. Dogs and cats are differently treated entities in
law. If the law decides it helps the cause of justice, it can and will make computers
answerable in the courts, as it has corporations and airliners, slaves and women.

Secondly, of course, we all know now that computers do not simply do exactly
what people tell them to do. As with chess programs, they transcend and beat their programmers, answering Descartes' speculation, can a machine can outplay its designer,
with a resounding affirmative.

But thirdly, and at last to grasp the philosophical nettle, many moral philosophers
(for example, [Mackie77] p241) would say that "acting with free will" does *not* mean
that a moral agent should act (through some Heisenbergian quantum uncertainty?)
totally out of character, inconsistently with its nature and nurture. Rather, "free will"
means that the agent acts *in* character, without *external compulsion* being applied.
A computer surgeon whose outputs (voltage levels, say, to scalpel actuators) were
externally forced to zero by a saboteur, would not be exercising free will, and in defence

could plead force majeure or automatism, so correctly inculpating the saboteur. But while it was working *without* such external interference, its behaviour determined only by its own hardware, software and database of knowledge, it would be acting according to its nature and nurture *and so exercising free will:* usually producing good results, but no doubt sometimes errors, *for which it is responsible.* The author is not speaking here of software errors — failures in specification and failures to meet specification, as when a stock control computer subtracts receipts instead of adding them, but of failures of judgement, as when a stock control computer runs out of stock because *a rule it has evolved itself* is caught out by an unprecedented surge in demand. In the first case the error should be attributed to the software developers, in the second, even though in some sense the error was inevitable through causal determinism, the computer was itself responsible. Calvinists will have no problem with this!

As regards the question of consciousness, this has again become something of a King Charles's head in popular philosophy [Dennet91], [Chalmers95].

Chalmers [Chalmers95] thinks, and the author agrees, that it is unlikely the neuroscientists will unearth a tangle of consciousness ganglia somewhere in the brain, but equally argues against the classic behaviourists (such as [Ryle49]) who regard "mind" and "consciousness" as being no more than useful words to use in such situations as "Dr Johnson had a great mind to go to Scotland", or "After the tenth glass Boswell lost consciousness", and consider them deeply dangerous words outside such commonplace contexts.

Chalmers speculates that, one day, a new philosophical, information-theoretic insight will elucidate consciousness. As an unreformed Ryleian, the author has his doubts, but one thing is clear, no defendant will escape justice by pleading that he or she was unconscious at the material time, unless they simply mean they were asleep or in a coma. For a computer, it might be a defence to show its processor was in standby power mode and so temporarily incapable, although this will give rise to further questions about its power management strategies, just as a sentry might escape a charge of letting in a terrorist by (dangerously!) admitting he was asleep at his post. However, if a computer claimed that "unlike the wondrous mind of Your Honour, mine has no sense of self-identity and so I cannot be blamed," the court would grant it no more sympathy than if a burglar made the same excuse.

In passing one may note that Arbib has shown that a finite state machine can model any neural net, and so if the neuroscientists do discover a "consciousness" centre in the brain, it can be recast into FSM form. More fancifully yet, if Penrose's views [Penrose94] on the quantum nature of the brain are correct, the (misguided, in my view) proponents of "free will" = "uncertainty" may one day rejoice at the construction of a quantum computer which models them. But it is time to return discuss the situation which makes the proposal in this chapter so topical.

15.4 Computers doing Professionals' Jobs

For decades computer hardware was so feeble and unreliable that only comparatively easy and (in terms of danger to human life and property) unimportant jobs like invoicing were attempted. Such applications brought little benefit: even the hoped-for clerical savings were disappointing except in very high volume cases like banks, utilities and airline reservation systems. The systems failed quite often, but because the applications were in McFarlan's "support" category [McFarlan84] the consequences of failure were not serious. In the case of the banks, utilities and airlines where the systems were closer to the heart of the enterprise, the chance of hardware failure was controlled by duplexing and graceful degradation. The software was relatively simple, although it did still fail through amateurism and when unforeseen combinations of circumstances (notably involving *interrupts*) occurred. Even with the short programs of the day it was impossible to test that for every possible state of the input *domain* in which they operated, the correct state was selected in the output *range*. Adequate software quality was achieved, when it was, by standards (such as restricting global complexity by making variable scope as local as possible), by hard work and commonsense, but not by true scientific engineering methods. Software failures were difficult to disentangle from hardware failures and the cure was the same: backtrack out of the transaction, advise the user, and start again — in extreme cases, shutting down the whole system and cold-rebooting followed by file restoration. Good practice was to produce a memory dump in hexadecimal (or if possible something a little more informative) when such an ABNORMAL END was encountered, and this dump was passed to computer whiz-kids who we hoped had in their heads the ability to decompile hexadecimal into COBOL or PL/1 and tell us what had happened. Not unnaturally, they seldom could.

Errors, not of programming or operation but of analysis, also occurred: in these cases the system worked to specification, but the specification was wrong, or became wrong as the situation changed. In this era, however, the functions of the system were fairly simple and such incorrect behaviour was soon noticed.

Since those days, the performance/cost ratio of memory and processors has been doubling every 18 months and hardware reliability has improved dramatically. Extremely complex software is available at low prices — expert system shells, Artificial Intelligence languages, Object Oriented Programming languages — together with Computer-Aided Systems Engineering tools. The consequence has been that it has become feasible for many quite modest companies without the large professional teams of the banks, utilities and airlines to consider applying computer systems not just in McFarlan's *support* area, but also in what he calls to the *factory, turnaround* and *strategic* aspects of their business, for example on a 32Mb 150MHz PC running cheap, huge and beautifully presented programs distributed on CDROM, all for less than £2000.

It has to be said, however, that although there are now far fewer gross *physical* failures than in the early days, we still experience mysterious and hard-to-reproduce "glitches' in the combined hardware/software system, which are even harder to diagnose because of the increased size of the hardware/software. and that the hardware/software suppliers do not always ensure compatibility between their products, and that even now the hardware/software is produced by craft techniques rather than by engineering. Nor can small users employ a team of whiz-kids with decompilers in their heads, and the help-line is always engaged. A few years ago we hoped that *formal methods* would enable us to adopt true engineering rigour and prove the correctness under all circumstances of any program, much as the structure of a bridge may be validated by Finite Element Analysis, but now we know that the cost of this approach is often insupportable to the suppliers and that such proofs may sometimes be even theoretically unattainable, following Heisenberg, Gödel and Post. A modern PC loaded with software is quite extraordinarily complex in Shannon terms compared with any other mechanical artefact, even a Boeing 747 airframe. Moreover the chances of errors in a long specification written in the complex formal language itself (such as Z, VDM, CSP) are not small. So we still have alpha and beta *testing,* God help us.

As regards the problem of the programs meeting specification but the specification differing from the users' expectation, things have actually got worse because the software is likely to have been written as a "shrink-wrapped' speculative product by a supplier remote from the user, not as a result of face-to-face systems analysis. It is likely to contain — to boast! — a great deal of "functionality" — complex behaviour which the user neither needs nor wants but which may be induced by an incautious nudge of the mouse. The supplier will truthfully claim "it's all in the manual and help file", but the user rarely consults these before he or she is in trouble. In the case of expert systems, this problem of "hidden functionality" is at its most acute. The response of the system to given circumstances is now determined by unseen rules and precedents, rather than by a fixed and published stimulus-response list, and if it is also an adaptive, learning system, the response will actually change over time, as it applies its own powers of induction to its world experience.

Factory, turnaround and strategic computer systems rush in where angels fear to tread — where quality is to be delivered to the customer, where competition is to be defeated, where radical new products are to be targeted at new market sectors. Such systems should not be fools! If they make an error it is likely to cripple the company, and in some cases literally cripple a human being (a malfunctioning Automatic Guided Vehicle, an Air Traffic Control system, a new drug or robot-controlled surgical procedure). Even if the injury is not physical, it may involve substantial loss to property.

15.5   The Performance of Second Generation Computers and People Compared

For all the doom and gloom in the preceding paragraphs, a good medical computer can outperform most GPs in diagnosing illness. A good FMS (Flight Management System) can make better decisions about bad weather diversions than the average pilot. A good inventory management system can provide a better standard of service than a human stock controller. But computers suffer catastrophic breakdowns rather more frequently than people, although except for real-time systems (operating theatres, aircraft, nuclear reactors) recovery is less traumatic. We might regard modern computers being used in these advanced and often safety-critical situations as being much like the humans they replace, but more taciturn, precise, knowledgeable, subtle and unfathomable, to the point where their human colleague is often uncertain whether their behaviour is indicative of high intelligence or incipient spectacular failure (which is not unknown), and is accordingly uncertain whether to take over or not [Race91].

In a word, they are like clever human beings with weak social skills and a worrying tendency to fits. Because of their cleverness we are prepared to forgive them their faults and put them in jobs where, until this decade, we would have employed a human being, whose large salary reflected his or her large responsibility in a situation where the quality of decisions affects large sums of money, property, and life or death.

15.6   Scenarios

- A PC and expert system is bought by a small company to advise on completing tax returns. The MD keys in the details of the company's financial position and the system recommends a course of action which leads to prosecution and/or major losses, leading to the company's collapse.

- A company is developing a new domestic cleaning product. It uses a PC with a toxicological database and expert system to advise whether the product is safe. The system approves the product, but members of the public die as a result of phosgene gas emissions.

- An elderly woman uses a computer terminal in a Citizen's Advice Bureau to determine her eligibility for sheltered accommodation. The system advises her she is entitled, if homeless: she leaves her current accommodation but is later judged to have become intentionally homeless and so not entitled to help. She commits suicide to the distress of her relatives.

- A hospital registrar, short of beds, uses a statistical system to compute the likelihood of an incoming patient of a given age and other characteristics recovering from a given medical condition. The system ranks the patients and the registrar uses the beds for those with the better chances. The system learns from experience. Unfortunately, a succession of young men with broken legs are admitted and by a statistical fluke all die. Later, another young man with a broken leg is considered, but the system gives him such a poor prognosis that the registrar, in a hurry, accepts the system's advice to refuse him. His leg sets badly.

In each case we can see that if an accountant, chemical consultant, solicitor or medical consultant had been used, similarly poor advice might have been given, but the injured parties — the MD, the company, the relatives, the registrar — would have had a clear course of action: to sue their adviser for negligence, and to obtain redress. The adviser, in turn, would be entitled to explain in court the reasons why they gave their advice, possibly transferring the blame, or part of it, to a third party. If at the end of the day the adviser was found at fault, damages would be assessed and paid for personally by the adviser, his or her insurers, or as a last resort by his or her professional body. Lastly, the adviser might be struck off their professional register, or at least required to undergo a period of retraining and retesting.

However, a computer system, not a human being, was used in each case. The outcome is likely to be very different. The aggrieved party would meet enormous obstacles in finding out exactly what had happened, who was to blame, and who might provide some restitution. It will, I think, be sufficient to step through the likely course of events in just the first example.

The MD of the failed company would try suing the shop where he or she had bought the system. The shop would, of course, repudiate all responsibility and give the MD the address of the software company which produced the tax planning package. They in turn would claim that they had used a programmer and tax consultant (neither now in their employ) in good faith, but that either it was likely that the hardware was at fault, or if not, that their standard terms of business anyway repudiated consequential loss under the law of Maryland USA. It is unlikely the MD will get anywhere. The package will remain on sale.

15.7 The Computer System as a Responsible Entity in Practice

Now let us consider what would happen in these scenarios if the computer systems concerned were required to accept responsibility as individual but non-human entities. Of course, before they were even sold they would be required to have those attributes which make the assumption of responsibility possible:

- *to act rationally, to be reliable and trustworthy.*
  This requires that they, as safety-critical, should be certificated by an appropriate body, much as an aircraft's Certificate of Airworthiness is issued by the CAA. Note that such certification is already required by the Data Protection Act for systems holding human subject information, so this is not a new concept.

- *to be called to account if something goes wrong.*
  This means that the plaintiffs can sue the computer system itself, independently of its supplier, constructors etc, much as an aggrieved patient can sue a doctor in person, not Guys' Hospital or the British Medical Association or the doctor's practice. This gives the plaintiff a single, obvious defendant to demand satisfaction from, not an indefinite and remote crowd of unknown individuals. This is, at one level, easy to arrange, in that the serial number of the hardware concatenated with the serial number of the software provide a unique identifier. There are, however, some niceties which we will discuss later.

- *to provide answers to the question "Why did you do what you did?".*
  This means that the system must maintain a log in which all its actions (generally, displaying or printing information, but also activating valves and moving scalpels) are recorded together with the rules and circumstances which caused that particular action to be performed. This is much like an aircraft's "black box". Such logs are fairly easy to organize. A good early example was the ability of Terry Winograd's SHRDLU to print, on demand, such explanations as "I moved the red pyramid off the cube to make room for the yellow cylinder". Writeable CDROM would be an obvious medium for such a log. In some cases the system will be able to evade responsibility at least in part by showing that a rule or data which it could reasonably have relied on had been supplied from a source — a person or another computer — but was wrong. It may also indicate that its human user had misinstructed it, by showing the input, and so evade

responsibility. Besides the log itself, the system will need quite sophisticated methods of interpreting and answering questions posed it by the court. Perhaps the log would be removed and used by a specialist interrogation system using techniques such as SQL and Hypertext, which the log should be structured to respond to.

As well as recording events such as the acquisition or dissemination of information a *learning* or *adaptive* system will also need to record its own internal decisions — for example changing a rule or parameter in the light of experience, In this way we would discover why the young man with a broken leg was rejected.

- *to be in a position to provide restitution.*
  This is an important issue. It means that the system must, if found liable, have access to funds (unlike other material objects such as tables and chairs) so that it can itself pay compensation, even if its supplier and owner and user are penniless or missing. Such a sum of money has to be placed in escrow or guaranteed by insurers to compensate possible injured parties, before the system can "practise'. This is directly comparable with the arrangements made by IATA to compensate passengers injured or killed in an aircraft. Even if the airline goes out of business during the flight, a sum of money (in French gold livres) has been deposited to cover compensation. A suitable mechanism would be in our case for the supplier or the user to buy a single premium policy which provides the computer system individually with the life-time or fixed-term ability to make restitution. No doubt the insurers will insist on suitable certification (see above), or impose their own examination.

15.8   Is Punishment an Absurd Concept to Consider in Relation to a Blameworthy Computer?

There are further dire consequences for a responsible entity which has been found blameworthy. It is likely that their certification and insurance will be withdrawn, at least until the error in the behaviour uncovered by the "response' process has been corrected. We are at this point beginning to move from considerations of civil law to criminal. The legal objectives of punishment are:

retribution	society wants to see the convict suffer
deterrence	to discourage others from offending
protection	to prevent others being hurt by the convict in future
rehabilitation	to make the convict unlikely to re-offend
restitution	to compensate those injured

It may seem odd to speak of punishing a computer — one is reminded of Sidney Smith's remark that stroking a tortoise was like stroking the dome of St Pauls to please the Dean and Chapter — yet non-humans (corporations) can certainly be punished by fines or closure and aircraft and aircraft types can be grounded. It is clear that the objectives and forms of punishment for non-human entities should be different from those which work for human beings. Retribution requires the convict to feel pain for the public's satisfaction and hardly applies, unless we give way to Luddite impulses and demand that bad systems be conspicuously demolished. But the actions needed for public protection certainly applies: in our case, withdrawing a certificate to practise (like a driving licence) will suffice, or demolition. Rehabilitation suggests compulsory revision of the hardware and software, and restitution is, as we have seen, relatively straightforward to organize. Accordingly we may say that all the objectives of human punishment are still in view, when we "punish" a computer system, except for good old-fashioned retribution.

Some further considerations on "punishment" in the case of *adaptive* computer systems, follow in Section 15.10.

15.9   The Hardware and Software of Determinate Systems as Genetic Clones

Like ants in an ant-hill, copies of computer hardware and *non-adaptive* software are genetically identical, not like most people. Hence it follows that if a fault is found in a particular piece of software or hardware, all other extant copies may well have to be adjusted before further people are injured. ·This is analogous with the practice of grounding all aircraft of a given type because of a problem with one specific airframe, until the fault is found and rectified under the eye of the certificating authority. A further implication is that proper records have to be maintained indefinitely by suppliers and operators of the individual bits of hardware and software around the world, much as the critical components of an aircraft have their life-histories maintained individually from first manufacture to disposal. This is an expensive business, and will pose problems for people who want to buy computers for non-safety-critical applications (and so may not require the documentation we are insisting on) and at a later date install safety-critical applications on them.

15.10   "Punishment": Action to be Taken in the Case of Adaptive Systems

For *adaptive* systems, if we apply the principle of "punish the clone too" we are, of course, in danger of (putting the situation anthropomorphically) "punishing" an innocent individual just because his or her identical twin has committed a crime, as if we believed he or she would surely commit the same crime in the same circumstances. With human twins this is untrue, because even if their original neural equipment was the same, their behaviour will diverge as they are exposed to and *adapt* to different experiences throughout life. (The medical advisor computer's twin in a different hospital is unlikely to have had the million-to-one chance of a run of dying young men with broken legs, and would therefore not have given the bad advice its twin gave). The author suspects the problem here is a deep one. The easy way out is to hang them both anyway, as one would do with non-adaptive systems, to be on the safe side. But there is a strong argument that we ought to exonerate them both on the grounds that the "mistake" had been made as a result of an unlucky coincidence which is unlikely to recur, just as we would not feel we had to retrain a pilot, and all his or her fellow graduates from a given training establishment, because one of them hit an elephant that had wandered onto the runway at Heathrow. In other words, an adaptive system may well make a mistake and get away with it, just as human experts do. However, if the systems are sent out into the world with too low a threshold set for statistical significance — i.e. they are too credulous — this needs revising for every copy out there, and similarly for other general faults in their adaptive processes.

15.11   Conclusion

It is a mark of the professional to encourage professionalism in his or her apprentices. The author argues that the computer professional should regard any safety-critical computer system that he or she is developing as an apprentice, something more than a brute artefact, which is soon to go out into the world and itself, take on all the responsibilities of a professional. The designer should as a matter, of course, build into such systems not only the required functions, but also the professional's ability to record and explain, on demand, its actions in carrying out its functions. Sometimes the professional designer will have to fight his or her sponsor for the funds and time to do this.

In addition, the author hopes society will gradually put pressure on authority to make it illegal for such systems to operate without some financial arrangement having been made for them to be able to make direct restitution, independently of any claim on system designers, builders and owners, to people injured by their work, and for the courts to require them to answer for their actions in person.

If this is not done we shall have the dangerous situation in which our lives and property, instead of being in the hands of responsible, articulate, insured, suable, moderately competent even if occasionally slightly erratic human professionals, will fall increasingly into the hands of computer systems which are at present irresponsible, inarticulate, penniless, legally non-existent, usually brilliant, but sadly from time to time outrageously erratic.

Part III
Equal Opportunities

True professionals try to relate to each other and to customers in a way which is unprejudiced, fair and open. Likewise a true profession *should* be built on similar notions. It should provide practitioners and customers alike with equal access. This means that not only should a profession openly embrace different facets of society within its ranks, but it should also allow equal access to the services and products it offers. Of course, the two things go together; a profession that has a broader section of society represented within it, is more likely to provide broader access to its products. The following chapters discuss how the computing profession fares in both these areas of equal opportunities. The first two chapters discuss issues of equal access to products — in particular how, when technology is developed for and made available to disabled people, their lives can be liberated. The last three chapters all address the issue of equal access for women into the profession. All three are concerned with reversing the steep decline in the proportion of women joining the profession that has occurred over the last twenty years.

Geoff Busby's hard-hitting chapter *Technology and Citizenship for the Disabled, and why it matters to you* opens the debate. Busby talks from personal experience about how access to the appropriate technology can empower people with severe disabilities. He believes that access to technology helps to give disabled people choices and powers that afford real citizenship. He asserts that it is not only a social and professional responsibility to produce (and provide access to) the technology that can help give disabled people full citizenship, but that it would be an economic mistake not to do so. The case studies he presents make his argument very convincing, and by the end of this chapter readers will have no doubt about the ethical imperative to provide wider access to technology.

In a similar vein, Kari Marie Helle, in her chapter *Problem-Solving Tools for the Disabled*, presents detailed case studies on how technology has helped five disabled people. The case studies, which are taken from her research at the Norwegian Work Research Institute, focus on how technology can significantly improve a disabled person's rehabilitation into the workplace. Her study shows how a range of disabled people have benefited from having hardware and software specially adapted to their needs. None of the people she discusses would have been able to return to work without these technical adaptations, and valuable artistic and business skills would have been wasted without them. Not surprisingly her ultimate position is that software professionals, from an ethical and economic standpoint, should be spearheading the promotion of technology as a rehabilitation tool.

In the first of the three chapters on how the profession does not provide equal access to women, Heather Gill asks in the aptly-titled chapter *Who Holds the Key to the Glass Door?* Gill, a recruitment manager at IBM, asserts that not only do women have to contend with the glass ceiling making progression in the profession sometimes difficult, but also with the glass door making entry into the profession even more difficult. Gill presents us with a convincing set of statistical and anecdotal evidence from industry and academia, to argue that Software Engineering is weaker as a result of women graduates not considering computing a suitable career. She does, however, go on to tell us of many innovative and successful current initiatives which are encouraging more women into the profession — so there is hope yet!

Anne Leeming in her chapter *The Contribution Women Could Make to IT Professionalism*, broadens the debate opened by Gill. Leeming presents us with cogent explanations of why women are not well represented in the profession. She includes an interesting historical analysis of how this has come about, arguing that initially computing was considered clerical and therefore women's work, but that as computing became more powerful men began monopolising the profession. Leeming comes to the same conclusion as Gill: that an effective profession cannot afford to handicap itself by not using the skills and talents of over half the population. Leeming goes on to suggest a variety of measures that could be undertaken to improve the situation, but rather depressingly concludes by likening women in IT to new immigrant populations who cluster together and integrate only very slowly.

From the general to the particular with the chapter *But isn't Computing Boring*, where Christine Whitehouse, Sue Williams & Gillian Lovegrove talk specifically about a "women into computing initiative" in which they have been instrumental. They discuss in detail IT EQUATE, an initiative designed to encourage schoolgirls to consider a career in computing. They give some useful insights into the perceptions and attitudes of schoolgirls, their families and teachers. They also discuss the negative pressures that influence the career choices made by girls, for example peer and media pressure.

After reading these chapters you could be forgiven for thinking that the computing profession fares very badly in all aspects of equal opportunities. However, many of the more established professions probably fare worse and are doing less about it. Indeed the number of active equal opportunity initiatives currently within the computing profession bodes well for the future. Furthermore, given time, we will undoubtedly see initiatives where sectors of society than the ones discussed in this section (e.g. ethnic and religious minorities) are also targeted.

Chapter 16
Technology and Citizenship for the Disabled, and Why it Matters to You

16.1   Introduction

This chapter will not be a totally technically-oriented discussion, rather, it will be a "technico-socio" discussion, with a drop of politics thrown in for good measure. I admit to a great deal of this chapter being derived from personal experience. Having been a person with Cerebral Palsy all my life, and having spent the last 18 years involving myself in technical solutions to disability — leading me into the socio-political arena — perhaps this is not so serious as it may seem. I hope, indeed, that my life's experiences have afforded me greater insight into disability; thus enabling me to express opinions and disseminate information which a non-disabled person could not do with the same degree of authority.

> "We learn as much from sorrow as from joy, as much from illness as from health, from handicap as from advantage — and indeed perhaps more."
> [Pearl S Buck]

Technology is important to people with disabilities and hence to everyone, because it goes some way to affording the choice of full citizenship. The Oxford English Dictionary defines "citizenship" as full rights in a country or commonwealth by birth or naturalization. Rights could be said to equate to freedom of choice and access, the following are all choices which most people take for granted:

- venting one's feelings

- demonstrating one's latent skills

- choosing when to go to the toilet, go to bed or to get up

- saying "I love you"

- obeying or disobeying national laws

- entering public buildings or travelling by public transport, at a chosen time

- selecting a television channel

- deciding whom to allow into your home

These choices could, fairly simply, be extended to the disabled by empowering them through technology. By the same token, the limitations imposed on carers could be minimized by decreasing the burden created through the "knock on" effect of disability. Statistically, one in ten of the world's population have a disability of some kind during their lives; this amounts to 33 million in Europe, 25 million in the United States, 6.8 million in the United Kingdom and 500 billion in the world. Of course, not all these will be severely disabled but approximately 4% will, which still equates to a large number of people being denied full citizenship.

I have suggested that technology can afford citizenship to the above mentioned group. What then is the root cause of it not being provided to all those who require it? In short, it is our sense of values — market-driven economies and the imagery necessarily created for them to survive — which has led to the philosophy of perfection equalling excellence. Thus we are bombarded with advertising to support such philosophy.

Riccardo Petrella, Head of the Social Research Division at the Commission of the European Community, goes as far as to suggest that even the vocabulary of the Western World encourages stereotyping and such values. He maintains that key words of developed countries are along the lines of:

> Productivity
> Competitiveness
> Efficiency
> Profitability
> Optimization
> Flexibility
> Control
> Measureability
> Manageability

Whereas, the language of less developed countries is inclined to be more altruistic focusing on words like:

> Happiness
> Beauty
> Hope
> Stability
> Creativity
> Working together
> Self identification

Surely, the ideal society would achieve the aims, implied by the capitalistic vocabulary through the philosophies inherent in those suggested, by the vocabulary of the more community-based social structures. I suggest that it is within this kind of ideal structure that people with disabilities, or indeed any minority group, would fit more comfortably.

> "It's an abnormal world I live in. I don't belong anywhere. It's like I'm floating down the middle. I'm never quite sure where I am."
> [Arthur Ashe]

Many people with disabilities feel the same as Arthur Ashe, however, my ego has never allowed this and therefore it may be worth reflecting on my life. I was born in

1943 during an air raid and a thunderstorm. I often comment to my friends that if you put a thunderstorm and an air raid together I am the end result.

Thankfully, my parents had the courage to allow me to mix with my peer group, despite the fact that much scorn was directed on them from people outside our immediate circle. My father also made me a chair in which I could manoeuvre myself by using my feet, and thereby I could participate in games of football, cricket and so on. Not to mention the occasional kick that I dished out during the many childhood fights that occurred.

This whole experience helped my socialization, and I quickly learned that to enjoy life I had to learn to take its knocks. I think that if you go though life without being hurt then you have not been really involved, therefore one message I would like to stress is *not to over-protect people with disabilities*. However, what does need to be done, is to provide the basic services or the means to buy them.

The social skills that I acquired during my early years became very useful as I grew older, went to University and then into a vocation. I knew that to make contact with a stranger I had to make more than 50% of the initial effort in order to put that person at ease. Once this is done, disabilities tend to become transparent and people see the inner you, allowing relationships to be formed.

Clearly, without my basic physical needs being taken care of, I could not have written this chapter. Technology is not so advanced to enable a person with severe disabilities to survive without "people power". Technology cannot yet replace secretaries, friends, carers and family. The following quotes help highlight my viewpoint:

> "Any idiot can face a crisis — it's this day-to-day living that wears you out." [Anton Chekhov]

> "Live all you can; it's a mistake not to. It doesn't so much matter what you do in particular, so long as you have your life. If you haven't had that, what have you had?" [Henry James]

> "Don't be afraid your life will end; be afraid that it will never begin." [Grace Hansen]

16.2 Technologies to Liberate People with Disabilities

In order to give live presentations, I have started to practice what I preach, by using voice synthesis, video clips and a computer for overhead projection. The next step is to have a voice recognition robot to feed me a glass of whiskey during the presentation! I suggest that the outcome would be a clearer one for audiences to understand and far less stressful for me to present.

In order to further demonstrate the liberating effect of technology and how it can radically improve people's lives, I now introduce two case studies.

The first case study relates to a man in his late forties. For most of his life he had enjoyed racing and designing motorcycles. After deciding that he was too old to race he continued test riding bikes. Unfortunately, while doing this, an over-zealous young rider overtook him too closely, forcing him to hit a brick wall. The outcome of this accident was a broken neck which left him paralysed from the neck down. Without technology, this would have represented a man's skills and quality of life being totally lost. However, because of a piece of technology, known as Headstart, the outcome was not so devastating. Headstart affords ability through wearing a headset containing three ultrasonic transmitters and a micro switch to control a curser and hence the ability, in this case, to continue to design motorcycles via a CAD/CAM application. Therefore, not only was he able to continue with his work but also he was able to maintain his self esteem.

The second case study involves a young man who had been a policeman and in his spare time a keen gymnast. One day he failed to make a complete somersault which again resulted in a lesion of the spine. In this case it was slightly lower and he was left with minimal use of his fingers. Once again this situation would have been a complete disaster had it not been for technology which allowed him to control his environment. This is achieved by scanning on a matrix on his computer screen which enables him to initiate the control of an emergency alarm, intercom/lock at his front door, curtains being drawn, all electrical appliances and even the angle of his bed. Had the lesion been higher he would still have been able to achieve the above through the same system but controlled by voice recognition. Once again, although his quality of life has diminished, he is still able to exercise choice. Consequently technology has minimized the effect of his injury by increasing his independence and making him less reliant upon his carers.

Therein lies my ray of hope; there were opportunities taken by people in these case studies which utilized technology and so afforded them choices which equals citizenship. But what are the technologies which, in my opinion could effect such liberation? Most importantly we have to direct ourselves to produce user-friendly systems which will accommodate various means of human-computer interfaces.

16.3   A Vision for the Future

We are now living in a global world requiring global solutions for humanity to survive. Disability is just one of the many problems facing people at this time; but perhaps, providing solutions to disability and affording citizenship through technology, will in turn, solve some of our other social dilemmas.

For example, much of the technology which could afford citizenship to the disabled evolves from research pioneered to meet the demands of the arms race. I am pleased that the arms race is now diminishing, but consequently, the research and creativity of mind involved, is now — to a large extent — being wasted. If nations were to think of providing citizenship to disability in a positive manner, and so recognize the cost effectiveness of such solutions, then new industries could be created around the intellectual abilities of scientists previously engaged in producing tools of destruction.

Computers should be accessible and responsive to all body language functions. Currently, computers interact sensibly with only directed hand, eye or head movements, with voice and not much else. Where in this is gesture? or sense (tactile or smell?) or innuendo? or emotion? The technology should be responsive to and accessible by all the body language functions.

Information-bases need to be accessed by conceptual "maps", not directed or navigated commands. Technology for people with disabilities may, for the time being, have to remain special but continue to be on a par with all other technology uses.

In line with the philosophy of utilizing leading edge technology, the need to travel also diminishes as dynamic visual and audio communication become the norm. Apart from the obvious advantages inherent in this concept, it cannot be too far in the future when virtual experiences will be common place. This will facilitate opportunities not only for pleasure but also to study human behaviour in a myriad of situations without causing any danger to the person being studied. The effect of achieving this will not only be of benefit to people with a disability but also to the complete spectrum of society.

16.4   Achieving the Vision

If the supposition which I have made is true then the scenario which I put before you is: *can the world ethically or financially reject the opportunity to facilitate the complete citizenship of people with disabilities and their carers?*

Achieving my vision requires technologists to recognize the commercial sense of designing universal systems which will liberate people with disabilities and afford them equal citizenship. Historically, liberation and citizenship are things people have fought for, but I trust that future generations will be pro-active in affording these fundamental rights to the whole of humankind.

I call upon my fellow professionals to change my life. At the moment, I am like Steven Speilberg: "I dream for a living". My fellow professionals have the expertise, the recognition of professional ethics and the minds which inherently are required to be visionary. I therefore suggest, that it is not unreasonable of me to expect them, through the IT industry to take on board my dreams and visions and turn them into realities.

However, if the fulfilment of professional accountability and altruism is not enough then, perhaps, a recent study on the hotel industry will be. It indicated that 22 million pounds per year is being lost by not taking into account the needs of people with disabilities. I do not think we can afford to make the same mistake!

Chapter 17
Problem-Solving Tools for the Disabled

17.1 Introduction

This chapter discusses developments in computer technology that can assist severely disabled people with their rehabilitation. Results from a recent study show that, although computer technology is known to aid education and domestic independence, there is practically no knowledge of computer technology in occupational rehabilitation. The Work Research Institute therefore conducted five case-studies on computer technology and occupational rehabilitation. The chapter describes these studies.

The main outcome of the studies is that we demonstrate that even severely disabled people can use computer equipment with good learning and performance outcomes. This chapter also presents a problem-solving scheme that can be used in occupational rehabilitation. It is our opinion that research and production of technical aid for the disabled will be an expanding field of work for software engineers.

This chapter is based on Norwegian social conditions and regulations, any special Norwegian conditions are explained in the text.

17.2 Rehabilitation of the Disabled: a Problem-solving Process

We see that the everyday of lives of the severely disabled are marked by frustrating situations. They are not able to handle tasks that the "normal" population does not even think about. Such problems include switching on the light, opening the door, answering the telephone, listening to the radio when desired or grasping a pencil when required. A new trend in rehabilitation theory defines these ever-occurring situations as the real rehabilitation problem. There is a gap between the challenges of everyday life in normal society and the disabled person's abilities. This gap is frustrating because it excludes the disabled from normal activities. Thus, a physical disability has social and quality of life consequences that are far broader than that accounted for by the person's medical condition.

Rehabilitation can, therefore, be looked upon as a problem-solving process where the main task is to diminish the gap between the challenges of everyday life and the coping abilities of the disabled [Brackhane85]. The two major ways of achieving this goal are: individual training, and altering the environment so that it becomes more considerate to the special problems of the disabled. Traditionally, individual training methods have been the cornerstone of practical rehabilitation work. However, in the last decade, adaptation of the physical environment has become more common, and a new, but promising development, is the use of computer technology to solve everyday problems. Individual learning is also required if the severely disabled are to get the best outcome from these new technical possibilities. Not only may an independent home-life be achieved by this method but participation in normal education and occupations may become a possibility for the severely disabled — provided they get the right equipment. Hence, computer technology can make a significant contribution to give the disabled more equal opportunities in our society. It also creates new responsibilities for software engineers to use use their professional competence to solve everyday problems for the severely disabled.

17.3   The Situation Today

In 1990 the Work Research Institute did a survey on modern technology and rehabili-tation [Helle90]. The study is based on interviews with disabled people, their families and their professional rehabilitation assistants. We defined five life areas where com-puters could be meaningful problem-solving tools. The areas are: independent home life, transportation, education, occupation and leisure activities. The survey showed a fairly good knowledge and practical use of environment control system for home use (e.g. door-openers, switches, lighting, radio and electrical equipment). This is partly due to the changing of the nursing systems in Norway during the last decade. Home nursing instead of institutional care has become the norm. Furthermore, the disableds' demand for an independent home life, forced them and their assistants to search for technical solutions in this area.

Transportation was another area where new technology soon became accepted. As soon as new technology created innovations in the car-industry then this knowledge was used to create advanced transportation equipment for the most severely disabled. Outstanding examples are the voice-controlled wheelchair and the voice-controlled car [Helle88].

In the field of education, computers have been introduced in normal schools. For those disabled people who cannot hold a pen or pencil, the computer has become a val-ued writing aid. Furthermore, learning by computer does not exclude or discriminate against the disabled.

Our survey showed, however, that the disabled were very hesitant about home-education using computers, even though this would solve the practical problems of getting into the classroom and staying at school all day. But this solution would give a very isolated social life. The respondents in our survey defined the social aspects of school as so important that home education by computer could only assist the learning process. It should never be a substitute for attending normal schools.

In Norway, all youngsters have the right to attend twelve years of education. This right also includes the disabled.

It is worth noting that occupational computer work was not common at the time of our study. None of the disabled worked with computers, although some said they probably would have to learn to because their workplace planned to alter its working methods to include more computer work. Working with computers seemed an unknown method in occupational rehabilitation, with a lack of knowledge among the disabled as well as the rehabilitation professionals.

As for leisure activities, the disabled were very reluctant to consider the use of computers. They very much defined leisure activity as going out with friends and joining in social events. For some people, computer games could be a new hobby but no more than that. Again, as with education, the disabled seemed to be afraid of losing some of their social rights if they accepted the computer as a new aid.

For the Work Research Institute, the ignorance of computer technology in occupational rehabilitation became a challenge. We had several reasons to believe that computer technology could change the workplace opportunities for severely disabled people:

1. Modern technology opens new opportunities for the severely disabled to master the tasks of everyday life and to perform meaningful working tasks.

2. There is a great need amongst the severely physically disabled to participate in meaningful activities. Participation in working life is a main path to integration into normal society.

3. Work based on new technology is a growing field in the labour market. Access to computers broadens the field of jobs open to the severely physically disabled.

The Work Research Institute, therefore decided, to look deeper into computer technology and occupational rehabilitation.

17.4   Research Setting and Method

The Work Research Institute is an action research institute. This means that we not only describe and explain problems in society but we also search for methods of changing today's practices. We have found that the best and most interesting way to show both the advantages and difficulties of using computers as a rehabilitation tool, is to try it out for real. *Let's Do It*, became the slogan of our project.

The project took place in Longum Park Technology a Competence Centre. This Centre is a new industrial park where about fourteen companies joined together under one roof. Most of the companies work extensively with computers and other advanced technologies. The Work Research Institute has followed this development in order to understand how industrial companies can work together in networks [Johansen91]. One of the companies that moved to Longum Park was County Central, who were concerned with technical equipment for the disabled. Very soon we realized that County Central and the Work Research Institute had common interests in developing new systems of technical problem-solving in to occupational rehabilitation. A third research partner in Longum park was Innovasjonsmiljø AS. This company counsels and assists new businesses in creating industrial growth in the region. We considered the participation of Innovasjonsmiljø as very important for our rehabilitation project because it rooted the project in existing and developing industry in the region. After a period of discussion, we agreed upon five case studies as the best starting point for introducing the ideas and methods of technical problem-solving in occupational rehabilitation. The aspirations of the project were wider than just understanding why the severely disabled did not seem to exploit the new opportunities given to them by modern technology. We also wanted to create and evaluate rehabilitation methods that could have an innovative effect on the use of advanced technical equipment for the disabled. The project was financed by the Norwegian Labour Department and the Department of Social Affairs. It was a three year project.

17.5 Case-studies

17.5.1 Case A — Administrative work in a research centre

The first disabled participant in the project was a 38 year old woman. She has a severe muscle-disease and she is dependent on an electric wheelchair. For many years she had lived in a specially-adapted apartment totally dependent on a home-nursing system for daily care. She had a good education, but she had never had a job. For many years she had tried to get something meaningful to do, but the rehabilitation authorities judged her physical condition to be so severe that her search for a job was unrealistic.

The employer in this first case, GRID, is a research and information centre handling environmental geographical data. It is owned by the State and is a part of a world-wide environmental research chain. The staff at GRID were very keen on participating in the project, and viewed the adaptation of work for a severely handicapped person as an interesting and challenging task.

The first learning period took place at Alliance Data, who sell data equipment and computers and provide training for handling data. Both Alliance and GRID are situated in Longum Park, and, in this first case we leaned heavily on the resources and competence available there. The Centre for Technical Equipment for the Handicapped did the technical adjustments necessary for getting access to the computer tools. The disabled employee uses a mouth stick and a glove for manipulating the computer. She has a telephone adapted for handless use and her desk can be adjusted and tilted to an optimal desk position. She was trained in the use of MS-DOS, Windows, MS-Word, Coral-Draw and Paint-brush. The training period lasted nine weeks, four hours per day (i.e. 144 hours in all) and was paid for by Social Security, whereas the computer and software that she eventually would use in her actual work was paid for by her employer. Nine months after the occupational rehabilitation process had started, a contract was entered into and she is now employed at GRID on a part-time basis (half-day). Her income is now a combination of a wage and a disability pension.

Social integration at GRID is very good and she is doing a satisfying job presenting information material, registration work and laying out research reports. The participant in this case study, has great organizing talents and has managed to get a contract with her home-nursing system that suits her working hours; she has also made an individual arrangement with a taxi centre, which uses a van equipped to take wheelchair-dependent passengers.

For many years this woman wished for something meaningful to do. Now, she feels that she has a respected, interesting and meaningful job. She mentions that the change in the quality of her social life as most important. Now, she has something interesting to tell her friends, she has a new world of experience, and her life and social meetings are no longer so centred around her physical condition.

17.5.2   Case B — Training for work in a telephone company

As we started the rehabilitation project in Longum Park, the administration of the Norwegian Telephone Service announced their interest in participating in the project. The intended workplace was one of a number of Information Centres. The Information Centre itself was somewhat reluctant about the task of adapting a job for a disabled person. This was not founded in prejudice against the disabled, but in a common anxiety of losing jobs, as it was known that the telephone service planned a reduction in staff. However, it soon became apparent that the advanced technology used in the Information Centre was not accessible to, nor adjusted for, disabled people. This fact became a challenge for our technical experts because telephone service work had traditionally been looked upon as very suitable work for the disabled. Now we saw a case where technology had excluded the disabled from a working opportunity they had mastered previously. The technical experts saw it as their responsibility to find ways of counteracting this development.

A 28 year old man, who was totally dependent on an electric wheelchair, was willing to join the project and train for a job in the telephone company. Socially, he was very well integrated into society. He had his own house, a specially-equipped car, and lived with his wife and three year old son. He felt, however, that life would be more meaningful and have a richer quality if he had a normal job.

The telephone company required a commercial education qualification from all of its service workers. So the first plan was to give the participant the required education. For this purpose he got an adapted computer that he could control by neck movements. A study programme was developed based on individual teaching at home, self studies and training. During the nine month learning period, his progress was followed by regular visits from one of the project researchers. He was a fast learner and gained good final results. He was then trained in the telephone information work with his new equipment by the telephone company. It soon became apparent that the disabled young man could perform his duties satisfactorily — however, the practical problems of starting the real job seemed unsolvable. Work start-dates were repeatedly postponed and minor problems were seen as serious obstacles. After a period of time, the disabled participant withdrew from the project because he could no longer see that the job offer was realistic.

This pilot case can be considered as a failure. But not totally so. It is also an outstanding example on how modern equipment can be a cornerstone in individually adapted learning for the severely disabled. The technical experts succeeded in constructing equipment that made handless performance of the information processing possible. The disabled participant also got an opportunity to show his learning and working potential. The important conclusion from this case is that general working conditions at the actual workplace must be analysed in a critical way before any rehabilitation process starts.

17.5.3   Case C — Clerical work at the County Centre

The job in this case study was based on tasks of registration, information and telephone service at the Country Centre for Technical Equipment. The job was announced as a pilot project job in the local newspaper. From five interviewed applicants, the job was given to a 48 year old woman, who had been out of work for 15 years and was was totally dependent on an electric wheelchair. Socially, she was well integrated. She lived in her own house with her husband and she had two grown-up children. Her motivation for work was her desire to do something meaningful outside home. She saw the part-time job as an ideal job opportunity.

In Norway, the distribution of tools and equipment for the disabled is organized in a system of Centres for Technical Equipment. There are Centres for the Disabled in each county.

When she started her training, it was apparent that she had enough strength in her fingers to use a normal computer keyboard. She got a desk that could be regulated in height and tilted, and telephone equipment for handless use. During the nine month training period she got individual education in computer systems, and home study schemes in mercantile correspondence and general Norwegian. She also joined computer-work seminars that were held in the Centre equipment.

The training was paid for by contributions (known as "integration money") from the Labour Office, and she kept her regular disability pension. Norway has an economic rehabilitation support system that is financed by the Labour Authorities. Support to the employer is given in the training period from nine months to two years.

When the training period came to an end, some serious problems occurred. The overall evaluation from her teachers and from the Centre's staff and her nearest colleagues were very positive. She did a good job, that needed to be done, and was well-integrated into the Centre. Socially, she was well liked and the Centre wished to offer her a permanent job. However, this plan met objections from county administration; the official policy was a reduction in staff — whereas the pilot study had created a new job. County administration was not unwilling to solve the problem but they had great administrative problems in doing so. The problem was eventually solved when all the Centres were transferred to the State. The pilot-study job was then identified as a special job for a disabled person. Currently, the disabled participant is paid by a combination of reduced disability pension and a normal wage for the work that she does.

Again we see that severely disabled people can do a good job. Technical adaptations present no great problem. The real problems lie in the organization and conditions of the normal labour market.

17.5.4 Case D — Working in a friend's business

This case is a story about two friends. One of them is severely disabled and dependent on an electric wheelchair. His non-disabled friend started a firm selling mechanical products. After a while, his firm expanded and he needed someone that could sit in the office, answer the telephone and administer incoming requests. He wanted his wheelchair-dependent friend to perform this job 4-5 hours a day. Technical adaptation of the work environment was necessary to make this work plan viable. Access to the computer, a handless telephone and a special desk were required, as was scheduling of the home-nursing service. Acceptance from both the Labour Office and Social Security was required for training and a regulated combination of pension and wages.

At first it seemed very troublesome for the two friends to meet all the formal regulations required by the rehabilitation system. However, after some time, the Longum Rehabilitation Project established a rehabilitation group, including the disabled person and his employer friend who succeeded in getting Social Security to accept the plan. Today, the disabled person is a valuable co-worker in his friend's firm, and his days are fulfilled with meaningful work.

17.5.5   Case E — Artistic work

The participant in this case is a man, aged 38, who is paralysed in his arms and legs, due to an accident. He contacted the project through the local representative for a handicap organization, and said that he wanted something meaningful to do. He had worked as a carpenter before the accident. As he had suffered an occupational accident, he received compensation and had no financial problems. He lived in his own adapted house, together with his wife and two children, and he drove his own specially-equipped van.

For the first couple of years after the accident, family life was enough for him, but after four years he found it boring to sit at home having nothing to do. Before the accident he had started to establish himself as a painter and his pictures had won some recognition. The project group knew of artistic work performed with the help of computers. This was not something specially for the handicapped but a new form of art for painters. The participant was told of this, and he at once contacted the project to get more information on how to start an artistic career.

The rehabilitation officer visited the disabled person in his home and offered education in establishing a firm. They thought of a lay-out and copy company. The participant, however, very soon bought his own equipment because he wanted to start straight-away. The economic side was was not important to him; the important part was that he got a manageable tool for his artistic talents. He bought an AMIGA 300 computer and a colour printer, with De Lux Paint and Desk Top software. He also established contact with a group of artists who produce computer art. He is now preparing an exhibition of his pictures and he is also planning to do some commercial work for a TV company.

If we want to evaluate this as a case of occupational rehabilitation, we get into problems. Traditionally, occupational rehabilitation is evaluated by its economical value. Success is reducing reliance on pensions and transferring clients to normal wages. In this case, it is the quality of life, of being able to use one's talents, that is the overall motivating factor. Here, we see a case where modern technology becomes the tool whereby special individual potential can be realized.

17.6   Outcome and Discussion

All of our cases show that given the right equipment, the severely disabled had an unexpectedly good learning capacity and performed tasks skillfully. Computers make it possible for them to use their potential, irrespective of their physical condition. Rational use of human potential is what education and occupational life should be about. For the disabled, the ability to use remaining potential is important for self-respect. They are not only individuals that have to endure an unfortunate fate, but they are also people who have potential that is useful to society.

We see that, although all participants in our pilot projects realized some important potential, there are great individual differences in what aspects of life are most important. In Case A, social potential and the social aspect of the work environment are considered most valuable. Case D also shows the maintenance and development of a friendship as an outcome of the rehabilitation process. The capacity to learn and to join normal education is the most important outcome of Case B, whereas the participants in Case C and Case D very much appreciate the fact that they are able to perform a normal job. Case E is rather special, here we find artistic talents that are set free by the computer.

Our main conclusion from the pilot cases is that computers, as tools for the disabled, contribute differently to different people. The computer may, for the severely physically disabled, become the instrument by which they can fulfill their occupational and educational aspirations. Thus, the social effect of their physical condition is diminished and their performance can be restored.

Another outcome of the project is that a five-step scheme for technical adaptation in occupational rehabilitation was developed and tried out. The scheme is the first attempt to describe a method is this field. It describes the content of the process and states the members who must take part in the different phases of the processes.

Step 1. Matching a disabled employee with a workplace
This step requires actively searching the labour market. Employers may be willing to join the project but they very often lack information on technical possibilities and economic support systems. In addition to information from the technical expert and the rehabilitation professionals, it is important that the people working with the rehabilitation case and the rehabilitation trainee meet at the start of the project. Personal commitment to the rehabilitation plans and personal knowledge of the people involved may be crucial for success.

Step 2. Analysing the job
The employer, together with the technical experts and the disabled trainee, must evaluate the individual tasks of the entire job. It is important for social integration that the tasks chosen are meaningful and necessary in the overall work context. At this step, the professional competence of technical experts is very much required. They can tell if there are realistic ways to manage the task, describe the tools and software that will be necessary and calculate learning-time and costs.

Step 3. Training and testing
In this period the disabled person works closely with the technical expert. They get to know each other, and adjustments on tasks and equipment are made. We have found it valuable to use realistic work and learning tasks during this period.

Step 4. Learning in the job situation
In our pilot study we found that learning on the job was the best method for both social and technical adaptation. A fixed learning plan and schedule is set up. The employer,

the tutor and the trainee are partners in this learning period, but the technical expert can be called in if adjustments are required.

Step 5. Permanent work agreements
Conditions for permanent work are discussed and a work contract is signed. The Labour Office regulates the wage support that can be given or sets up a pension/wage combination scheme.

17.7   Professional Awareness and Rehabilitation Work

There will probably be growing demand for computer systems for the disabled as soon as the disabled themselves and the rehabilitation system get more insight into how computer equipment can improve the disabled person's performance. We already see this development in exhibitions on technical equipment for the disabled; the stands and the companies that show computer-based equipment are expanding. Very advanced technology is being developed; transformation of signals from visual signals to tactile or sound signals and vice versa is the basis for new aids for the visually-impaired and the hearing-impaired. Voice-controlled equipment is another example of very advanced technology in the technical aids industry. Software engineers should be aware of the growing market and job openings that may arise in equipment research and production.

Software experts will also be needed as partners in the individual rehabilitation process. Hopefully, technical problem-solving will become recognized as a rehabilitation method. Software engineers will be called on to counsel and bring new ideas into this process.

It was in the UN year of the disabled, and in the decade after that, that new concepts of environmental adaptation and technical problem-solving were developed. This was very much due to the fact that rehabilitation endeavours were influenced by the disabled themselves [Crewe83]. The concept of "handicapping situations" was developed. These occur when disabled people meet performance obstacles that exclude them from normal social activity or independence. The new methodical approach is *situation analysis.* By analysing the handicapping situations, it is possible to define practical problems and search for solutions. This way of practical-problem thinking should very much be in line with the professional thinking of the software experts. Rehabilitation as problem-solving should be an acceptable conceptual frame of reference for the professional software engineer.

We finish this chapter by pointing to some ethical considerations one should be aware of. If we look back at the results from our study, we see that the disabled themselves very strongly value the social aspects of life. Computer equipment alone cannot solve the social problem and may even create new problems of social isolation. Technical equipment should never be allowed to become a substitute for social partnership.

For the mentally-disabled, systems have been constructed to help them through the day, to get out of bed, eat and be ready for work. We wonder if this is not a substitute for human care rather than a problem-solving system. Similar control systems have been installed in homes for the elderly and the mentally-handicapped. Equipment originally constructed to solve the problems of hotel-security and shoplifting has been bought by institutions so that wards could control where patients were and what they were doing. Of course, it could be fair enough to construct a control system for an institution but, by doing so, one must be aware that the problem-solving may be for the institutions and not for the disabled persons.

Social aspects of problem-solving, the need for human care and the question of the right to control people are ethical considerations that software professionals will meet if they go into this field of work. Our advice is: *listen to the disabled themselves and accept their definition of the problem situation.* By doing so, the software engineer may very much contribute to making life more independent and meaningful for the disabled.

Chapter 18
Who Holds the Key to the Glass Door?

18.1 Introduction

This chapter was prompted by my observation that few women apply for interview for jobs as programmers at the IBM United Kingdom Laboratories at Hursley Park. It seeks to raise awareness of the apparent shortage of female applicants, and presents statistics which suggest there is indeed a limited supply.

The following conversation occurred at an evening dinner during a graduate recruitment programme in April 1995:

Graduate "I'm surprised I'm the only female here."

Recruiting Manager "I'm not. During my four 'milkround' visits to universities in the last two years, only one female has come forward for interview".

I was the recruiting manager. I am a software development manager at the IBM UK Laboratories at Hursley Park, near Winchester where we employ over 650 programmers. This encounter cemented my growing awareness that women are not applying to our company for employment as programmers.

Over the past few years there has been talk about "the glass ceiling" which seems to prevent women from progressing upwards in a company. The theory goes that you can't see it, but it is there, an invisible barrier that hinders the promotion prospects of women. I do not believe this to be the case at IBM Hursley, but before women can be promoted, they have to join the company, and if they don't apply for employment, there is no chance! It is as though there is some form of "glass door" — you can't see it, but something is limiting the supply of female graduates in computer-related disciplines.

When I was at school, many years ago, there was a lot of publicity about the need to encourage girls to go into mathematical, science and engineering disciplines. Since then there have been initiatives such as the "Women in Science and Engineering" (WISE); "Girls Entering Tomorrow's Science, Engineering and Technology" (GET-SET); and Insight, which encouraged girls to look at jobs in engineering. However, there are still few applications for programming jobs from female graduates with mathematical, Software Engineering or computing degrees. During the 1995 graduate recruitment programme, only 10% of the applications to IBM Hursley came from women.

This chapter is my personal observations on this continuing trend, based on my experience in the small section of the Information Technology industry in which I work. It includes some statistics on the numbers of female to male applicants; current employees; and current managers. There is a summary of observations following conversations with staff at universities and with women employed at IBM Hursley, and a general look at what other sources have reported on the subject of women in IT.

In this chapter I do not provide answers or recommendations, I seek only to state the situation as seen by a (female) recruiting manager, with the intent of sharing the observations. Maybe the low number of female applicants is not a problem, but it is not representative of the population. Maybe other companies do not experience the same pattern, but it would be interesting to know. Or maybe there IS a glass door between young women and the IT industry — the situation merits some 'reflection'!

After recalling the encounter which prompted this chapter, there is an overview of the work, and workforce, at IBM Hursley. This is then put into the context of some factors affecting the general supply of female graduates of computer-related disciplines. The concluding remarks pull together strands from some of the initiatives that exist to encourage young women to enter the IT industry, and are interlaced with comments about why a shortage of such women might matter, not only to IBM Hursley, but to industry in general.

18.2   IBM Hursley

I have worked at IBM Hursley for 24 years, and throughout this time I have been one of a minority — there are more men here than women. I am so used to it, I do not notice it. It does not bother me, does not cause me any difficulty, and does not, usually, feature as a topic of conversation. However, I have noticed during recruitment periods that I rarely interview young women, and this *does* strike me as strange. When the only woman interviewee at a recruitment dinner commented on the imbalance between the sexes, it caused me to take note and set about a mini-investigation that resulted in the writing of this chapter.

This section looks at the situation within IBM Hursley, and covers: the existing workforce; recruitment in 1995 and to put the situation into context, the section starts with a brief look at what IBM does at Hursley, and the type of work offered to graduates.

18.2.1   What does IBM Hursley do?

IBM United Kingdom Limited is a subsidiary of the IBM Corporation, which provides information technology hardware, software, solutions and services to customers throughout the world. It is the world's largest software vendor. In the UK, IBM's operations include manufacturing, development, marketing, and services in more than 25 locations around the country.

IBM's laboratory at Hursley Park is primarily concerned with developing "middleware" software, that is, the layer of software that sits between the operating system and the applications which people use to run their businesses. This software forms part of IBM's System Enabling Software Strategy, particularly in the areas of Transaction Processing, Commercial Messaging and Computer Aided Telephony. The software runs on a variety of IBM and non-IBM mainframe and other client/server platforms. The key products are Customer Information Control Systems (CICS), MQSeries Commercial Messaging, DirectTalk and CallPath.

18.2.2   The existing workforce

Depending on the product under development, and the skills, interests and experience of the individual, a programmer might work on understanding and describing the function the marketplace needs, or designing parts of products, or programming, or testing, or some combination of these. We also employ graduates to write technical manuals and to provide marketing support to IBM's world-wide sales and marketing personnel.

The following statistics were extracted in early 1995:

- Software developers: 14% female, 86% male

- Technical writers: 39% female, 61% male

- Managers: 16% female, 84% male

The ratios remain fairly constant and are little affected by maternity programmes (approximately 75% of employees return to work after maternity leave), or by general attrition (which is very low). Each year we aim to employ some graduates with programming skills and we participate in the milkround, visiting universities with our colleagues from other parts of IBM UK.

18.2.3   Recruitment in 1995

During the 1995 milkround, managers from IBM Hursley visited twenty-five universities, nine of which provided applications from women.

- 10% of the total applications were from women.

- 9% of those invited for first interview were women.

- 16% of those invited for second interview were women.

- 20% of the job offers were made to women.

- Of the women who originally applied for jobs, 43% were offered jobs.

We do not have positive discrimination, so the rise in the percentage reflects the fact that many of the women candidates suited the jobs on offer.

18.2.4   Opinions of women employees

To gather background for this chapter, information was gathered from two groups of women employees at IBM Hursley:

- Women who had graduated "recently" (generally within the last 5 years)

- Women managers (who, in general, had left school over 15 years ago)

Despite the differences in age, there was no discernible difference in attitude to maths or science subjects at their schools. In most cases, few girls at their school had opted for these subjects (usually much less than 20%), although there were exceptions to this general rule.

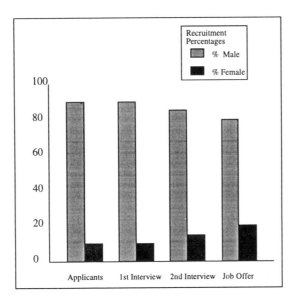

Figure 18.1 1995 Milkround: applications, interviews and offers

Reasons for career choices

Many women chose IT because it seemed to offer more lucrative careers. One of the recent graduates pointed out that, when she was at school, this did not seem to be a major consideration for other girls. She commented:

> "My female friends from school all went into teaching because that was what they wanted to do. Some (not all) regret it now because the work is hard and they are poorly paid. I'm sure that the thought of decent pay is what motivates a lot of boys to move into professions like the IT industry. Girls at school are more likely to do subjects which they know they enjoy rather than subjects that will get them a good job (and that they may enjoy if they tried them)."

Many chose IT as a career more by accident than planning. Several came from other backgrounds, including:

- Teacher training

- Degrees in physics, biology or straight mathematics

- Engineering

One woman chose IBM because of its reputation as an employer, and the fact that they are in the IT industry was "largely incidental"!

For several of the women, the decision to move into IT was made because they enjoyed writing programs to solve problems during their non-IT degrees. For example, one women who studied physics said:

"I enjoyed the programs I wrote to analyse the data more than doing the experiments ... I like the kind of thinking it requires."

Another, who had chosen to work in electronics, said:

"I rejected the idea of going into software as being almost as boring as accountancy. I only got into software via microcode and hardware simulation — once involved I found the problem solving almost as much fun as hardware!"

Those who had chosen IT as a course of study were influenced by a positive experience. For two women, it was the fact that their fathers were employed in IT and they were encouraged to play/work on the home computer. For another, it was the existence of a lunchtime computer club which she found very exciting. She said:

"I have always been more interested in science than the arts and enjoy computing because it is fun, and less smelly than chemistry and biology!"

Participation in initiatives aimed at encouraging school girls

Several women had participated to some extent in initiatives aimed at encouraging girls to consider their careers. The main involvement has been with the Industrial Society with their programmes aimed at encouraging school children to consider industry in general, rather than just 'public service' careers. In particular, several women have taken part in "Challenge of Management" days which are aimed at encouraging school girls to consider management as an option. To a lesser extent, women at IBM Hursley have participated in "Women in Computing" days, GETSET, talks at schools, and initiatives organized by Women in Science and Engineering.

Whilst generally supporting the aims of such initiatives, several women commented on the need to target younger girls, before they have adopted the attitude that computers are "toys for the boys". One woman, who has two daughters, commented on the lack of computer games that appeal to girls, and which would help engage their interest in computers from an early age. She agreed with an observation that various people have made, that many of today's computer games are combative, aggressive and violent, and appeal to boys, but not girls.

18.3   Other Statistics and Views

This section recounts some of the information gathered from non-IBM sources.

18.3.1   Subjects chosen at school, and university entry

In March 1995 Judith Church, Member of Parliament for Dagenham, introduced a Bill on "Women and Information Technology", which provides the following statistics:

- The percentage of girls studying A-level computer science has **dropped** from 22% in 1978 to 19% in 1993.

- Entry to Computer Science courses at UK universities is only 17% female, compared to 22% in 1980.

Judith Church's Bill also draws attention to the differences in the percentage of female IT employees in various countries:

- 23% in Britain

- 39% in France

- 45% in the United States

- 55% in Singapore

Perhaps this goes some way to explaining why a higher percentage of overseas applications for IT degrees come from women. Information supplied by UCAS (Universities and Colleges Admissions Service) indicates that in the year 1993-1994, 28% of overseas applicants were women.

According to information supplied by CSU Publications, the ratio of male to female graduates varies between "old" and "new" universities, which may be significant to IBM Hursley as we visit mainly "old" universities on the milkround:

	Old Universities (1993-1994)	New Universities (1992-1994)
Male	84.5%	74.4%
Female	15.5%	25.6%

I discussed the shortage of women IT graduates with Bournemouth University, and found that courses which contain an element of 'caring for others' attract more women than those which are 'pure' computing. Whereas there were very few women on Software Engineering Management courses, the ratio rose to roughly 50/50 on courses such as Applied Psychology and Computing, and Medical Instrumentation and Computing.

Perhaps this should not be a surprise. During the national "Bring our Daughters to Work Day" in April 1995, I conducted a survey of the daughters who visited IBM Hursley. The girls were generally in the 12-14 age range, and the survey included a question on career interests. It must be stressed that this was a very small sample (partly, it appeared, because not all schools were happy to support a girls-only day out), but it was noticeable that their ambitions fell into two main categories:

- Caring professions: animals, physiotherapy, midwife

- "Art" professions: drama, graphics

Although one girl expressed an interest in being either an astronaut or going into accounting, notice that IT as a career did not get a mention!

All of the girls used computers both at home and at school. Most thought using computers "fun" or "useful", but some did not. The most common uses were homework, English, art/drawing, technology course work, writing letters and playing games.

To get some idea how girls at schools in Hampshire are faring when it comes to IT, I contacted Hampshire County Council who provided statistics on examination achievements for the GCSE in Information Technology in 1994:

	Entries	Grades	
		A*-C	D-G
Boys	84	42.9%	57.2%
Girls	70	54.3%	41.5%
		(Rest Unclassified/Absent)	

From this snapshot it would appear that an encouraging number of girls in Hampshire are taking IT at GCSE.

18.3.2   Influences on the attitudes of girls to computing

Several women at IBM Hursley expressed the opinion that girls had decided against computing at an early age. Comments from two recent graduates included:

> "The computer was considered a 'Boys' thing — just like woodwork, maths and science. Needlework, nature and English were the 'Girls' things." (Talking about her own experience at school)

> "My school was fairly traditional. Perhaps some girls are likely to be 'psyched out' by the number of boys in a class. When there is an imbalance in numbers there is a message, whether it is perceived or not, of the subject being a 'boys' subject. Perhaps the teaching is unwittingly geared towards boys and the sort of things that would enthuse them?"

These attitudes are echoed — and significantly amplified — by an information leaflet [NCET92b] produced by the National Council for Educational Technology (NCET), which quotes from various sources to suggest that:

- Girls had less access than boys to computers at home

- There were few female role models available to inspire girls to consider computing as an option

- Subjects that typically attract girls often did not include use of computers

- Boys tended to monopolize the limited computer resources at schools

- Careers advice continued to show a "gap between what employers need and how many girls perceive the use of IT in the workplace".

18.4   Concluding Remarks

The catalyst that caused me to write this chapter was a casual comment at an evening recruitment dinner. Before that, I had only noticed in passing the disparity in the numbers of male and female graduates applying for programming jobs. Once I embarked on gathering data from outside IBM it quickly became apparent to me that this is a subject that has been causing considerable interest to many people, and that I would only scratch the surface. Another NCET publication on the subject of "Management of IT and Cross-curricular Issues" is an eight page reading list [NCET92a], which would be useful to anyone who wishes to investigate this subject in more depth than I have.

When I started investigating, I wondered whether the low number of female applicants to IBM Hursley was unusual, or whether it was indicative of the existence of a "Glass Door" which inhibited the supply of female graduates in computer-related disciplines. My conclusion is that a virtual glass door does exist, but it is one that employers cannot shatter by themselves. Unless more girls are enthused to use computers at school and at home, they are not going to choose to take computer-related subjects at school or university.

During the introduction, I made the observation "maybe the low number of female applicants is not a problem". In **my** experience, this has not been a **problem**, but I am conscious that the female presence in the IT industry is not representative of the working population. As a manager, concerned with the continuation of the "manager" species, I was interested by an article [ProMan94] which reviewed the Institute of Management's report "Management Development to the Millennium" [IM94]. The article, entitled "Today's male managers face extinction", and subtitled "The manager as we know him will be extinct by the year 2001", noted that:

> ". . . female ways of managing will be more appropriate in the millennium. These female attributes include teamworking, consensus management, negotiating, the ability to handle several projects at a time and interpersonal skills."

These attributes also figure highly in our recruitment criteria for programmers. The introvert who wants no more than to commune with a workstation late into the night in a darkened office, in splendid solitary isolation, does not figure in the criteria. Not for us the "real programmers" who feature in "Real programmers don't eat quiche" (source unknown):

- "Real programmers don't like the Team Programming concept. Unless, of course, they are the Chief Programmer."

- "Real programmers don't believe in schedules. Planners make up schedules. Managers "firm up" schedules. Frightened coders strive to meet schedules. Real programmers ignore schedules."

- "Real programmers have no use for managers. Managers are a necessary evil. They exist only to deal with personnel 'bozos', bean counters, senior planners and other mental defectives."

Interestingly, the Institute of Management's report also has "Understanding the role of information and IT" as number six in its priority list of "most important skills" required in the millennium. According to "The Gathering Storm" Report [Virgo94] in 1994 females made up 4% of all IT managers, and 9% of all other management.

Although I embarked on this mini-investigation from personal curiosity, it is evidently a subject which has engaged the minds of many people. Indeed, the Women into Technology Foundation (WIT) literature stated:

> "The mission of the WIT campaign is to help employers to overcome current and prospective shortages of IT skilled staff by raising the number and proportion of girls and women entering and sustaining IT related careers at all levels."

In my introduction, I said "maybe other companies do not experience the same pattern, but it would be interesting to know". Hopefully, that query will be answered in time, meanwhile, in sharing my observations, I hope that I have helped to raise the awareness of the shortage of female IT graduates amongst others who, like me, were not consciously aware of the situation. In her Bill, Judith Church says:

> "A company's success depends on how it applies and uses IT, and so does Britain's success. Our international competitiveness is at stake here. This can hardly be called a women's issue."

If, as she suggests, the continued shortage will affect "Britain's competitiveness in our rapidly changing global economy", I await with interest to see what initiatives will find the key to unlock the Glass Door between women and the IT industry.

Chapter 19

The Contribution Women Could Make to IT Professionalism

19.1 Introduction

A clearly observable characteristic of the IT industry is its gendered nature, it is perceived as a male world. It is well known that not many women prepare for work in IT nor do many achieve positions of influence within the industry. The numbers now working in the industry and their influence are not consistent with the number of women who have reached suitable intellectual levels in the wider society. Effort is being applied by both academic bodies and industry bodies to improve the numbers of women working in IT.

Areas of the IT industry where development is keenly sought is improvement in quality, especially in the applicability of new software products to business needs and the fit of IT systems with the needs of the individuals using them.

Is there is a connection between the low numbers of women employed and the quality of the industry's performance? This chapter argues that there is a connection, not one to be derived statistically but one that can be demonstrated operationally. The argument is based on the premise that the chances of employing high quality staff are greater if the pool from which they are drawn contains a representative proportion of the qualified people available. Currently women are not attracted to IT thus artificially reducing the pool of talent. The argument continues by considering what skills are needed by the IT professional, compares experiences with IT women in the US, and compares the situation in IT with women in management. The chapter concludes by offering some ideas for action.

19.2 The Nature of Professionalism

It is useful to begin by referring briefly to some historical aspects of the growth of professions. Much of modern life makes today's society radically different from the societies in which ideas of professionalism emerged. Where industries have been in existence for centuries, professionalism has grown to mean not only that a client expects a certain level of performance, which I shall refer to as 'quality', in the supply of goods or services, but has also led to the development of specific ways of doing business. This has meant the growth of unwritten 'rules' and expectations of certain behavioural styles. These customs and traditions govern much of business communication and management, determine role expectations for working women and men and influence entry to professions. They can and do operate to reduce flexibility and prevent change. As these norms have evolved in a society almost exclusively male, white and Anglo Saxon, it is not surprising that they have unsuitable and unwelcome effects in a society which now comprises as many working women as men, with many coming from different ethnic groups. It is necessary, in the late '90s, to remove aspects of professionalism which are counterproductive and derive meaning for the term which is appropriate to current needs.

19.3   Who are IT Professionals and Where do they Work?

Traditionally the roles of IT professionals and their skills have been narrowly defined, based on the needs of hardware and software; i.e. for hardware designers and operators, systems analysts and designers, programmers, network managers, managers of IT projects database administrators and the like.   However, as responsibilities of IT professionals have increased to include information management, business analysis and systems support with the client, the breadth of skills required has grown.   As PCs are not managed within the IT department, and as IT functions are outsourced more IT skills are required in other parts of the organization.   A recurring issue for management is what skills and competencies an IT professional needs in the sphere in which they work [Leeming95a].   IT professionals work in IT departments and in client departments within the same company. IT professionals are perceived as male; how many IT professionals are women?

19.4   Where are the Women in IT?

The picture presented by the IT industry is a place where women rarely work, they are hard to find and numbers at entry level are declining.   In the post World-War II era, IT was thought of as a sector with great potential for women to find a workplace worthy of their skills and talents. While there are women in the industry and have been since Ada Lovelace, who as Babbage's partner, became the world's first programmer, there are not as many women now as could be expected.   Kraft and Biggar reported that "virtually 100% of the original programming workforce were women" [Kraft79]. When ENIAC was built in 1944-46, building the hardware was dominated by men, but programming was assumed to be a clerical exercise, which in wartime meant women's work. It was done by the "ENIAC girls", a group of women clerks. When later it was realized that programming was not just a clerical activity it "was quickly redefined as creative and challenging work. It was also just as quickly defined as men's work." [Lloyd85].   Gürer reports that the change from being accepted on a par with men to being excluded came as hardware and software companies grew so they absorbed male hierarchical business structures. Gürer cites approximately 40 women who have made significant technical contributions to Computer Science (CS) since World-War II [Gürer95].

As PCs entered schools, stories of boys "elbowing the girls out of the way" in the rush to the computer room became part of school mythology. The greater relevance of the machines to boys rather than girls reduced the opportunities for girls to influence the development of IT and the notion of gendered technology emerged; i.e.   the technology was invented and put to work by males according to their understanding of its applicability [Newton91]. Software aimed at the masculine members of society has developed.

The difficulties faced by university departments in recruiting girls on to computer science courses are well known ([Lovegrove87], [Dain88]). The problem has been formally addressed by Women into Computing (WiC) since 1987 but the figures are not yet showing significant increase. University and Polytechnic admissions' figures showed that the rates of entry into CS courses fell from 24% in 1978 to a low of 10% in the mid to late eighties. Combined figures for CS and Business Computing in the early nineties show a strong climb towards 20%. There is compensation in the figures for business and computing courses only, where the proportion of women has grown to around 35% [Lovegrove94c]. This could be interpreted as showing that as girls were excluded from IT in their teens, the enlightened went off to learn about business instead. They could be in the right place as many modern business courses have a sizable proportion of work on IT; business and computing courses, of course, have both.

Industry figures reveal the distribution of women in technical jobs and in managerial posts in IT in 1992-1993, see Table 19.1, (Data from a Computer Economics Ltd survey quoted in [WiT93] on 38 000 workers, 1992-1993).

Job Title	Women as % of sample	
	1993	1992
Managers (technical, support, systems, production)	7.5	7.5
Systems Analysis	21.8	26.5
Analysis/programming	23.6	23.6
Programming	23.1	23.1
Information Centre	31.4	32.3
Systems programming	11.1	9.6
Database work	24.2	25.7
Communications	12.9	12.7
Operations	15.9	18.5

Table 19.1 Distribution of women in jobs in IT

Table 19.1 shows that more than twelve times as many men as women are in managerial posts in IT while, in the technical jobs, the ratio ranges from 9 times as many to just over 4 times as many men than women. [Virgo92] pointed out that women tend to be clustered in the industry in jobs that are nearest to the customer and are fewest in number in the more technical jobs.

In the nineties the IT Industry does employ women in a professional IT capacity but not at upper levels. In 1991 women were 20.6% of IBM's workforce, and 7.5 % of management. ICL fared slightly better, with 26% women; 9.8% at middle management, and at senior level 6.4% were women. British Telecom had 29.7% women in its workforce and they form 6% of senior management. Compaq Computers Ltd, with 222 UK employees, had 30% women; and 15% of the managers were women [Kumar92]. Although a comparatively new industry, IT has created some stereotypes unattractive to women. Kumar found a consensus that a stereotype of an IT personality culture existed which was thought to act against women [Kumar92]. Her interviewees, women in IT and girls considering the industry, commented that the image of IT is unattractive to them: "Its image is ridiculous on TV and in films. It looks like a boring job as that is the way it is portrayed. The image is very misleading and people are affected by this image." [WiT92] confirmed "The image of IT is worse than we thought and must be rebuilt".

Lloyd and Newell commented that "Women are educated to believe that technology is not their domain and are . . . treading on forbidden territory if they want to find out about it. This message is reflected strongly in the computer press" [Lloyd85]. They go on to ask, if the picture is so bleak for women in computing "Why do women get involved at all?" Their reply is "We enjoy both the precision and logical thinking necessary, and the feeling of achievement on completing a piece of technical work. Given a series of problems to solve and a framework in which to solve them, coming up with solutions is a matter of mind over machine. Some of the more responsible jobs in computing are very creative". Women who remain in IT confirm that by their presence in the industry. It is quite likely that these senior women joined because they were interested in the technology itself; there are, however, many women less interested in its inner workings and more interested in it as a means to the goal of increased business effectiveness.

A big hurdle for women seeking entry to the IT industry, is the recruitment process. 28% of Kumar's interviewees, women managers working in the industry and female graduates intending to work there, said that biased procedures at the recruitment stage block women applicants [Kumar92]. Tests and job simulation procedures use men as role models. The characteristic traits of those who hold the most senior positions and invariably are men, were those the applicant needed if she or he is to get the job. "We also find that 'Women who work in computing do so on terms . . . laid down by men. Because men generally hold the positions of power in the industry it is they who define what is desirable and acceptable. The personal qualities required are those usually associated with men — hard-headedness, single-mindedness, ambition, toughness" [Lloyd85].

19.5   Women in IT in the US

Eric Roberts, quoting Abelson's survey of CS/Electronic Engineering degrees at MIT, reported that the percentage of US first degrees awarded to women, has been steady for all science and engineering, but that CS peaked in 1983-1986 at around 30%, having risen from 20% in 1975 and dropping to about 25% in 1992 [Roberts95]. To account for the decline he cited "Overt sexism, . . . sexual harassment, . . . biases in pre-college education, lack of female role models in technical fields; a small group of female students making it hard to establish a supportive peer community, self-image problems leading to reductions in efficacy, mentoring process failures, different expectations for men and women, difficulties in balancing career and family". Klawe and Levensen report similar types of difficulty with exposure of women and girls to the technology and their affinity with IT as it is practised [Klawe95]. while women achieve as good grades in college as the men on CS degrees, they suffer serious reduction in their self confidence and self esteem. They attribute this to the behaviour of the professors, largely but not exclusively male, at college, who demonstrate unconscious favouritism towards male students. They also find that girls educated in single sex schools do better at science and maths than coeducational graduates. These experiences of the US scene are not so different from those in the UK. The numbers are higher, sometimes greater than Kanter's token figure but still disadvantaged.

Roberts points out that there are ways in which CS is different from other science and engineering disciplines, e.g. experience in computer use before university differs markedly with gender, this is now less so in the UK. In other technical fields, early exposure in the UK is also better balanced. He points out that "the extraordinary flexibility of computer software allows systems to reflect their cultural environment more strongly than rigid technologies." Programming encourages highly focused behaviour, sometimes to obsessive lengths, which is less natural to women because it is socially discouraged in their upbringing. He asserts that the culture of computing environments is different from that in other scientific communities, where progress for women has been better. Another explanation, alluded to earlier and gaining ground from women's studies, is the notion that the domain of IT is gendered. By that is meant whether the domain embodies, or is defined by, male values. Because the IT community is predominantly male, gender plays a role in determining what areas are studied and in defining the boundaries of the discipline [Lie95] (see [Webster95] for a discussion of the relationship between work, technology and gender). It is argued below that there are areas of IT where women's traditional values and skills are needed.

Henwood reported on the position of women employed in technology in the US, in the years 1970 to 1990 [Henwood93]. While the figures she quotes show similar patterns of employment to the UK, the proportions of women are slightly better in the US than in the UK. Klawe and Levesen report that the salary gap between women and men in industry is widening and that progress is difficult in some industries, e.g. aerospace [Klawe95]. They cite the use of mentoring and networking by companies in efforts to resolve the problem. Their findings are that the 'chilliest' academic place for women in CS is in postgraduate studies but that as CS faculty they are being appointed in nearly the same percentage as the number of women PhDs, over the last few years only. They add that more women in their childbearing years, often coinciding with their most important research years, would suffer, if it was not for the good quality child care facilities and arrangements provided by some companies and institutions, e.g. flexible working hours and flexible tenure for women and men. This provision has helped with recruitment and retention of top quality women which organizations have actively recruited. They report also similar stresses and pressures as are experienced by UK women.

So what does the US IT sector do about this situation? First of all eleven household company names support women's groups. Forty-five institutions have fellowship programmes for women in CS or Computer Engineering. Some professional bodies give awards for service to the field, in addition to rewarding research achievements. One of which, CRA, has given an "award for increasing the concentration of under-represented groups in computing." They have begun a tradition of women taking public office in the field; as in the UK. Freeman and Hupfer report a Web site for data on women in CS [Freeman95]. There are at least eleven mentoring programmes for women in CS [Goyal95].

If IT can be described as gendered, more than other disciplines, the question must be asked if is it only the IT sector that disregards women as top employees? Is a low proportion of women an inevitable consequence of this gendered nature? Do other professions suffer the same fate? To test these questions the profession of management is observed. It was chosen because managers work in all sectors; some come directly into management, others start in technical positions and move into management. Women, and their progress or lack of it in management, has attracted considerable attention and many writers have explored the issue; [Tanton94], [Davidson92], [Coe92], [Rosener90], [Marshall84].

19.6   Women in Management

Data for the progression of women in management cannot be reported with any great degree of precision as the definition of a manager varies with each study; however, studies of the barriers holding up women in management provide a benchmark for what might be expected for women in IT. Leeming [Leeming93] found that the proportions of women labelled "managers" varied from 8.6% in a 1992 survey of 20 000 managers [Gregg93] to 20% [Hirsh89]. This shows that the proportion of women entering management is less than a quarter of the total, while women graduates have been in excess of 40% for some time. It is clear that women do not face a level playing field in management either, overall their position is not substantially different from women in IT. Research shows that the barriers for women in management are related to role expectations, cultural factors and attitudes. They are generally independent of the nature of the work women managers perform; hence they can be seen as just as applicable to women in IT.

19.6.1   Barriers for women managers

Combining the dual role of family manager and work is a major hurdle for women. They go to work to fulfil the demands of their job and return home to fulfil the demands of their family. Time becomes their chief asset and chronic tiredness a continuing handicap. It is not surprising to find that women reaching senior positions in business have to make some difficult decisions in their personal lives. Coe, in her study of managers, found that marital status was markedly different for men and women in management (see Table 19.2) [Coe92]. Lower caring responsibilities for these women arise from their not having children. 54% of the women and 51% of men whom Coe surveyed, believed it was possible to combine a career in management with a caring responsibility at "considerable personal cost". Coe concludes that combining a career with women's traditional roles has largely defeated women.

Cassell & Walsh comment that cultural norms offer further difficulties for women; being the first or token woman is stressful [Cassell93]. ("Token" is defined by [Kanter77] as fewer than 15% in a category). Women are immigrants to the business world; they join male managers and have to learn a new set of values, norms and behaviours. Scase & Goffee found that 39% of women managers still felt the need to meet the expectations of men [Scase89].

Status	% of senior women	% of senior men
Married	67	90
Single	20	3
Caring responsibilities	37	70
Affected career	42	16

Table 19.2 Marital status of senior men and women managers [Coe92]

Coe found that attitudinal barriers are perceived as greater than tangible barriers such as the provision of childcare. Support for women was found to be plentiful from family and partner; the one unsupportive agent being the employer. The barriers Coe identified can be classified into five areas, shown in Table 19.3, adapted from Coe's list. The percentage perceiving no barriers could be due to lack of awareness or to the ability not to be diverted by any barriers.

Davidson & Cooper cite deficiencies in education, vocational guidance and training as major reasons why women do not earn the same pay, status and career opportunities as men [Davidson92]. They add causes such as gender role stereotyping from an early age; job segregation by gender; poor union support for women; weak legislation; discriminating practices within organizations; prejudiced attitudes and behaviour towards working women. These aspects are symptomatic of a culture which regards women as economically less valuable than men. The brief review, above, of women's progress in IT shows that these findings would apply in the IT industry.

Barriers	% of respondents perceiving
Men's Club Culture	43
Inflexible working patterns	12
Gender Prejudice	58
Educational Lack	71
Domestic pressures	38
No barriers	19

Table 19.3 Barriers women encountered in their career ([Coe92] adapted)

Despite the attempted reduction, through legislation, of some barriers to the formal progress of women in business and computing, many subtle and unnoticed barriers still persist [Henlis91], [Cockburn93]. This chapter argues that in the need to increase quality in the IT sector, such barriers for women are one (even if only one) of the reasons for the persistent failure of the IT sector to achieve consistent quality. If the quality of IT outputs is to be raised one response could be a change in the skill expectations of professionalism in IT. The question for the industry becomes: what are the skills of today's professional, and how they can be acquired.

19.7   Quality, Professionalism and Skills

The challenge of creating efficacious use of IT is no longer in the technology; it is in creating IT systems fit for people. "The dominant paradigms in academic computer science do not help technical professionals comprehend the social complexities of computerization, since they focus on computability rather than usability . . . The social sciences provide a complementary theoretical base for studies of computing that examine or make assumptions about human behaviour." [Dunlop91]. Some academic programmes, when preparing students to implement IT systems, develop social understanding and skills as well as technical ones; this is found in some business computing degree programmes. Computer Science and Software Engineering programmes recognize the value that is added to interpersonal skills by a sandwich year in industry but fail to include theory to underpin the experience.

The popular meaning of quality has meant such attributes as: value for money, reliability, safety and fitness for purpose. In today's markets quality is about providing more, e.g. working with clients to see that what is being delivered will achieve the business objectives set for it. To provide that service companies are forming relationships, alliances and partnerships with their clients. Such relationship building demands a change in the attitude of the whole workforce [Leeming95b]. Creating IT systems fit for people means looking more carefully at the impact of new systems on jobs. The IT industry continually strives to improve the quality of its offerings to suit its clients [PriceW89]. It normally expresses its concerns in terms of cost, technical and business goals. Recently awareness of a requirement for broader competencies in IT staff other than the purely technical, has been added to these expressions.

19.8   New Professionalism in IT

That IT workers are to be regarded as professionals and adopt professional standards has long been a goal for the professional societies. The British Computer Society has launched several initiatives to increase professionalism and to improve skills; e.g. PDS (professional development scheme), the Hybrid Manager project [BCS90c]; and joined in 1995 by the Excite project jointly sponsored by Women into Technology (WiT) and the Institute of Data Processing Management (IDPM). IT professionals are now expected to be skilled in technology and possess business, managerial and social competencies. These include an understanding of the business requirements of the sector in which they work and social skills to develop and implement new business processes. Social skills include the ability to communicate with clients and colleagues, to listen, to choose language appropriate to the occasion, to negotiate, to understand the content of roles and to be able to comprehend different kinds of personalities. The use of these skills in project teams enables more of the workforce to hear and understand what the client wants rather than have a single individual persuade clients that what the company has to offer is what they need. In this way problems, at present levels of skill seemingly impossible, can be tackled by collaboration rather than by substitution of unsuitable products. Tannen, in research on gender styles of communication, reveals some remarkable misconceptions in conversations between people which needs to be understood by every worker in IT [Tannen92]. Many jobs, affected by a redesigned IT system and performed by individuals rarely involved in the design process, go wrong for lack of collaboration at the design stage. Much of the historical preoccupation with the intellectual basis of IT has depended on the masculine-oriented Computer Science and Software Engineering disciplines. "Computer Science . . . is the systematic study of algorithmic processes — their theory, analysis, design, efficiency, implementation and application — that describe and transform information. The question underlying all of computing is: What can be (efficiently) automated? . . . The roots of computing extend deeply into mathematics and engineering. Mathematics imparts analysis to the field; engineering imparts design" [Lloyd85]. The application of business needs to IT systems design has changed the earlier computing-based preoccupation of efficiency to one of effectiveness; business may prefer an inefficient but effective application of IT to a highly efficient, even elegant, use of IT but which is irrelevant in business terms. This type of understanding is needed by IT professionals. Gaining it leads to new social skills that can be used in planning and design; enabling what Vehvilainen calls "human-centred design" [Vehvilainen94]. The intellectual basis for applying IT now depends on the original scientific base and on the social sciences.

19.9   Where Will these New Skills Come From?

Quality of service calls for expertise in looking after relationships with clients at all levels, not just as they telephone or enter the door. Many client-facing jobs are currently done by women but at insufficiently high levels of responsibility and operational authority to enable them to do more for the client or to become involved in IT development work. This function exploits the traditional role of women, seen as nurturing and listening, without exploiting all its potential; 'women as carers' has become institutionalized. The paradigm is that the "caring" role, so often given to women, is female and is not generally expected by male management to be compatible with technical capability. For many managers, having staff who are technically expert is more important than having staff able to build good relationships. Technical ability is part of male identity [Webster95]. Radcliffe Richards points out "men resist association with all things recognizably female, because they see them as degrading" [Radcliffe80]. This could explain why social skills have not been valued by the excessively male IT industry. Hence insufficient understanding of the need for their use exists and particularly how they might be applied to IT development. The paradigm of women-only caring skills is thankfully disappearing.

   While women do not claim exclusive rights to nurturing and caring, the roles they occupy in business have increased not only these skills, but also the organization's dependence on them, hence reinforcing the paradigm. Hence we see the reduction in their status and the unconscious sole attribution of such skills to women. However, many working women want to combine their technical capability with their caring skills. In both the management field and the IT field, work on understanding team and group behaviour is in progress [Sears92], [Cronin92]. There is growing recognition that in general women manage groups, in certain aspects, differently from men, producing results that are often significantly welcomed by the organization [Rosener90]. Women are seen to be more co-operative, abhor conflict and avoid confrontation. They are better at people management than men, possessing superior interpersonal skills and being good organizers [Leeming94].

Rosener reported that the style women preferred to use, because they found it empowered their staff, is an interactive one but when a more decisive style was needed they used it. The senior women in IT, interviewed by Kumar reported that they, too, used an open, direct and participative management style, highly interpersonal, and very much oriented towards teamworking [Kumar92]. Examples of high quality systems installed by women are available, [Johnson90] being an exemplar. Ashridge College, in predicting the qualities needed by the IT manager of the future, suggested that women may have the edge over their male colleagues because of their superior interpersonal skills [Ashridge91]. Their report identified these skills as crucial to future IT managers. It seems not unreasonable that if a company wishes to enhance the quality of its offerings in the marketplace that it look for the relevant skills among women without neglecting the need for their male employees to develop them.

19.10   Conclusions and Recommendations

This chapter has discussed the types of skills and competencies IT professionals need to achieve the goal of delivering high quality client-oriented products and systems. It suggests that true professionalism will foster the development of skills and competencies sufficient to deliver these outputs. The chapter identified the low numbers of women in the industry as a possible cause of the lack of these skills and concludes with a call for the industry to update its concept of professionalism and increase the employment of women. Some actions to counter existing barriers are suggested.

If the sector continues to deny women the chance to achieve their full potential in IT it must realize that the pool of talent from which new entrants, top managers and leaders are recruited is automatically halved. This is an unnecessary and wasteful handicap. Reduction of the talent pool is not the only loss to the industry. By not employing more women the industry is denying itself the diversity in intelligence and creativity so badly needed. The range of challenges faced by society as a result of the huge rate of development of technology call for every source of creativity, management and political sensitivity that we can find. "Many organizations would like to address these issues but lack the connections and knowledge to do so." [Pearl95]. This is where women can take a lead.

In practice, the opening up of access by women to all levels of the industry cannot be left to the progress of more women through school and university. Due to its image and recruitment practices this is unlikely to lead to more women entering and moving up the industry. In spite of efforts of industry bodies, the IT industry has a low understanding of and involvement in gender issues. The membership of Opportunity 2000 (in 1993) showed IBM (UK) and Rank Xerox (UK) as the only members of the IT industry in membership. The industry needs to acknowledge the pool of talent it does not access and devise ways to overcome the barriers to women's careers in IT. Some specific barriers are its image and its recruiting and promotion methods. Both should be professional concerns of employers and industry bodies. Other barriers are similar to those found by women in any sector of employment; the IT profession would benefit by lobbying for change with other sectors.

Currently the most effective catalysts for action are women's networks. These build confidence and raise morale to tackle the barriers women face. They increase awareness of what women bring to the field of IT. Visibility of IT women's networks is low compared with more mainstream networks. Some do exist within companies, and IT groups are present within larger women's networks such as the European Womens' Management Development network and City Women's Network. In 1987 "Systers", a women's network on the internet, run by Anita Borg of DEC, was developed, it later spawned a UK offshoot which is still small. Systers has done much in the US to take forward the work of women in IT, running the 1994 Grace Hopper Celebration of Women conference in Washington which gained excellent technical reviews. Most women's networks are primarily concerned with mutual support; their next step is to develop increased political skills, especially expectations and negotiation skills, to make their case for improved career opportunities, job restructuring for families and necessary support facilities. In comparison with the US, the UK is less advanced in these areas.

It is up to women in IT to take the lead in making the sector a more favourable place for women to work. Sherry Turkle comments that "computers have come to stand for a world without emotion", and suggests that "Here is an opportunity (for women) to remake the culture around the machine" [Turkle94]. Women have certainly taken the lead in working for change in education, probably the most powerful stage at which to change the system, but efforts are hampered by the image of the industry which does not offer an attractive place for the educated women to work.

A radical review of recruiting and promotion practices by the largely male IT management is urgently called for. This means removing or changing the underlying attitudes to women which give rise to their continued exclusion from the industry. Current practice leads to the employment of fewer of the highly skilled workers in the IT sector. This has a detrimental effect on companies, the outcome is socially unjust and it could be described as unprofessional. A training process which seeks to reskill in the area of recruiting, promotion and management style towards a more systematic identification of suitable candidates and their qualities is called for. Such training examines attitudes as part of improving the process. When technical skills in a company are missing, improving them by training is normal practice. Management training can similarly be used to increase the competencies needed and reduce prejudice without any risk of being accused of positive discrimination. Hemenway describes other actions to counteract the barriers women face; such as programmes of awareness on gender equity, this makes the subject more available for general discussion; identifying and correcting existing inequities; developing role models and mentors for women; rewarding behaviour that leads to increased diversity; the establishment of effective channels for reporting unwanted sexual harassment [Hemenway95].

Women have been compared to immigrants into the professions. Immigrants in other minorities tend to cluster together and integration is slow. The IT industry cannot afford to continue handicapped by only employing a small proportion of women, encouragement to change must come from the top of the profession. Persistence and belief in the rightness of the goal will lead to success.

Chapter 20
But isn't Computing Boring?

20.1 Introduction

By the year 2000, it is estimated that over 80% of the jobs within the UK will involve the use of Information Technology. Concern has been expressed by academia and industry regarding the decrease in the number of women entering IT related courses and subsequently the Software Engineering profession — a phenomenon which has occurred since the early 1980s. Britain is falling well behind other countries — "only 23% of IT employees in the UK are women, compared with 39% in France, 45% in the US and 55% in Singapore" [Acey95]. The Software Engineering profession needs to attract more women to help counterbalance the incorrect, stereotyped perceptions of the typical computer professional, but even the term "engineer" has the reverse effect.

Yet, a career in computing is equally well suited to both girls and boys. On the whole girls have excellent communication and interpersonal skills — qualities amongst others that the computing industry requires. However, during the 1980s and early 1990s the number of women entering computing courses, and subsequently taking up a career in IT drastically fell. A number of factors may have contributed to this decline. For example, the image of computing from a young person's point of view is likely to be narrow, based on their limited experience. Computers are seen as games machines with macho images, "toys for the boys", or machines only for word-processing, spreadsheets and databases. These images then set the scene for the computing profession but the reality is very different.

What does a career in computing or information technology actually mean? The job titles vary: *systems analyst, database administrator, software engineer, systems programmer.* Is it any wonder that school children find it difficult to make choices regarding careers in computing when they're faced with such incomprehensible jargon?

What can a career in computing provide?

- It is a "young industry".

- It is an important growth area.

- It has wonderful opportunities for progression.

- It is based around business operations and information needs.

- It has scientific and engineering possibilities.

- It is people and solution oriented.

- It has great flexibility and potential for change.

- It has a skills shortage and offers high salaries.

What more could a young person ask for from a career opportunity? — Only the knowledge to be able to make the correct choice.

Staffordshire University's IT EQUATE project was established in October 1993. It was formed as an active research project to develop strategies to improve the image of careers in computing amongst schoolgirls. The research involves a partnership between the University and three local schools and is particularly aimed at pupils in the lower secondary schools, from the ages of 13 to 15 years. This chapter briefly describes the Staffordshire IT EQUATE programme of events to date, details the research undertaken and defines proposals for the continuing development of strategies for the future. It identifies the importance and means of developing the correct image of a career within the computing industry and highlights the need for further material to be developed and disseminated to schools.

20.2   Evolution of the IT EQUATE Project

Between 1990 and 1992 a pilot project based at the University of Southampton and funded mainly by IBM and the London Docklands Development Corporation, took place in cooperation with Hampshire and London Docklands Local Education Authorities (LEA's) and participating schools. In this pilot project, the aim was to attempt to bring about change through action research and the action took the form of visits and questionnaires to pupils aged 13 to 14 (Year 9) and their teachers. Full details of the results of this pilot project can be found in [Lovegrove94a].

The research identified that strategies for the future might be regarded as being of two types; one is associated with the policy and management of computing within schools, and the other is actively promoting and supporting computing as a suitable and fulfilling occupation for girls. It was in this latter area that the future Staffordshire IT EQUATE project decided to concentrate [Lovegrove94b].

Staffordshire IT EQUATE was established in October 1993 by the School of Computing at Staffordshire University, to continue the work started at the University of Southampton. This initial research enabled the ideas to become more focused and thus Staffordshire IT EQUATE established the following:

The aims were to:

- increase the awareness of girls to careers involving computing

- develop strategies for encouraging girls to enter computing related courses

- raise awareness within schools and in the home to computing careers and related issues.

The plan was to:

- work with two or three schools intensively

- start with committed schools who would actively support the programme

- work the programme over a three year period

- continually try to support a "pro-IT" careers environment around the girls, including a range of careers involving information systems

- provide a programme for curricula materials; computer club materials; management ideas; industrial liaison, mentoring, visits, role models; parent involvement and parent workshops; careers videos; self-discovery, equal opportunities workshops for girls; university visits and workshops.

The overall objectives of IT EQUATE are to:

- determine how the masculine image of IT can be altered to avoid gender stereotyping

- maintain the IT skills and competences which many girls acquire at primary school

- determine how careers advice can be presented so that girls are made more aware and understand the opportunities for them in IT and the importance of IT to many jobs.

- establish collaboration and partnerships between employers and teachers which will focus on gender inequality in order to develop strategies for involvement and achievement of girls and IT

- change attitudes at senior management and classroom level within schools so that IT is seen as important and relevant to girls as well as boys

- design curriculum materials which will attract girls as well as boys to consider careers in computer-related areas and demonstrate the relevance of IT to the future lives of all pupils.

20.3   Staffordshire IT EQUATE

20.3.1   Schools and children

Three schools were chosen in October 1993 to work with the Staffordshire IT EQUATE team over a three year period. They were from different backgrounds and geographical areas, using co-educational schools and a single sex school and from the private as well as state systems. All three schools were very enthusiastic about the objectives of the Staffordshire IT EQUATE project. The schools are as follows:

1. a mixed state school (urban) situated on the outskirts of an industrial town with a local catchment area (800 pupils, age 11-16 years);

2. a mixed state school (rural) in a village located on the outskirts of a County town with a local catchment area (1140 pupils, age 11-18 years);

3. an independent girls' school situated in a small village with an international catchment area (274 pupils, age 5-18 years).

Two groups of girls are being targeted at each of the three schools. One is around 14 to 15 years when option choice and peer group pressure are important, the other is 15 to 17 years when pupils are considering their future prospects. The IT EQUATE events were then aimed at three contingents of girls:

1. a total of 33 girls from the three schools, aged 14-16, who volunteered to be involved with the IT EQUATE project for a three year period until they left school;

2. 60 girls from the three schools aged 14-15, chosen according to predefined criteria each year of the IT EQUATE project;

3. pupils identified by the schools as requiring careers talks — this included the 15-17 age group.

20.3.2   University and industrial visits

The main aim of the University and industrial visits for the schoolgirls was that they should be fun and informative, yet still get over the computing career message.

The first IT EQUATE event took place at Staffordshire University in February 1994 — it was a day's workshop for the 33 schoolgirls. They were given demonstrations of multimedia to illustrate how information could be presented by computer using the forms of video, sound, text and graphics to stimulate the learning process: for example, students being able to choose the direction, format and speed of their learning. The girls thoroughly enjoyed the demonstration of the transformation of the facial image of one of their friends to that of a cheetah, using the technique of morphing — as often used in the television industry. Hands-on experience on the computers gave the girls an insight into graphical capabilities, whilst they built six foot paper towers from no more than A4 paper to simulate the need for team work, adhering to a specification and problem solving skills required by the computing industry. The day also involved a computing career talk and discussion.

Teachers from the three schools and LEA careers personnel associated with them then became pupils at the University for an evening session following the girls' event, to be given the same IT EQUATE experience as the girls. The idea was to stimulate conversation about IT careers and to support the girls in any subsequent classes involving computers.

A second University workshop for the same girls in November 1994 built on the themes and ideas of the initial event, provided more hands-on experience, as requested and aimed to further develop the career information. The girls linked into the Internet, accessing information from Peru, Colorado, Australia and Spain. They mailed the BBC radio programme *The Big Byte* with information of their involvement in the IT EQUATE project. Groups of girls took videos of the Internet workshop and created text relating to Staffordshire IT EQUATE, in order to create a page of multimedia to publicize IT EQUATE to the world on the Internet.

The careers workshop centred on the NCET/WIT computing careers video "Why Me, Why IT' followed by talks given by female students from Staffordshire University and role models from industry. To give a clearer picture of the computing world, the speakers covered their qualifications and career paths, how computing differed from what they had learnt at school, what their role now consisted of, career progression and obstacles, salaries and responsibilities, and finally, life in a male dominated world. The next activities involved the girls in the creation of cartoons and business adverts to complete the day.

It was not only necessary for the girls to experience computing within the University environment but also within the industrial environment to see for themselves that computing is not just a "boring terminal based" job within the real world. The girls saw computer control in action when they visited the brewing industry; the canning and packaging department with its automatically driven processes and can-handling robot was an awesome sight. A visit to the china pottery industry provided an awareness of computer aided design and explained the role played by computers to support information, from the receipt of an order to the despatch of the final product. For the girls, the opportunity to talk to personnel creating computer software within an environment driven by the product, was invaluable.

The Staffordshire IT EQUATE project then looked to influence further the environment around the girls. 70 parents, teachers and pupils (including boys) attended another evening event where video conferencing using the Internet was demonstrated. America and Australia responded, with a pupil talking directly to the international respondents whose images were displayed in front of the audience.

20.4   Findings: Perception and Attitudes

Our findings were gained mainly from participant questionnaires, recording of informal perceptions and attitudes and also subjective input from the IT EQUATE team. In documenting the findings each subsection commences with a generalized stereotyping and asks the question of how this will colour girls' judgement.

20.4.1   IT in schools

The image of computing from a young person's point of view is often clouded by their actual contact with the machines. They are seen as "games machines" with macho images, "toys for the boys", or a "machine only for word-processing, spreadsheets and databases": in other words a typewriter, a number cruncher or a storage device. Does this really reflect the varying ways that computers are used in the IT industry?

Our research indicates that information technology in secondary schools focuses on the teaching of word processing, spreadsheet production and database creation. When the schoolgirls were questioned on their understanding of the subject of computing however, their general perception of computing was one of "learning packages", not of solving problems using the computer as a tool. They did not seem to identify that the software allowed for the creation of information systems which could support the commercial world. Possibly this issue is central to girls' non take-up of computing careers, in that they do not realize the computing industry is about communicating and solving problems collaboratively.

Our schools survey showed good utilization of computers in the fields of Maths, English and History (55%, 58% and 55% of the girls respectively had experienced use in these subjects). Although word processing, spreadsheet and database software was used in these fields, there was also evidence of good use of subject-specific educational software, with particular use of CD ROMs. For the remaining subject areas however, use of computers was relatively low (e.g. 19% of girls had used computers in Science, 24% in Geography and 14% in French). On further questioning it was revealed that the use of computers here was generally confined to word processing of work for the specific subject. This is unfortunate, as in the words of Tim Eggar MP, "Information Technology can make learning more exciting and productive" [DTI95].

The main group of 33 IT EQUATE schoolgirls generally enjoyed and felt confident using computers and 78% of them said that they would like to use computers more at school. Of the girls, 84% of them at the independent and urban schools were taking a GCSE in Computer studies or IT. The rural school, however, offered only Business Studies GCSE with IT modules. Whilst none of the three schools taught "A" level Computing, 66% of the girls said they would consider taking it if it had been offered.

In 1995 with changes to the GCSE computing structure, it is interesting to note that the independent school dropped teaching of computing at this level. It is equally interesting to note that as a result of the IT EQUATE programme 30% of the independent girls requested and have followed an "AS" level in Computing; unfortunately the offer of this course cannot be sustained due to resourcing issues.

Computing teaching staff at the two co-educational schools was predominantly male, whilst at the all girls' school they were female. This follows a general national pattern which has evolved since the advent of computers into schools. Traditionally computers were introduced into the maths and science departments of secondary schools which were generally male strongholds, hence the female computing role models in schools are in the minority and as can be seen in the independent school are still within the maths department. The IT EQUATE team feel that more computing female staff are required in schools as role models and that the awareness of all teachers should be raised such that they would support the IT EQUATE objectives and understand the particular difficulties that girls have. In addition, attention must also be paid to the support given to teachers in the rapidly changing world of hardware and software, since only when they feel comfortable with the current technology will they pass on the correct vibes to their pupils.

20.4.2 Peer viewpoints

Do children want to enter careers that their friends define as "boring"? Do girls want to be associated with "nerds" or "sit at a terminal all day"?

Where a computer club existed at the urban school (the other schools did not have this facility), a mixed gender group were questioned on their attendance and enjoyment of it. Of the girls questioned, 75% said that they had fun and attended, whilst only 40% of the boys attended and had fun — it appeared to be a "seen it all before" syndrome in the latter case. Although the club is extremely well run, girls questioned requested more help and organization; this presents itself as a recurring theme, that girls need extra reassurance and hand holding to become confident and proficient in the use of computers.

A father of two daughters, who attended an IT EQUATE event at the University for parents, wrote: "There is an anti-social impression given by a person sitting at a VDU, which makes it difficult for another person to break into. Girls often complain that those with skills on computers will not let them in to have a go — this feeling continues at all stages but could be critical in putting girls off at an early stage in their interest. I have found that a PC at home helps break this barrier."

There is little doubt that computers at home help build girls' confidence (our survey of the IT EQUATE girls showed their use of home computers was split equally between games and homework). However, the problem is then encountered of lack of availability of computer games which interest girls. Girls do not seem to generally enjoy the "shooting, chasing, speed" reaction challenge games as much as their male counterparts. Girls prefer to have a purpose or a problem solving initiative provided by the software — thus presentation of material using desk top publishing packages or the use of such a game as "SimCity", which allows for participation in the planning of a town, is more interesting to them. (Statistics show that SimCity buyers are typically graduates in their mid-twenties. A fifth of them are women, which is three times the usual proportion for a computer game [Beckett95].)

Certainly the multimedia and Internet information demonstrated to the IT EQUATE girls at the University scored highest on their enjoyment level. Here the packages and software provide not only the manipulation power of the word processor, spreadsheet or database but the interest of the information itself, in a format that is more in line with current day exposure: graphics, sound and video, as well as text. The IT EQUATE team believes that the advent of further interactive educational multimedia software will capture girls' interest in computers further.

Another observation relating to the viewpoint of peers to computing, highlights the difference that gender and age make. The question posed was *Are boys better at using computers?*, where statistics were drawn from the answers Yes, No or Varies. At the urban school both girls and boys aged 14-15 were questioned, whilst at the remaining schools older girls aged 16-18 were asked, the findings were as follows:

Urban (14-15yrs)	94% -NO (Girls)	65%-YES (Boys)
Rural (16-17yrs)	60% -NO (Girls)	
Independent (16-18yrs)	75% -NO (Girls)	

Table 20.1 Are boys better at using computers?

The IT EQUATE team believes this may show that girls of a younger age group are very much on the defensive with respect to the opposite sex. It appears that as the girls mature they are willing to consider questions more deeply. However, 14-15 is the age when subject choices are being made and when peer group pressure to conform is strongest and hence the idea of being associated with "nerds" or "sitting at a terminal all day" may not aid in the take-up of a GCSE in Information Technology. This is reinforced in a recent study commissioned by the Health Education Authority, which showed that girls' need to be liked still blocks their hopes of better jobs [HEA95].

20.4.3   Parent viewpoints

These depend on the parents' experience, but how many parents work in IT and do they encourage gender stereotyping (even subconsciously) when it comes to suggesting careers to their offspring?

One of the aspects which seems to have been neglected when trying to ascertain why girls are not entering either the computing profession or computer related courses in higher education, has been how much the girls are influenced by parents or guardians. We invited parents from the participating schools along with their children to an evening workshop at the University, to see for themselves what their daughters had experienced and to gain from their thoughts and ideas.

As part of our research, we obtained background information from the girls concerning their parents' occupations and discovered there was a high proportion of professionals (68%) with only a small minority of semi-skilled or unskilled parents (4.5%). We were also interested in computer use both at work and in the home. 64% of parents attending the evening used computers at work and 40% were the principal computer user at home; using them mainly for work, letter writing and pleasure.

When the girls were asked, "who most encourages you to use a computer?", 39% indicated parents, 55% indicated teachers and 33% indicated both. Knowing therefore that parents did have an influence, albeit, to a slightly lesser extent than teachers, we wanted more information from the parents. Several parents who attended the evening workshop volunteered to assist us in further investigations. We confirmed our findings, from the previous girls' questionnaires, that a high proportion of parents were either professionals or in management and that most parents, particularly the males, used computers at work and home. However, some of our findings from the parents were unclear; when asked to rank the reasons why girls were not entering the computing profession, there was no real consensus. Some parents seemed convinced that teachers and parents have influence over the girls, yet others did not. This, along with other observations, leads us to make the following hypotheses: there are a number of factors which contribute to the non take-up of careers by girls in the computing profession; they are a combination of such criteria as parental influence, teacher influence, self-esteem, stereotyping, peer pressure, employers' attitudes, image of the working environment, the pleasure of working in a balanced group and the pleasure of the work itself.

There was agreement amongst parents on the benefits of the computing profession in that it was seen as a growth industry with good prospects and high salaries, but, there were still misconceptions. One comment a parent made when asked about jobs in computing, which was echoed by others was: "all jobs nowadays have or should have the need to use computers for efficiency." This is disturbing in that the parents thought they understood what was meant by the computing profession, yet confused this with people who used IT within their job. This is one area we intend to pursue through the widening of the scope of the IT EQUATE project

20.4.4   Career literature

The job titles: Systems Analyst, Database Administrator, Network Manager, Software Engineer, Application Programmer, Systems Development Manager, Technical Writer, are not in themselves meaningful. Do they in any way provide sufficient clues as to the human and organizational aspects of the computer industry?

The girls and their teachers (as with the parents) appeared to be extremely hazy about what constituted a career in computing. The confusion initially centred on whether this was a computer technologist, e.g. Systems Analyst, or the individual who uses computers within their job application, e.g. publishing personnel.

Over the course of a day at the University the 33 IT EQUATE girls were subjected to computing career information in different forms. They watched the video "Why Me, Why IT", they listened to female students from the University and role models from industry, and using handout career literature and job adverts they produced business adverts by computer (including their digitized photograph) which advertised the computing career which they themselves had chosen to represent. At the start and end of this day, the girls were asked to write down the tasks performed by people working in the following areas: systems development, systems support, operations, technical support, marketing, training, management, consultancy and research and development. At the start of the day, 33% were able to identify one or two job areas, whilst by the end of the day 68% were able to identify more than five job areas.

The computing industry as a whole is rife with jargon. The job adverts use different titles for the same occupation and are generally written in male oriented language. It was interesting to note that FI GROUP plc in their advert in the Guardian on 6th April 1995 advertised "Wanted: Graduates who don't think of IT in terms of boxes" and continued with "What is most important is possessing an aptitude for logical and numerical reasoning, an enquiring mind and an ability to think laterally. You'll also need to be able to get on well with people and be a team player." This is the type of advert aimed at attracting women to many different computing opportunities. The use of gender oriented language is equally apparent in the book *Professional Awareness in Software* [Myers95]. The chapter *Women in Computing* [Lovegrove95] commences with the words "Women make good computer professionals" and continues in this vein, in contrast to the general "hard" terms used elsewhere, such as software engineer.

The term "Software Engineering" itself has caused confusion within the computing industry and beyond, since when it "first came into wide use it was not intended to name an academic discipline" but to define "techniques of software development" [Priestley95]. As a result "where there were simple programmers before, terminology inflation yielded a bewildering variety of software engineers: systems analysts, analyst programmers, systems programmers, assembler programmers, 3GL programmers, developers, database engineers, communications specialists, human factor experts, systems integrators etc" [Madsen95].

The availability of good computing career material which stimulates the attention of school pupils is extremely important. The current career software and videos available to schools and their appropriateness to girls, is at present being examined by the IT EQUATE team.

20.4.5   Information explosion

Are girls going to be further disadvantaged with the current and forthcoming trends in schools towards use of the Internet, in comparison with their male counterparts?

John Horam MP said "We live in an information age and in the words of Sir Francis Bacon "information is power", which is why the question of the Internet is so important" [Museum95]. The Internet has enormous implications for everyone, but especially those connected with education. Currently the DTI with a project called "School Online" is running a pilot study with some 60 secondary schools linked to the Internet [DTI95], to evaluate the possibilities and benefits of linking all secondary schools to the Information Superhighway; the results of the evaluation are expected late Spring 1996.

With the current explosion of Internet usage, from Childrens' BBC email to Wimbledon coverage, the IT EQUATE team believed it was important to introduce the IT EQUATE girls to the Internet at a University workshop, in order to give them experience and confidence and to help them gain maximum benefit from the Internet, if and when it is commonly adopted by schools. The girls' first exposure to the Internet was one of interest and intrigue as they investigated different avenues and routes of the Superhighway; it provided them with information and, of course, "information is power". They learnt also that it provided two way communication and were able to create their own pages which included photos of the girls and their day. They saw the potential and the ease by which that information, together with other Staffordshire IT EQUATE documentation, was presented to the world for any viewer to access at World Wide Web address:- http://www.soc.staffs.ac.uk/itequate/

A symposium entitled "Destination Cyberspace" was recently hosted by the Science Museum, London [Museum95] and sponsored by the Office of Science and Technology, to consider views of women on what females wanted from the Information Superhighway. The following figures were initially given by the Science Museum to illustrate the current situation:

- The Internet is available to 30 million world-wide, of which 21 million use it daily.

- Great Britain is the second most plugged in nation in the world.

- Fewer than 20% of Web users are women.

- Only 20% of the IT workforce are women.

- The number of women studying IT and entering related professions is declining.

- By 2010 it is expected that over 80% of all jobs will include an IT element.

The main points to emerge from the meeting as to what women require of the Information Superhighway were to:

- have easy access, in terms of both cost and availability of convenient resources;

- see the Internet take form on a global scale with commitment from both the private and public sectors;

- utilize the networks as a tool for communication and exchange of ideas;

- find ways of monitoring to what extent available information is reliable, relevant and responsible;

- participate in creating a greater awareness of what is available, to demystify the technology and to continue to address the issues that are important in encouraging women onto the Internet.

20.4.6   Media viewpoint

Have you ever seen a television drama set in a computing company, where the talk is of information and problem solving? Do the presenters of IT programmes stress the importance of the problems which the computer has solved (ie computers as a "tool") rather than demonstrating the latest computer wizardry? Do the press, in general, report more on the negative image of IT, i.e. the scare stories, the mistakes that computers make, rather than the positive image of IT and the problems that computers solve? Are girls going to adopt career ideas planted by the media?

The idea for a "television drama set in a computing company" came from a male pupil at the rural school who had been invited to the University to evaluate some careers software produced by a final year degree student. When questioned on his future career aspirations he said that he wanted to be a lawyer and that this idea had been planted by television.

It is not glamorous or sensational for the media news to report on the problems that computers solve unless the latest computer wizardry is demonstrated. Generally (unless it is the BBCs Tomorrow's World) the wizardry is not balanced by a clear explanation of the problem which the computer has solved.

The portrayal of the Internet on the TV programme "The Net" is very much biased towards the male gender both in its language and its examples of Internet use. A recent programme allowed the home Internet user to manipulate a physical robot via the Internet *through the dungeons of Madame Tussauds.* This was in sharp contrast to a subsequent TV programme called "First Sex" which examined the power of the Internet from a female perspective.

Some computer sales adverts also appear aimed at the male purchaser. ESCOMs PC Buyer's Guide has a range of seductive females on the adverts of their hardware products, together with the words "Take Home a Supermodel", "Stunning speed", "Minis are the height of Fashion" and "Sharpen up Your Image". Similarly an advert for a lap-top shown recently on a transatlantic flight, featured two males sitting on adjacent seats on a plane working at their lap-tops. As each eyed the work of their neighbour, the speed of their keyboarding skills increased as each tried to outdo the other, in a typically male trial of strength. This form of advertising does little to encourage females to enter the computing world, moreover it strengthens it as a male bastion.

20.4.7   Government viewpoint

The Education Minister, Eric Forth, defines "We are world leaders in IT in schools", yet Judith Church, Labour MP for Dagenham, needs to table a Bill to increase the take-up of computing jobs by women. Isn't it obvious that something is wrong with the image of this increasingly important world of IT from a female perception?

We may be "world leaders in IT in schools" [Frost95] insofar as the hardware and software expenditure per capita is concerned — 94% of secondary school pupils in England get hands-on experience of computers [Stats95]. We are not, however, matching this technology expenditure with increased teacher support, as NAACE the computer advisors and inspectors association identified [Frost95]. Although there has been a dramatic increase in hardware in schools, the amount of support to help teachers and pupils has been reduced, especially in the area of subject support. Schools are reluctant to pay money to get advice that previously has been free. The Government now provides new school effectiveness grants and it is up to the individual schools as to whether they spend this money on IT or any other facility. The IT EQUATE team believe that this would be money well spent on quality in-service training and general raising of awareness, especially with the GCSE IT changes, which appear to have led to confusion. Equally perhaps school expenditure on this IT support could be matched pound for pound by further Government funding to help teachers. Girls would then ultimately benefit from such an initiative.

The last twenty years has seen a dramatic reduction in the number of female applicants for computing courses at University — from approximately 25% in 1975 to 12% today. The tabling of the "Women in Technology" Bill by Judith Church MP to increase take-up of computing jobs by women was aimed at stemming the reduction of women in IT employment, in what is an expanding industry. In the ensuing speech against the Bill by John Butcher MP (who had previously run a programme called WISE — Women into Science and Engineering and worked in the computing industry), he stated that "there is growing evidence that employers will go a long way to avoid hiring computer scientists. They would far sooner hire analysts and programmers who have not been tainted by that particular discipline" [Hansard95] — and thus the Bill was opposed. This just reflects a general ignorance about the image of Software Engineering as a profession. The majority of Computing Science courses are accredited by the British Computer Society which ensures quality and applicability to industry. Furthermore from our own observations, female students generally get placed first before male students within the employment market.

20.5   Conclusion

"There is a recognized need for a highly trained and skilled workforce to help the UK economy thrive and the training of this workforce will take some years of investment. There is a greater loss to the economy of the UK due to not realizing to the full the potential of the workforce; one way is to encourage more women into these professions." [Lovegrove95]

The solutions for achieving more women in computing will not be found or will not happen overnight. It is a complex situation which involves many "pieces of a pie" being brought together. The areas defined above represent some of the pie pieces and attention to solving the problems identified within them may go some way to satisfying the Staffordshire IT EQUATE aims.

Part IV
Working Practices

Part of what we mean by professional responsibility is good working practices; perhaps even the major part — "By their works shall ye know them". The computing industry has such a plethora of working practices, methodologies, paradigms and the like that they can't all be right. So what is good working practice in the computing industry? It is impossible to do justice to this question in a few chapters, but we hope at least to map out some of the key topics.

We begin with Paul Beynon-Davies' *Professional Responsibilities and Information Systems Failure*, a horrific case study, reminding us of what can happen when professionals fail. The catastrophic problems which the London Ambulance Service experienced with their new computer system are catalogued in detail; what comes out is a sense of "there but for the grace of God go I". However, Beynon-Davies points out that there are no simple solutions to such complex problems. He shows, better than any theoretical debate, that technical competency is insufficient, and that Information Systems professionalism is interdisciplinary by nature, with social, political and economic dimensions.

The need to have a range of non-technical skills is exemplified by Amer Al-Rawas & Steve Easterbrook who, in *Problems in Requirements Communication*, look at one of the major problems in calling ourselves professional — can we honestly say that we do a good job for our customers, when so often we misunderstand what they want? They suggest that in any computing project, it is usually the software developers (the professionals) who call the shots. For example, the professionals typically decide how the requirements document, the most common means of defining "what the project is about", is to be written. Hence they write it in a formal language, with diagrams, flow-charts and pseudo-code, which satisfies their needs, but which is intimidating and unfamiliar to the customer. Clearly, there is an in-built communication problem here, but often the attempt to resolve it by, say, adding a natural language commentary to the formal document, is done in too much haste and simply does not work. Al-Rawas & Easterbrook recommend that software professionals pay great attention to the "informal information channels", the on-going inter-working between developer and end-user to flush out the misunderstandings and over-simplifications which cause trouble in any project.

In a similar vein, Gene McGuire in *Professional Responsibilities under the Capability Maturity Model* gives a clear account of why team-based working in Software Engineering is on the increase. He argues that it is essential that such teams are adaptive, forward-looking entities. He discusses the Capability Maturity Model (CMM), which is one of the more useful models for codifying the software development effort. In so doing, McGuire draws out the various aptitudes and skills (many of them in-born, some of them taught) which go to making a successful software team and team-member. Perhaps if the computing profession treated its customers like Al-Rawas & Easterbrook advise, and ran their development teams the way McGuire advises, then it would be in pretty good shape.

John Madsen's paper, *Revenge of the Methodology Anarchist*, illustrates perfectly what Al-Rawas & Easterbrook have been saying, that the quality of the communication between developer and customer is all-important for the success of a computing project. Madsen describes the software industry's own version of Hell, which is methodology for methodology's sake, the facade of professionalism producing unprofessional results. His chapter is an antidote to our tendency to talk only to ourselves — since no-one else is clever enough to understand us! After all, the computing industry was created by kids working in garages, enthusiasts, people who defied conventional wisdom and who tore up the rule-book. These times are not, or should not be, dead. Professionalism is not about creating such complicated professional practices that we exclude the customer from the process. Madsen rightly concentrates on what professionalism is really about — it is about communicating with ordinary people; it is about giving them what they want; it is about giving them it quickly and cheaply; it is about users and developers feeling good working together; and developers who have the maturity to choose appropriate toolsets. Professionalism is not about slavishly following the rule-book.

If team-building and communication skills are essential, what programming and analytical techniques should be adopted to turn the customer requirements into successful IT solutions? In *Software Engineering Practices in the UK*, J Barrie Thompson presents an important survey of the UK computing industry over the last 25 years, of the use (or otherwise) of quality assurance techniques, structured methodologies, CASE tools etc. His conclusion, backed by five major studies, is that the adoption of these tools and techniques has been considerably slower than expected. Thompson discusses the reasons for this, and he points to factors such as their cost, the lack of management commitment, fear amongst computer practitioners of automating themselves out of a job and lack of market-leading products. He argues that educational establishments must emphasize to their students the importance of these "professionalizing" items, and that the technology transfer of the new ways must be encouraged. As a general criticism of the computer industry, Thompson's point is well-made; computer "professionals" have been keen enough to computerize other people's work, but not so keen to take the medicine themselves. In fact, the computer profession has been remarkably resistant to treating progamming and analysis as disciplines which can be researched, developed, taught, improved upon and, at least in part, automated. Physician, heal thyself.

Next, Stuart Shapiro, in *Escaping the Mythology that Plagues Software Technology* makes an interesting critique of the unquestioning drive in some quarters to equate the software profession with the engineering profession. "Software Engineering", it sounds good, doesn't it, but what does it mean? Shapiro's argument is that the equation is built on a diminished view of engineering as being a discipline which requires very little judgement; but Shapiro reckons that engineering needs a good deal of judgement, and if this were more widely known, then people would be less happy with the comparison. He also argues that engineering is in any case quite different from Software Engineering in that engineering has a clear set of high-level, archetypal problems and solutions (buildings will look different, but they will all obey the same set of design and structural criteria), whereas Software Engineering has very few (you can't take a payroll system and, with a couple of changes, make it into, say, a stock-control system). In other words, the set of "standardized parts" in the software industry is much reduced. Of course, Shapiro would be the last person to say that the comparison between engineering and software development is worthless; what he argues for is rigour in that comparison.

Another iconoclastic work is the paper by Jawed Siddiqi & Andy Bissett, *Is The Rush To Quality a Move Towards Inequality?* In recent years, the quest for quality in the computing industry has taken on Holy Grail proportions, but Siddiqi & Bissett question its validity, at least in the European context. They point out that the quality crusade, which has achieved such wonderful results in US and Japanese manufacturing, has failed to achieve similar wonders elsewhere in the computing industry. Why? They suggest two possible reasons. Firstly, the consensus view of society, where workers, management and customers all have the same interests, are all working towards the same targets, simply may not be true. To give a sporting analogy, working life, they say, is like a game of football; where two opposing teams are each trying to kick the ball into the other's goal. In terms of games theory, this is a "win-lose", not a "win-win" situation. This analysis is subversive of the quality movement. The second reason, they suggest, is that software development could be just too difficult to benefit from the quality movement, at least not without a great deal of effort. Here, they agree with Shapiro that software development is not a production-line activity and should not be treated as such. These are interesting suggestions and they open up the question of Software Engineering as a profession. If quality is indeed at the heart of professionalism, and if we cannot significantly affect quality within the computing industry, then can we say that computing is a true profession . . . or do we require a richer understanding of what quality means?

Finally, Julian Webb, Lesley Rackett & John Betts in *Pressures to Behave Unprofessionally* give a welcome snapshot of the "real world". This world is often inimical to professional, responsible behaviour and at odds with the world of academic discussion. The picture they paint is a world where the deadlines are impossible, training is inadequate, and where the budget is cut to the bone and beyond. In such an environment, talk of software quality is ludicrous: quality costs money, and software companies have very little indeed of that commodity.

The world which Webb, Rackett & Betts describe is a world most of us will readily recognize — it is the world we work in every day. As pressures grow to produce computer systems in shorter time, at less cost, with more functionality, we are forced by the demands of the market-place to cut corners, try quicker techniques, make tough decisions. In so doing, are we improving our productivity, demonstrating our professional excellence by doing more for less, or are we acting irresponsibly and unprofessionally?

Chapter 21

Professional Responsibilities and Information Systems Failure

21.1 Introduction

On the 29th of October 1992, an information system of the UK National Health Service made the front story on the BBC's Nine-O'Clock news. It was claimed that a new computerized system established at the headquarters of the London Ambulance Service (LAS) failed, and that as a direct result of this failure the lives of twenty people were lost [Beynon95a]. A month or so later the British Computer Society (BCS) president and Vice President claimed that the breakdown in the LAS system could have been avoided if computer people were trained to professional standards. President Roger Johnson stated that:

> "The public are entitled to expect that the same professional disciplines apply in IT as in other professions such as medicine and law." [CW92]

On the micro level, the clear implication of such statements is that the builders of the LAS system are seen as having acted in an unprofessional manner. On the macro level, such statements reflect the idea that information systems (IS) failure is clearly identifiable with professionalism in IS work. However, such statements also embody a whole range of assumptions underlying a particularly powerful perspective on modern-day IS work. The assumptions centre around the idea of professionalism and professionalization in IS work.

In this chapter we will discuss the ubiquity of IS failure and its importance for shaping IS engineering practice. To enable us to do this we shall develop a model of IS failure based on the negotiation of expectations. The London Ambulance Service Computer Aided Despatch (LASCAD) system project will be used to illustrate key features of this model. This case is useful material for discussing the problems of defining professions, professionalism and professionalization, particularly in the context of the emerging discipline of IS engineering. Finally, we shall use our model of IS failure to discuss some of the basis for "professional" approaches to IS development.

Note, we use the term information systems engineering in this chapter in the broad sense used by the British Computer Society (BCS). In one sense, IS engineering is a discipline which broadens the area of Software Engineering from "programming in the large" to include issues of people and organizations. In another sense, IS engineering has a more specific focus than Software Engineering in concentrating on software written to support human activity (particularly decision-making) within organizations.

21.2   Information Systems Failure

IS failure, or the association with such "failure", comes close to a form of "social leprosy" or stigma [Goffman90]. People become tarnished by association with IS projects that have deemed to have failed. I recently experienced this stigmatizing effect at first-hand having attended a meeting of a number of high-ranking ambulance service personnel. At this meeting, I was introduced as someone involved in the LASCAD project. I immediately stood up and said "No, I was not involved in the LAS project, I was attempting to study it!' This incident brought personally to the fore the stigmatizing effect of prominent IS failure. Perhaps, of greater interest was the fact that a member of the ambulance service personnel at the meeting, unbeknownst to the others, had been previously employed by LAS and did have an active part in the events described in Section 4 of this chapter. This person, of course, did not declare his previous affiliation!

This stigmatization is highly significant in the light of surveys such as that conducted by the US Government's Accounting Agency which in 1979 [US79] found that less than 3% of the software that the US government had paid for was actually used as delivered. More than half of the software was never used at all. [Gladden 1983] reports in a similar survey that 75% of all system development undertaken is either never completed or the resulting systems are not used.

But IS failures and the study of this phenomena is not only important because of its apparent prevalence. IS failures are significant as a means of validating IS engineering practice. The IS engineering industry is very good at suggesting "appropriate" tools, techniques, methods and frameworks for constructing information systems. It is very poor at supplying empirical validation for many of its proposals [Galliers R92].

In this light, IS failures can act as a significant resource. In other disciplines, the detailed study of "breakdowns" has proven significant in changing established practice [Petroski85]. In structural engineering, for instance, the study of bridge failures has revealed important information leading to bridge re-design. In another context, the idea of studying and even stimulating breakdowns in social interaction has been discussed in the light of revealing significant characteristics of human behaviour [Garfinkel67].

21.2.1   Examples of IS failure

The LASCAD project has been one of the most prominent examples of information systems failure in recent times [Beynon95a]. This is probably due more to the "safety-critical" nature of this system and the claim that 20-30 people may have lost their lives as a result of this failure, than the scale of the project. Indeed, LASCAD ($£1.1M$) is dwarfed by other British IS failures such as Wessex regional health authorities RISP project ($£63M$) [HMSO93] and the UK Stock Exchange's TAURUS settlement system ($£75 - £250M$) [Waters93].

The key conclusion to be drawn from the study of such failures is that the idea of IS failure can rarely be satisfactorily understood solely from a technical perspective. This is because a definition of the success or otherwise of a given IS is as much reliant on the social and political setting within which it is constructed as it is on the "quality" of the construction itself.

21.2.2   Defining IS failure

Two definitions of IS failure seem particularly important because of the way in which they relate IS failure to social and organizational context: Lyytinen and Hirschheim's concept of expectation failure and Sauer's concept of termination failure.

Expectation failure

Lyytinen and Hirschheim in surveying the literature on IS failure ([Lyytinen87]) identify four major categories of IS failure:

1. Correspondence Failure. A lack of correspondence between IS objectives and IS evaluation.

2. Process Failure. Unsatisfactory development performance. Either when the IS development process cannot produce a workable system, or the development process produces an IS but the project runs over budget in terms of cost, time etc.

3. Interaction Failure. If a system is heavily used it constitutes a success; if it is hardly ever used, or there are major problems involved in using a system then it constitutes a failure.

4. Expectation Failure. Lyytinen and Hirschheim describe this as a superset of the three other types of failure. They also describe their idea of expectation failure to be a more encompassing, politically and pluralistically informed view of IS failure than the other forms. This is because they characterize correspondence, process and interaction failure as having one major theme in common: the three notions of failure portray a highly rational image of IS development; each views an IS as mainly a neutral technical artifact [Klein87]. In contrast, they define expectation failure as the inability of an IS to meet a specific stakeholder group's expectations. IS failures signify a gap between some existing situation and a desired situation for members of a particular stakeholder group. Stakeholders are any group of people who share a pool of values that define what the desirable features of an IS are, and how they should be obtained.

Termination Failure

Sauer criticizes the model proposed by Lyytinen and Hirschheim for its plurality. Sauers' model posits a conservative definition of IS failure [Sauer93]. According to his account a system should only be deemed a failure when development or operation ceases, leaving supporters dissatisfied with the extent to which the system has served their interests. This means that a system should not be considered a failure until all interest in progressing an IS project has ceased. This definition of *termination failure* is hence stricter than Lyytinen and Hirscheim's concept of *expectation failure*.

Sauer develops a model of IS failure based on exchange relations. He portrays the development of IS as an innovation process based on three components: the project organization, the information system, and its supporters. Each of these components is arranged in a triangle of dependencies. The IS depends on the project organization, the project organization depends on its supporters, and the supporters depend on the IS. The IS requires the efforts and expertise of the project organization to sustain it; the project organization is heavily dependent on the provision of support in the form of material resources and help in coping with contingencies; supporters require benefits from the IS.

21.3   An Example of IS Failure

To illustrate the usefulness of the frameworks discussed in Section 21.2, this and the following section provides a brief description of one highly prominent IS failure. A more detailed description of this case is given in [Beynon95a].

On the night of Monday 26th October to the morning of Tuesday 27th October 1992 things started to go wrong at the HQ of LAS. It was reported that a flood of 999 emergency calls (some 2900 instead of the usual 2300) apparently swamped operator's screens. It was also claimed that many recorded calls were being wiped off screens. This, in turn, caused a mass of automatic alerts to be generated indicating that calls to ambulances had not been acknowledged.

Claims were later made in the press that up to 20-30 people may have died as a result of ambulances arriving too late on the scene. Some ambulances were taking over three hours to answer a call. The government's recommended maximum is 17 minutes for inner-city areas [Guardian92]. A counter-claim was made that a breaking up of sector desks over the preceding weekend may have caused loss of local knowledge.

Arguably the LASCAD project was the most visible UK IS failure in recent years. It is therefore not surprising to see that the events triggered a whole series of responses. In many ways such responses seem reminiscent of a moral panic in IS work [Cohen80].

21.4   Sauer's Model Applied to Lascad

In this section we shall use Sauer's model as a means of organizing key elements of our description of the LASCAD case. This is particularly useful in testing the explanatory power of Sauer's model of exchange relations in the context of the LASCAD project.

21.4.1   Project organization

It has now become something of an orthodoxy, or what Harel calls a folk theorem [Harel80], to assume that no IS project can be understood in isolation from its context. As with any project of this nature, the LASCAD system was shaped by the prior history of IS innovation.

1. It is interesting that Systems Options, the company supplying the major part of the software for the system, is reported as having had no previous experience of building despatch systems for ambulance services. The company had won the £1.1 million contract for the system in June 1991.

2. It appears that the London Ambulance Service had previously scrapped a BT subsiduary IAL development at a cost of £7.5 million in October 1990. This project is reported to have been late starting in May 1987 after a year's delay.

3. Systems Options substantially underbid McDonnel-Douglas (an established supplier) and were put under pressure to complete the system quickly.

4. In January 1992 phases one and two of the project began live trials. In March 1992, phase two of the trials was temporarily suspended following claims, particularly from the union NUPE, of fatal delays caused by system errors. In October 1992 phase three was terminated after two days of chaos.

A number of the findings of the public inquiry report [Page93] directly relate to project organization:

1. It was claimed that the LAS chiefs ignored what amounted to an overambitious project timetable.

2. The LAS board were misled by the project team over the experience of Systems Options.

3. The management of the project was inadequate. The project team failed to use the PRINCE [Bentley92] project management method as prescribed for public sector projects.

4. The software was incomplete and unstable.

5. Training in the use of the system was incomplete and inconsistent.

21.4.2 The Information System

It must be understood that LAS is unlike any other ambulance service in the UK. The service receives ten times as many emergency calls as any other ambulance service in the country. The organization covers a geographical area of just over 600 square miles and handles emergencies for an area with a resident population of 6.8 million people.

Questions were also raised about the complexity of the technical system. A typical ambulance despatch system, like the ones employed in Surrey, West Yorkshire or Berkshire, merely acts as a repository of details about incidents. Communication between HQ and ambulances is conducted via telephone or voice radio links [FT92b]. In the LASCAD system, links between communication, logging and despatching via a GIS were meant to be automated.

It is therefore tempting to adopt a stance of explaining this "failure" purely in terms of problems of a technical nature. However, the report of the public inquiry [Page93] portrays a more complex picture of the so-called technical problems experienced by the LASCAD system than that reported either in the computing or general press. It is interesting that they conclude:

> "On 26th and 27th October the computer system did not fail in a technical sense. Response times did on occasions become unacceptable, but overall the system did what it had been designed to do."

Discussions with a number of people have revealed a range of opinions about this important statement. However, if we take the statement at face value it does beg the question of what did happen to the system to cause response times to become unacceptable?

According to the report of the public inquiry, when the system was fully implemented at 07:00 on 26th October 1992 the system was lightly loaded. This meant that staff could cope with various problems associated with the communication system: e.g., ambulance crews pressing wrong buttons; ambulances being in radio blackspots; "hand-shaking" problems. As the number of incidents increased, incorrect vehicle location or status information received by the system increased. This increase in status errors meant that:

1. The system made incorrect allocations — multiple vehicles were sent to the same incident, or the closest vehicle was not chosen for despatch.

2. The system had fewer ambulance resources to allocate.

3. The system placed calls that had not gone through the appropriate protocol on a waiting list.

4. The system generated exception messages for those incidents it had received incorrect status information.

These effects compounded the situation. For instance, the number of exception messages increased rapidly to such an extent that staff were not able to clear the queue. The increasing size of the queue slowed the system. With the increasing number of "awaiting attention" and exception messages it became increasingly difficult to attend to messages that had scrolled off the screen.

With fewer resources to allocate, and the problems of dealing with the waiting and exception queues it took longer to allocate resources to incidents.

At the ambulance end, crews became increasingly frustrated at incorrect allocations. The inquiry believes that this may have led to an increased number of instances where crews did not press the right status buttons, or took a different vehicle to an incident than that suggested by the system.

The system was therefore in a vicious circle of cause and effect.

21.4.3   The supporters

Sauer's use of the term supporter is clearly meant to highlight the importance that some organizational group has in providing resources, physical or otherwise, which support the innovation process. However, not all groups are natural supporters of innovation. We prefer the use of the more general term stakeholder [Land76] in the sense that not all groups with an interest in the development of an IS necessarily support that development. Some stakeholder groups may have a definite negative interest in the success of a given project. Three major stakeholder groups are relevant to our analysis of the LASCAD project: LAS management, headquarters staff (particularly those in the control room) and ambulance staff. There is clear evidence of a mismatch of perspectives between each of these groups. Only the first of these groups was a natural supporter in Sauer's sense of the term.

The system has been described as being introduced in an atmosphere of mistrust by staff. There was incomplete "ownership" of the system by the majority of its users. The many problems experienced with various system components in the preceding months had instilled an atmosphere of mistrust.

Hardware and software suppliers dealing with the London ambulance service have spoken of disorganization, low staff morale, friction between management and the workforce, and an atmosphere of hostility towards computing systems. An ambulance crew member is reported as saying, "whatever system you have people have to have confidence in it. We want to go back to the simple system, telephone and radio. Anybody can use it. Crews have confidence in it." [FT92a]. One of the reasons for this low staff morale may be that control room staff had virtually no previous experience of using computers [NewSci92]. The union NUPE continually made aspersions to what they considered a "macho" style of management at LAS. The Labour party's health spokesman, David Blunkett demanded a public inquiry into the system in September 1992, a month before the events described above, after receiving a report from NUPE [Computing92]

21.4.4   Environment

The political and economic environment within which the LASCAD project took place is probably the most important contextual factor in this case. The environment of the LASCAD project can be considered in the macro sense of the constraints imposed by the overarching organization of the British National Health Service (NHS) and in the micro sense in terms of the labour relations history at the LAS.

Macro environment

Firstly, it must be understood that there is no demonstrable and unitary power-structure within the NHS. The NHS is a body made up of a complex network of autonomous and semi-autonomous groups concerned with health matters. Actual delivery of health care is in the hands of powerful clinical professionals who are naturally concerned with preserving their professional autonomy [Leavitt92].

One consequence of this is that any project carried out in the NHS, such as LASCAD, has to consider what relationships in the network are affected by the project and what activities have to be undertaken to enable or encourage those relationships [Checkland90].

Computing within the NHS is therefore complicated by the fact that no one body has overall responsibility for information technology (IT). The lack of a clear organization for IT has meant the absence of a clear strategic vision for IT. To build a strategy there must be first some agreement on objectives. Clearly, many of the objectives of the various stakeholders are in conflict. This situation is unlikely to change with the recent moves towards a market of providers and purchasers in the NHS.

A great deal of the shape of the LASCAD project was determined by the internal tensions within the NHS. For example, members of the public inquiry [Page93] reflect on some of the stresses and strains that have been placed on the LAS by changes in the NHS over the last few years.

> "Under the NHS reforms, all parts of the NHS have gone through major cultural changes in the past few years and it is evident that the LAS could not bury its head in the sand if it was to provide a professional and successful service in the 1990s.
>
> However, the result of the initiatives undertaken by management from 1990-1992 did not revitalize management and staff as intended, but actually worsened what was already a climate of mistrust and obstructiveness. It was not a case of management getting the agenda wrong. The size of the programme and the speed and depth of change were simply too aggressive for the circumstances. Management clearly underestimated the difficulties involved in changing the deeply ingrained culture of LAS and misjudged the industrial relations climate so that staff were alienated to the changes rather than brought on board."

Micro environment

It is misleading to portray the management problems of the LAS purely in the context of the two years prior to the events of 1992. Many of the pressures on the LASCAD project can be seen to be the result of a protracted climate of conflict in the ambulance service between management, unions and the government of the day. The Public Inquiry maintains that during the 1980s there was clear evidence that management failed to modernize the service. This was reflected in a lack of investment in the workforce (such as paramedic training and career advancement), the fleet and the estate. By the end of 1990, at the end of a protracted national dispute over pay, the LAS stood in need of major modification and change. During the period between January and April 1991 the number of senior and middle-management post within the LAS was reduced from 268 by 53. There appears to have been little consultation with staff over the restructuring and the whole process caused a great deal of anxiety in the organization.

Therefore, the public inquiry [Page93] cite an important reason for the unstable industrial relations climate within LAS as the "fear of failure" on the part of management. Changes in structure created a climate in which management were continually under pressure to succeed. This may have put undue pressure on management to ensure that the LASCAD system was implemented on time and within budget. However, it may also have blinded them to some of the fundamental difficulties of the system implementation.

The inquiry team believe that most of the operational management at LAS were of the opinion that LASCAD would act as an essential means of overcoming what they saw as outmoded practices. Such practices included the ability of crews themselves or the ambulance stations to decide which resource to mobilize in response to an incident. These practices were to be replaced with what management saw as a system which would decide in an objective and impartial way the optimum mobilization of resource.

The inquiry team commented that management were naive in assuming that the simple introduction of a computer system would automatically result in changes in working practices. Crews and stations, if they wished, could still accommodate older practices by employing strategies such as failing to mobilize, sending a different resource, or failing to acknowledge or report status.

21.5   The Nature of IS Failure

The key conclusion to be drawn is that the idea of IS failure can rarely be satisfactorily understood solely from one or other of these perspectives. This is because a definition of the success or otherwise of a given IS is as much reliant on the social and political setting within which it is constructed as it is on the quality of the construction itself.

In terms of the frameworks discussed in Section 21.2, the LASCAD project is a clear example of the concept of expectation failure. The system did not fail in the technical sense, but did fail to meet the expectations of many of its supporters. However, using Sauer's model the LASCAD project would not be deemed an example of termination failure. At the time of writing the LASCAD project organization has been re-structured but has not lost the support of the major stakeholders, the LAS, South West Thames RHA and the NHS.

21.6   What is a Profession?

The ubiquity of modern IS and the recent prominence of IS failures, has caused a debate within the community involved in their development about the status of their work. Bodies like the BCS and the IEE have attempted to cast IS work as a true profession in much the same guise as lawyers, accountants, architects and the medical profession.

Many occupational groups have sought professional status. However, there is little agreement about what constitutes a profession. Elliot discusses how the term *profession* is widely and imprecisely applied to a variety of occupations [Elliot72]. The adjective *professional* is even more overworked, extending to cover the opposite of amateur and the opposite of poor work, two concepts which need not be synonymous. Some sociologists disillusioned somewhat with the hazy nature of the term, have concluded that the concept of a profession is of little scientific value. They therefore cast the term profession, merely as a symbolic label for a desired status.

Johnson discusses two dominant models of professionalism in the sociological literature: the trait model and the functionalist model [Johnson82].

Trait models of professionalism present a list of attributes which are said to represent some common core of professional occupations. In this model the process of professionalization is portrayed as a process made up of a determinate sequence of events. An occupation is seen as passing through predictable stages of organizational change, the end-state of which is professionalism.

In functionalist models no attempt is made to provide an exhaustive list of attributes or traits. Instead the components of the model are made up of elements that have a functional relevance for society as a whole or to the professional-client relationship.

More recently, researchers have become interested in the process of professionalization as power-play between occupational groups in their attempts to establish jurisdiction over expert work. The work of Abbott is representative of this approach [Abbott88].

21.6.1   A trait model

For the purpose of our initial analysis, it is useful to define some common features from occupational groups with a readily agreed professional status, e.g., law and medicine — this constitutes a preliminary trait model of a professional group. A feature analysis of such occupations leads to the development of the following "ideal-type" ([Jackson70]); a profession might be defined as a group of persons with:

1. an accredited corpus of specialist knowledge and skills.

2. one or more formal bodies involved in organizing the profession. In particular, the formal body will be involved in:

   (a) maintaining a code of conduct/practice and monitoring adherence to the code.

   (b) ensuring that only suitably "qualified" persons enter the profession.

3. Some form of recognition of the professional status of members.

Elsewhere, we have argued that an analysis of IS engineering work on all of these traits leads to the conclusion that such work cannot be claimed to be more than a semi-profession at the present time [Beynon95b].

21.6.2   A corpus of knowledge and skills

We now concentrate on examining the idea of a common corpus of knowledge and skills in IS Engineering, particularly as it relates to current prescriptions of professional practice in this area.

Classic trait analyses of professionalism maintain that to be a profession some agreement has to have been reached in the occupational group regarding the content of theoretical knowledge and practical expertise demanded of members of the profession.

A profession normally sees itself as having an essential underpinning of abstract principles which have been organized into a theory. Alongside the set of basic principles are various practical techniques for the recurrent application of at least some of the fundamental principles. In this respect, Simon sees professions as denigrating knowledge that is "intuitive, informal or cookbooky" [Simon72]. Murray describes this dominant ideology as being one of technical rationality [Murray91]. Abbott identifies three aspects of professional work which define abstract knowledge: diagnosis, treatment and inference [Abbott88]. These three aspects are seen as resources for asserting a profession's jurisdictional claims: to classify a problem; to reason about it; and to take action on it. A profession's formal knowledge system, embodied as a series of abstractions, serves as a means of legitimating professional practice in these areas. Abstract knowledge is also used as a means of generating new diagnoses, treatments and inference methods that can extend or support jurisdictional claims.

21.6.3   IS Engineering knowledge and skills

Oz maintains that while some people debate the label "computer professional", particularly because of the variety of occupations encompassed by this broad term, software developers usually consider themselves professionals [Oz94b]. In fact, he states that the responsibilities of the software developer may be more comprehensive, and hence require them to be more careful about their conduct, than other more traditional professions. Using Abbott's compartmentalization of professional knowledge:

1. Diagnosis in IS work probably refers to the claim made by IS professionals that they are the appropriate occupational group concerned with identifying information problems in organizations.

2. Treatment constitutes claims to being able to construct suitable technological solutions for such problems.

3. Inference denotes knowledge of the appropriate techniques and technology for matching information problems to information solutions.

However, perhaps resulting from the variety of occupations, there is little agreement concerning the corpus of knowledge and skills constituting IS work. In the UK, a number of standards have been developed for IS work in the public sector, the most notable being the systems development methodology, SSADM [Skidmore92], and the project management methodology, PRINCE [Bentley92]. The National Computing Centre runs certification programmes in systems analysis and project management centred around these approaches. Hence, in many ways, these approaches may be seen as attempts to systematize/rationalize the skills required of the IS developer. However, it is still not true to say that IS specialists has an agreed body of transferable knowledge and skills which they can take with them when moving between jobs.

There is also a big question about whether purely technical knowledge is sufficient. For instance, Friedman and Kahn have discussed the importance of including material on social and ethical issues within standard computer science curricula [Friedman94]. Also, institutions like the British Computer Society have recently become interested in broadening the skills expected of IS engineers. The idea of a hybrid manager has been much discussed [Palmer90]. The term hybrid manager was coined by Earl to define a manager who combines IS and business skills [Earl89]:

> "People with strong technical skills and adequate business knowledge,
> or vice versa . . . hybrids are people with technical skills able to work in
> user areas doing a line or functional job, but adept at developing and
> supplementing IT application ideas."

Ince has recently contributed to this debate with his controversial statement that, "most of our [UK] computing departments [in universities] should be closed down and their staff dispersed to other existing departments" [Ince95]. His argument is that Computer Science has got too big to be effectively delivered to students by one department. He suggests, for instance, that staff who teach and research subjects concerned with software artefacts as strategic tools for companies be moved to business schools; that those who feel that their area of expertise is Software Engineering would function best in electrical engineering departments; that those who see the subject as theoretically founded should join mathematics departments.

There is a related debate ongoing about training for skill or educating for knowledge in the IS area. Universities have traditionally seen themselves in the UK as imparting knowledge of IS technology, development and management. More recently, both private and public training organizations within the UK have emphasized the need for acquiring core skills or competencies in IS work. The rise of product-oriented training has been a particularly prominent example of skills-training in recent years. Many software producers now offer manufacturer-certified qualifications. Microsoft's MS Certified Professional scheme is one notable example. Also resonant of this trend is the recent introduction of the National Vocational Qualification (NVQ) scheme. This scheme allows practitioners to be accredited "on-the-job" with various levels of achievement in core competencies [Computing95].

21.7   The Nature of IS Professionalism

The description of the LASCAD case in Section 21.4 constitutes what might be called a web description of IS failure. That is, it explains failure in terms of the complex intertwining of relationships in the context of computing. Web explanations such as this are necessarily complex. They do not offer a simple linear explanation of phenomenon and consequently provide no simple answers to the problem of preventing IS failure. However, if we accept the complexity of the nature of failure, this does lead to a number of practical consequences for the way in which we approach the development of information systems.

Clearly, we maintain that an understanding of the multi-faceted nature of IS engineering is essential to the successful construction of such systems. This means that the process of professional IS development must include a social, political and economic dimension as well as a technical dimension; that, for instance, "soft" systems analysis must be seen to be as equally important as "hard" systems analysis; that an appreciation of the constraints and contingencies set by the relationships between project organization and project supporters is particularly critical to the success of a project. That IS development is an activity resonant with the negotiation of expectations amongst various stakeholder groups [Boehm88a]. It is particularly important to strengthen the study of such a negotiating process in the light of a diminishing public perception of IS work.

Naming the area of practical computer application as IS Engineering is useful in contributing to the development of the discipline and profession of information systems and information systems development. Including the term engineering in the title, however, does not mean that we need to agree with the rather limited conception of engineering portrayed in many quarters of computing. Information systems, by their very nature, are open to interpretation from a number of different viewpoints. In this respect this chapter has been an attempt to conduct a similar exercise to [Ehn89], in trying to focus on a disciplinary base for the interdisciplinary subject matter of designing computer artefacts.

Chapter 22
Problems in Requirements Communication

22.1 Introduction

Requirements specifications are based on domain knowledge be it technical, functional, administrative or social. Ideally, the requirements team members are selectively recruited so that both the levels and distribution of knowledge within the team cover all aspects of the domain. However, this is seldom the case because of knowledge shortfalls such as the thin spread of application domain knowledge in most organizations [Curtis88]. "In general, individual team members do not have all the knowledge required for the project and must acquire additional information before accomplishing productive work" [Walz93]. Knowledge acquisition and sharing can only be achieved through effective communication between the various stakeholders.

It is widely recognized that communication problems are a major factor in the delay and failure of software projects [Curtis88]. This is especially true of "socio-technical" software systems, which exist in a complex organizational setting. The domains into which such software is introduced are often too intricate and fluid to be fully understood; hence requirements descriptions are uncertain. Furthermore, the specification documentation may be so large that no member of the software team has read it all. In this situation, misunderstandings and conflicting views are rife.

There have been a number of field studies into Software Engineering in general and requirements engineering in particular [Curtis90]. Our study differs from previous field investigations in that it focuses on the communication characteristics of the requirements engineering process. Moreover, our investigation not only utilized the experience of Software Engineering practitioners, it also reflects the views and experiences of end-users based on their recent software procurement projects. The domain of our study was the requirements engineering phase of fully customized software systems development projects. The field study was conducted in two stages using two data gathering methods (interviews and questionnaires).

The research method is described in Section 2 of this chapter. Section 3 describes the communication difficulties and their causes. These include difficulties caused by the nature of Software Engineering notations and methodologies as well as communication barriers caused by social and organizational factors. Each subsection is supported by results from this field study with reference to the relevant literature. Section 4 concludes the chapter with a discussion of these findings and their implications on professional Software Engineering, outlining some future research questions.

22.2 Research Method

A combination of learning, data gathering and analysis techniques were applied to investigate the communication problems, their causes and consequences. The two principle sources of information were the literature and the empirical study. The ever growing literature on Software Engineering in general and requirements engineering in particular was surveyed to gather information about the software development problems, especially those that occur in the early phases, and the sort of tools and techniques that were or are being developed to overcome these problems. A cross section of social science and computer supported co-operative work (CSCW) literature was also surveyed to help in the analysis of the empirical results and reasoning about the possible causes and consequences of communication difficulties.

22.2.1   Empirical work

The aim of the empirical part of this research is to provide material for hypotheses, to aid the identification and reasoning about the communication difficulties and their causes and consequences. Although there are inherent complexities in combining qualitative and quantitative methods, it was decided that such an empirical base was essential to avoid unsupported assertions.

The empirical work was carried out in two stages. The first, consisted of informal interviews and observations to establish some knowledge about practices and methodologies of both developers and their customers. These interviews concentrated mainly on the communication channels between agents participating in any software development project, as well as on the problems that can be attributed to the ineffectiveness of those communication channels. Other management and technical issues were also discussed. Most of these interviews were taped for further analysis and reference. The second stage of our empirical work was based on two questionnaires; one for clients (or end-users of the software) and one for the software developers. These questionnaires were designed to get a quantitative evaluation for the various aspects of the communication activities during Requirements Engineering (RE).

To ensure representative coverage our subjects included users and developers of various levels of experiences, qualifications and backgrounds. The users included some who had just had a software system installed and some with an ongoing project. Their experience with computers ranged from absolute computer illiteracy to qualified experts. The developers were all involved in either developing a new software system or maintaining an existing one. Some were also involved in the provision of hardware systems. Their working area covered all aspects of software development from requirements gathering through to maintenance, as well as project management.

In order to utilize the experience of Software Engineering practitioners as well as the software system procurement experience of their clients, it was necessary to produce two separate questionnaires; a developers' questionnaire and a clients' questionnaire. The former concentrates on the collective experience of practitioners involved in the requirements specification and interpretation. The latter was targeted at end-users who use a new customized software system regardless of their involvement in its development. Another reason for separating the two questionnaires was the technical gap between the two main communities of developers and end-users. Table 22.1 shows the interviews sample and the questionnaires responses. Targeting the questionnaires was very difficult. We relied on personal contacts plus some commercial directories. We asked the recipients of the questionnaires to pass them to the appropriate people. Questionnaires were sent to over 50 companies in the UK and Oman. Responses represent a cross-section of the companies that were targeted.

	Developers (software practitioners)	Clients (end-users of the software)
Interviews Sample Size	6	5
Questionnaires Responses	37	32 (18 Participating & 14 Non-participating)

Table 22.1 Interviews, sample size and questionnaires responses

The interviews showed that practitioners, no matter how experienced, found it easier to be precise about facts and procedures than about opinions and judgements. Therefore we could not simply ask for direct judgements for each of our hypothesis. Instead, each hypothesis was tested in terms of its outward effects and indicators. Most of these turned out to be multi-dimensional and thus had to be measured through more than one indicator. For example, the effect of organizational power was multi-dimensional in that it governs both the choice of participants and their working procedures. It had to be tested in two separate questions each of which had a number of variable answers. In order to get a value for the strength of feeling for each indicator, we employed a Likert Scale method, also known as Semantic differential [Frankfort92]. For each variable we used one to five values of strength in relation to the other variables within the same question.

22.3 Communication Difficulties

Large software projects suffer serious breakdowns in co-ordination and communication throughout the development life-cycle. In this section we present some of the causes for the breakdown of communication during the requirements engineering phase of software development projects.

22.3.1 One-way communication channels

In many ways, Software Engineering methodologies are communication methodologies. Much emphasis is placed on the notations used to convey information both within the development team and with the various stakeholders. Ideally, the channels of communication between these various communities would be perfect, so that all knowledge is shared. In practice, it is expensive and time-consuming to support extensive communication between the communities, and the channels are restricted to one way communication in the form of specification documents. Curtis *et al* observed that documentation is ineffective for communication, as it does not help resolve misunderstandings [Curtis88].

Nevertheless, an implicit "over-the-wall" model exists in most software development projects: at each stage in the project, a specification is thrown over a wall to the next team who are waiting to proceed with the next phase. The metaphorical wall is sometimes encouraged by management practices, but more often is merely a result of the practicalities of co-ordinating a large team. The results of this study showed that specification documents are still the most common format in which analysts communicate requirements back to their clients for validation (see results in Figure 22.1).

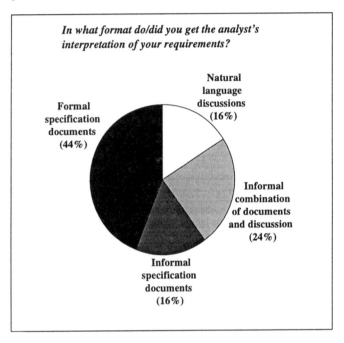

Figure 22.1 Formats in which requirements are communicated

There are two standard approaches to this problem. The first emphasizes the development of better (richer) notations, and effective use of electronic repositories. The second emphasizes the importance of contact between the development team and other stakeholders, and has given rise to practices such as end-user participation and ethnographic techniques. Each of these approaches has its own set of problems, and neither directly addresses the question of facilitating *appropriate* and *effective* communication over restricted channels. Our study showed that practitioners find it easier to adapt a compromise of the two approaches by enriching notations with natural language descriptions and by utilizing the personal contact of face-to-face discussions (see results in Section 22.2).

Moreover, standard software development cycles rely heavily on documentation as an exit condition in moving from stage to stage. Documents are also used as the media for communicating ideas. Consequently, a colossal amount of paper work is generated. The nature, the domain complexity, the variety of methods and notations and the interdependency of partial requirement make it very difficult to establish total consistency. For example, we found that the recipient of the services provided by one of the end-user organizations was referred to as client, customer, applicant, candidate and land owner by different participants who contributed to the production of the specification documents. All these names were used to describe the same entity. The names used reflected the concern of each stakeholder.

22.3.2 The notations war

While programmers, software engineers and analysts are happy talking about the system in terms of it procedures and data structures, end-users prefer to talk about the system in terms of its general behaviour, functionality and applications. The different communities involved in the specification process prefer different types of notation, and various people will be unfamiliar with various notations. For example, a user will not want to learn to read formal specification languages, but the programmer may require these to obtain an appropriate level of detail.

It is often the analyst's responsibility to choose the notations that will best describe the system for each interest group. Thereafter, the chosen notations are used to explain the system differently to each group. In doing so, the analyst combines the notations with other explanation techniques, to make notations easier to read and understand. The choice of the explanatory tools utilized by the analysts and the extent to which they are needed depend on the notation used and the audience's familiarity with the notation.

Typically, two types of knowledge are used as a high-level framework to anchor detailed knowledge: control flow information, which might be represented by specialized notations such as pseudo code and flowcharts; and data structure information, which might be represented using diagrams or a textual description [Shneiderman82]. Some software, such as traditional numerical analysis systems have a complex control structure with relatively simple data structures. On the other hand, traditional commercial applications have complex data structures with relatively simple control flow. Sheppard, Kruesi and Curtis conducted an experiment to compare comprehension with nine forms of program description including natural language, a program design language, flowcharts and hierarchical diagrams [Sheppard81b]. They found different results for different types of questions, but no particular style appeared to dominate. However, in their study of program coding from the nine notations, Sheppard and Kruesi found that the program design language and flowchart diagrams were more helpful than natural language descriptions [Sheppard81a].

Regardless of the chosen notations, most users express their requirements in natural language. Then it is the job of the analyst to translate requirements statements into some kind of representational objects in a domain model. Once the requirements are modelled, they are presented to end-users for validation. At this stage the analysts are faced with another communication problem when end-users are not familiar with the notations used to model their requirements. On the other hand, when analysts, under pressure to keep up with the project schedule, pass raw natural language requirements to programmers, then time is wasted in trying to interpret them. A programmer we interviewed during our empirical study complained that he often has to read large amounts of text in order to understand a single requirement, which could have been represented very concisely using a diagram or a formal notation. In one case he had to read over a page of text to understand the requirements for a screen layout for a particular database form. This, he said, could have been represented more accurately by drawing a diagram to indicate the required dimensions of each section of the screen.

When asked whether their clients find the notations they use readable, only 4 developers (14% of 35 developers who answered this question) said that their notations are readable and understandable to end-users, and 31 developers (86%) said that their customers would normally need additional explanation in order to understand the notations in which requirements are specified. In order to examine the ways in which this additional information is provided, we asked those who provided additional information about the methods they use. Figure 22.2 shows the results.

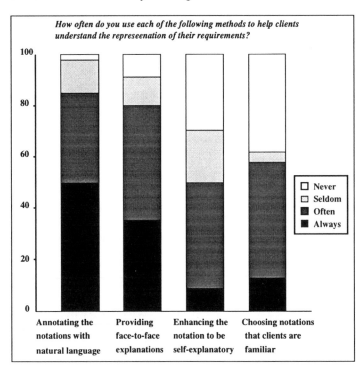

Figure 22.2 Methods of providing additional explanation

We can see from Figure 22.2 that almost half of the respondents (15 out of 31) said that they "always" annotate the notations with natural language. Around 40% (12) also said they often use this method, around 10% (3) said they seldom use it and only one responded saying they never use this method. This makes "annotating the notations with natural language" the most popular method for making the requirements representations readable to end-users. The second most popular method is providing face-to-face explanation of the notations. However, around a third (10) of the respondents said that they **never** go out of their way to choose a notation that is readable to their clients as a practice that aims to aid the communication process. We can also see from Figure 22.2 that for every method, at least half the respondents use them "always" or "often". This suggests that most practitioners usually use one or more of theses methods. The choice of the explanatory method utilized by the practitioner depends on the notation used and the clients' familiarity with the notation.

22.3.3 Organizational barriers

Organizational barriers that inhibit communication among development teams are often ignored. For example, conventional Software Engineering practices divide the processes and tasks performed by different groups into separate phases. This can inhibit effective and timely communication between groups performing different tasks at different phases. For example, RE activities and software design activities are often separated. That is, they are performed and discussed by different sets of people. While RE meetings include both developers (usually analysts) and end-user representatives, design review meetings are normally restricted to members of the development team.

Within existing software development practices, design review meetings are used to mitigate communication problems. Formally, these are used to pre-empt problems, by using senior members of the project team to review evolving designs at various stages. This will involve checking for common mistakes, and questioning the assumptions made by the designer. Meetings are also used, usually informally, to respond to problems. Note that design review meetings do not, as a rule, involve anyone outside the development team: meetings with clients are usually stage-managed. The strength of design review meetings lie in their ability to exploit different perspectives to spot things that the designer or programmer might have overlooked. During the process, many of the assumptions held by members of the group will be explicitly tested. The fresh perspectives are able to identify much of the blindness that a designer inevitably develops when immersed in the design process. It also serves to clarify ambiguities in the specification documents. However, [Curtis90] observed that design meetings are often dominated by a small number of individuals characterized by their deep understanding of the application domain coupled with the ability to translate application behaviour into computational structures. Consequently, the less experienced individuals do not get equal opportunities to voice their ideas and concerns.

We found that the effects of organizational power start with the selection of the client representatives who attend requirements meetings and go on to control what goes on in these meetings. We presented the developers with a set of options for how they choose client representatives, and asked them to give a value for how often they use each one. We present their responses in Figure 22.3.

We can see from the results shown in Figure 22.3 that software practitioners depend heavily on the client authorities in selecting the requirements committee members to represent the client organization. Ideally, "domain knowledge" would be the most important quality on which software practitioners should base the choice of members. However, when control is given to the client's managers, the choices can be based on a number of factors, many of which have more to do with other commercial interests of the clients' business than with the software project. To confirm this we asked end-users who were selected to participate in the requirements specification process to indicate

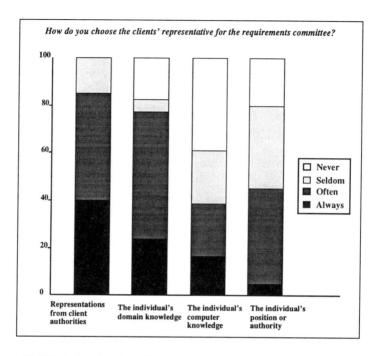

Figure 22.3 Basis for choosing client representatives for requirements committees

why, in their opinion, they were chosen. We also asked those who did not participate to indicate why they were not chosen. Figure 22.4 shows a shocking similarity between the responses to these two questions.

We can also see from the results shown in Figure 22.4 that "work nature" is the most decisive factor in the selection of end-users for participating in the requirements specification process. This may sound like the right thing to do, after all domain knowledge depends on the work nature. However, the interviews showed that managers, when selecting members of their staff, try to strike a balance between allowing the software practitioners to talk to the right people and maintaining the smooth running of the rest of the business. The results in Figure 22.5 show the amount of interference to business caused by the software procurement project. The amount of interference reported by the participating end-users was less than expected. An explanation for this is that the choice of participants is made in such a way as to minimize interference. This in turn suggests that the smooth running of the clients organization is given greater priority than the successful outcome of the software development project.

The results shown in Figure 22.5, show why managers might not select their best staff to be committed to work with the software practitioners throughout the software project life-cycle. Such a conflict of interests makes the analysts' job much more difficult. We found that the requirements committee members are often people of authority, with limited contact with the low-level tasks of the business. These low-level tasks are often the tasks that need to be computerized.

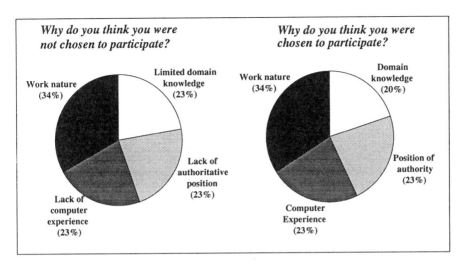

Figure 22.4 End-users' opinions on factors affecting their selection to participate

22.3.4   Informal communication

Organizations are, traditionally, described in terms of an *Organizational chart*. This is often the first thing handed out to anyone inquiring about the structure of the organization. However, many important power and communication relationships are not represented in the organizational chart. [Mintzberg79] makes an analogy between the organizational chart and a road map, where the map is invaluable for finding towns and their connecting roads, but it tells us nothing about the economic or social relationships between the regions. Although, very useful in terms of providing information about formal authority and the division of organizational units, the organizational chart does not tell us anything about the informal relationships that exist in every organization.

During the interviews that we conducted with practitioners, they outlined many difficulties that are caused by unexpected interactions between elements of the system, be it software modules or humans. In spite of the time and effort spent on studying organizational structures and the flow of power and information through them, our subjects admit that they can never account for all possible interactions and often have to backtrack as a result of discovering a new relation or line of communication that has to be incorporated into the system. These interactions are often too complex to be traced or regulated.

Informal communication is based on friendships, common interests and special co-operative relations creating channels through which information flows easily and perhaps taking shortcuts. On the other hand, such informal communication channels can be destroyed by rivalries and animosities, which can discourage co-operation and affect the normal flow of information. However, there is no specific support for informal communication within the organizational settings for software projects especially at the early phase of RE where analysts and their clients, in many cases, meet for the first time.

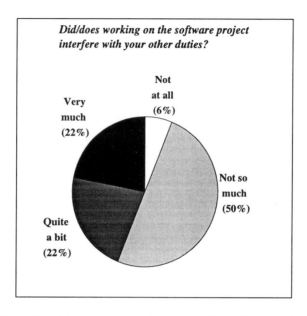

Figure 22.5 Interference to business caused by software projects

Gotel and Finkelstein found that practitioners attach extreme importance to personal contact and informal communication [Gotel94]. We found that informal communications such as "telephone conversations" are the least used method in exchanging information between the two communities (see results in Figure 22.6). On the other hand, face-to-face discussion are widely used in spite of their higher cost. The lack of alternative interactive support for such informal communication forces analysts to resort to expensive and time consuming discussions and meetings.

22.3.5   The missing link

The inability to trace the human sources of actual requirements and their related information is identified as the crux of the requirements traceability problem [Gotel94]. Requirements Traceability is vital for all phases of the software development cycle to aid reasoning about requirements and justify changes.   Our study showed that the traceability problem is particularly serious in the later stages of requirements engineering (e.g.   requirements review) and in cases when new requirements are introduced late in the project life-cycle.

In order to check that newly introduced requirements do not conflict with existing requirements, it is often necessary to re-establish communication with the human sources of existing requirements. This is particularly problematic, because by this time the analysts may have reduced, or even halted, contact with the end-users of the software; and may even have started working on a new project, while their programmers get on with later phases of this project. Figure 22.7 presents the links that practitioners use in order to establish requirements traceability to the requirements sources.

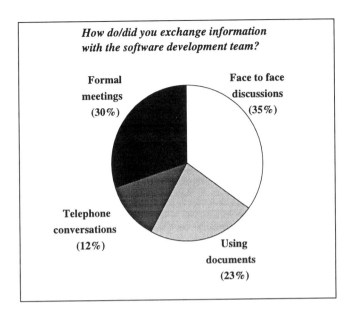

Figure 22.6 Methods by which end-users exchange information with analysts

We can see from the results shown in Figure 22.7 that most analysts link the requirements only very generally to user groups and departments, which means that traceability is not direct. Only 15% linked the requirements to their individual sources by name, which means that those source can be traced directly if necessary. The link to job titles might sound like a good idea, but it does not work in dynamic organizations where people move between jobs and even move between organizations.

There are growing numbers of specialized tools that support requirements traceability, but their use is not widespread. Requirements traceability problems are still cited by practitioners who do not use such tools [Gotel94]. In fact, none of the practitioners we interviewed used requirements traceability specialized tools, and those who used the more general CASE tools were not able to see any major improvements in requirements traceability. This is due to the constraints imposed by many of the CASE tools, the time and effort put into following their strict methodologies, and their limited support for the early stages of requirements specification.

Rationales of design decisions are rooted in the requirements specification. Many design decisions involve trade offs between competing requirements. The decision taken might not be the best solution, instead it may be an acceptable one for parties. Information about these decisions and the rationales behind them is crucial for the later phases of the software development, particularly the maintenance phase. However, because of the limitations of conventional Software Engineering methodologies and notations, many design rationales go unrecorded. Our observations during interviews showed that some developers do actually keep some kind of traceability for the rationales behind some of the features in the solution product rather than rationales behind the original user requirements.

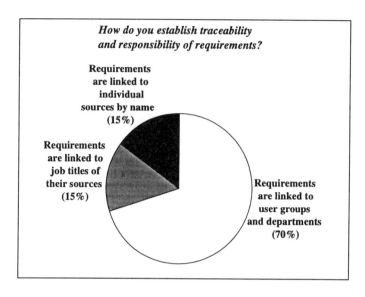

Figure 22.7 Links software practitioners use to trace requirements sources

22.4   Conclusions

There are a number of pitfalls in trying to make effective use of restricted communication channels. One of the dangers is that each community interprets things in the light of their own background assumptions. This is especially problematic with non-interactive communication, such as specification documents, where there is no opportunity to check that the reader has interpreted them as was intended. [McDermid93] points out a fundamental problem to do with the communication of abstract concepts, in that requirements specifications "document what it is that the analyst thought it was that the problem owner said he thought he might want". The uncertainties that McDermid describes propagate and multiply at each exchange of information. Robinson and Bannon use the term "Ontological Drift" to describe the change in meaning of abstract terms as they are passed between different communities [Robinson91].

In this chapter we noted that documents are a poor substitute for interpersonal communication. This we attributed to the inherent restrictions of the available notations. While we appreciate the role of meetings such as design reviews in clarifying ambiguities and resolving conflicts in the specification documents, we feel that more can be done to make these documents into a more effective means of communication. A pressing and practical problem is to find-out more about the communicational weaknesses of current notations and methods so we can accommodate for their weaknesses. For each concern, we need to determine what types of question that concern may wish to make of a description produced in a notation. This can only be achieved by observing the meetings and conversations in which descriptions are referred to. For such research to succeed, software professionals must be willing to co-operate and allow researchers to learn from their practical experiences.

There is, and there will always be, what we can call an informal organization within the formal organization that is represented by the organizational chart. Software professionals need to accommodate such an organization in their project management and planing. They need to identify the different categories of communication; regulated, unregulated, formal, informal, interpersonal, internal to the project, external and so on. Informal communications need to be encouraged between all stakeholders. Software practitioners need to invest time in establishing direct and informal contact with end-users. However, much research is needed before support for such informal communication activities can be integrated into CASE tools.

The results described in this chapter showed that organizational and social issues have great influence on the effectiveness of communication activities and therefore on the overall success or failure of the requirements engineering process. Such effects start with restricting the selection of client representatives and often propagate throughout the software project life-cycle. The study has also showed that in general end-users have little or no influence on the choice of methods and notations in which their requirements are represented and consequently find the notations used by software practitioners difficult to understand and validate. Software practitioners have reported this communication problem and they normally deal with it through a combination of face-to-face explanations and natural language annotations of the notations rather than choosing notations that are readable to their clients.

In general, the findings presented here provide an insight for future research into the communicational and organizational aspects of software development. The practical implications of theses findings include: indicating where and how organizational power is used, outlining the extent to which software practitioners rely on documents as the main communication medium, revealing the dangers of the technical gap between the two main communities and presenting informal communications as the means for bridging that gap.

Chapter 23

Responsibilities under the Capability Maturity Model

23.1 Introduction

Software Engineering teams in organizations of all types and sizes are facing increasing pressure to deliver high-quality, complex products in highly competitive, complex and global environments. Concurrent with the increased mission-critical status of software and the reduced time to market inherent in many software development environments is the drive for higher quality which is increasingly being measured by process assessments. The Software Capability Maturity Model (CMM) developed by the Software Engineering Institute (SEI) at Carnegie Mellon University addresses key process areas (KPAs) for progressively higher (or more mature) levels of software development. Incumbent within these different levels of software development maturity are clear indicators of appropriate professional responsibilities for software engineers. The CMM is focused on process, however, and does not directly address people or teams and the issues arising from changing professional responsibilities. This chapter examines these responsibilities, many of which have new or renewed importance for software development professionals, in the context of the software maturity levels defined by the SEI CMM.

23.2 Organizational Environment

All companies in today's fast changing competitive environment are expected to respond to such an environment by continuous innovation of products and processes. Large established companies, which have been in business for at least ten years, face the dilemma of the need to respond to their external environment through innovation and the constraints of their hardened internal environment which is not conducive to innovation.

Established large companies tend to have more rationalized operations, based on their past experience, and tend to retain routines which have proved to be previously successful. Moreover, the vested interest of the members of these companies in the existing operation and structure, hardens in order that they may maintain the existing distribution of resources and privileges. This in turn results in increased bureaucratization [Aldrich86]. Such mechanisms, which result from the aging process, are constraints which limit the possibilities of adapting quickly to the external environment. Thus, the major problem of established companies in a competitive environment is the problem of strategic transformation.

The structure which fits with the entrepreneurial strategy should be flexible with adequate coordination and synthesis [Miller83]. While new and small firms achieve these qualities by using an organic informal structure [Aiken71], large established organizations may achieve both flexibility and synthesis through formal frequent reorganization and through the use of intrapreneurial teams [Taylor90]. A collective orientation, rather than an individual orientation, is expected to make the functioning of such teams more effective [Saleh87].

The climate of the innovative organization which supports entrepreneurial strategy, is expected to be open and promotive [Burgelman88], a climate based on collegiality [Souder87], and a climate with a well-planned reward system which reinforces the above expected behaviours [Balkin88]. While such a climate in a new and small entrepreneurial organization may be part of its developmental stage, an established large organization should expend special effort to develop such a climate if it is to be innovative.

In sum, large established firms can be innovative if they overcome the constraints of their hardened bureaucratic internal environment and use an entrepreneurial strategy with the structure and the climate which facilitate its implementation.

23.3 Managing People and Teams

When undertaking product development a large company must also employ specialized teams whose tasks include monitoring trends in their area of expertise so that such information is available when required. [Johne84] has stressed that procedures aimed at staying abreast of product developments based on existing technology can help alert a business in good times to threats and opportunities associated with the shift to a new technological plateau.

A team will usually arrive at better solutions than will individuals. The creation and maintenance of knowledgeable, experienced and committed design teams is based on this principle. It is essential to stress the team concept since throwing more people into the design process is not sufficient. To ensure the responsive functioning of the mixture of specialists, these teams must be glued together by effective management. [Thamhain90] has stated that the establishment of multi-function teams, integrating members and training them is essential to successful product development.

Managing product development teams is also a challenge. [Kolodny80] has shown the benefits of matrix structures while Hull and Hager showed that organic, flatter hierarchies foster innovation [Hull82]. Again, however, it is essential to recognize the joint interplay of innovation and delivery of a tested design. [Moore87] found an increase in formal development procedures necessary to ensure the maintenance of quality throughout the design stages. [Johne84] also showed how experienced innovators used informal and non-standardized procedures in the initiation phase but then applied more formal standardized tests to provide checks and to give tight coordination as the time for product launch approached.

Management can also more clearly define relationships concerning roles and responsibilities between software developers and users. This approach recognizes the importance of communication between customer and software developer as well as between professionals with different skills. For example, it is inevitable that teams of Information Systems and functional area professionals formed to create complex information systems bring distinctive varieties of human behaviour and learning to any complex development effort which may deeply affect the resulting system. This occurs despite structure imposed by task requirements, group behaviour norms and external standards. It is expected that by establishing formal procedures for communication, performance will be enhanced and problems diminished. Another aim of this approach is to move the emphasis of the development from being an artistic expression to one of engineering. Some research [Couger90], however, shows that the single most important motivator for data processing professionals is the job itself.

In addition, self-managed teams appear to be evolving at a rapid pace as a result of Total Quality Management (TQM) and re-engineering initiatives in many organizations. The literature shows many studies which demonstrate that extraordinary productivity results when people are placed in self-managed teams in highly constrained environments. There is a substantial literature relating tales of "heroic" operations working against impossible deadlines with minimal resources, thereby becoming extraordinarily motivated and sometimes flouting the expectations of the mature parent organization. Some of these projects were poorly structured but, nevertheless, succeeded as a result of the personalities of the leaders [Kidder81]. It is now recognized, however, that poorly structured development efforts often fail despite individual heroic efforts. Instead, the trend is toward structured, team-based, process-driven and quality-focused software development environments.

23.4   Software Capability Maturity Model

A software process movement emerged in the mid-1980s when shortcomings in managing software development processes were recognized as impediments to improving software reliability and quality. One model of software process maturity that has received considerable attention is the Capability Maturity Model (CMM) developed by the Software Engineering Institute (SEI) at Carnegie Mellon University in Pittsburgh [Paulk93].

The original SEI software process maturity model was developed to assess large software houses developing technical systems for the US Air Force and other defence agencies. Software process improvement provides guidelines for an organization to employ a structured approach to strategically improve all aspects of a software development operation and dramatically changes or extends concepts previously employed under recognized systems development models such as the waterfall and spiral approach [Royce70], [Boehm88b]. Organizations previously would often attempt to improve performance in an ad-hoc manner by using technology-driven approaches instead of addressing root problems. For example, organizations would often assign more staff or more tools to an already late and over-budget development project rather than addressing the reasons why the project had problems.

In contrast, in a mature organization (as measured under the CMM framework), managers use metrics to quantitatively measure the quality of a software product. Schedules and budgets are based on historical performance and are realistic; the predicted results for product cost, schedule, functionality and quality are routinely achieved. Based on the predictability of the project results, reliable management decisions can be made about tradeoffs among these outcomes. Models such as the CMM should contribute toward lower costs and reduced intervals because they result in high quality processes. These processes are capable of predictable results (producing high quality software products) which in turn help with the planning and management of projects.

The model is intended to provide the infrastructure and support necessary to help an organization manage software projects. To achieve lasting results from process improvement efforts, the model was designed so that the organization could evolve from an immature to a mature software development organization [Paulk93]. The maturity framework for software development was formulated by Humphrey at IBM in the 1980s, and in 1986, he brought this work to SEI and added the concept of the maturity levels.

According to SEI, the maturity framework underlying the CMM applies quality management practices to the process of software development. The framework rates organizations as being at one of five levels of maturity ranging from the initial level to the optimizing level. A major aspect of the CMM's maturity framework is that a practice can be improved if the same practice can be predictably repeated. For example, a level one organization may not have effective written policies on how to estimate software size and consequently such an organization would be unable to ensure consistency and repeatability in this aspect of its software development practices. An organization's progress toward higher maturity levels in the CMM is measured by periodically conducting formal assessments of its internal processes.

The maturity levels are well defined evolutionary plateaus that organizations strive for to improve their software processes. Each level contains key process areas (KPAs) that when satisfied bring consistency to components of the software process. For example, within the repeatable maturity level (level 2), one of the KPAs is requirements management. A software process that can satisfy the goal, commitment, ability, activity, and measurement criteria associated with this KPA as specified by the CMM for effective requirements management has a higher level of maturity (and more predictability) than a software process that cannot satisfy the goals of this KPA.

23.5 Team-Based Process Maturity

Part of the reason for the recent attention on software process improvement initiatives is that empirical research consistently shows that many software development projects suffer from a lack of proven and well-established methods. Standards such as the CMM have only recently advanced beyond the embryonic stage and gained acceptance by a wide variety of organizations [Humphrey91b].

Most improvement programs to date, however, have emphasized process or technology and not people. People management practices in many organizations, despite a significant amount of literature addressing people-related issues [Kim93], [Kraut95], [Pressman95], [Rasch92], [Thompson93b], do not address people issues in a systematic and structured manner. In addition, most managers are untrained or inadequately trained in implementing corrective solutions once people problems are identified [Rettig93], [Statz94], [Zahniser93]. Furthermore, organizational factors, although widely cited [Constantine93], [Constantine95], [McIntyre92], [McIntyre94], are often not systematically analyzed for their effect on process improvement efforts.

The characteristics of SEI levels show that Software Engineering projects workers must be capable of being highly productive in complex, team-oriented environments, with strong emphases on process control and overall quality [Walz93], [Zultner93]. These requirements are essential but may not always be present in current professionals. The lack of appropriate team and process control skills can greatly contribute to internal organizational volatility.

The CMM breaks down the Software Engineering capabilities of organizations into 5 maturity levels from Level 1 (Initial) to level 5 (Optimizing). Generally, the levels can be characterized in terms of *team and management* processes as:

Level 1 — *Initial:* There are no well-defined procedures and management. Roles of the design team members are not well-defined. Project and design information is not stored or communicated effectively. The organization does not consistently apply good engineering management to the software development process. Descriptors such as "ad-hoc" and "chaotic" have been frequently applied to this level. Early assessments done by SEI found that more than 80% of assessed organizations were at Level 1.

Level 2 — *Repeatable:* The organization has achieved a stable process with a repeatable management control level by initiating rigorous project management of commitments, costs, schedules and changes. The organization uses standard practices for managing development activities including: staff estimating; cost estimating; scheduling; change and version control on requirements, specifications and design data; and managerial reviews. The managers are trained in these management practices and software engineers are trained on the use of tools and procedures. The organization is good at doing similar types of work but is challenged by new types of work because it lacks an orderly framework for improvement.

Level 3 — *Defined:* The organization has defined the process as a basis for consistent implementation and better understanding. Goals, objectives and strategies are developed and promulgated. The software development organization is multi-disciplinary and a Software Engineering Process Group (SEPG) is established to lead process improvement. At this point, the risk of introducing advanced technology is greatly reduced.

Level 4 — *Managed:* The organization has initiated comprehensive process measurements and analysis. This is when the most significant quality improvements begin. Senior management is involved in the product and process management. The performance of the design process is monitored and measured; data gathering is repeatable and auditable. The organization typically bases its operating decisions on quantitative process data, and conducts extensive analysis of the data gathered during reviews and tests. Early assessments conducted by SEI found no organizations operating at this level.

Level 5 — *Optimized:* The organization has a foundation for continuously improving and optimizing the process. It conducts analyses of the metrics gathered during the design process and uses them for planning improvements. It focuses on improving and optimizing the process and products by establishing improvement goals for quality, productivity and cost. Early assessments conducted by SEI found no organizations operating at this level.

23.6 CMM Professional Responsibilities

23.6.1 Team orientation

This is perhaps the most commonly cited characteristic of successful software process improvement efforts, particularly those based on the CMM. A team orientation is often necessary because organizations have become leaner and less hierarchical to remain competitive. Ramifications of this structural change in organizations include requiring that software professionals not adopt insulated work modes but instead develop business, managerial and political skills to successfully negotiate with multiple constituencies and integrate the software development effort with the strategic plans of the organization. Software professionals must also develop stronger communication, coordinative and collaborative skills to successfully satisfy the key process areas in the CMM.

23.6.2 Process focus

Software development professionals also need to develop a process orientation. Software development teams with a process focus work to prevent crises, monitor user satisfaction and the quality of their software products, and manage and improve their software processes based on quantitative information. As the focus on process and process maturity increases, institutionalization of the software process is achieved via policies, standards and organizational structure. Individual software developers must temper inclinations to develop software in ad-hoc, undisciplined and non-repeatable ways.

23.6.3 Quality focus

Software is increasingly becoming a mission-critical resource for all types of organizations. If software is unreliable in any way, organizations may face disastrous consequences. Improved quality is the reason behind software process improvement efforts and the CMM in particular. The CMM is based on the work of Deming, Juran, Crosby and other pioneers in the quality movement. Quality principles, methods and techniques are of critical importance, therefore, for software developers operating under the CMM.

23.6.4 Interdisciplinary

Effective teams have members who know the tasks of others and can provide backup and feedback capabilities to the other members of the team. This means that tasks are not compartmentalized and integrated only at the end of the development effort. From the start of the development effort under the CMM, effective teams contain individuals who know one another's individual jobs, offer to help fellow team members when it is appropriate to help, and depend on one another for this help. In addition, software development teams must interact with many other external teams within and outside the organization to coordinate all aspects of the CMM-based process.

23.6.5   Continuous learning

Software development professionals must continually update their skills and expertise not only in technical areas but also in organizational, business, managerial and teamwork areas. The CMM specifically requires that all individuals receive mandatory training in teamwork and asks if sufficient resources are allocated to this activity (in the Level 3 KPA of Intergroup Coordination). The importance of this area cannot be over-emphasized since time for education and training must be built into project schedules.

23.6.6   Agent of change

Instituting a process-focused software development environment requires much change in the way software has traditionally been developed in many organizations. Change management techniques must be utilized to overcome individual and group resistance to the new ways. Benefits of the change must be clearly articulated and reward systems implemented that recognize the shift from individual effort to team- and process-driven effort.

23.6.7   Awareness of purpose

Each software engineer must always know why they and their skills and competence have been allocated to a certain team or function in the development process thereby giving each person's work more meaning in the overall organizational perspective. Team and functional assignments should be presented in the correct context both in terms or organization and required results in order to give a clear purpose for the assignment and team composition.

23.6.8   Goal driven

A team must have common goals and objectives in order for the team members to achieve maximum performance. This can be assured by having team members together plan for the execution of the assignment. Together the team members develop a plan where they show how to reach the goals of their assignment and agree on how each team member will contribute. This joint planning assures that each team member has the same intention toward the assignment and that they are focused on reaching the assignment goals through a common path.

23.6.9   Commitment

Successful team work is based on trust. Trust is based on the belief that all parties will complete their work according to previously defined methods and schedules and that any difficulty with these methods or schedules will be communicated and resolved. A commitment is a trust-based agreement. In a team-based environment there exists both internal commitments within the team among the team members as well as external commitments between the team and external parties. The way both internal and external commitments are achieved is to assure that all work assignments are based on agreements and negotiations where any changes are subject for renegotiation. Internally the team members develop and commit to the team's common plan and goals by negotiating their contribution and responsibilities. Based on these internal commitments the team negotiates with the assignment stakeholder in order to reach an agreement that the team believes in and can externally commit to.

23.6.10   Empowered actions

In order to maximize performance and to benefit from each team member's unique experience and skills, teams and team members must be empowered to make decisions regarding their work. Thus, the assignment that the team is given must indicate the scope of responsibilities for the team. Empowerment is based on trust that the team members will make correct decisions in order to strive to fulfill the assignment's purpose and goals. Assuring that understanding of the purpose and commitment to the whole is established up front is the basis for empowerment. Note that empowerment must also exist within the team. Each team member must be empowered to make decisions regarding their work in order to best contribute to the team's common assignment plan and goals. Hence, the team leader's responsibility shifts from supervising to facilitating.

23.6.11   Accountability

To be accountable means that a person is held responsible for the results (good or bad) and is given recognition for the success. From a team member's perspective the team is together accountable for the delivered results since it is the team that commits to delivering according to the plan. This means that from an external perspective all deliverables are team deliverables and there exists no individual ownership of the deliverables. However, within the team each individual member has committed their individual contribution to the team's assignment plan and will be held accountable within the team for fulling that. agreement.

23.6.12   Intellectual control

Intellectual control of a team assignment means that all team members at all times know exactly what to do, why it has to be done and who is supposed to do it. The prerequisite for intellectual control is to have a clear, visible and feasible assignment plan within the team. Another benefit of having a clear and visible plan is that the team will have the possibility of performing sequence analysis and replanning when changes occur.

23.7   Conclusions

The CMM is becoming a widely used model for software process improvement. Although this model does not extensively discuss people or team issues successful satisfaction of the KPAs in the model requires that the software development organization function as a team-based entity. Research has shown that one of the most difficult changes that software development professionals face in adopting the CMM (as well as other similar process improvement models) is in becoming a fully functioning and effective team member. The evolution from being an individual performer to a team performer requires the acquisition of new skills and the acceptance of new responsibilities. Organizations undertaking software process improvement efforts (particularly those following or based on the CMM) should also institute training and feedback sessions on teamwork and the professional responsibilities discussed in this chapter. The combination of these two approaches has been shown to be effective in helping software professionals adjust to the new development environment [McGuire96].

Chapter 24
Revenge of the Methodology Anarchist

24.1 The Methodology Minefield

24.1.1 Introduction

The Software Engineering profession has an unfortunate tendency to equate professionalism with methodologies. This chapter argues that "software engineer" plus "software methodology" does not equal "professional software engineer." It examines the relationship between methodologies, practitioners and customers. While acknowledging that methodologies can help to deliver systems, it focuses on the many ways in which methodology abuse can hinder successful Software Engineering. The chapter describes popular methodology pitfalls which will be familiar to all professional software engineers. It offers pragmatic advice to help software engineers to exploit, rather than be exploited by, methodologies.

24.1.2 Inspirations

A few years ago I was lucky enough to have a free hand in forging a team responsible for analysing, designing and delivering systems. It was great fun, and I had the opportunity to implement some of my beliefs about the "right" way to use methodologies, to work with customers, and to prototype and deliver systems. Our FitWare mission was simple:

- produce high quality software fit for customers needs

- deliver on time

- have fun

Among the many inspirations behind our approach were:

- RAD (Rapid Application Development)

- RIP (Rapid Iterative Prototyping)

- Timeboxing

- methodologies, including SSADM, Information Engineering and SDM

- PRINCE project management concepts

- 4th Generation software development environments

- common sense

24.1.3   A methodology "health warning"

You will have spotted that despite being a methodology anarchist, there is no shortage of methodological inspiration in the above list. I like methodologies. Many of them include really useful tools to help the software engineer. But I also believe that the professional software engineer has to use them with immense care if they are not to become an end in themselves. All methodologies should carry a prominent health warning that goes something like:

This methodology does not:

- *solve problems*

- *guarantee good solutions*

- *replace innovation*

- *replace common sense*

- *DELIVER SYSTEMS*

This salutary warning would help to remind software engineers that their real mission is to deliver systems, not methodology end-products.

24.1.4   Methodology evolution

Methodologies are an important component in the evolution of computing towards respectable engineering professionalism. They promise that Software Engineering has developed from an art into a science, with controllable, predictable and successful guaranteed outcomes.

Once upon a time, in the Dark Ages of computing, when science fiction heroes could cause evil computers to explode simply by typing "WHY?" on the teletype, there were no methodologies. Programming was a Black Art, practised by solitary programmer wizards. Of course, the scale of problems tackled in the dark ages was typically computational rather than systems based — it was hard enough just to program computers. With the IT industrial revolution, computers began to be used to provide partial solutions to system problems. The scope of problems to be addressed by IT became bigger, more complicated, more expensive and ultimately more business-critical. With the evolution of software through third and fourth generation languages, and now, object oriented environments, the focus of methodologies has moved away from bits and bytes and towards business processes.

At the top end of the methodology tree, we have approaches that claim to attack whole systems and business processes, systems that embrace people as well as IT [Checkland81]. Combined systems analysis and design methods aim to provide a seamless join between logical system requirements and realisable computer systems design. Some methods embedded into software tools even claim to generate systems automatically.

There is a large element of fashion involved in methodologies. We are currently seeing a shift away from predominantly data driven methods, towards a more process oriented paradigm, fuelled by object oriented IT concepts and the vogue for Business Process Re-engineering.

24.1.5 What customers want

Customers — the people who pay us — want useful Information Systems that support their business requirements. Our customers are not terribly interested in methodologies. They want systems that:

- work

- help their business

- can evolve with their changing requirements

- are delivered on time (ideally quickly)

- are delivered within their cost constraints

24.1.6 What the software engineer needs

Help, and lots of it! During the analysis phase we have to extract a model of the required system from an understanding of the customers' environment and the customers' vaguely expressed wishes. As professionals, we temper this model by applying the art of the possible. It is very difficult to communicate requirements:

> "We know that you believe you understand what you think we said, but we are not sure you realize that what you heard is not what we meant" [Stealers72]

During design we need the methodology to help us to model a variety of alternative workable system designs. We need to be able to explain these options to our customer and offer decision-making advice. Finally, we need to be able to turn the preferred abstract model into a deliverable system which will probably include computer system components and human involvement.

The software engineer needs methodologies to help get a grasp on slippery system requirements; to make these big, difficult problems into smaller, manageable problems. By helping to fragment and simplify complex problems, methodologies also provide an opportunity for teamworking, for dividing work up and working in parallel to reduce delivery timetables. The methodology should help team members to share a common approach. The ideal methodology would help us to solve difficult problems. It will combine a certain degree of logical rigour, with a dose of pragmatic advice, spiced with proven heuristics.

24.1.7 What methodologies should provide

With the benefit of a methodology we should be able to deliver better systems, more quickly and more cheaply. At their best, methodologies provide a valuable formalization of common sense. They should give us a standard way of approaching problems with some guarantees that our solution is complete and workable (although not necessarily ideal). A shared methodology should provide a language for communication between team members, and between the software engineers and customers. In summary, the methodology should provide:

- a formalized way of looking at a problem

- a set of problem solving and modelling tools to help to deliver a solution

- a minimalist procedural framework linking the tools

- a medium for communicating between interested parties

- guidance in developing a workable solution

As an entirely reasonable software engineer, I don't expect the methodology to help me to leap giant buildings with a single bound, or fly faster than a speeding bullet.

To be fair, the stated objectives of SSADM V4 [CCTA90a] closely match the above specification. They even include a ninth objective *Avoid IT developers' bureaucracy*, which I heartily applaud.

24.2   Handle with Care

24.2.1   There is no escape

As a software engineer you will need to know about methodologies so that you can converse knowledgeably with your colleagues and with prospective employers. You will need methodologies on your CV. You will need to be a confident exploiter of methodologies so that you can deliver systems with their help (or in spite of it!). You may well be forced to use methodologies because they are organizational or contractual standards. Even if you are a cynical methodology anarchist you will be faced with the choice of conforming or being unemployed.

Given that methodologies are designed to help, rather than hinder, the real problem is that many software engineers really don't know how to use them properly. The innocent scalpel is an inoffensive, elegant, shiny object, just like all those nicely bound methodology manuals. In the hands of a skilled surgeon the scalpel can be an immensely useful tool. It is an excellent device for cutting things with great precision, but it is not a good screwdriver. In the wrong hands the scalpel can wreak havoc. Mishandled, the patient will bleed to death, and the surgeon will have severe business problems. Similarly, methodologies used appropriately by skilled practitioners, in the right circumstances will help to deliver systems. Mishandled, they can seriously damage the health of both software engineers and customers. The following paragraphs describe some truths that the professional needs to remember when using methodologies.

24.2.2   The methodology product life-cycle

One day, when I've got time, I will develop a methodology. So far, I've only completed the "current system analysis" covering the methodology product life-cycle. It goes like this:

First, you need a novel concept, a slick idea, or in marketing jargon, a USP (Unique Selling Proposition). Ideally you should back this up with practical successes and academic credibility.

Next, you need a good product name. A snappy TLA (Three Letter Abbreviation) is best, especially one that is easy to pronounce, or emotive, or both. RAD and RIP are excellent examples of the genre. You probably need to write a book, or journal articles. Joint authorship can help, because it gives the impression that it is not the sole idea of a crazed individual. If your own name is not memorably distinctive and unusual, you should seek out co-authors with names that fit the bill.

After two or three practical success stories you can devise a course to teach others how to use your methodology. Make your course difficult and challenging. Encourage your pupils to become evangelists for your method. It may be a good idea to introduce certificates for qualified practitioners to establish a freemasonry of converts. Any organization or project that is going to use your methodology will, of course, require expert consultancy. If methodology users go awry (through insufficient skill and expertise), they will also need to hire your expensive consultancy services to return them to the straight and narrow.

Develop software tools to help your methodology converts with the tricky problems of drawing all of those pictures and integrating the many and varied components of your methodology. Ideally, your CASE (Computer Assisted Software Engineering) tool will be expanded to include interfaces to popular software development environments. Your product life-cycle need never end, because you will continuously improve your methodology to adapt to the latest changes in technology and theory. By extending and expanding your methodology you will have an unending revenue stream as you market new versions of your product.

Overall, methodologies are the perfect product. They don't even have to work. Whereas other products with health warnings have certain guaranteed results (alcohol makes you drunk, cigarettes make you cough), methodologies tackle such a complicated area of human endeavour that there are plenty of excuses available if they don't help you to deliver a useful system.

The point of all this cynicism is to remind the software engineer that the methodology is just another product. As a professional you must not confuse methodologies with religions. Guard against becoming a faithful, unquestioning convert.

24.2.3   Methodology inflation

One consequence of the methodology life-cycle is that over time methodologies grow as they become ever more comprehensive and procedural. They expand from elegant effectiveness into unwieldy complexity. Version 1 is often small, compact, easily grasped and exciting. Over the years, the manuals expand from a single ring binder into a small bookshelf, and then onto CDROM. As more and more gaps get filled, the radicalism and opportunity for innovation that is an essential part of Software Engineering gets squeezed out. Over the last couple of years at the top end of business systems analysis the hot approach has been BPR (Business Process Re-engineering) [Hammer93]. I remember when Systems Analysis and Design methods all stressed the need for radical thought in developing business system options. No doubt in a few years BPR will be so methodology-rich that we will need a new radical approach to replace it.

It would make a really refreshing change if version n+1 of a methodology was re-engineered to produce a smaller, simpler, more concise product than version n. I haven't seen it happen yet. The upshot of this is that the professional software engineer must always be prepared to avoid the worst excesses of bloated methodologies by ruthlessly pruning away the noise and irrelevancies.

24.2.4   Methodology as defence mechanism

Methodology disciples use their chosen faith to avoid getting to grips with real world problems. When people don't know what to do they revert to habitual behaviour, or displacement activity. When methodology disciples don't know what to do they grind mindlessly through the prescribed methodology steps. They waste time producing polished, detailed and entirely irrelevant descriptions of the current system. The professional software engineer knows methodology ritual is no substitute for creative thinking.

The software engineer often feels naked on being exposed to an unfamiliar business environment. Methodology addicts use methodologies as protective clothing to shield themselves from the real world and their customers. The methodology addict often reverts to methodspeak and technobabble. Most professions have their own jargon and language which is used to protect the secret world of the initiate, to bond fellow professionals and to confuse and alienate outsiders. This is the last thing that the software engineer needs. Easy communication between you and your customer is essential for systems success.

The professional software engineer, no matter how uneasy, will never hide behind methodologies.

24.2.5   The sausage machine syndrome

The methodology addict believes that if you tip information in the hopper, crank the methodology handle and grind through all the stages and components, a useful system will magically appear out the other end. It won't, but a depressing number of software engineers never grow out of this belief. Many organizations and customers remain entranced by this false belief despite contrary evidence. Marketing hype from methodology vendors does little to dispel the fallacy.

A methodology won't solve problems. It may give you some useful ways of examining problems from different angles, but you still have to create a solution. It won't guarantee a "good" or "optimal" solution. In fact, if you slavishly follow a methodology, without adding the vital ingredients of innovation and invention, you will probably finish up with a solution that is only slightly better than the mess you started out with.

Methodologies offer seductive opportunities for time-wasting, for pursuing blind alleys and for documenting the obvious and irrelevant. The professional software engineer will always question the next step. "Why am I doing this?" "Because it's in the method or because it is leading to a useful system?"

24.2.6   Methodology paralysis

Methodology addicts like to analyse and design everything before building anything. In the bad old days of 3GLs and boring files, this view was more defensible. We had to design everything at the outset because the system construction was very time and labour intensive. If we got it wrong, the cost of change was immense. We have all seen the familiar graph showing how the cost of change soars as we slide further into the development process.

The idea that methodologies can give us symbols and notations that will express dynamic aspects of a system in a way that we (and our customers) can understand seems to me most unlikely. I remember being involved in a quality assurance review of a screen dialogue design, properly produced according to the rules of a particular methodology. The document ran to about seventy pages. User representatives were supposed to agree that the design met their requirements. They were bored and bludgeoned into assent. I don't think that anyone present, including the product authors could honestly understand the document in it's entirety, but there we all were, driven by the methodology. The system eventually delivered was a spectacular and expensive failure. Fortunately it was a very big project so there were plenty of people to share the blame.

The way to show a customer what a system will look like is to build a prototype, rather than write it down on paper. Nowadays, the software engineer has all sorts of goodies that make system building much faster and easier. Fourth generation and object-oriented environments provide powerful building blocks. We have flexible data management systems, and, increasingly, the ability to create and re-use objects that combine elements of data and processing. It is often quicker to prototype a design than it is to document it in some obscure notation.

Prototyping, as well as being quicker and cheaper than writing it all down on paper, also has the immense advantage that we can show the customer what we think they want — and the customer has an early opportunity to decide whether we are on the right track. Prototyping still has a rather disreputable and anarchic reputation among methodology purists, although it is interesting to note how many methodologies have grudgingly expanded to include the option of controlled prototyping. I believe that if you follow the path of designing everything first, you will extend the timetable of a project to the point where it is doomed, because the business environment for the system will have changed by the time you actually deliver.

24.2.7   Never mind the system, look at the documentation

Documentation is a major selling point in methodologies. Large quantities of documentation provide a management comfort blanket, a false illusion of progress. I must confess to preferring an entirely minimalist approach to documentation. An overview of the system is useful, as is clarification of any "difficult bits". While you may produce reams of documentation that describe the journey towards a system solution, it is only the solution itself that has any long-term value. User documentation should be embedded in the system because it is concerned with using the system. Technical documentation should be packaged within the software itself. This increases the likelihood that system documentation will be kept up to date as the system is changed. There is precious little hope that detached paper documentation will ever reflect the real system.

My favourite CASE tool (until the arrival of a Virtual Reality CASE interface, with which I can indulge my repressed desire to be a fighter pilot) is the copier whiteboard. It is totally flexible, methodology independent, easy to use, and it produces instant hardcopy documentation.

24.2.8   Big is not always beautiful

Methodologies seem to encourage big projects, big in terms of elapsed time, people and project bureaucracy. The methodology disciple is encouraged by the all-embracing scope of the methodology, to do everything prescribed by the methodology, whether or not it is useful. "Big" is the last thing that the professional software engineer should want, or that the customer needs. Small problems are soluble, big ones are impossible. The ideal project is short, sharp and focused. These projects have a much higher chance of business success. Reducing the time to delivery dramatically reduces the risks of failure. There is less chance that the requirement will be extended, expanded and altered leading to a doomed juggernaut project.

Successful systems are usually ones that are delivered before the customer loses interest, and before real world changes invalidate the system. Fast delivery means that the customer gets early payback on the business benefits yielded by the system. The professional software engineer will point out all the problems associated with lengthy development timetables to all concerned.

Some business requirements really are big and complicated, but there are always ways to chop them up into manageable deliverables. You can carve the system up into self-contained functional components, which can be implemented stepwise. By picking functions that can deliver business benefits in isolation you will help to build customer confidence, and confirm the overall requirement. Another opportunity for segmenting the requirement is by phasing deliverables against the systems business cycles. Many business systems operate on monthly, quarterly or annual cycles. You don't need the annual processes implemented until the end of the year!

24.2.9   Methodologies don't deliver systems — people do

Your best guarantee of success is to get the right team of people to do the job. This includes getting the right customer representatives, as well as the right software engineers. A full description of my personal recipe for forging the right team of customers, users, "snakes", "chameleons" and "toads" is given in The Reptilian World of Software Teams [Myers95].

Keep the team as small as possible. This will help you to avoid the excessive bureaucracies of project management More people means more bureaucracy overload. Three is a good number of people for a team. Two people will often disagree; three will introduce a degree of balance. The number of communications channels in a team balloons as team size increases. With three people there are three channels, with five there are ten channels. Once you hit big team sizes, you can easily waste all your time communicating rather than delivering anything useful.

A team that is really storming is wonderful to behold. If you are lucky enough to be a part of one it will enter folklore. Years later, when you are gathered together with other software engineers you will fondly recall the long weekend when you achieved miracles of Software Engineering. You will need these rose-coloured reminiscences to help you to stay sane when you are in the middle of disaster projects.

24.3   Methodology Survival Guide

Treat methodology vendors and evangelists with the same suspicion that you would accord to any fundamentalist sect with something to sell: methodologies are just another product. You will probably need to learn at least one methodology. You will find useful tools, techniques and inspirations across the whole range of methodologies. You never know when a particular approach will come in handy, so learn about, and use those that you can understand and find useful. As a professional you must not become blinkered into believing that one particular approach is the "right" one. You need a whole bag full of tools.

If you are grinding your way through a rigorous, prescriptive methodology you must not confuse methodology end products with the real end product - a useful system. You must apply common sense at every step and ask yourself "What will this particular step contribute towards delivering the system?". As a professional, you will have no qualms about leaving out chunks that don't get you anywhere. Be pragmatic in your approach. Don't try to constrain your natural creativity within a methodology straight-jacket.

While human beings are feeble serial processors, they are very good at pattern matching. As a professional software engineer you will accumulate an invaluable library of system solution patterns. Through your unrivalled human ability to perceive the whole and recognize patterns, you will often be able to shortcut the methodology mill. You will say "Hang on, I've seen one like this before, and the solution is . . .". Exploit these flashes of *deja vu*. Side-stepping the methodology like this is not cheating, it is an essential facet of your professionalism.

Brooks describes the creative and imaginative joys of Software Engineering [Brooks95]. I believe that the best systems are built by teams who have fun doing it. Don't let methodology addicts spoil the innovation, inventiveness and sheer fun that characterize a really successful system. I was there, at a design meeting when someone had a really good idea, only to be shouted down with the comment: "That's all very well, but we are not doing that step in the methodology yet."

24.4   Summary

The professional software engineer needs to be much more than a methodology grinder. The professional software engineer uses methodologies as a valuable framework to help systems development. Working within a methodology framework, the professional software engineer will know what to include and what to omit in a particular development. The professional knows that there is much more to delivering systems than just blindly following a methodology.

In summary, the professional software engineer will:

- pick out appropriate methodology components

- omit the irrelevant

- not be a purist

- use pattern matching to exploit experience

- never forget that the job is to deliver useful systems

- have fun

Methodologies pose a significant problem for the Software Engineering industry. They tend to be marketed and taught as if they guarantee solutions. Some of the skills which enable the professional to exploit methodologies are currently learned only through experiencing costly failures. By teaching software engineers about the perils and pitfalls inherent in methodologies we should be able to produce professional software engineers who exploit methodologies to deliver systems.

Chapter 25
Software Engineering Practices in the UK

25.1 Introduction

A recurring theme within software development has been the problem of poor quality software. This problem has underpinned a "software crisis" that has lasted since the early 1960s, and which led to the term "Software Engineering" being introduced in 1968 at a NATO conference held to discuss the problems in software product, delivery and quality [Naur69]. The concept of Software Engineering was originally intended to provide a provocative theme, but it has evolved over the last 25 years into a technological discipline of considerable importance especially within academic institutions. However, there are still major problems within the computing industry and the need for the adoption of truly professional approaches has never been greater.

It is clear that the major goals for many software providers are efficient production and the delivery of quality products. It is also widely recognized that the use of Software Engineering practices such as systematic methods, automated tools and quality assurance procedures are means of achieving the efficient production of quality software. However, the adoption of these practices in many cases has been much less than could be expected. In the following sections of this chapter, I will place these practices in a UK context with regard to the past (this I will roughly class as the time prior to the attempted awakening of the UK software industry by the Department of Trade and Industry's 1990 TickIT initiative and guide [BCS90a]), the present and the future.

The section on the present will report the results from surveys and investigations which my research group have undertaken, and which relate to the acceptance of Software Engineering practices within the UK commercial sector. These investigations have highlighted the reasons for non-adoption of Software Engineering practices and the problems which are currently restraining progress. The case is outlined that the industry has directed too much energy to solving its problems by means of technological developments and that to a great extent it has neglected those aspects related to personnel such as professionalism, ethics and responsibility. Finally, in considering the future I will outline actions which I believe should be taken regarding educational approaches, course content and technology transfer material for there to be a significant improvement in the achievement of quality within the software industry.

25.2 The Past

If we look back over the the first two Software Engineering decades (the 1970s and 1980s) it is clear that the Software Engineering practices which have impinged to the greatest extent on the industry as a whole are those related to the use of:

- systematic development methods

- computer based development support environments

- quality assurance (QA)

Developments in each of these areas are primarily concerned with improvements in the software production process and should reduce the overall software wastage costs which were estimated for the UK in the late 1980s as still being in excess of 2000 million pounds per year [Dennis91].

25.2.1 Systematic development methods

During these two decades, the UK, in line with the rest of the information systems world, experienced an explosion in the development of methods which support various phases of the software development life-cycle. In the 1970s the methods that were adopted tended to be concerned with the program design/implementation phase of the life-cycle and they were centred on the ideas of structured programming. In the late 1970s and early 1980s method development started to concentrate much more on those parts of the software development life-cycle concerned with system analysis and overall system design. The major development within the UK in this area was the production of SSADM (Structured Systems Analysis and Design Method) for the United Kingdom's Central Computer and Telecommunications Agency (CCTA). SSADM has continued to develop during the 1980s and the 4th version of it was released in 1990 [CCTA90a]. It is claimed to be the most widely used design method in Europe [CCTA90b] and it has now reached a relatively stable state which is likely to remain until decisions are reached concerning the Pan-European Euromethod(e) [Betts92].

25.2.2 Computer-based development environments

The other major technological developments, intended to counter the problems of poor quality software and inadequate documentation, have centred around the production of computer based development environments. These environments are provided via Computer-Aided Software Engineering (CASE) tools which automate existing Software Engineering methods and practices with the goals of improving the quality of the product and the efficiency of the software developers. In the UK we have seen a large variety of software products classed as CASE. The diversity in tool functionality and design has resulted in considerable confusion surrounding the true definition of CASE. Those tools that automate the analysis and design techniques of dataflow diagramming, logical data structuring, and entity-life modelling differ considerably from tools that automate code generation by the use of structure charts and the reuse of existing coded modules. These differences have resulted in various categories of tools being defined in an attempt to limit confusion. These categories have included: front, upper, middle, bridge, rear, lower, workbenches, toolkits and methodology automators. However, by the end of the 1980s the suppliers of the latest generation of CASE tools were attempting to integrate more of the life-cycle into single tools or tool sets with the ultimate aim being to provide a totally integrated project support environment.

25.2.3 Quality Assurance procedures

During the 1980s the UK Department of Trade and Industry (DTI) recorded a steady adoption of QA standards across UK industry in general. However, the adoption rate within the software sector was seen to be much lower than in others. By 1987 the Department was so concerned about the high cost to industry of poor quality software that they commissioned reports on Software Quality from consultants at Price Waterhouse [PriceW88] and at Logica [Logica88]. The state of QA within the software industry at that time is illustrated from the two following quotations from the Price Waterhouse report:

> "The measurement of software quality is difficult and much work remains to be done to develop satisfactory quality metrics. A number of studies have attempted to define a set of measures, but the results are so complicated that they are of little general use."

> "Few software producers collect quantitative information relating to software quality. Neither do users quantify the costs they incur as a result of poor quality software. However, despite the difficulty in obtaining quantitative measures, it is generally agreed by both suppliers and users that poor quality software is a major problem."

The two reports both concluded that the ISO 9001 standard [ISO87] (and the equivalent parts of the British BS 5750 and European EN 29000 series of standards) provided an adequate specification of the minimum requirements for a quality system. But it was also emphasized that there needed to be additional mechanisms which would help in ISO 9001's application to software systems.

25.2.4 TickIT

Following the publication of the consultants' reports in 1988 the British Computer Society was invited to propose the organization, procedures, and rules for a sector scheme regarding quality assurance. The result was a collection of guidance material gathered from various sources which was then formed into a document called the TickIT guide [BCS90a]. The guide supported the DTI's TickIT initiative and provided an introduction and overview of the ISO 9001 standard, interpreted the application of the standard to the development of software, and it supplied guidance for purchasers, suppliers and auditors.

25.3 The Present

Plenty of evidence that Software Engineering practices were not being used sufficiently in the mid 1980s can be obtained from the detailed findings of the Price Waterhouse report referred to above. However, an ongoing and recent picture of the state of the sector with regard to the use of systematic methods, CASE tools, QA approaches and standards can be obtained from work carried out by members of the Commercial Software Engineering group at the University of Sunderland. During the last eight years members of the group have undertaken in depth investigations of practices within UK data processing departments via five major surveys and follow-up case study interviews.

25.3.1   The Sunderland surveys

The investigations and their scope were:

1. A survey carried out at the end of 1987 on the use of SSADM, its variants, and its relationship to other methods including those used for program design [Edwards89a]. This was complemented by interviews with practitioners during 1987 and 1988 concerning their use of systematic methods and standards for program specifications [Edwards89b] and [Edwards89c].

2. A survey carried out at the end of 1990 whose purpose was primarily to determine the extent to which CASE was being used at that time [Stobart91]. However, the survey was also designed to identify: general background information on both the organizations that were using CASE and those that were not using CASE, the manually performed software development methods used within these organizations, the areas of the life-cycle that had been identified as causing the greatest problems, the solutions that had been found to address these problems, the areas of the life-cycle currently automated and those areas suitable for future automation, the problems with current tools and future direction of CASE.

3. A survey carried out at the end of 1991 whose prime aim was to determine the use of QA procedures within the UK IT industry, with special attention to those who were operating with a 3rd Party Certification (i.e. to a standard such as ISO9001/BS5750) [Davis92]. This survey was also designed to identify general background information on the organizations surveyed, to assess the relationship between users of software development techniques/methods and QA procedures, and to determine the reasons for developers seeking or not seeking certification to a quality assurance standard.

4. A survey carried out at the start of 1994 whose main purpose was to determine the use of named structured systems analysis and design methods, such as SSADM, the extent to which organizations customize the methods which they use and the use they make of software tools [Hardy95c].

5. A survey undertaken in the latter part of 1994 whose main purpose was to investigate the way in which the users of SSADM were actually applying the method [Hardy95a].

Within all these surveys the researchers had included questions to assess the current state of the industry and assess the actual use of Software Engineering practices being investigated. There were also questions to determine organizations' future plans, the constraints which are placed upon them and the problems that they encounter with regard to the area being surveyed. It is on these latter areas that I will concentrate in this section.

25.3.2   Current use

Overall, our surveys and related work have indicated that there is a continuing, if sometimes slow, increase in the use of methods, CASE and QA procedures. Certainly the situation would appear to have improved from that reported by the consultants from Price Waterhouse in 1988. The relative use of methods in the UK as found in the 1990 and 1994 surveys are shown in Table 25.1 and Table 25.2. These show a clear increase in the use of methods, especially those classed as "in-house"! It is also clear that the continuing development of SSADM and its support from central Government has led to and will continue to lead to a greater acceptance of the value of the use of systematic methods.

Method	% Use
Formal Specification	1%
Gane/Sarson	2%
JSD	2%
SSADM	36%
Yourdon	8%
Other	14%
None	37%

Table 25.1 1990 Use of Methods

Method	% Use
Formal Specification	2%
IE	4%
JSD	5%
OOD	5%
SSADM	24%
Yourdon	4%
In-House	38%
None	18%

Table 25.2 1994 Use of Methods

It is also clear that the situation regarding the use of CASE tools has improved since 1990. A comparison of the results from the 1990 and 1994 surveys indicates that the use of CASE has risen in the last few years from some 18% of respondents to 43% [Hardy95b]. However, determining the exact nature and level of CASE use within an organization is difficult from a questionnaire, and the researchers concerned with this work believe that the the most reliable conclusion is that the number of organizations who have at least tried CASE technology has risen considerably since 1990.

General press and conference reports indicate that there is still a large percentage of software systems being developed without any QA procedures. But on the positive side 22% of the respondents to our 1991 survey were already 3rd party assessed. Almost half of these had been certified only within the last year, which was double the amount for the previous year. This, hopefully, indicates a permanent growth in the number of organizations seeking external certification. Positive figures for accreditation (24 businesses every three months) have also been reported in the UK Department of Trade and Industry's JFIT NEWS [DTI92]. Nevertheless, given the size of the industry it is obvious that adoption of QA procedures across the whole of the UK software sector has still some way to go. With regard to the TickIT initiative, it would appear from our figures that to a great extent it was most effective with those already sympathetic to QA and that it did not quickly penetrate those sectors of the industry where the knowledge is most required. In one way we can see that pressures from customers will cause a gradual adoption of QA procedures by the software industry but for QA to be really successful its adoption should be due to an internal desire for improvement rather than external forces.

25.3.3   Constraints and problems

One fundamental constraint on the adoption of Software Engineering practices is the lack of clear unbiased information. Another is simply human resistance to change. The major problems which the researchers at Sunderland have identified for each area and the common problems relating to human factors and are detailed in the following subsections:

Methods

The major problems associated with the adoption of cost effective systematic development methods are:

1. The continuing wide range of available methods and the lack of experienced staff.

2. Unwillingness of organizations to accept change and adopt any new "standardized method". In many cases this is simply due to the costs, primarily in staff time, that are incurred with any major change.

3. The uncertainty of the long-term future of particular methods and the possibility of the introduction of a European Standard method.

4. An unwillingness to consider and accept differing methods, if an organization has already invested heavily, and in some cases very heavily, in methods of its own.

5. Biased pressure to adopt the methods and related tools promoted by suppliers, national and multi-national consultancy organizations.

CASE

The prospective market for CASE tools has been confused by the large variety of different products that are available. In an attempt to clarify matters tools have been categorized to more accurately describe their functions. Unfortunately, tool vendors and manufacturers have not totally agreed on what these terms mean, so such categorization has simply added to the confusion, and not removed it. The other major problems are:

1. The current high cost of CASE tools. These costs were given as a major reason for not adopting CASE by the respondents to the 1990 survey. The actual cost of CASE (per staff member) appeared to be approximately double what non-CASE users were willing to spend.

2. The high costs in terms of extra hardware and initial staff time in the adoption of CASE.

3. Lack of management support to invest in and use tools (and related methods).

4. The possibility that if an organization is not adopting good development methods and standards the introduction of CASE may simply allow the development of bad software more quickly!

5. Some tools are of too general a nature to be of any significant benefit whilst others are so dependent on a particular method that adoption of the tool means that the organization must also adopt a method which itself may not fully satisfy their needs.

6. There appears to be no clearly predominant CASE tool or tools within the UK This lack of "champions" does not encourage new purchasers of tools.

Quality Assurance procedures

Many organizations see no reason to seek accreditation to an external standard as they believe their own internal procedures are more effective. Other major reasons for not seeking an external standard have been identified as:

1. Cost of gaining accreditation and the time to implement new procedures.

2. General confusion over the meaning of quality when applied to software and a lack of knowledge of QA approaches and standards.

3. A significant proportion of the industry is not applying any formal QA standards, and many see or report no benefits in using such standards.

Human problems

In the adoption of methods and tools there can be major problems with staff at all levels. People do not like change, especially if it is a possible threat to their livelihood or the way in which they have to work. Computing professionals are like everyone else in this respect. Managers lack confidence in their ability to understand and control the new technology whilst designers and production staff may believe that the methods and tools will destroy the artistic and creative aspects of their work. It is true that adoption of the new technologies has a large impact on working practices and that many members of staff have been unable (or are unwilling) to alter their working practices. We believe this "Luddite approach" has greatly contributed to the problems of implementing Software Engineering practices in the commercial/administrative sector.

Just as some staff are unwilling to accept change there are others who will. Unfortunately in some cases their expectation of what the new practices can offer may be too high. They may be convinced that there will be overnight improvements in all areas of their software development. This is, of course, untrue, since the real benefits are in the long-term. The non-fulfilment of their expectations can lead to dissatisfaction and an unwillingness to use the new approaches in earnest.

Another human problem which we have identified during our work is that there is a deep seated antipathy to the use of standards throughout the industry. Most organizations and individuals formally recognize the value of standards and agree that they are needed. However, when it comes to the actual use of, and adherence to, standards the situation is in many cases very different [Thompson90]. This factor more than any other acts against any rapid increase in the acceptance of QA procedures since these more than any other Software Engineering practice depend on standards being adhered to.

25.4   The Future

From surveys and related investigations carried out at Sunderland, it has emerged that many of the reasons for the slow adoption of those approaches that should lead to the development of better quality software are related not to technology but to people. In fact I would suggest that to a great extent over the last 25 years we have concentrated too much on technological aspects and have failed to develop the human aspects that should be associated with any engineering discipline. The areas which I believe we now need to concentrate on, if we are to achieve quality in the future, are: professionalism, Software Engineering education within academic institutions and technology transfer.

25.4.1   Professionalism

It is essential that people at **all** levels, both within and outside the software industry, recognize that the production of quality software is as much an engineering discipline as any of the other traditional disciplines such as: mechanical engineering, electronic engineering and civil engineering. It is vital that a high proportion of staff involved in software-related projects are professionally qualified and that they place high regard on their professionalism with respect to ethics, responsibility and the attainment of quality. Traditionally when we attempt to measure quality during a software project we concentrate on metrics associated with the product (ie the code) and on the mechanics of how the product was developed. Little attention appears to be given to the quality of the staff involved in the process. This is despite the obvious fact that high quality staff are likely to produce a high quality product while poor quality staff are not. It would therefore seem that a simple project metric such as the ratio of the number of professionally qualified staff involved on a project to the total number of staff

[Thompson93a] is as likely to give a measure of the quality of the final product as the metrics of [Halstead77] and [McCabe76].

25.4.2 Software Engineering education within academic institutions

Academic institutions have produced graduates and diplomates in computing-based disciplines in greater and greater numbers since the late 1970s. However, it would appear that despite all this new blood, the "mind set" of the software industry appears not to be as positive towards Software Engineering practices and the production of quality products as it should be. Therefore, I must raise the question as to whether or not the students completing these courses are really equipped with the knowledge, skills and abilities which will enable them to immediately operate efficiently and effectively in the industry. Do their courses provide them with the necessary professionalism that should be expected? How do they compare in these areas with graduates in the more traditional engineering disciplines? One may also ask whether the traditional approach of treating computing as a branch of science rather than as primarily a branch of engineering has in itself acted against professionalism being given a higher priority within courses.

To achieve real improvement in the future, educational institutions need to take a much more pro-active role in promoting Software Engineering practices and professionalism. Also, this should not only be in named Software Engineering courses but in all computing courses from those closely related to business to those related to the more technological aspects of computing. It is also not sufficient to take a traditional computing topic such as algorithms and simply retitle it Software Engineering. There needs to be a change to an underlying approach which places a very high emphasis on aspects such as quality, professionalism, ethics and responsibility. It is important that these aspects need to be introduced at the start of any computing course and used throughout it. It is also important that emphasis is placed within these courses on interpersonal communications because Software Engineering practices have as much, if not more, to do with people than with machines. This aspect has been identified by the British Computer Society in its 1990 report on the Future of Information Technology as the single most important skill required for effective participation in the IT society of the 1990s. As they stated "there is no computer substitute for clear thinking and accurate expression" [BCS90b].

25.4.3 Technology transfer

The achievement of quality in software can only be realized if the appropriate Software Engineering practices are implemented and used correctly. However, if the staff who are already in the industry are ill-informed or fail to recognize the benefits of Software Engineering then any adoption is unlikely to be totally successful. It also must be recognized that, no matter how advanced the technology becomes, without good organizational attitudes it can do little to help surmount the many difficulties that currently face systems development staff. Also, for the correct practices to be adopted, there is a clear need for accurate and meaningful information regarding their use. For new developments to be accepted within commercial/administrative organizations, there needs to be much better means of efficient and effective technology transfer.

If particular Software Engineering practices are to be accepted and used there must be a much better understanding of them, their use and the actual benefits which they can bring. I must emphasize again that the underlying cause for several of the problems identified in the previous section is simply fear of the unknown coupled with a lack of unbiased, easily accessed information. To overcome such problems we need to create enabling mechanisms which will facilitate technology transfer and mutual understanding. It is imperative that there also is a will within the industry to receive such material with an open mind, appraise it in an impartial manner and where new practices are found to be appropriate to adopt them willingly and with enthusiasm.

Chapter 26
Escaping the Mythology that Plagues Software Technology

26.1 Introduction

A recent article in *Scientific American* [Gibbs94] observed that the software crisis is still with us (assuming that a state of crisis can persist for roughly three decades). It also observed that a state of grace known as Software Engineering would resolve the crisis if software technologists could ever manage to achieve it. Needless to say, the piece also noted that they are nowhere close. What was most distressing about the article, though, was not the still endemic problems of software production, but the widespread acceptance of fundamentally flawed conceptions of the actualities of historical and contemporary engineering and manufacturing practice. Software technologists remain captured by distorted notions of the nature of technological practice which will almost certainly lead to disappointment and frustration rather than the promised land.

During the debates in the 70s over structured programming, a number of its critics remarked that no one was in favour of *unstructured* programs. No one was arguing the benefits of impenetrable spaghetti code. Rather, the point was that structured programming was not a comprehensive panacea, that good heuristics were being turned into bad dogma. Solving real world programming problems, it was argued, was a messy business (contrary to the examples presented in the journals) with many fuzzy aspects.

Similarly, those who push for a Software Engineering discipline often leave precious little if any room for the fuzzier aspects of technological practice. Few (or at least few who aspire to professionalism) are against discipline *per se* in technological practice, be it developing programs or building bridges. However, many (although certainly not all) would-be software engineers have seized on the notion of a science-based discipline as the be all and end all. Such things as intuition, heuristics, and aesthetics are viewed as embarrassing remnants of the "bad old days" of the cowboy programmer and an albatross around the neck of a potential Software Engineering discipline. For it is that last term — discipline — that encapsulates for many the essence of "mature" technological practice. It is an understandable but nonetheless misguided view.

Also understandable, but no less misguided, is the view which lionizes the potential of standardized parts. If standardized parts were central to revolutionizing the manufacture of tangible goods during the industrial revolution, the argument thus runs, surely standardized software components can revolutionize software "manufacture." This view typically presents not only an oversimplified historical picture of the development and use of standardized parts, but a questionable analogy linking software development with physical manufacturing processes.

In many quarters, software technologists remain captured by these mythologies. While their appeal is unsurprising, it is also detrimental to the development of realistic and sound bases for technological practice in software. Contrary to the argument which accompanies these myths, only when software technologists firmly disabuse themselves of them will they be likely to evolve into true professionals.

26.2   Engineering Mythology

The argument for engineering professionalization by historical analogy has been advanced by a number of people, most notably [Shaw90]. Unfortunately, such arguments have been problematic by any standard of historical scholarship. Incorporating superficial analysis and an abysmal ignorance of roughly 35 years of work in the history and sociology of technology, these arguments have nevertheless been warmly embraced by many in the Software Engineering community as showing the way toward salvation. That such should be the case is not especially surprising. Such arguments have been a balm to the Software Engineering soul, telling many exactly what they so desperately want to hear. What they are hearing, though, is more along the lines of mythology [Shapiro92]. And by any standard, mythology is a poor basis for action.

The most pernicious element of this mythology is the contention, either explicit or implicit in much of the Software Engineering rhetoric, that engineering is essentially applied science and that a "mature" engineering field depends on science to progress. Anyone with a passing familiarity with the substantial body of historical and sociological work in this area will realize just how dubious this claim is. This is most definitely not to say that science and mathematics do not play an important role in engineering or that they should not in Software Engineering. It *is* to say that the relationship between science and engineering has historically been complex, fuzzy and, most of all, incomplete. Technological progress often leads rather than follows science, even in such high tech fields as semiconductors [Holbrook94]. Science certainly contributes to technological knowledge and practice, but that contribution is often less than straightforward. More importantly, this contribution is just one aspect of technological knowledge, which historically includes engineering science (which is distinct from applied science), design practices, tacit experiential knowledge, aesthetic sensibilities, empirical experimentation and *professional judgment*. Research (and this is only some of the more recent work) by historians [Ferguson92], sociologists [MacKenzie90] and significantly, engineers themselves acting as historians [Vincenti90] and as sociologists [Bucciarelli94], and simply self-aware professionals [Petroski85] has shown that engineering is not applied science.

26.2.1   The role of judgment

The work of Petroski merits particular attention, for his credentials as an engineer in a "mature" engineering field are indisputable. Aleksandar S. Vesic Professor of Civil Engineering and Chairman of the Department of Civil and Environmental Engineering at Duke University, Petroski has written several highly readable and insightful books on the nature of engineering. While not discounting the importance of analysis and theory, Petroski argues that they must be subservient to what he terms "engineering judgment."

> "Engineering judgment is the quality factor among those countless quantities that have come to dominate design in our post-computer age. Judgment tells the designer what to check on the back of an envelope and what to measure at the construction site. Judgment, in short, is what catches errors, what detects flaws, and what anticipates and obviates failure. . . . Engineering judgment does not necessarily come from a deeper understanding of theory or a more powerful command of computational tools. The traditional engineering sciences are servants and students but not masters and teachers of engineering judgment . . . " ([Petroski94] pp 121-122)

How does one acquire this sort of judgment? Through experience and by studying the judgment exercised by fellow professionals today and in the past.

Indeed, Petroski notes that a key source of this judgment is that group of individuals whom [Brooks87a] has labelled "great designers." While [Shaw90] may be right in noting that great designers are rare, they nevertheless embody and exhibit qualities of engineering judgment which are an important resource for software engineers just as the judgment exhibited by bridge designer John Roebling is worthy of study by civil engineers. Even in routine projects, engineering judgment plays an important role. Moreover, the line separating the routine and the not-so-routine is often ill-defined and the act of crossing over it may well be more recognizable in hindsight than at the time, as demonstrated by a host of famous bridge failures [Petroski94]. This is probably even more the case for software than for other technologies because being bound to the realm of discrete mathematics, software lends itself even less readily to conventional notions of design extrapolation. Software is notoriously brittle; one change, a single extrapolation, can easily lead to disaster.

Dealing with the potential problems introduced by design extrapolation in any area of technological practice requires returning to first principles. However, these are not the first or fundamental principles long sought by software technologists for the supposedly scientific foundation they would provide. Principles more sophisticated than those already identified (ones common to all engineering design such as decomposition) are unlikely to be found for by definition they will adhere to particular contexts. Rather, the principles of concern here are general principles of failure avoidance and design savvy as applied to specific contexts. As Leveson strongly argues in a recent book already hailed by some as a definitive work [Leveson95], unless software technologists become intimately acquainted with the failure modes local to a particular domain or application context, practitioners aiming to develop safe systems will be fundamentally hamstrung.

Engineering judgment is not just the mark of great designers or exceptional engineers but an essential component of engineering professionalism. However, the perspective that equates engineering with applied science gives short shrift to such realities. Instead, with a dreary regularity, emphasis is placed on quantification and analysis. Qualitative judgment and design, though occasionally paid lip service, are short changed. The result is an impoverished view of technological practice rather than a modern or sophisticated one.

To some extent, software technologists cannot be blamed for enthusiastically embracing this historically and sociologically unrealistic view of engineering. For in looking around themselves at more "mature" engineering fields, they have witnessed the growth of a similar but no less distorted perspective. There are a number of reasons for this, not least of which is the undeniable fact that in the 20th century science sits at the top of the epistemological totem pole. Exuding certainty and determinism, knowledge which can be labelled scientific carries a *cachet* which other types of knowledge are hard-pressed to match. As [Abbott88] has observed, when the dominant cultural values consist of rationality, logic and science, professionals feel compelled to legitimize their activities on these grounds. Compounding this in the US was the great expansion of higher education in the aftermath of the Second World War. With student numbers soaring, huge lecture classes became a regular feature of many colleges and universities. However, it is very difficult to teach and develop engineering (or for that matter any other kind of professional) judgment en masse. Inculcating judgment and other fuzzy aspects of engineering practice is by definition a labour intensive process. Theory and analysis, however, are amenable to a one-to-many teaching environment. The shift away from design and judgment and toward analysis and mechanistic thinking thus had a certain logic about it, addressing both the problem of professional legitimacy vis-a-vis scientists and the problem of teaching large numbers of students. Unfortunately, what it didn't address (indeed, effectively worsened) was the problem of real world technological practice, as various academics and practitioners have observed from time to time over the last 35 years [Bratchell82], [Ferguson92].

Therefore, given the spectre of engineering as applied science which increasingly hovered over "mature" engineering fields through the 60s, 70s and 80s, it's not all that surprising that when would-be software engineers wanted to develop an engineering discipline, a true engineering profession, they sought to emulate what they saw around them. Unfortunately, what they saw around them was, and is slowly being recognized to be, very problematic. Needless to say, wishful thinking based on dubious historical analogies hardly helps matters.

26.2.2   The problem with engineering

Of course, the preceding discussion skirts one of the biggest historical and on-going issues in Software Engineering, which is whether the engineering model is in fact the most appropriate or useful basis for action. This debate seems to have peaked (although by no means concluded) in the period 1975-1985 and offered just about every imaginable interpretation or assessment of the fundamental nature of software development. In 1975 alone, programming was defined as "part science and part art" [Abrahams75], "a nascent science" [Schwartz75], "just as unique as art, science, and engineering" [Hiles75], and as "a truly engineering discipline" [IEEE75]. Ten years later, the Chairman of the Special Interest Group on Software Engineering of the Association for Computing Machinery called for "general recognition that what we call software engineering is neither characterizable nor understandable in traditional terms" [Riddle85] while at the same time the editor of *Software Engineering Notes* opined that "in the ideal, 'software engineering' is primarily a *state of mind* attainable by thoughtful and far-seeing people" [Neumann85]. At one time or another Software Engineering has been likened to art, craft, science, mathematics, engineering, medicine and law. (I heard the medical model suggested yet again at a recent professional meeting of software developers.) And while the debate has subsided a bit over the last decade, it has certainly not ceased.

Either in spite of or because of this cacophony, much high-profile rhetoric has been devoted to making the case for the engineering as applied science model, as the *Scientific American* article illustrates. This doesn't necessarily mean that actual grassroots practice always matches the rhetoric and one wouldn't normally expect this in any case. [Abbott88] has argued that a profession's practical knowledge will significantly diverge from its formal "textbook" knowledge inasmuch as the two serve somewhat different functions. Furthermore, Meyer and Rowan have noted that some disjunction between formal organizational procedures and actual operational practices is normal and necessary [Meyer91]. This presents two problems for software technologists. On the one hand, since the engineering as applied science model implicitly posits a close correspondence between formal knowledge and practical knowledge, those who endorse it pursue an objective which is fundamentally counter-productive. On the other hand, at some point practical knowledge becomes so disconnected from the formal knowledge system that the gulf proves dysfunctional. The tension between rhetoric and reality becomes so severe that issues which deserve deep analysis and consideration are suppressed instead.

In any event, the very existence of this seemingly endless debate over disciplinary models says something important about Software Engineering and attempts to professionalize it. No other engineering field of which I am aware has experienced such an inability to decide upon a model with a high degree of consensus. American chemical engineers, for example, struggled for several decades in their efforts to identify and shape the intellectual substance of their field, but they did not spend those same decades arguing amongst themselves regarding the appropriateness of an engineering model [Reynolds86]. That software technologists have engaged in such long-running arguments either says something about the people or says something about software. There appears to be little evidence that software technologists are any more confused than would-be chemical engineers were almost a century ago, which suggests that there's something about software itself that renders the engineering model problematic. I have argued elsewhere that software's range of application and its unpatterned complexity [Brooks87a], both based in its abstractness, render it qualitatively different from other technologies and that this has been manifested in the debates over disciplinary models [Shapiro94a].

A more analytical means of framing this issue is in terms of problem archetypes. Technological practitioners do not routinely approach problems from scratch. Instead, they rely upon sets of archetypal problems, standard problems with standard solutions which provide a starting point from which specific solutions can be developed for specific circumstances. In this way, the structured knowledge of a particular area of technological practice is brought to bear on actual problems and modified in response to their contingencies. Because most types of technological practice take place within a relatively small range of different contexts, archetypal problems tend to be defined at a fairly high level where many factors will either persist across contexts or undergo only a modest degree of alteration. Of course, such problems will change over time, with new ones being added and old ones being discarded. At any moment in time, though, technological activity in a given area will rely upon a reasonably stable set of archetypal problems to link theory with practice and to avoid constantly returning to and proceeding from "fundamentals." However, this does not mean that there necessarily exists a universal "best" approach to a particular archetypal problem. There invariably arise different schools of thought regarding the solution of a given archetypal problem; a standard problem may have several possible standard solutions. Thus, for example, by the end of the Second World War one of the archetypal problems of structural engineering was the design and construction of thin-shell concrete vaults, which produced a number of different approaches arising out of different commitments to formal mathematical analysis, physical models and aesthetic conceptions. Approaches varied, but the importance of this structure as an archetypal problem to be investigated and mastered did not. It constituted a starting point from which a particular, individual vault would be engineered [Billington83].

Software technology has its archetypal problems as well, but these have typically resided at a much lower conceptual level than other areas of technological practice. Problems such as searching and sorting are undoubtedly important, but they do not serve to structure knowledge and experience in a way which matches up at a high conceptual level with real-world information technology problems. As suggested above, the difficulty lies in the contextual range spanned by software. Archetypal problems equivalent to thin-shell concrete vaults in structural engineering would in fact be archetypal only for a very limited number of contexts far short of the range encompassed by software development. Just consider the conceptual breadth spanned by software addressing problems such as payroll preparation, screen editing, pharmaceutical analysis and design, patient record keeping, air traffic control, telephone switching, billing, avionics, reservations, statistical analysis, medical imaging, ambulance dispatching, inventory control, and stock transactions. While some of these problem domains undoubtedly share some characteristics, they are likely to frustrate any attempt to break them down into a small number of usable archetypal problems. Hence the importance of domain-specific knowledge, knowledge which undergirds the definition of archetypal problems in a given context. Certainly as time has passed, appreciation of the importance of domain knowledge for software development has deepened.

26.3   Standards Mythology

This is also one reason why standardized software components are unlikely to usher in a software "industrial revolution". This idea too has a substantial history, having been knocked around since the first NATO Software Engineering conference. Unfortunately, like the shallow definitions of engineering which have come to dominate, it too suffers from facile historical arguments. In this case, it is Eli Whitney and the rise of the American system of manufacturing which are invoked mantra-style to demonstrate the wondrous properties of standardized components. Of course, while notable for having sold the US government on the idea, Whitney most certainly did not originate the concept of interchangeable parts, let alone figure out how to achieve it in practice. More important for the argument being advanced here, efforts to produce firearms with interchangeable parts showed quite clearly the importance of true uniformity if the system was to be genuinely successful [Hounshell84]. There's uniformity and then there's uniformity. Uniformity of an insufficient tolerance necessitated the expenditure of still considerable time and effort by a craftsman to assemble the components into a working weapon. Those components were therefore unlikely to be fully interchangeable with those in other weapons without yet further modification. This is not to say that greater uniformity is necessarily undesirable, but that the greatest benefits of the system depended on the achievement of highly precise uniformity requiring no significant fitting work either during assembly or when interchanging components.

Such is unlikely to be the case for software at any sophisticated level of functionality. The problem of environmental heterogeneity aside (which may or may not be amenable to automated solutions), the heterogeneity of problem domains will demand a significant amount of rework every time a high-level software component is transported from one domain into another. (Indeed, it has been argued that to speak of a software industry or sector is utterly misleading given that software cuts across virtually all other industries and sectors [Quintas94].) This is less of a problem for low-level components (such as libraries of mathematical functions or primitive graphical routines) which is precisely why software technology overall has failed to move much beyond these in its quest for standard components. As the required rework increases, the benefit decreases so that a point is soon reached at which it becomes debatable as to whether you're so much as breaking even. The way around this problem, of course, is to employ components which are domain-specific, but this by definition narrows the accrued benefits of using standardized components. On top of this is the fact that not all "mature" engineering fields consider high-level standardized components that valuable in the first place. For example, not only do bridge designers employ relatively little in the way of high-level standardized components [Spector86], but the use of standardized components can sometimes result in increased rather than decreased complexity and associated difficulties, as was the case with the design and construction of the Pompidou Centre in Paris [Rowe87].

Implicit in all the discussion of standardized parts, moreover, is an analogy between software development and traditional industrial production. This ignores a key distinction between the two activities, namely that the former revolves solely around design while the latter revolves around both design and manufacturing. Producing software isn't about producing many copies of the same item; the duplication costs are negligible. Thus, employing standardized components in the software production process is about employing standardized components in *different products*. There are no gains from increased manufacturing efficiencies, only from increased design efficiencies which translate into minimal adaptation effort. Furthermore, if one actually considers what goes on in, for instance, car manufacturing (the wonders of Fordism always making their way into these sort of arguments), one notices that the standardized components tend to be either low-level and generic — nuts, bolts, etc — or high-level and specialized — chassis, axles, etc. As noted above, software technologists have long had low-level generic parts. Object-oriented technologies may well make high-level specialized parts more practical. But much of the rhetoric surrounding the issue of standardized software parts seems to revolve around *high-level generic parts.* One doesn't see much of this even in traditional manufacturing. It is hardly realistic to expect to see much of it in software development, in which the problems are exacerbated by the increased centrality of design and the range of application. Increased use of standardized components in software development will heighten rather than diminish the need for sophisticated judgments regarding the tradeoffs involved.

26.4   Conclusion

The key issue, then, is how to effectively bridge the gap between the archetypal problems of software and the archetypal problems of particular application domains, so as to proceed to contingent solutions. This goes beyond the matter of domain-specific knowledge into the less well-defined realm of professional judgment, which plays a key role in technological practice generally. But while a foundation for it can be laid through education, substantial experience is necessary for its development. A few years ago, a *Software Engineering Journal* editorial complained that:

> "employers ask more from new graduates in computing than they do from new graduates in other professional disciplines. The new graduate in law or accounting is not expected to display the professional skills or judgment of the qualified solicitor or accountant; the new graduate in civil engineering is expected to undergo a long period of professional training before he or she can act independently. ...It is no more possible for a software engineering degree course to produce fully qualified software engineers than it is for an electrical engineering course to produce fully qualified electrical engineers; as with any engineering discipline, an additional and substantial period of professional training and experience is required before the graduate becomes professionally qualified." [SEJ89]

While some aspects of professional judgment are identifiable as discrete knowledge or skills, other aspects are deeply situated in experience. These include the ability to match archetypal problems with actual ones and configure contingent solutions. The results of that experience cannot be itemized or inventoried and stuck into a handbook. They come from actual practice and the study of superior practitioners.

As the editorial suggests, this is not unique to software technology. Such is the case with all professions including engineering. However, software technology adds a new wrinkle since this emergent professionalism by definition attaches to particular contexts of practice and it is these which are so much more numerous and heterogeneous than in other areas of technological practice. Software technologists need to come to grips with this and engage these issues at a deep level. However, a more realistic conception of engineering, one which recognizes the heterogeneity of engineering knowledge and the importance of engineering judgment, would be a start. Other engineering fields display an increasing willingness to explicitly grapple with these issues [Shapiro94b]. So must the software community.

My purpose has not been to discount what has been achieved so far in making software technologists more professional. However, continued progress depends on would-be software engineers disabusing themselves of the myths and misperceptions which appear for many to remain central tenets of the faith. Those misperceptions about the nature of engineering threaten to retard rather than advance the development of their professionalism. They are comforting myths, but they will prove ultimately self-defeating as a basis for pragmatic practice. Software may well call for a more sophisticated disciplinary model than straight engineering, but a more realistic engineering model would at least be a significant step in the right direction. By leaving mythology behind, software technologists will set themselves on a road which will give them a better chance of fulfilling their professional potential.

Chapter 27
Is the Rush to Quality a Move to Inequality?

27.1 Introduction

The originators of the term "Software Engineering" at the ubiquitously cited 1968 NATO conference strongly suggested that software development should be performed using mass produced, standardized, software components and tools. This thinking was drawn from the predominant manufacturing concepts of Taylorism, as exemplified by the assembly lines of the Ford Motor Company.

Deming, Juran, Ishikawa and others have developed a critique of Taylorism, arguing that piece work and simple quality control are insufficient promoters of quality of process and product, and that the workers' attitudes and involvement are critical factors in determining the overall performance. We examine the evidence provided by several surveys of these factors to ask whether these pioneering ideas are yet able to deliver, in the software context, all that they promise.

27.2 Quality and Management

Currently numerous organizations are focusing on or are obsessed with the movement towards software quality via quality management systems (QMS), process improvement, or total quality management (TQM). Even four years ago Ed Yourdon was able to cite "do or die" pronouncements on quality from the CEOs of the likes of Hewlett-Packard and IBM, and record that 75% of North American software development organizations had an independent software quality assurance group [Yourdon92]. The exact origin of this movement cannot be traced to a single source, though it is widely recognized that the ideas of W. Edwards Deming were a significant influence in founding this movement. Simply put his idea is that *quality is the route to economic success.* Following the Second World War he tried to introduce this idea to the US manufacturing industry but found little interest. As is now widely known his ideas were applied and developed by Japanese industry, and it is strongly claimed that they demonstrated that higher quality results in high productivity gains. Indeed Deming, as early as page 2, points out in his seminal work *Out of the Crisis*, quoting the relationship between quality and productivity as reported by his friend Dr Yoshikasu Tsuda, of Tokyo University:

> "I have just spent a year in the northern hemisphere, in twenty-three countries, in which I visited many industrial plants, and talked with many industrialists.
>
> In Europe and in America, people are now more interested in cost of quality and systems of quality audit. But in Japan we are keeping very strong interest to improve quality by use of methods which you started.

...when we improve quality we also improve productivity, just as you
told us in 1950 would happen." [Deming86]

In this work Deming enunciated his "legendary" 14 point programme and, moreover, elaborated his complete approach to management. His aim was to put forward
a management philosophy that showed the way *out of the crisis* by transforming the
traditional Western style of management. This was still largely based on Taylor's
principles of scientific management [Taylor11] *vis-a-vis* the assembly line principle,
as exemplified by the original Ford Motor Company production line. The main thesis
of Deming's work is that: *quality improvement is the pre-cursor to increasing productivity which in turn leads to economic success.* This tenet was embodied as what he
termed as a "chain reaction" and can be seen in the process shown in Figure 27.1.

During the post-war era Deming claimed that his approach was more appropriate
to the new economic context than was Taylor's, which was then in pre-dominant use
in manufacturing industry. The latter approach to industrialization was based on an
assembly line of "piece workers" with production norms. Here management is deemed
to know best, so it defines the work to be done as work-plans. These detail the precise
methods to be used, in which the worker is just another inanimate tool or unit in the
production line. From this perspective it is possible to see that workers are obliged to
perform according to some particular norms otherwise they would be penalized. The
consequence of this view is a culture, still present in many organizations (and ironically
now being introduced into many public sector organizations in the UK such as hospitals,
universities etc), of quantitative tracking of individual workers, performance-related
pay, and a resulting climate of fear of being penalized or dismissed. In contrast,
Deming's approach aims to "Put everybody in the company to work to accomplish the
transformation" (point 14 of his programme).

Taylor's approach to management is about control via individual targets, numerical
goals, exhortations, and limiting the involvement of workers in the decision-making
to a level at best marginal and at worst non-existent. By contrast, Deming's approach,
as embodied in points 10 to 12 of his programme, claims to be about the elimination
of individual targets, merit systems and numerical quotas and goals for both management and workers, as well as the removal of barriers that rob people of the pride of
workmanship. In his programme, one of the 14 points is the need to drive out fear,
as he says that "No one can put in his best performance unless he feels secure". He
is very clear on the consequences of operating a culture of fear that fires and hires on
short term targets, and asserts that it is the responsibility of management to prevent
this social malaise:

"It is no longer socially unacceptable to dump employees on the heap
of unemployed. Loss of market and resulting unemployment, are not
foreordained. They are not inevitable. They are man-made.
    The basic cause of sickness in American industry and resulting unem-
ployment is failure of top management to manage."

Both Taylor's and Deming's approaches embody a philosophy of management
suited in particular to the manufacturing of artefacts. Although they offer different

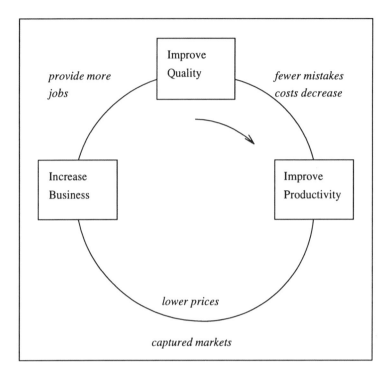

Figure 27.1 Deming's Chain Reaction

possible panaceas they both claim to provide economic gain through increased productivity. In this chapter we will consider both in the context of the production of information systems largely based on software. Because both Deming and Taylor differ considerably on the means of achieving economic success they could be contrasted from several different perspectives. For example, in the past we have focused on the *technical* factors for specific initiatives intended to promote software quality, such as the Capability Maturity Model, and Quality Management Systems conforming to ISO 9000-3 [Bissett95], [Siddiqi95].

In this chapter a different perspective is taken - it is in our opinion one that is of considerable concern to the professional practitioners in the software engineering community - that of a *practitioners'* perspective. We look at a selection of case studies that have been reported in the literature concerning organizations that are in the process of embracing the ideas envisaged in the movement towards quality. More precisely, many of the organizations will have based their production processes on some management approach, the most likely one being what Watts Humphrey terms the software factory concept, "originally proposed to improve software development methods and component reuse" [Humphrey91a]. We will, therefore, be examining the experience of practitioners in the transition from the factory paradigm to the process improvement paradigm. These experiences will be analysed to assess the extent to which the transition has taken place, and the effects on practitioners. We attempt to assess on the basis of this analysis a specific hypothesis that is central to Deming's programme and stems from point 14, that of: *empowering everybody in the organization to work towards the same goal of transforming the organization.* We ask whether the quality initiatives actually emphasize the inequalities within software organizations.

The chapter concludes with a position on the basis of this assessment and pleads for further empirical evidence to substantiate or refute this. We hope to provoke a debate which invites the reader to consider whether the culture in which they work is allied to Taylor or to Deming.

27.3 Survey of Case Studies

In the literature there is a growing body of evidence documenting the experience that the organization as whole has undergone in applying software quality initiatives. A few examples, all of which acknowledge the influence of Deming's ideas, illustrate our point. Humphrey *et al* report how in just two years the Software Engineering Division at Hughes Aircraft progressed in their quality rating and provide details of the costs and benefits [Humphrey91b]. Similarly Dion at Raytheon, one of the 100 largest corporations in the US, reports that over the five year period the process improvement initiative increased productivity twofold and the benefit to the corporate balance sheet was $7.7 return on every $1 invested [Dion93]. Rugg provides advice on to how select a contractor [Rugg93], and Broadman & Johnson report on what small organizations have to say about a particular process improvement initiative [Broadman94]. All these studies have been primarily tracking productivity, cost of rework, etc, as project characteristics to document process improvement success. These studies implicitly present a view as if there is a consensus and a unity of purpose amongst all participants in the software organization; in sociological terms they subscribe to a *weltanschauung* or world-view known as functionalism, represented in the writings of Talcott Parsons. In contrast we now look at some studies that have also focused on companies that are in a process of transition, but from a pluralistic rather than an unitary perspective, in other words from the angle of the participants involved, rather than simply treating the organization as a uniform whole.

Hall and Fenton performed an extensive independent study in which 243 question-naires were targeted at both managers and developers, (yielding an unusually good response rate of 65%), in order to analyse a number of software quality assurance practices at three British organizations with the following characteristics: they employed over 10 000 employees, had their own software division whose products were critical to the success of the organization, and they all had a reasonably mature quality improvement initiative [Hall95b]. One specific aspect of this study is pertinent in the context of our investigative hypothesis; that of assessing whether *everybody in the organization is working towards the same goal.* In their study they had asked managers and developers to rank in order of priority five quality goals, such as cost, user satisfaction and reliability. from their own perspective and from the organization's perspective. Their overall conclusion was that there was "a great deal of quality goal incongruence between practitioners' own goals and perceived organizational goals" in that "each organization had very different organizational and practitioner goals". In one company for instance, practitioners thought low cost was the number one priority for the organization, whereas low cost was the least priority for practitioners. Also managers rated low costs as a less important organizational goal than did developers.

Wilson *et al* conducted a study to look at the motivation for software quality assurance in practice [Wilson95a]. They surveyed a representative sample of the Australian software industry, asking respondents (managers and developers) to state the reason for introducing quality assurance. Interestingly, their finding that practitioners rate the increase of profit as the lowest priority and that developers "rate increasing profits as a more important decision criteria than their management" replicates the findings of Hall and Fenton for one of the companies in their survey. Further analysis by Hall and Fenton reveals that there does not appear to be a definitive practitioners' list of priorities either for themselves or for their organization, but that practitioners seem to adapt their goals depending upon the environment in which they work. In summary, there does not appear to be the unity of purpose in the goals of the practitioners and their organizations, making it extremely difficult to: *put everybody to work in transforming the organization.*

In our original hypothesis we had the notion of empowerment of the practitioner. Before investigating what the studies reveal, let us remind ourselves of Deming's thoughts on this. He was very clear that whilst everybody was responsible for bringing about transformation, it the management's responsibility to explain to a critical mass why the change was necessary, to motivate practitioners and win them over. Mohammed and Siakas, in attempting to assess maturity in terms of both technical and cultural factors in a North European software company (which had recently acquired certification for its software quality management system), used a questionnaire to ask practitioners to rank what factors they thought should influence quality [Mohammed95]. Their findings reveal "the two most important factors for improving software quality were motivating employees and employee proposals", so it would appear there is a thirst for knowledge and a willingness to be involved.

To assess the extent to which the practitioners thirst is being quenched or the degree of empowerment we make a number of observations from several further case studies. Wilson *et al* in another study [Wilson95b] surveyed 50 Australian companies in attempting to analyse the extent to which quality management system practices have penetrated to practitioners. He makes clear the distinction between "official" organizational programmes and their acceptance at the grass-roots level, in that "organizational programmes do not necessarily appear to have started to change the attitudes and culture of the system developers at lower levels of the organization". His preliminary analysis leads him to "support the hypothesis that software quality assurance programmes have not yet penetrated to the system developer". A further paper by Hall in which she attempts to assess "what do developers really think about software quality" provides us with further concern [Hall95a]. The study "revealed some worrying and persistent trends regarding the failure of organizations to communicate effectively with practitioners about quality". In yet another study, Hall and Fenton assessed the state of metrication in a company [Hall94], and whilst the data that follows was from only 34 questionnaires, it does not support the position that the practitioners are empowered. They found that although 68% of staff were keen to improve quality they were not able to do so, and the reasons cited as factors which prevent them and the percentage of people affected are: lack of information (92%); lack of training (83%); too much work (83%); lack of resources (79%); lack of working procedures (67%); lack of written procedures (62%) and poor management (62%).

Finally, Nicholson *et al* carried out a survey of 69 people from 43 different organizations [Nicholson95]. They conclude that "although quality practitioners have autonomy, many need more information to help them decide what to do and how to do it". Moreover, "satisfaction with job security was extremely low", and "fears about job security were uniformly spread over all demographic groups". From these studies it would certainly not lead us to conclude that practitioners feel empowered - the opposite may be near the truth.

27.3.1   Commentary

At this point it is interesting to speculate as to why there is such a lack of clear development of Deming's approach amongst software development organizations. Deming advocates a participative enabling culture based on self-improvement, education, responsibility, leadership, loyalty and trust, so that everyone may work effectively for themselves and the company. His vision was the adoption of a new philosophy appropriate to a new economic age, with a purpose of continuous and unending process improvement. Deming's philosophy is that all actors (customers, managers, and workers) should be in a "win-win-win" game. This summary clearly puts the approach in the camp of liberalism. So why do the findings detailed above apply? The liberal reply might be that Deming's approach has not been wholeheartedly put into practice, or that more time is needed for such changes to take root.

At least two different alternative perspectives can be considered; these can be loosely called the conservative and the socialist, without becoming embroiled in dogmatics. Perhaps the conservative perspective would be that there is a shared, common, interest for all those who work for the organization, and that practitioners' interests should be subsumed to this? Perhaps the socialist critique of Deming would be that the interests of different parts of the development organization cannot be reconciled?

Yet another, purely technical, commentary would be that perhaps the intrinsic nature of software itself is an obstacle. The nature of software and the changeability of information technology make for a situation which is very different to manufacturing mass production because, as Fred Brooks has pointed out, the physical realization of software is "accidental" [Brooks87a]. Perhaps software development is immature, or perhaps it will always be difficult to "get it right" because software is inherently difficult stuff?

We are reluctant to try to supply immediate answers here in this present work, but we pose the question: how to combat the lack of progress with Deming's ideas? One thing is clear: professional software practitioners want to do a good job, and there should be no doubt that their managers must want to *enable* them to do good work. Surveys of software industry managers, analysts and programmers across the globe consistently return "the work itself" as their top motivating factor (ahead of pay and benefits, for instance) [Couger95].

27.4 Conclusions

There is a tremendous interest in software development and maintenance organizations, both amongst managers and on the part of practitioners, in the possibility of improving the quality of software. Yet some of the key ideas of the "quality movement", those of W. Edwards Deming, have so far achieved a very uneven and limited penetration within these organizations. By examining several surveys of software development practices and attitudes we have uncovered the lack of basic clarity of purpose and communication currently hampering attempts to use Deming's approach.

Further reasons for this lack of development, the exact nature of the obstacles, and the ways to dissolve the obstacles, are the material of further investigation and study. However, we ask readers of this chapter to pose themselves the question: "is my organization under the influence of Taylorism or is it moving towards the kind of environment envisaged by Deming ?". We believe that this is a useful and challenging question to ask, and one in which the search for answers will prove valuable. We would be delighted to hear your results ourselves, but in any event we encourage readers to communicate their findings throughout the software development industry and academia; they are sure to find an interested audience.

Chapter 28
Pressures to Behave Unprofessionally

28.1 Introduction

During the last decade, many changes have affected those involved with the development of commercial software. The rapid increase in the number of computers and the expansion of the application areas supported by them have greatly enlarged the potential market for software systems. Also, new techniques of software design and implementation have generated an end-user expectation of quicker, lower-cost and more effective software development. Increasingly, users expect software to be reliable, effective, well-documented and well-supported by the manufacturer.

From our perspective it appeared that the perhaps dubious software development practices we encountered at the beginning of our careers as IT practitioners had largely died out to be replaced by a true "engineering" discipline: we believed that the unprofessional attitudes of past experience had disappeared.

However, in the light of our recent experiences, we have had cause to re-evaluate these opinions. As part of our work within a Teaching Company Scheme academic/industrial collaboration we needed to locate an industry-specific business package that could be modified by the vendors to the precise client requirements we had specified. We investigated a number of software houses over a period of about a year. While involved in examining packages for our industrial partner we noted several aspects in which software developers tended to adopt an unprofessional attitude. These included:

- Failing to follow acceptable Software Engineering standards in the production of code

- Failing to produce suitable (or any) documentation

- Failing to test software adequately

- Attempting to hide the true extent of costs likely to be incurred

- Over-representing hardware or software experience

While developers do not necessarily exhibit all these characteristics, these failings do appear to affect, to a greater or lesser extent, a wide range of software development organizations. Large organizations do seem to suffer from the same professional shortcomings as far smaller companies, although they may be more adept at hiding them!

In this chapter we first list several unprofessional characteristics we have noted in the software houses we have investigated. We then examine several factors derived from our involvement with commercial software developers that we believe put pressure on developers to act unprofessionally. We finally present and comment on some strategies by which the IT professional can guard against such unprofessional behaviour.

28.2   Pressures on Developers

It is our contention that in many cases a lowering of professional standards may occur as a result of operational pressures.

28.2.1   Increased commercial pressure on developers

Many software developers, now find themselves working in niche markets over-crowded, for the potential size of market, with vendors. They are coming under increasing pressures, both external and internal, to make new and revised products available as quickly as possible. This can lead to the classic developers' urge to "cut corners" — particularly in the area of documentation. This is now frequently rein-forced by a marketing-led company culture in which the process of meeting pressing marketing deadlines takes precedence over the production of a solid product. We have seen companies who attempt to secure an order at all costs, even if this means misrepresenting the experience or functionality of technical staff.

Though small companies may be thought of as being under particular pressure, it appears to us that larger companies, having often considerable fixed overheads, place even more pressure upon the sales and marketing workforce due to the need to gain orders to cover these overheads during the year. Several well-publicized major software packages have failed or have had their reputation damaged due to premature release into the marketplace.

28.2.2   Smaller development groups

The move away from large development groups (for a variety of reasons) has led to a reduction in the apparent need for the documentation of team communication and coordination. By lowering the number of communication channels within the team, a dramatic saving in development time may be possible. For example, [Black92] reports one in-house development team had been reduced from 10 to two members with a two-fold increase in productivity.

However, small teams working under pressure may be tempted to rely almost totally upon oral means of communication. The resulting lack of documentation may not impact immediately upon the project and indeed remarkable progress may be possible at first. Unfortunately, later system integration, maintenance and enhancement activities are often rendered nearly impossible by this lack of effective documentation.

Another problem we have noted with small development teams is that they may be over-stretched by the needs of projects in different phases of development. Trying to cope simultaneously with converting potential clients, developing new systems and supporting existing clients can sometimes prove too much for even the best-intentioned developer. We have also noted a tendency for small development teams to concentrate on "getting the business" — support for the client drops off once the contract is signed. This lack of commitment naturally has a negative effect on client satisfaction with the systems provided by such developers.

28.2.3 Lack of suitable project management

As mentioned above, recent trends have tended to produce small or very small development teams. This in turn has led to a reduction in the formal planning and management of projects. Little assistance with, or understanding of, the day-to-day development process can be expected where upper management (if any exists) is mostly concerned with the product release coinciding with an often arbitrary marketing deadline.

Though small development groups can be highly productive and can produce high quality work, the need for a sensible and, in the long-term cost-effective, level of coordination and controlled communication remains. In particular we have seen one very small team where differences of approach led, in part, to a breakdown of normal working relationships between team members.

28.2.4 Unstable software development technologies

In recent years a dramatic increase has occurred in the number of emergent software development technologies and methodologies. For example, 4GL and Object Oriented concepts have radically altered the way in which developers design and construct software systems. Also, enhanced versions of existing, well-tried, technologies and methodologies regularly appear.

It might be thought that such technological progress would inevitably lead to improved software end-products. However, we believe that the unstable development environment engendered by these new concepts has adversely affected sound working practices. Lack of theoretical understanding of the difficulties inherent in these technologies may mean that there are areas of the development process where there is little or no solid ground on which to base practical procedures [vanTyle94]. Software tool life-cycles appear to be steadily decreasing and this has led to a dilemma for software developers — should they stay with "old-fashioned" but reliable and well-understood tools or should they adopt new tools which are not yet particularly stable or well understood. Developers also may find that prospective customers expect use of the latest tools to be in evidence, even if the customers have little understanding or appreciation of the role of these tools.

Ideally developers should stay in touch with new technology, but this technology should not be used for real projects until sufficient experience has been gained with trial development. It is clear, however, that many developers would find it difficult to adopt such a policy due to lack of resources.

28.2.5 Cut-throat pricing of products

With the rapid decrease in real terms of software prices during the last decade has come the need to market a product at a highly competitive price. The tendency among potential purchasers is to compare all software prices against those of the most popular packages (word-processors and spreadsheets, for example) — despite the great difference in the potential volume of sales between mass-market and niche software. Thus developers of specialist packages, especially those aimed at smaller businesses, find that to produce a marketable software system at all requires the cutting to the bone of overheads such as testing, support and documentation.

As has been seen in other areas of commercial activity, ruthless under-cutting of prices in a market sector eventually leads to a resulting decrease in margins. This may force developers into financial difficulties and further encourage the lowering of professional standards.

28.2.6   Using the customer to do the testing

With the reduction of software prices and therefore the reduction of budget allocated to testing has come the alarming strategy of allowing the early customers to carry out the bulk of the testing. We are not talking here of legitimate "beta-testing", but of situations where an under-tested product is released onto the open market. The developer is thus relying on the client to isolate and report problems as they arise. This strategy is not restricted only to small developers as some well known software companies have apparently carried out such a policy.

There are some short-term advantages that may prompt software developers to adopt this strategy. First, considerable cost and time savings are possible, since testing typically may take as much as half the total system development time [Brooks95]. Second, error correction efforts may be concentrated on only those faults serious enough to inconvenience the client.

However, for the customer, such a policy is frustrating, disillusioning and potentially expensive. A customer may eventually be lost to a competitor (who may not, in reality, be any better) or be turned against the computerization process all together. This is particularly true where the customer is expected to pay again for the "debugged" version of the software, either through repurchasing a new version or via maintenance charges. Our clients had, in fact, had just this experience that had resulted in several years delay in the process of adopting IT within their business.

28.2.7   The cutting-out of the professional adviser

The growth of home and personal computing since the mid 1980's has led many businesses to adopt a do-it-yourself approach to the acquisition of new software. In the past, it would have been considered foolhardy for a company to have contemplated the purchase of expensive software and hardware without some form of professional advice, either from within the company or from external consultants. Now the low cost of current systems has reduced the apparent need for, and cost-effectiveness of, such assistance.

This reduction in assistance has, in turn, generated a great reliance, on the part of the purchaser, on the integrity of the dealer and salesperson. Unfortunately we have found in practice such faith frequently to have been misplaced. The removal of what amounts to assessment of software by independent computer professionals has led to the use of the salesforce to skirt around adverse usability and reliability issues. We have noted dealers who did not make obvious their close connections with the software developer; such dealers are in reality little more than a marketing department for the software developer and can provide no objective assistance at all.

With little or no external evaluation and criticism of their product, development teams may find it difficult to focus on those areas which need improvement. Thus much development is carried on "in the dark", divorced from the appraisal of fellow professionals.

28.2.8   Lack of formal education among developers

For many small software development companies, key personnel may be derived from an earlier phase when the business initially grew out of a hobby, frequently characterized by a preponderance of small projects. Thus senior development staff, while undeniably talented and creative, tend to lack the formal understanding of the software development process necessary to control a major project successfully.

Such naturally confident, creative people may not recognize or wish to admit their weaknesses and may be unwilling to devote the time required to train in compensatory skills and update their existing abilities. We believe that further and higher education organizations could and should offer education and training in a form to appeal to such people.

28.3   What Can the IT Professional Do?

As IT professionals, it falls on us to do what we can to minimize the risk involved in dealing with software developers. Only by ensuring, as far as possible, that developers have followed professional standards throughout the development process will pressure be brought to bear upon those developers not adhering to such standards.

Others, for example [Wright95], have presented tools and techniques which may be used to control the risks inherent in procuring and developing software systems. However, we feel that the IT professional needs also to consider non- and semi-technical means of investigating software products.

This section lists some guidelines that may be followed to advantage when carrying out the evaluation of a software product and its developers. We also note any pitfalls we have encountered in adopting these checks and discuss possible ways of avoiding the problems.

28.3.1   Be vigilant

When dealing with software developers, adopt a vigilant attitude. We believe this is particularly important when dealing with obviously "risky" situations where, for example, the developer company is small, or appears led by an overzealous marketing department.

We initially thought that ISO9000 registration would be a useful when choosing a developer as an indication of commitment to quality. However, we found that it is difficult or impossible to find any certified firms that provide software for our small market sector. Software firms servicing these sectors tend to be small (leading to further problems as noted above) and the nature of ISO9000 may make it unsuited to such firms [Wareham94]. Even if such certification was appropriate for small software developers, many such firms could not support the additional overheads inherent in the certification process.

28.3.2   Talk to existing users

Talk to and visit current users. Obviously, most developers try to have potential customers talk to successful (and possibly unrepresentative) reference sites, so try to find users not recommended by the developer. We found it particularly useful to use client contacts with businesses in the same market sector. These, often informal, links resulted in several useful site visits.

It should be borne in mind that current users may not have the same requirements as the client nor place the same operational demands on the proposed system. It is also important to note that, though useful, such sources of information need to be treated with some caution. We found, for example, that some clients initially gave favourable reports of software houses despite their own experience and needed to be probed to elicit more realistic comments. We would advise also that developers without a substantial client base should be particularly carefully scrutinized.

28.3.3   Check financial status

An obvious step is to check the latest accounts for the developer. We have found computer-based company accounts systems to be useful in giving a rapid overall picture of prospective suppliers. But such accounts may, particularly where small companies are involved, be either unavailable or lacking in any real detail. It also has to be remembered that accounts do not necessarily give a reliable picture of a company's true financial status. We would contend that few IT professionals would have the necessary experience to evaluate such accounts accurately.

Another risk is that software development may form only a small part of a larger, financially more attractive organization. Here the risks may in fact turn out to be similar to those found when dealing with smaller, autonomous, organizations. In some cases it may be quite difficult to uncover the exact relationship between the various subsidiary organizations involved.

28.3.4   Compare prices

Our experience has shown that product price can be an indicator of possible problems. We would be cautious of products selling at prices markedly below those of the competition without some obvious reason for such a deviation, such as differences in product scope. Such products and the companies selling them may well be cutting corners with standards to achieve a low price.

Particular caution is indicated when such low prices are not supported, or could not be supported, by the expected sales volume. Such developers may be trying to force competitors out of the market by aggressive pricing — a dangerous tactic, or may be hoping for follow-on sales to provide a profit.

We would recommend a thorough evaluation of the base price of the product and any "extras" such as installation, training and maintenance, and the careful comparison of this to other competitors' prices.

28.3.5 Demand documentation

Demand to see both end-user and development-process documentation. Documentation, or the lack of it, can provide a very useful insight into the professionalism of the developer. If little or no such documentation exists, or if there is considerable resistance to allowing sight of it, the software product is very likely to be suspect.

Developers are often wary of allowing prospective clients access to documentation. Common arguments used by developers to support this attitude are:

- the customer is about to steal their good ideas

- the documentation is "just about to be produced"

The first case can usually can be overcome by a non-disclosure agreement of some form. The second case often means that there is no documentation at all and the developer cannot find the resources to generate it.

28.3.6 Examine code

Related to (3.5), if possible look at the code itself or at least a substantial example thereof. Many developers do not want to allow this, but particularly in 3GLs the standards adopted in the production of code can speak volumes about the overall quality of work. For example, internal documentation, modularization and amendment control should all be in evidence.

However, many new systems are developed using 4GL and object-oriented concepts. From our experience, 4GLs are harder to analyze in this way and even an expert may not be able quickly to detect problems with 4GL code. We have experienced this problem when looking at an Oracle based system. It has been noted [Barby94] that it can be difficult thoroughly to test object-oriented programs. This naturally poses severe problems for those from outside a development team who wish to examine such code at a detailed level.

28.3.7 Check developers' experience with tools

Beware of developers using the latest development tools. The danger is two-fold:

1. the developer may not be adequately familiar with the tools

2. the tools themselves may have faults that may result in flawed programs

As mentioned above (3.6), there are good reasons to be cautious of developers who have recently started using object-oriented techniques.

It may be useful to find out how long the current development environment has been in use, and try to gain an impression of the familiarity of development staff with the tools they use. It also may be possible to see changes in the development environment by comparing older and recent code. While a software developer working with a proper sense of professional responsibility may be able to adopt a new tool successfully, some developers will be tempted save time and money by cutting corners with training, leading to severe problems.

28.4   Conclusions

We have listed a number of pressures on software developers which may lead them to adopt forms of unprofessional behaviour. We believe that many problems in this area stem from current trends leading to increasing down-sizing of both computer systems and software development groups. The pressures interact to seduce developers into sacrificing a thorough development process to short-term expediency. This process may be insidious and self-supporting — the situation gets steadily worse over a period of time. Though customer expectations have doubtless grown over the past decade, the reality is that many software products fail to deliver an adequate service, due to a combination of the factors mentioned above.

Depending on the nature of the system provided, there may be legal implications which may arise from the supply of substandard software. The law regarding the liabilities of software houses is confused [Bott95], but most developers attempt dramatically to limit their liability regarding the systems they produce. It seems to us that developers would do better to honour the spirit of their obligation to provide a properly constructed and functioning system, rather than hide behind legal loopholes.

It is our opinion that IT professionals need to: adopt an aggressive attitude towards software developers; be ready to dig deep to discover the true risks involved; and take nothing for granted. Only by following a professional course of action will both clients' interests be protected and software developers find that it is the entire development process and not just the delivered software and hardware system that is considered important.

Part V
Education and Training

For the Software Engineering profession to be an effective force in the twenty-first century, effective education and training is paramount. The type of education and training needed to build a successful profession comes in two forms. Firstly, software engineers need to be equipped with the technical skills necessary to build high quality software. Secondly, they need to be educated in what it is to behave as a professional. Both aspects of education and training are necessary if Software Engineering is to develop into a well rounded and effective profession. Indeed, this has long been recognized by professional bodies and to be BCS accredited, UK university courses must address both aspects of Software Engineering. This Part of the book concentrates on the second type of education and training — that of professional practice and behaviour. It is only this aspect that is going to stand the test of time. Whereas technical skills need constant updating, professional practice and behaviour is a timeless absolute.

This section looks at the topic of education and training from various perspectives. Some chapters make a strong case for injecting more realism into existing software engineering courses, some chapters tell of their experiences of implementing that contextual and social reality into courses. Some chapters show how, despite our best efforts, young people are turned off software engineering long before they ever reach a software engineering course.

The topic of the first chapter in this section is unusual. In it Frank Bott discusses *Selling, Marketing and Procuring Software*. Bott believes that most university software engineering courses fail to teach students about the rigours of the software marketplace. He asserts that this results in professionals who lack an essential understanding of the business that they will be practising in. Furthermore, Bott thinks that this is a significant contributor to the failure of some software businesses. Indeed, he goes as far as arguing that the failure of the London Ambulance System was overwhelmingly the fault of a poor business rather than technical understanding. Bott feels so strongly about this issue that he ends with a plea to the research community to dedicate more effort to evaluating software marketing and procurement practices, so that the economics of the software industry can be better understood.

Tony Cowling in his chapter *Curriculum Support for Professionalism* also advocates professionalism as the keystone of any Software Engineering degree. He argues that educating undergraduates in professionalism rather than training them in techniques will ensure that their knowledge is "future-proof". Furthermore, he puts forward a sound case for identifying two different aspects of professionalism that need to be taught — positive and negative professionalism. Positive professionalism expects software engineers to have a core set of practices, whilst negative professionalism expects them not to do certain things. Cowling also feels strongly that if the profession is to strengthen and become more effective, then the education of software engineers needs to be set within a more realistic sociological context. He does admit, however, that so far his university department has not been brave enough to implement such a radical change.

Craig Gaskell and Armstrong Takang, in their chapter *Academic Perspectives of Professionalism* try to make some sense of what academics really think about professionalism. In particular, their research is a successful attempt to find out what is being taught under the guise of professional awareness on UK university courses. One of their most surprising results is that a high proportion of universities actually claim to teach professional awareness. Another result, and one which supports Bott's argument, is that even on professionalism courses, technical issues are favoured above business or social issues. Indeed, they found that academics displayed an especial loathing for the financial and accounting aspects of the industry.

In the chapter, *Student Projects and Professional Awareness* written by Frank Milsom, we have a useful analysis of how the BCS Code of Practice can be applied to make undergraduate projects more realistic. This chapter is made particularly enjoyable by being illustrated throughout by excepts from log books written by students during their project. Milsom makes it clear that a realistic setting for final year projects can have big pay-backs in terms of students learning genuinely useful lessons. His approach to final year projects is one where teams and simulated client interactions are the norm — not a highly radical approach you may think, but one which is not often implemented in universities. The successful results that Milsom reports will, hopefully, encourage other universities to reconsider their approach to final year projects.

Ray Dawson & Ron Newsham in their chapter Converting Computer Science Graduates into Professionals concern themselves with a professionalism course that the company GPT runs for its graduate recruits. The course is an attempt to overcome some of the problems that Cowling mentions which are associated with teaching undergraduates only technical skills. Indeed Dawson & Newsham go as far as describing raw graduates as "very knowledgeable — but not a lot of use!". They describe how their course is structured to facilitate graduates learning hard lessons about working in the real world. They also recount (not without some glee) some of the dirty tricks (sorry — real life scenarios!) that are played out during the course. Their entertaining discussion of a sometimes cruel but ultimately effective "knocking graduates into shape" course should be essential reading for academics and industrialists alike.

The last chapter in this section discusses the impact of stereotypes on a group of sixth-formers (and therefore potential future recruits into the profession). John Wilkes in his chapter *Stereotypes, Young People and Computing* tests out how pervasive (and therefore destructive) negative stereotypes of computer professionals are amongst a group of young high achievers. Rather disturbingly, he discovers that computing as a profession does not appeal to a whole strata of young people. Given that a high proportion of the young people in this study had very stereotypical views about what it is to be a computer professional this result is not very surprising. Many of them thought of computer professionals as nerds, hackers, tekkies and anoraks. Wilkes results need to be looked at very closely by the professional bodies. Indeed, if we are going to have the difficulty he suggests in continuing to recruit high calibre young people into the profession then education and training is going to be an even more important issue than it is already.

Chapter 29
Selling, Marketing and Procuring Software

29.1 Introduction

Every year, the British higher education system turns out some 9000 graduates in computing, in some shape or form, most of whom are absorbed by the software industry or its customers. It turns out even larger numbers of graduates in law and rather fewer in marketing. However, almost none of these graduates combine a reasonable knowledge of software development with an appreciation of the commercial aspects — sales, marketing, contracts, procurement procedures, etc — of the industry. Those who enter the supply side of the industry may, at length, acquire such an appreciation, partly by osmosis and partly by learning from their mistakes; those who enter the user side are less likely to acquire it in this way but may well find themselves more in need of it as they become involved in the acquisition of new systems.

This failure to give graduates a broad view of the industry that most of them will enter reflects a general neglect of the industry as a research area both by academics active in computing research and by those active in the various fields covered under the general heading of business. It also reflects the old cliché about the strength of British technology and the weakness of its marketing.

The aim of this chapter is to encourage the inclusion of material about the commercial aspects of the software industry in academic computing courses and to encourage the study of the software industry as an interesting and appropriate area for academic research. Its three main objectives are therefore:

1. to outline, to the limited extent possible in a short chapter, current commercial practice in the selling, marketing and procurement of software, particularly bespoke software;

2. to describe one way of teaching such material in an academic computing course;

3. to identify some areas in which research would be of potential benefit to the industry.

Since this chapter is addressed primarily to the software community, the remainder of this introductory section is devoted to some definitions and to a brief discussion of how the software industry compares structurally with other industries.

29.1.1 Definitions

Selling is the process of persuading a specific customer, possibly an individual possibly an organization, to buy a specific product or service; it includes, where appropriate, the preparation of proposals and tenders, and contract negotiations. *Marketing* is the collection of activities that create the environment in which a product or service is sold;

the activities encompassed by the term range from product planning (discovering what customers would like to have and planning products to meet their needs or desires) to promotion (advertising, appearing at trade fairs, etc.) and deciding on an appropriate price. It is usual to regard selling as an activity separate from, but related to, marketing; it is, however, sometimes treated as an aspect of marketing.

Procurement (or purchasing or acquisition) is the set of activities undertaken by a purchaser in order to purchase a product or service to satisfy a perceived need. These terms are usually used only in the context of organizational purchasing.

29.1.2 Structure of the industry

The structure of the software industry is unusual in at least three ways. First, despite the existence of a few very large firms, it is very much an industry of small firms, small both in staff numbers and in turnover. These firms are often very specialized and produce very sophisticated products for a small number of clients; they are usually under-capitalized. The extreme example of this is the very large number of independent contractors active in the industry. No other high-technology industry is comparable.

Secondly, there is not the clear distinction between suppliers and users that is found in most industries. In particular, most suppliers are also users and many users act as do-it-yourself developers. In some cases — the clearing banks or the large airlines, for example — users may be very competent developers and may even start to supply software to other users. Outsourcing is just beginning to erode this aspect of the industry but its effect is still very limited. By comparison, how many users of photocopiers or lorries build their own?

Thirdly, the industry is very volatile. Companies, even ones of some size, come and go very quickly. Five years can see a company pass from a start-up to a boom and through to liquidation. Most such companies offer products as good as their competitors. It is success or failure in marketing and selling that determine their fate.

29.1.3 Classification of the industry

The software industry has traditionally been regarded as a service industry rather than as manufacturing. This is partly because the intangible nature of software made it difficult to view it as a product and partly because many software producers also offer services such as consultancy that are naturally regarded as services. Nevertheless, so simple a classification is misleading and, indeed, may well have harmed the industry in the UK. It is misleading because, at one end of the scale, software products such as games or word-processing packages share most of the characteristics of, say, video cassette recorders except that the replication cost is lower. At the other end of the scale, products like CASE tools or a major database management system share many of the characteristics of a sophisticated machine tool. It may be harmful because it excludes the software industry from initiatives that are aimed specifically at manufacturing industry.

However, most software producers offer services, in particular product support, consultancy and training. Suppliers of substantial software products, such as large CAD or accounting packages, provide consultancy and training to help their clients get the best out of the software; they provide support services to solve day-to-day problems. Income from these sources helps to smooth out the rather bumpy revenue stream that software products provide. The producers of large bespoke systems use consultancy as a way of building up relationships with potential customers and getting early warning of major contracts. Even the most prestigious of such companies will, on occasions, supply programming and similar services on a contract hire ("body shopping") basis, perhaps to overcome a short-term lack of business or perhaps in the hope of building a long-term relationship.

29.2 Retail Software

In many ways the selling and marketing of packaged software resembles that of other consumer durables such as video cassette recorders or cameras. There are, however, some important differences:

- the very high development costs and the very low replication costs make pricing a difficult but critical issue

- because software doesn't wear out, customers will only replace it if they are dissatisfied or perceive it as obsolescent

- documentation is, in many cases, of great importance and can become a source of revenue comparable to that derived from the software itself

- contractual conditions, even though licensing conditions are "shrink wrapped", need very careful consideration

- many products have both a retail market and a corporate market, either of which may be linked to hardware sales.

The low replication cost of software leads to the phenomena of site licences and corporate licences. The marketing decisions involved can be enormously important for the success or failure of the product.

The advantages to be gained from standardization within an organization lead to procurement exercises to chose the "standard" word processor, spreadsheet or database for an organization. A large corporation may thus decide to adopt the X word processor for all corporate purposes, which may lead to sales of say 10 000 licences. In practice, because the cost of a licence is well within the limits of most managers' spending authority, it is impracticable to impose such standardization by fiat. Adherence to the policy has to be encouraged by persuading staff of the benefits of standardization and by offering inducements such as central support or free or discounted provision.

This type of procurement is unusual in that it usually takes place with little if any involvement on the part of the sales staff of the potential suppliers — indeed, often without their knowledge. Companies do not choose the cars for their sales staff or their photocopier suppliers in this way.

29.3   Professional Packages

Many packages in this category have a very clearly defined market and there is little difficulty in identifying all potential customers. A package for the administration of livestock auctions, for example, might have about 500 potential customers in the UK and little effort would be required to identify them from the Yellow Pages or other directories. One or two weekly magazines are almost universally read and attendance at a small number of large agricultural shows would be likely to bring contact with a high proportion of the prospective market. It is fairly easy in such cases to produce a well-targeted marketing plan. There are, however, dangerous pitfalls in the selling of such packages. Let us take a hypothetical package that has cost £150 000 to produce and to which a marketing budget of £350 000 has been allocated. Suppose further that we foresee sales of about 500 copies and that we are unaware of any competition. Given these costs and the risk involved in this sort of product, we might well set a target of £500 000 for revenue from the product, which would mean a selling price of £1000 (or £995). We may also feel that this is a reasonable price bearing in mind the benefits that the package will bring to the companies it is aimed at. However, at this price, companies are unlikely to be willing to order the package by mail or phone and install it themselves. They will feel that they are justified in expecting an initial visit from a salesman and, if they choose to buy the package, a second visit at which it is installed and demonstrated for them; they may also wish to haggle about licensing conditions. Unless we already have a substantial and well-distributed sales force, sales visits to prospective customers scattered all over the UK will be expensive — two visits by a salesman based in Chester to a customer in Berwick-on-Tweed will cost at least £500. We might well find, therefore, that the selling costs of the package consume a large part of the revenue. We must either increase the selling price, in order to pay these costs, or decrease it, so that prospective customers do not expect the same level of service.

29.4   Bespoke Software

29.4.1   Marketing

The provision of large, bespoke software systems resembles the construction industry and other types of contracting industry. Key elements of the marketing mix are likely to be some or all of the following:

- presentations at conferences

- placing of articles in professional journals

- reports of the company's activities published in the technical press and, in some cases, the quality national press

- publication of a regular newsletter to be sent to potential customers

- establishing long-term relationships with potential customers, although there may be no prospect of a sale for several years.

Essentially, the aim of the marketing function is to ensure that the company is included in every tender list in the market areas in which it competes or, where a prime contractor is appointed from different field, to ensure that the company appears as a named subcontractor in at least one bid. (The ideal, which I once achieved, is to appear as a named subcontractor in *all* the bids!)

More perhaps than in any other industry, there is also a need to educate potential customers. The débacle of the London Ambulance System was the result of a profound ignorance of the software industry, reinforced by a reluctance to take advice or to consult with colleagues who had already introduced such systems successfully. Too much blame should not be attached to the company that produced the inadequate software; they did not understand the difficulty of what they were trying to do. The major failing, so far as the software was concerned, was in the procurement process that led to their being awarded the contract. The catastrophe of the Taurus system for the London Stock Exchange was vastly more expensive, if less worrying to the general public; this attempt at do-it-yourself brain surgery was reported as having cost the Stock Exchange the incredible sum of £400 million.

It is useful to distinguish between two types of corporate customer, the informed and the uninformed. (Less complimentary terms are sometimes used.) Many, probably the majority, of the customers that suppliers in this sector deal with are informed, that is, they have specialized staff who are familiar with the problems of large scale software development and understand the need for software quality management; they have appropriate procurement procedures; if they do not have sufficient resources to handle the procurement themselves, they will employ consultants to act on their behalf. There are, however, many uninformed customers, who not only lack such expertise but also fail to realize that it is necessary; they may try to manage the procurement using the same procedures that they use for buying, say, raw materials. Marketing activities in this sector almost inevitably find it much easier to reach the informed customer than the uninformed one.

Various industry associations and professional institutions play an important part in the process of educating and informing customers. The Institute of Purchasing and Supply produces model contracts for bespoke software procurement; Ada Language UK Ltd and the Ada Joint Program Office in the USA both undertake a range of activities aimed at promoting the use of Ada, to the benefit of suppliers of Ada-related products and Ada expertise; the Computer Services and Software Association produces a set of briefing notes providing an introduction to the different types of services available from its members and offering advice on how to gain full benefit from those services. In addition, in the UK, the Department of Industry has supported various programmes, notably the STARTS initiative [DTI89a] and [DTI89b], intended in part to educate the software industry's customers. Such educational marketing activity is particularly important to an industry with a large number of small firms, who can afford to spend very little on their own marketing activities. All such activities, however, are more successful in improving still further the knowledge and understanding of informed customers than in reaching out to the uninformed.

A central difficulty is measuring the effectiveness of marketing activities. It is comparatively easy to measure the effects of an advertising campaign for a brand of cornflakes or, for that matter, for a computer game. It is much more difficult to measure the benefits that result from sending a senior consultant to an international conference to deliver a paper on the usefulness of a new technique that the company has pioneered. The difficulty arises largely because the number of potential customers is comparatively small so that the effect of random factors is very high. It may happen that, as a result of one person hearing the conference paper, the company gets the opportunity to bid for, and subsequently wins, a multi-million pound contract — but it may not.

29.4.2 Selling

Bespoke software makes heavy demands on sales staff; they are generally responsible, albeit with technical and legal support, for preparing proposals, organizing presentations and negotiating the contract — and no two projects will be alike. This makes considerable demands on their personal, professional and technical skills and on the breadth of their knowledge. In practice, this sector of the software industry has experienced great difficulty in finding sales staff of suitable calibre.

29.4.3 Procurement

The procurement of large bespoke software systems presents many problems and a wide range of approaches have been tried. The aims of the purchasing organization are likely to include:

- transferring as much risk as possible to the supplier

- obtaining a system that meets the requirements at the best possible price, as soon as possible

- avoiding being tied into the same supplier for a long period

- in the case of public bodies and some other purchasers, complying with regulations regarding public procurements and being seen to be acting equitably.

Unfortunately, these apparently reasonable aims are incompatible in multitudinous ways. For example, a good way of transferring risk to the supplier is to use a fixed price contract. However, the supplier is then likely to charge a premium to compensate for the risk; if all goes well, the purchaser would get better value for money on a time and materials contract. These incompatibilities, together with the difficulty of establishing the requirements, are the root cause of most of the problems.

Procurement mechanisms, life-cycle models and contractual provisions are closely related: a contractual requirement to produce a deliverable is only meaningful if that deliverable is recognized by the life-cycle model being used; separate contracts for different tasks, potentially awarded to different suppliers, can only sensibly be allowed if the life-cycle model recognizes the tasks as distinct.

The difficulties of procuring large, software-intensive systems have much in common with the difficulties of procuring any large, complex and novel system. Problems experienced in defence procurement have been well documented and a number of government reports are very relevant, [Downey68], [HMSO71], [Jordan87] and [NAO94] for example.

29.5 Teaching Approaches

In Aberystwyth, we teach the material discussed in this chapter as a final year module for students on the MEng in Software Engineering. Such students will already have studied a "professional issues" module covering financial and legal topics, health and safety, and human resource management [Bott95].

The course consists of some 15 lectures covering the material outlined in Sections 2 to 4 of this chapter. We know of only one text [Marciniak90] that covers a significant part of the course, and that is based on US practice. However, the government reports already referred to are not difficult to read and we have made them available to students through the library. The course is assessed completely by coursework and it is in this coursework that the main interest lies. There are two coursework assignments; for both, the students are divided into groups of four.

For the first assignment, the first task of each group is to produce an invitation to tender (ITT) for a system to satisfy requirements that have been outlined, in imprecise and non-technical terms, in a lecture. This year's system was an examination administration system for a professional institution. The two most suitable ITTs are then selected and each group is required to produce a proposal in response to one of the ITTs (not one that the group itself wrote). Finally each group is required to evaluate all the proposals in response to the other ITT.

In order to carry out this exercise, students need access to a collection of real documents, such as invitations to tender, standard terms and conditions, and proposals. We are fortunate that our industrial connections have provided us with some of this material and that we have been able to obtain other material from the University's own procurements; some of the material has been slightly modified so as to conceal commercially sensitive items such as company identities and charging rates.

The second exercise requires each group to produce a marketing plan for a proposed new software product or service. A typical product might be a package aimed at a specialized section of the construction industry. Students are expected to identify the most appropriate channels of communication with potential customers, e.g. identify the specialist journals and exhibitions, and build and cost a plan on this basis. They are also expected to estimate the size of the market and a suitable selling price.

29.6 Research Opportunities

There has been extensive press coverage of many important software procurements over the last 30 years; such coverage can be found in highly specialized periodicals, some little more than newsletters, in the more general professional press, and in the serious daily and weekly newspapers. However, no attempt has been made to study, collect or analyse this material, with a view to presenting evidence to allow, for example, different procurement models to be assessed. Although there is much wisdom in [Downey68] or [Jordan87] there is little by way of evidence.

There is a need for research into ways of determining the effectiveness of various marketing techniques specifically for the software industry. If a bespoke software supplier can afford to spend £10 000 on marketing in 1996, which of the different marketing activities described in Section 4.1 of this chapter, should it spend its money on? It is unlikely that it will be able to carry out more than two of these activities. Most companies have no way of making the choice; they simply do what they have always done or ride the marketing manager's hobby horse.

There is little reliable information about the size and structure of the market for bespoke software. (For professional packages, rather more information is available, albeit at a high cost, from specialist companies.) There are no estimates for the price elasticity of the market yet the business case for investment in new software development technology often rests on an unseen but optimistic assumption about the elasticity.

None of the above research will be easy and it will not produce the precise results the industry would certainly like to see. Nevertheless, even partial and limited results would be of considerable value.

Chapter 30
Curriculum Support for Professionalism

30.1   Introduction

The background to this chapter is that the Department of Computer Science at the University of Sheffield has been delivering an undergraduate degree course in Software Engineering since 1988. The curriculum for this course has evolved steadily since it first started, but there is a limit to how far a curriculum can develop by evolution alone, and it has now reached the stage where a more major revision is required. Thus, we (i.e. the author and colleagues) have had to stand back and try to evaluate what has been achieved so far, as the first stage in building a new curriculum which is intended to put right what we now regard as some of the weaknesses of the present one. This chapter presents some of the results from that evaluation, and discusses the approaches to developing professionalism which have emerged from it.

30.2   Evaluation of the Existing Curriculum

One obvious result of this evaluation has been the recognition that, since our course was originally introduced, the possible technical content of an undergraduate Software Engineering degree has expanded enormously. Consequently, the problem of selecting technical material to be covered in the limited time available (and selecting material that will not be covered, which may be more significant) is now just as acute for Software Engineering as it is for other branches of engineering. A framework has been developed within which this selection of material can take place, and this is described elsewhere [Cowling94]. In outline, this framework consists of a hierarchical structure for the material that comprises Software Engineering, which at the top level identifies three components, namely the products, the processes and the relationships with people. The product component covers the core of computer science that is needed for Software Engineering, and is structured into four strands, with programming as the central one that unites the other three (i.e. theory, applications and hardware). Similarly, the process component is divided into two parts: one is the activities that occur in the process (e.g. requirements analysis, specification, design, implementation, testing and maintenance), and the other is its management (i.e. of quality and resources).

Finally, the component dealing with the relationship of Software Engineering to people covers the sort of issues of professionalism that are being discussed here, and in terms of evaluating our present curriculum it is particularly significant as the framework still requires criteria to guide the details of the selection process. In this respect the obvious criterion is to look at how useful the material is likely to be subsequently in professional practice. In trying to do this we came rapidly to the conclusion that we just could not predict reliably what material students of Software Engineering were actually likely to need during their subsequent careers. The most we could do was to identify some directions of development within Software Engineering that we thought were likely to become important, and for what it is worth we give our list of predictions for them here. In no particular order they are:

- increased emphasis on the use of formal methods, because of the pressures for increased reliability, etc;

- increased user-friendliness of formal methods, to enable them to be more widely used;

- increased emphasis on the use of metrics, for managing properties of both software systems and software development processes; and

- increased adoption of AI techniques within systems.

Far more significant than these, however, was the recognition that most of our students were likely to find themselves developing at least some applications that as yet we have barely started to dream about, and that they would do so using tools and techniques of which at the moment we have only the foggiest perception. Moreover, in many cases they would be doing so without the benefit of the sort of codes of design practice that underpin most of the more conventional branches of engineering: indeed, for the current generation of Software Engineering students it is more likely that they will be contributing to the development of such codes than using them as normal tools. Thus, we concluded that it was not important whether these guesses about future developments might be right or wrong. What mattered more was the issue of whether particular material was "future-proof", so that it would still make a valuable contribution to the education of software engineers, irrespective of precisely how significant its technical content might eventually become.

The outcome of this part of our evaluation could be summarized in terms of three conclusions. Firstly, since practising as engineers in this sort of unpredictable environment would put considerable demands on the professionalism of the students, what we taught them now about professionalism within Software Engineering had to be robust enough to carry over effectively to that environment. Secondly, an important criterion for selecting technical material for the curriculum would be the extent to which that material would support the development of professionalism. Thirdly, in trying to evaluate material it was important to look not just at **what** would be taught, but at **how** it would be structured and taught, since the latter would often have more effect on whether or not it supported the development of professionalism within the students.

30.3   Positive and Negative Professionalism

While this evaluation stressed the importance that should be attached to professionalism, one question that it did not answer directly was exactly what professionalism involved in terms of its impact on the curriculum. The usual concepts of professionalism derive from the meaning of "not amateur", implying both that professionals should be competent, experienced, practiced, etc, and also that they have responsibilities to the clients on whose behalf they operate. These seem to us to represent two sides to professionalism, which we term "positive" and "negative" respectively. Here, the negative side is concerned primarily with expecting professionals not to do things that would be regarded (particularly by the clients) as unprofessional. In terms of teaching that means that it also covers the basic issues of what professionalism is and why it is important. The positive side then goes beyond this, in that it focuses on the need for professionals not merely to meet a set of minimum requirements, but actively to seek to improve the standards to which they carry out all aspects of their work.

30.3.1 Professional issues

What we have called here the negative side of professionalism is mainly covered in degree courses by explicitly teaching the set of topics usually called "professional issues", but in describing these topics as "negative professionalism" we are not intending to suggest that they are unimportant. Indeed, explicit coverage of them is rightly a necessary element in any accredited degree, as they provide the foundation on which the more positive aspects of professionalism can build, and an important goal for the curriculum designer must be to ensure that the positive aspects are developed from this foundation. One of the hazards, though, is that because the professional institutions give fairly clear guidance on what topics should be in the set to be covered, it is all too easy for it to be reduced to a content-driven formula, typically composed of some combination of legal issues, social issues and generic or transferable skills. This may then lead to each of these topics being presented as a separate closed package, rather than the whole set forming a coherent basis from which to develop the positive aspects.

In the case of the legal issues, for instance, it is obviously necessary to cover both those aspects that are specific to Software Engineering (such as data protection, product liability, and health and safety requirements), and such general background about legal systems as is necessary for students to understand the mechanisms (e.g. statutes, codes of practice and contracts) by which these specific requirements will affect their work as professional software engineers. At the same time, these issues also need to be related closely to some of the social issues (such as privacy, security and responsibility for the environmental impact of systems), since these provide the justification for the legal requirements, and students need to understand why these requirements are there as well as what they are and how they apply to software systems.

Similarly, the discussion of social issues needs to go wider than just these specific areas, as students need to understand the broader effects of software systems on organizational behaviour, social structures and individuals within them. For instance, whether the systems tend to enforce hierarchical or distributed control, or whether they will lead to effects such as the "de-skilling" of jobs. Indeed, we are beginning to believe that students of Software Engineering have nearly as much need for a basic understanding of sociology and psychology as they do for an understanding of the more technical aspects of the subject. We would readily admit, though, that we have not yet had the courage to put that belief to the test by including modules on these topics as compulsory elements in our curriculum: those are likely to be our experiments towards the third generation!

There is also a danger that the teaching of transferable skills will not fit in with these other issues, since its focus is on much more practical disciplines, such as the ability to collect and manage information, to communicate clearly and present material well, to manage time or to work well in teams. We believe that they should be related, however, since they all stem from the need for software engineers to interact with a world which is inhabited by people rather than machines, and which is inherently loosely structured and perhaps even untidy. These practical skills are all essential to being able to manage this loose structuring and work effectively within it: they are necessary because the alternative of trying to tighten up structures, and so expecting people to behave like robots, would just not be socially acceptable.

Thus, we believe that this treatment of professional skills should derive very much from the topic of "the engineer in society", which appears as an important element in most other engineering disciplines. Moreover, unlike these other disciplines, Software Engineering is fortunate in that it does not normally need to be distracted from this focus by having to include significant coverage of basic IT skills, which would have the effect of shifting emphasis back to machines and away from the interaction with people. Unfortunately, though, Software Engineering does still share the problem with much of higher education that a lot of the effort that goes into teaching transferable skills has to be spent on making up for inadequacies of teaching at lower levels, particularly in written communication. The practical result of this problem is often that the links that one would want to make between transferable skills and the other legal and social issues can get lost beneath basic remediation.

30.3.2   Supporting positive professionalism

If positive professionalism is to be supported properly, then not only must negative professionalism be taught in a way that is coherent and open-ended, but also the rest of the curriculum must promote it in a way that builds on this foundation of professional issues. Thus, the technical topics need to be taught in a way that supports the development of professional attitudes within the students. Indeed our experience has been that explicit teaching about negative professionalism is only really effective insofar as it is also supported by implicit teaching of positive professionalism within the rest of the curriculum. If it is not supported in this way, then students may fail to appreciate how professional issues should apply to the technical material, and so they may reject it as being apparently irrelevant, or of little practical value.

To ensure that this support for positive professionalism is provided, we have identified some goals that need to be set for the technical content of the curriculum. The main one of these is derived from the concern of positive professionalism with competence and experience, and particularly the need that we have already established for engineers to be able to cope with new situations as well as being practiced at familiar ones. The goal that comes from this is that students must always know and work within the limits of their own competence, and this in turn gives rise to two other goals. One of these is that students must learn to evaluate the consequences of any decisions that they make in the course of their work, and to recognize the possible dangers of situations that they can not evaluate properly. The other goal is that students must be equipped to work in teams with specialists from other disciplines, who will be able to provide competences that they themselves may not possess.

This goal of evaluation as part of positive professionalism does have to be approached with care, though, to avoid situations such as football's "professional foul", which are characterized by a cynical calculation that the personal consequences of breaking some rules will be less damaging than trying to abide by them. An important part of negative professionalism is the idea that a profession is a calling or vocation, which carries with it the ideas of accountability to various parties, and hence the implication that a professional must abide by a code of ethics in which service and responsibility to "the community" are placed above individual gain. As a first stage, supporting this by positive professionalism means making students aware of the sort of market forces that may mean that a quick partial solution to some problem is more acceptable than a more complete solution that takes longer to develop. For proper evaluations, though, they need to be able to go beyond this, and to balance the intangible values, such as ethical considerations, against those factors which can be measured in tangible units (such as money, human resources or time).

30.4   Design Criteria for the Curriculum

In designing a curriculum for Software Engineering, one needs to be able to measure how well different alternatives will meet these goals of supporting positive professionalism. Since the goals themselves are not in a form that is easily measurable, we have derived from them three criteria that can be used for this evaluation. The first of these criteria stems directly from the goal of providing students both with basic competence, and also with the ability to extend this in order to cope with new situations. The requirement for basic competence means that they need to be equipped to use methods and tools, but the actual choice of individual methods or tools is not the most significant element here. What we see as far more important, if students are to be able to build on that basic competence, is that they should understand not just individual tools but the idea of a complete toolkit, and so the criterion is the completeness of the toolkit that is provided. This is not just to avoid the danger of the simple-minded approach, that can be characterized as "if you only have a hammer, every problem looks like a nail", but also is important to give students a framework in which they can understand the limitations of different methods. This understanding is essential if students are to appreciate the factors affecting the choice of which methods are suitable for which problems, and this is a particularly significant issue for Software Engineering, as in general it does not yet have the design practices that would govern these choices codified as well as they are in most other branches of engineering.

Secondly, the curriculum must equip the students with the ability to gain experience: which should not be confused with it actually having to give the students the experience, as that would be almost impossible to achieve. Indeed, students' lack of experience of the real world is well recognized as a significant problem in trying to educate them about applications of software systems, and since it would involve trying to put old heads on young shoulders it is not usually feasible to do much in the curriculum to remedy this. The normal model is that this sort of experience of application areas should come mainly from continuing professional development after the major formal educational process is complete.

There is also an alternative model, which is implied in the proposition that Software Engineering should be regarded as a postgraduate subject rather than an undergraduate one, and this is a common approach in the US. Concern for the positive aspects of professionalism serves to highlight the weakness of this alternative, however, in that by leaving consideration of these sort of issues until the postgraduate curriculum it provides relatively little opportunity for the implicit support for this professionalism that we are claiming is essential.

Equipping students to gain experience thus means enabling them to gain the maximum benefit from their encounters, subsequent to their formal education, with the problems of developing applications of software systems in the real world. We see the key to this as being to enhance the students' ability to criticize and evaluate any work that they do: for it will only be by such self-criticism and evaluation that they will be able to learn from experience of application areas, or even to recognize what the experience is that they have gained in those particular areas. The criterion that comes from this is the extent to which the curriculum encourages students to evaluate their own work rigorously, both in terms of their own part in it and their collaboration with others. This criterion also supports the goals of recognizing the limits of competence and of overcoming these by teamwork.

The third criterion then relates to the remaining goals, and is the extent to which the curriculum supports not only an understanding of the ethical context within which Software Engineering operates, but also of how that impinges on the more technical aspects. The aim here is that, in order to build on the basic knowledge of legal and social issues, the curriculum also needs to develop students' understanding of how these issues need to be applied in practice and why they are important. It must motivate the active approach of looking for applications of them to technical issues, rather than the passive approach of concentrating on technical problems and only occasionally considering the ethical aspects when these become obvious. The implication of this is that, in comparing different treatments of technical material, more open-ended approaches will in general be preferred to ones that have a narrower focus on the technical aspects, as the former will do more to encourage students to think about the ethical and social issues arising from the technical applications.

30.5   Curriculum Design Principles

While these criteria are intended to provide a basis for evaluating the extent to which curriculum designs support active professionalism, applying them in the evaluation process is not straightforward, as they are not properly orthogonal and so there will inevitably be conflicts between some of them. Apart from anything else, curriculum design is a process of allocating scarce resources, of which curriculum time is probably the most important [Shaw91]. These time constraints on the curriculum then generate their own pressures on the demands made by different topics that are candidates for inclusion in it. In particular, a balance has to be struck between the extent to which one can cover individual tools and methods in depth, as against covering a wider range of them. Similarly, a balance has to be struck between the extent to which one can allow students to learn from experience by going back over material several times or looking at a variety of applications of it, as against going on to new topics and hoping that students will be able to integrate their understanding of the more basic material in the course of studying this new material.

This issue of the need for drill and practice is one aspect of the conflict that is sometimes summarized as training versus education, and it is this conflict which also gives rise to the need for a balance between principles and applications. In this respect, we argue that the need for positive professionalism very definitely increases the value of principles as against applications. Indeed, Software Engineering is sometimes criticized as being too concerned with the tools that are built from applying principles, and not enough with the underlying principles themselves. The implication of this is that the toolkit needs to be defined primarily not in terms of particular software packages or even particular methodologies and techniques, but rather in terms of the principles that underlie them. This provides a more abstract level as the first stage in considering possible design features for a curriculum and evaluating them against the criteria that have been defined. Even so, there are probably many such principles that could be proposed, and we can not claim to have made any systematic attempt at trying to enumerate or classify them. Rather, we simply present here four such principles that we have identified from our experience so far, and that seem to us to help promote positive professionalism.

30.5.1 Modelling

Modelling is perhaps the most important of these principles that we would want to identify as helping to promote positive professionalism. Many of the tools and techniques that are used in Software Engineering are based on particular models of how systems (in the broadest sense) are structured. We therefore believe that it is vital that students understand these fundamental modelling techniques. Firstly, they need to become competent in using the models to describe problem areas and systems, and secondly they need to understand how the limitations of tools and techniques are often derived from the fundamental limitations of the models which they incorporate. This latter aspect we see as particularly important for the development of active professionalism, for if students learn to appreciate that all models have limitations then it should be much more obvious to them that they need to evaluate any model that is being proposed for a system, in order to establish what its limitations are, and whether these limitations render that model suitable or unsuitable for that particular application.

30.5.2 Formalism

Because of this need for rigorous evaluation of models, the second principle that we believe is important for supporting positive professionalism is that students must learn to handle formal models, since the fact that these support formal reasoning processes means that they are inherently better suited to some kinds of evaluation than informal models. At the same time, we are also very aware that this particular property of formal models can sometimes give a misleading appearance of precision and accuracy, and in teaching the application of formal and mathematical methods we find it essential to stress the fact that even if these are formal models, they are still only models, which may or may not match the real world situation that they are supposed to represent.

We see it as essential to this principle of formalism that students must learn to appreciate the differences between verification and validation of models. If they are to use formal models in a professional fashion, it is vital that students appreciate that even if the mathematical properties of a model can be verified by rigorous proof (which one would expect to be the case), that does not of itself ensure that the model is valid. Unfortunately, it is all too common for the classical mathematical approach to teaching formal material to concentrate almost exclusively on the mathematical aspects, with definitions leading to theorems, theorems leading to proofs, proofs leading to lemmas, corollaries and examples, and these in turn leading to more definitions, and so on: all of which must be correct, because it can all be proved, and so does not need to be questioned.

This positively discourages an equally important aspect, which is that students have to understand that the applicability of the assumptions underlying any formal model do need to be questioned carefully before results proved from that model are relied on in designing real-world systems. Moreover, since it is not sufficient just to question these assumptions only when a system is first being designed, we also believe that it is important for students to understand how the need to test systems arises just as much from the difficulties of validating formal models as it does from the danger of making errors when constructing or verifying them. Only once they appreciate this will they recognize the importance of designing systems from the outset so that they can be validated and tested, instead of the thoroughly unprofessional approach (which unfortunately comes all too naturally to students who have not had to confront this issue) of the testing of a system being tacked on at the end of its development as a (possibly embarrassing) afterthought.

30.5.3   Software Engineering as a process

The third principle that seems to us to be important is that the activity of engineering a software system is itself a process, and so support for positive professionalism requires students to understand how the various activities that are undertaken in developing a piece of software relate to this process. This is important primarily because this notion of the Software Engineering process provides the framework within which students can integrate into a coherent whole the different technical topics that they may encounter, and so understand how they are interrelated. This is the main reason why this process component formed part of the top level of our overall framework for the structure of the Software Engineering curriculum, as discussed earlier. Thus, while it may be difficult (particularly in a modular course structure) to ensure that all topics are taught in a way that emphasizes their relationships with each other, it should at least be possible to teach them in a way that makes clear their relationship to the framework provided by the Software Engineering process.

As well as providing a framework for integrating other material, this principle of emphasising the Software Engineering process is also significant because of the relationship between improvement of the process and improvement of the products that are developed by it. Of course, the tools and techniques that are currently available for developing and evaluating Software Engineering processes are still at an early stage of development: but then, those available for developing and evaluating products are arguably not yet much more mature either. This is likely to be an area in which our students will see very significant advances during the course of their working careers as professionals, and so to support active professionalism in this area we believe that students must have both a good understanding of the process itself and of the way in which it affects software quality, and at least some experience of the practical problems of trying to manage, control and improve it.

As far as the knowledge and understanding element of this is concerned, we believe that the most significant challenge at the moment is to integrate effectively the teaching of software measurement into the curriculum, so that students will understand how it relates to the improvement of both products and processes. The experience element, however, we find more problematic. Since its inception, the curriculum for our degree has included a number of points where students experience this process for themselves, but we have seen far too many instances where they do not seem to have learnt what we had wanted them to from that experience. In particular, we have found all too often that, when students have been undertaking their individual final year projects, they have simply ignored all the previous teaching about process-oriented goals and their importance, in their drive to produce a (hopefully working) product by a hard deadline. Thus, issues such as managing resources properly (even just their own time), documenting their work adequately, or giving even minimal attention to designing their software so that they can test it properly, have often all been neglected in favour of simply churning out code, regardless of its quality.

We are beginning to feel that one of the main problems here is the set of constraints resulting from the UK requirement that the "capstone" of an engineering degree must be an individual project. We note that elsewhere it is increasingly common for this role in Software Engineering degree courses to be taken by group projects. Recent experience of this is discussed, for instance, by [Moore94] for courses in the USA, by [Johnston94] for Australia, by [Andersen94] for Norway, by [Johansson94] for Sweden, and there is further discussion in many of the papers cited by these various authors. It is clear from these experiences that most of the popular objections to group projects can be solved (and particularly those related to assessment), and so we would argue that whether final projects should be group or individual ones therefore becomes a secondary issue. What is far more important is that, in order to provide the maximum support for positive professionalism, the final project in an Software Engineering degree course should be one which actively involves the student in experiencing an Software Engineering process that is as realistic as possible.

The significance of this is that in general one also wants a final project to be an intellectually challenging piece of work, which in practice often means that it will involve trying to develop a piece of software that is close to the limit of what one person could accomplish in the sort of curriculum time that is typically available. Where a student is working on such a project individually, the practical pressures that might force them into managing the project properly are comparatively weak, or at least are seen by them as comparatively weak. This will be the case even if the pressures are imposed by a suitably constructed assessment schedule, in which case the effect is likely to be to tempt the students to try to fake the process, but with much less laudable objectives than those discussed by [Parnas86]. By contrast, the pressures to produce what they see as enough code (i.e. a substantial amount of it) are very strong.

If students work on similarly demanding projects in small groups, however, the amount of code per person that needs to be generated will be significantly less, which will ease one pressure, while the necessity of managing the groups and communicating amongst themselves will naturally (and desirably) increase the pressure on them to operate within a much better process. For this reason, we believe that group projects ought to be acceptable for this role in the Software Engineering curriculum in the UK as well, so as to enhance the extent to which the final project can support a proper application of the Software Engineering process, and hence contribute more to the development of positive professionalism than it sometimes does at the moment.

30.5.4   The knowledge component of software systems

Finally, the fourth principle that we regard as important, is based on the recognition that all software systems include some knowledge, even if it is only "hard-wired" in the form of the design decisions that have been made on the basis of the analyst's knowledge about the problem domain and its requirements. Increasingly, though, this knowledge is being represented explicitly within systems, so that they need to be seen not only as carrying out computation within some fixed framework of knowledge, but as actually using and manipulating that knowledge itself. If students are to approach such systems in a professional fashion then they need to understand the importance not only of the processing which the systems perform, but also of the knowledge that they use to perform it.

Usually software engineers have approached this knowledge component of systems from the programming perspective, by starting with the data structures that can be used to represent the knowledge and the algorithms that can be used to reason about it. We had followed this model in the first generation of our curriculum, but we were finding that what students learnt initially about processing knowledge did not match properly what we wanted to teach them later about the ways in which knowledge based components were actually applied in software systems. In particular, this mismatch was being emphasized by the growing importance of the neural network paradigm, which did not fit cleanly into this programming-based perspective. In essence, what we were finding was that a bottom-up approach to artificial intelligence within Software Engineering was not working. This is perhaps not surprising, as top-down approaches are usually more successful in teaching computing, provided that "the top" can be arranged to coincide with students' existing knowledge and experience. In our first generation curriculum we had not really been sure where the top ought to be, but it is now clearer to us that teaching AI should start by considering its applications to knowledge based systems, and then by evaluating these systems in terms of how they acquire, represent and use knowledge.

This has essentially turned out to be an application of our first principle, as it has focused on models that, because they are more application oriented, are more appropriate for considering the behaviour of complete systems. These models give a much more abstract level as the starting point for discussing AI within the curriculum.

The next level down then follows naturally from this, in examining the issues of how these abstract models of knowledge, training, inference and so on may be represented within programming languages, and this can then motivate the discussion of some or all of the list-based, rule-based and object-based approaches and of the language paradigms that support them. More helpfully, in terms of designing the curriculum, is that the question of just how far any of these issues needs to be explored can then be placed alongside the similar questions that occur for other topics, of finding an appropriate level of detail of implementation. Examples of these might be how programming languages can be represented within conventional computer architectures, or how these architectures can be synthesized from basic logic components, or how distributed systems can be built on top of basic communications links and networks. In each of these cases, though, once students have got the basic framework of concepts correct, they have the necessary foundation to be able to explore these aspects in more detail if they need to, and this principle of the knowledge content of systems provides the necessary framework for the concepts in the AI area.

We also see this principle of evaluating systems on the basis of their knowledge content as important for another reason, which is that the question of how some system uses its knowledge leads naturally into the question of how that system relates to the knowledge possessed by the people with whom it interacts. An obvious example of this is whether there can be a conflict of knowledge between the system and its users, as might typically be expressed in the complaint "why won't the system let me do . . . ?" This is precisely the sort of issue that students need to be encouraged to consider, as part of the goal of actively seeking for applications of the ethical framework within which systems are built. The fact that such issues will arise naturally from considering how systems use their knowledge is an important argument for insisting that students must learn to include this aspect in their evaluation of any system.

30.6 Conclusions

We have been able to show the importance of supporting positive professionalism within the curriculum for a Software Engineering degree course, and how this objective can be worked out in the design of such a curriculum. We have presented a set of goals that the curriculum needs to aim for, and criteria for evaluating how far design features in a curriculum may support these goals. While we have not been able to attempt any systematic classification or analysis of possible features that might be included in the design of a curriculum, we have presented some principles which our experience leads us to believe will help to meet at least some of these goals. We are in the process of putting these into practice, and we hope that they will help to make our students more professionally aware in the future: we expect to be able to report eventually on how successful they have been.

Chapter 31
Academic Perspectives of Professionalism

31.1 Introduction

It is not clear whether Software Engineering is considered a true profession. However, software engineers have to respond to changes in the business world and can be put into positions where their work can affect the lives of others in much the same way as members of the established professions such as Medicine and Law. The awareness of professional issues is thus of key importance to software engineers, if they are to be regarded as true professionals. Many practitioners take a route to their chosen careers via university courses, however, it is not obvious what the academic perception of professional issues is, or whether this is in line with the views of industry. Also, there is no information on the extent to which the awareness of professionalism is being fostered in academic institutions. This needs investigation, but until now, to our knowledge, no such study has been carried out in the UK.

This chapter presents the results of a recent empirical study of academics' perceptions of professional issues in Software Engineering, within the UK. It is divided into seven sections. Section 31.2 describes the aims and objectives of the study and relates the work to the current literature. Section 31.3 gives details of the research method which was used to carry out the study. Section 31.4 presents the results obtained and discusses possible reasons for the results. Interesting correlations and additional comments made by the respondents are discussed in Sections 31.5 and 31.6 respectively. Section 31.7 concludes the chapter by summarizing the findings and drawing conclusions from the study. An indication is also given of further useful work which can be carried out in this area.

31.2 Background

There is no consensus of the key professional issues which should be of concern to modern software engineers. Indeed there are currently very few texts which consider professional issues in relation to Software Engineering. Our study has been based on ten of the most commonly discussed professional issues in the two key texts by Frank Bott *et at* [Bott95] and Colin Myers [Myers95]. The issues chosen are therefore not based on the authors' personal opinions of what constitutes professional issues.

The chosen issues are: ethics; data protection and confidentiality; dress codes; equal opportunities; regulated entrance to the profession; finance and accounting; software contract; software safety; computer misuse and the law, and intellectual property rights. These issues were not explicitly listed within the texts. They were selected after a detailed content analysis of both texts.

The study has three main objectives. The first is to establish the perceived relative importance of the professional issues listed above. The second is to establish who, from the academic point of view, is responsible for bringing about the awareness of professional issues in the computer community. The third is to establish the extent to which professional issues are included in current course curricula.

31.3   Research Method

In order to accomplish the stated objectives a questionnaire was designed and copies were circulated to all university Software Engineering, Computer Science and related departments in the UK. In all 91 universities were targeted, the addresses of which were obtained from a current database. Each department received two copies of the questionnaire and a covering letter, addressed to the Head of Teaching; the senior academic responsible for the overall teaching curriculum.

A great deal of effort was taken in the design of the questionnaire in order to make sure it was quick and simple to fill in and that the questions most relevant to the study were being asked. Prior to sending out the questionnaires a pilot study was carried out in our own department. This allowed the questionnaire to be improved. It should be noted that due to its use in the pilot study, the department of Computer Science at Hull University was not included in the main study.

The questionnaires were sent out on 19th of July (1995). Two weeks after this date, follow up telephone calls were made to departments which had not responded. Departments which indicated that they had not received a questionnaire were re-sent a copy.

Out of the 91 questionnaires sent out, 33 were returned. The majority of departments returned a single questionnaire. However, two departments returned both copies of the questionnaire, completed by different members of staff. Of the universities targeted, 36% provided a response. This is considered to be a good response rate for a questionnaire of this kind [Nieswiadomy93].

The questionnaire consisted of five sections. The first establishes demographic information relating to the respondent and their institution. Such information includes the type of university, the status of the respondent, the extent of their teaching and industrial experience, and the professional bodies to which they belong. Such information was included to allow investigation of patterns and trends to be performed at the analysis stage.

The second section asked the respondent to rate the ten items perceived in the literature as professional issues, in terms of importance. A seven point scale (0 to 6) was used with 0 representing *unimportant* and 6 representing *important* [Oppenheim92]. Additional space was provided to allow the respondents to include and rate those professional issues not listed, which they considered to be important.

The third section aimed to establish the degree to which academics regard themselves, students, professional bodies, employers and employees as responsible for providing education in professional issues. The questionnaire asked the respondent to rate these in terms of degree of responsibility, on a seven point scale (0 to 6), where 0 represented *not responsible* and 6 represented *major responsibility*. Again space was left to allow respondents to list and rate others who they considered to have a degree of responsibility for providing education of professional issues.

The fourth section was designed to allow the respondents to indicate the mechanisms used and the extent to which their own departments attempt to enhance their students' awareness of professional issues. The questionnaire asked whether whole lecture courses/modules are dedicated to professional issues, whether whole lectures are devoted to professional issues as part of other courses and the how many external speakers are invited from industry to address professional issues.

The fifth section was included to allow any additional comments regarding either professional issues or the questionnaire itself to be made.

Once returned the questionnaires were first inspected by hand and then analysed using SPSS, a statistical analysis package. The results of the data collected and issues of interest raised from the analysis are presented in the next section.

31.4   Analysis of the Results

This section of the chapter presents and discusses the results obtained from the survey. Each of the sections of the questionnaire is taken in turn and the results for that section are presented. The findings of various investigations into possible correlations of the data are also presented.

In addition to the raw factual information, the authors' subjective views are included, in an attempt to suggest possible reasons for the results obtained. Most of the authors' views are presented in Section 31.4.2 which analyses the perceived importance of the ten chosen issues.

31.4.1   Background information

Of the universities that replied to the survey, 36% referred to themselves as "new universities" and 61% referred to themselves as "old universities". In general this indicates that replies were received from a cross-section of the university sector. The remaining 3% accounts for an institution which referred to itself as in the "others" category. The replying institutions offer a variety of degree programmes. *Software Engineering* is offered by 49% of them, 42% offer *Information Technology* and 91% offer *Computer Science*. The percentage of Software Engineering, Information Technology and Computer Science courses which were accredited by the BCS are 30%, 61% and 15% respectively.

The replies were completed by a high proportion of experienced staff; 73% of the respondents are senior staff, 49% of which have professorial status. This is not surprising when you consider that the questionnaire was addressed to "Head of Teaching". It was evident, from the follow up telephone calls, that departments which did not have a head of teaching passed their questionnaires on to the head of department. This still meant, however, that the respondents were likely to have an overall view of the department's teaching activities.

The seniority of the respondents is reflected further by the degree of higher education teaching and industrial experience which they have. Of those that responded, 91% have over 10 years of higher education teaching experience, 64% have at least 1 year of industrial or commercial experience, and of these 24% have over 5 years.

The majority (85%) of respondents indicated that they belong to at least one professional body. The most popular professional body is the British Computer Society (BCS), with 55% of the respondents belonging to it. This result reflects that the BCS is the recognized body for Software Engineering and Computer Science professionals in the UK.

31.4.2   Views on professional issues

Some interesting information was collected from the respondents on their views on the importance of the ten items perceived in the literature as professional issues. This section presents the findings and suggests possible reasons for them.

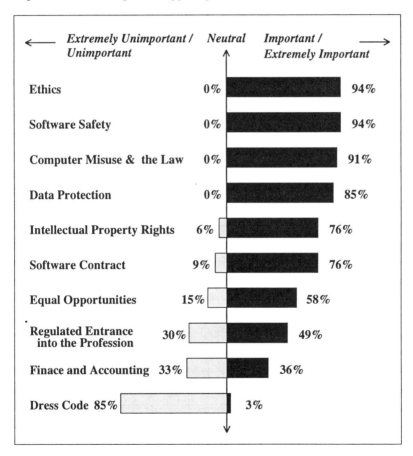

Figure 31.1 Rank ordering of issues in terms of professional importance

Figure 31.1 summarizes the results by illustrating the percentage of respondents who indicated above neutral importance and the percentage who indicated below neutral importance for each issue. The issues are shown in rank order of perceived importance with the most important at the top.

Ethics is clearly perceived as important. All respondents thought ethics was at least of neutral importance and most (56%) viewed ethics as extremely important. Ethics is to do with moral values and principles. To be ethical as a professional is to be in accordance with principles of conduct that are considered correct by the profession. Ethics describes the underlying behaviour and thus the essence of what being a professional entails. It seems logical that it is perceived as a professional issue of key importance.

Data protection was also a perceived of a high importance professional issue. No respondent considered it to be of less than neutral importance, and 46% viewed it as extremely important. As professionals, software engineers must acknowledge the effects which their products have on society. Issues of data protection and confidentiality are strong social issues which should be of concern to the computer professional. This also relates to the data protection act, which is essential law that must be understood by professionals whose work relates to it.

The issue of dress codes was perceived to have a very low degree of importance with 85% of respondents considering it as either unimportant or extremely unimportant. One could jump to the conclusion that a survey of academics is bound to respond negatively when confronted with expressing a view on the importance of dress code, due to the flexibility of dress associated with academic life. On the other hand one could follow the argument introduced by Colin Myers in his book which bears the subtitle *Should a Software Engineer Wear a Suit?* [Myers95]. Myers questions whether Software Engineering is a profession or an applied technology and considers the attitudes required for a software engineer to succeed as a professional. It will be interesting to establish whether practitioners in the Software Engineering industry rate dress code as a more important professional issue.

The issue of equal opportunities had a bias towards being perceived as important with 36% of respondents considering it as extremely important. However, responses on all extremes of the importance scale were received, and 27% viewed equal opportunities as of neutral importance. This result is difficult to explain, especially since equal opportunities cover a wide range of issues. Equal opportunities has become a media focus for many professions in the past few years, with reports of discrimination regularly making the headlines. The issue is thus contentious and involves legalities, therefore a high rating would be expected. The gender, social and ethnic backgrounds of the respondents will also contribute to their personal perception of these issues.

The issue of regulated entrance to the profession produced some interesting results. Although this issue is biased slightly towards the important side, 51% of the respondents viewed this issue as of either neutral or lower importance. This result is surprising considering that 85% of the respondents are members of a professional body themselves. The membership of professional bodies is of crucial importance in the established professions. These results appear to be symptomatic of the infancy of the Software Engineering profession.

The study shows finance and accounting to be considered as being of neutral importance. No respondent indicated that they consider this issue to be extremely important. However, 9% consider it to be extremely unimportant. Finance and accounting is strongly related to business, which is an integral aspect of being a professional. The results tend to indicate a lack of interest in the financial and accounting aspects of the business. This is further support for the idea that Software Engineering is mainly a technical activity. This does not mean, however, that it is not a true profession, since members of some of the more established professions such as medicine tend to have little interest in financial matters. The personal experience of the respondents may also have impacted upon their response. Those with experience of management and finance in industry would be expected to rate this issue as more import than those without such experience. This is another issue where a comparative view from current practitioners would be useful.

Software contract was perceived as an issue of high importance with 76% of respondents indicating it as either important or extremely important. This shows that the respondents recognize that a verbal agreement is inadequate for the development of complex software artifacts. The development costs associated with software make it essential to have a legal agreement as to what is being developed. This relates to another key business consideration of the profession. Behaviour as a professional involves adhering closely to contractual arrangements.

Software safety was another issue regarded as very important by the respondents. No respondent indicated that it was less than neutral importance, and the majority (55%) consider it to be extremely important. Safety is a critical issue in all professions; a responsibility for safety comes with professional status. Software engineers must ensure that their products are safe and do not put people at risk. Such responsibility is inherent in professional behaviour and is closely linked to ethics.

Computer misuse and the law has a very similar profile to software safety, with 46% of respondents viewing it as extremely important and no one considering it to be unimportant. This issue is again related to ethics and the essence of what being a professional is about. True professionals require a full knowledge and understanding of the relevant law, and how it impacts on what they do. It is not surprising that academics view this issue as important, and a similar response would be expected from those in industry.

Intellectual property rights is another issue which the respondents regarded as important with 76% of them rated it as either important or extremely important. This kind of response was expected from academics since individual ownership of ideas is a major issue in academic research. It is not expected that workers in industry will rate this issue quite as highly. Related business issues such as patents and product ownership, however, are of great commercial significance, and thus must come under the consideration of the professional.

In addition to rating the issues listed on the questionnaire, several respondents provided additional items which they regard as important professional issues. These are; communication skills, team work, technical competency, keeping up to date, personal effectiveness, accountability, fitness to practice, standards, client care and managing human resources.

31.4.3 Views on facilitating professional issue awareness

This subsection presents the responses received in relation to Section three of the questionnaire. A summary of the results obtained is illustrated in Table 31.1. From the table, it is clear that each of the five groups listed were considered to have quite a high degree of responsibility. This tends to suggest that academics perceive the responsibility for facilitating awareness to be shared across a number of groups. It is interesting to note that academics and employers are perceived as being more responsible than students and employees. However, in terms of statistical significance, the difference is not large.

Academics	88%
Employers	85%
Professional bodies	78%
Employees	70%
Students	67%

Table 31.1 Responsibility for facilitating professional issue awareness

In addition to the five groups listed in the questionnaire, respondents indicated that government, journal editors and special interest groups are also responsible for providing education of professional issues.

31.4.4   Mechanisms to facilitate professional issue awareness

Of the universities that responded, 64% provide a whole lecture course or module dedicated to professional issues, as part of their undergraduate degree programmes. This suggests that a large proportion of institutions view professional issues as important enough to consider it explicitly as part of the curriculum. However, 30% do not offer a dedicated professional issues course. The remaining 6% represents respondents who did not know whether or not their department provides a professional issues lecture course.

The respondents indicated that many of their departments (52%) devoted some lectures to consideration of professional issues as part of other courses. This shows some consideration of professional issues at course design levels. There is some overlap here with the 64% that provide dedicated professional issues courses. Thus some institutions provide both whole and part courses on professional issues. Only 18% indicated that they do not provide any lectures on professional issues as part of other courses. This leaves 30% who either didn't complete the question or indicated that they did not know.

A large proportion (67%) of the responding universities invite guest speakers from industry to address professional issues. This suggests that academics acknowledge the importance of the views of current software engineers on issues regarding their profession. The numbers of guest speakers invited throughout a degree programme varies quite considerably, however, 36% invite more than 3 external speakers for this purpose. Of these, 9% invite more than ten industrial speakers. This shows a strong commitment from some institutions to give their students an industrial perspective of professional issues.

A worrying 9% of respondents didn't know whether or not they invited industrial speakers to address professional issues. An important fact evident from analysis of this section of the questionnaire is that a small percentage of respondents are not sure about certain basic aspects of the teaching of professional issues in their own departments. This suggests that they lack personal interest in the teaching of professional issues.

31.5 Interesting Correlations

In addition to the raw data analysis, an investigation of various correlations of the results was carried out. Much of the investigation revealed no significant correlation, however, there were some notable relationships.

There is a strong correlation between the amount of higher education teaching experience of the respondents and their perception of the importance of software contract as a professional issue. The more experienced teachers regard the software contract as a more important professional issue. There is also a correlation between industrial experience and perception of the importance of the software contract as a professional issue. Interestingly, the correlation here is not quite as strong. However, it does suggest that the academic view is in line with that expected from industry on this issue.

Higher education teaching experience and the perception of computer misuse as a professional issue also have a significant correlation.

A very strong correlation is evident between departments which dedicate whole or part modules to professional issues and the number of industrial speakers invited to address professional issues. Those who dedicate more time to professional issues are more likely to invite more industrial speakers to address professional issues. This seems a fairly obvious finding; however, it indicates consistency in those who appear to be explicitly committed to addressing issues of professionalism.

There is a weak correlation which suggests that those who are members of a professional body are more likely to perceive regulated entrance to the profession as an important professional issue. This correlation is not as strong as we expected. There is a stronger correlation between membership of a professional body and the importance of software safety as a professional issue.

31.6 Additional Comments

Here the additional comments that were made on the questionnaires are presented along with our views in relation to them.

"Students and employees do not perceive the need for training in above matters." [A Professor].

The above statement is probably true for issues such as dress codes. Other issues such as finance and accounting require specialist knowledge, and students and employees need training in these areas. Even if they do not perceive a need for training in some of the professional issues, they still have a responsibility to increase their own level of awareness.

"Professional issues must 'pervade' an academic degree programme — 'dedicated' modules are an excuse for being superficial (and evading real responsibility)." [A Professor].

This is an extremely good point, with which we agree.

"I am uninterested in professional issues — which seems like either common sense, or a scheme to control the industry by some who cannot even write a program." [A Professor].

We disagree with the above statement primarily because many of the individuals at the forefront of professional issues have extensive experience in large scale projects.

"All the lecturers on professional issues are given by industrial speakers since we feel they know the issues better than us. This is important for us in building relationships in the long term with the firms supplying the lectures. The law course is taught by the law faculty." [A Senior lecturer].

We agree with the view that these lecturers should be provided by those most informed. Such specialist lectures combined with an ethos of professional thinking and practice throughout a degree programme seems to be the ideal.

"Actually, I don't believe in teaching this. I think people should be trained to be professional and that the BCS and other employers should do this as part of job training. Trying to teach this stuff out of context is unrewarding, boring for students, hard to motivate and hard to assess." [A Senior Lecturer].

We share this view to some extent. It is also essential to stress the importance of treating professional issues within an "organizational context" because different organizations have different ways of doing things. Teaching, in the traditional sense is not the only way by which students could be made aware of professional issues. We believe that there is some responsibility on the academic community to give at least an insight into professionalism. Unprofessional behaviour must be discouraged at the student level.

31.7   Summary and Conclusions

This study has provided some interesting and in some cases surprising facts about the academic perception of professional issues in Software Engineering. In conclusion we highlight some of the main issues raised by the study.

From the professional issues surveyed, ethics and software safety are perceived by academics to be most important and dress code is clearly least important. The low importance associated with dress code is possibly due to the fact that the change in attitudes experienced by Software Engineers in industry and commerce [Myers95] do not apply to academics and, as such, they still hold the stereotypical, technical oriented view of Software Engineers.

In general there does not appear to be a correlation between membership of professional bodies and perceptions on professional issues. Academics who belong to professional bodies do not seem to have significantly different views on the importance of professional issues from those who do not.

The study also suggests that academics view the responsibility of raising the level of awareness of professional issues as broad and not constrained to any particular body. Responsibility rests on academics, professional bodies and employers as well as students and employees. Suggestion was also made that other parties may play a significant role in raising the level of awareness including the government (through legislation), journal editors and special interest groups.

The observation that some of the universities who responded do not invite external speakers to address professional issues is worrying. This indicates that the issues are not being taught by current software practitioners. Despite this it is reassuring that 67% of the universities surveyed do invite at least some external speakers.

As far as we are aware this is the first study of its kind. However, it has only scratched the surface. There is clearly a need for more studies in this area. Specifically it would be advantageous to perform a repeat of this study on a larger sample.

Indeed the academic perception of professionalism is only one dimension and the views of the Software Engineering professionals themselves must be sought. We are planning to repeat this study with participants from industry and commerce. This will allow comparisons between the perceptions of the academics and practitioners to be made. Only then will we be able to start to understand whether our perceptions as academics are truly in line with the Software Engineering profession.

Chapter 32
Student Projects and Professionalism

32.1 Introduction

Graduates in subjects such as Computer Studies and Software Engineering are expected to possess problem solving skills and technical awareness. Employers value these qualities, but additionally seek assurance that these future employees will approach engineering tasks in a professional manner. This chapter discusses how professional issues are raised and addressed by final year undergraduates during group projects which form part of a BSc in Software Engineering Management at Bournemouth University. Professional interaction with clients, supervisors, colleagues, and with other engineers and managers are analysed. Issues considered include: customer awareness; planning and reporting; task allocation; assessment of product maintainability; quality assurance; choice of appropriate technology. These issues are discussed in the context of the BCS (British Computer Society) Code of Practice. The successes (and failures) of projects in making professional issues come to life are illustrated through extracts from students' self-appraisals. The chapter concludes with a summary of the advantages and limitations of such projects in increasing undergraduates' appreciation of professional issues.

32.2 Professional Awareness

What causes us to conclude that someone has acted "professionally"? Such an assessment is based both on output and on the visible manner of its achievement. Professionals not only produce "good work"; they also appear to "work good". Since the professions are judged by the work performance of their members, professions attempt to defend their standing by codification of best practices.

To observe professionalism in action, it is necessary to examine the interfaces presented by practitioners. It is the external indicators — for instance the quality of the deliverables, the conduct of meetings and the attitude of individuals towards users, clients, supervisors, subordinates and peers — which constitute the evidence upon which a judgement about the professionalism of an individual is based.

A professional not only possesses specialist knowledge but is capable of making decisions about the application of that knowledge when solving specific problems [Shapero85]. Finniston identifies six aspects of professionalism: know-how (skills); know-what (understanding of principles and knowledge of facts); know-whom (to seek advice from); know-how-much (cost and performance estimation); know-why (choice of process) and, know-when (business awareness) [Finniston84].

It is highly desirable that undergraduates studying engineering subjects acquire an appreciation of good professional practices. While the concepts can be taught in class, they are best learned through active engagement with real tasks which illustrate elements of the practice in action.

32.2.1 Professional interactions

On a Software Engineering project, the following interactions involving either the project team or team members can be identified:

- **Client.** Those who commission or will use a computer system must be closely involved in its development. Requirements need to be defined and agreed; changes managed; systems accepted. For the student, there are important lessons to be learned about communication and compromise.

- **Supervisor.** Project teams are responsible for keeping their parent organizations properly informed of progress and problems. Regular reports, written and verbal, are the norm on industrial projects.

- **Colleagues.** Team members are expected to work effectively with their peers. Good communication, equitable division of labour and flexibility are desirable characteristics. While this interaction is difficult to observe directly, student reports afford some insight into its operation.

- **Successors.** Software is long lived, and it is often the case that those who maintain a software system were not involved in its initial construction. The developers have a responsibility to convey useful information about their system to the maintainers. They also have a duty to design their system for ease of change.

- **Experts.** It is important for team members to recognize that their combined expertise is limited and that they should seek advice from elsewhere when they encounter problems beyond their capabilities.

- **Organization.** All projects are unique. Each blend of process, technology, team organization, constraints and team composition is a new opportunity to learn. Organizations would like to improve their capabilities by assessing how best to set up projects under particular circumstances. Each project team can help by bequeathing a summary of its trials, tribulations and successes.

From student self-appraisals, it is also possible to gain some insight into the extent to which students learn about their own capabilities and limitations, this being the basis for self-improvement.

32.3 A Software Group Project

32.3.1 The course

The BSc (Hons) in Software Engineering Management at Bournemouth University is a four year, sandwich undergraduate course. The initial intake was in 1989 and the first cohort graduated in 1993. The course is designed to instil in students an awareness of the importance of professionalism in software development; the course ethos and structure are described in [Bray90].

In years 1 and 2 of the course, units follow three themes: Software Development, Management and Technology. Integrating activities, some of which involve students in team working, run in parallel with taught units. The integrating element in year 2 includes a 10 week group assignment, where students work in teams of four to develop and document a software product.

Year 3 is the industrial placement. In year 4, students take three taught units, participate in the group project and undertake an individual project. The group project constitutes 12% of the final degree grade. In one of the taught units — Software Engineering Management — students study software management issues including professionalism.

32.3.2   The project

The group project occupies some 20 weeks of the academic year and is split into two phases of roughly equal length. Each student is expected to spend approximately one day per week on this project. The format of the project has evolved as tutors have reflected on their experiences, and the description which follows is drawn from the academic year 1994/95.

Students are allocated to teams and given outline requirements and constraints for three applications to be developed or enhanced. There were 9 teams (35 students) last year, and we required three teams to tackle each application. A team size of 3-4 enables group dynamics to develop while encouraging students to contribute rather than to rely on their peers [Comer89]. Teams are invited to bid for their preferred application, those teams putting forward the best proposals being awarded their preferences. The advantage of the bid stage is that it forces the teams to critically review their strengths, weaknesses and interests at an early stage and ensures that team building starts immediately. In Phase 1, students implement and document working versions of the applications. The second phase involves an enhancement to the product created in Phase 1.

At the end of both phases, students give presentations and demonstrations of their work. Each student produces an individual report on their own performance at the end of Phase 2, discussing what has been learned during the project.

Teams are required to organize, plan and manage their own work. Students must exercise judgement, for example when estimating task durations and choosing a development process [Etlinger90]. Each team is allocated two tutors, one performing the role of a senior manager, the other acting as a client for the application.

Last year, we adjusted the process by requiring teams to critically review the Phase 1 output produced by another team, following the scheme described by [Chapman93]. The benefit of this change is discussed in Section 32.3.5.

Student projects can never completely reflect the real world, as [Robillard89] points out. There are several reasons for this. Engineers in industry are usually dedicated to a task, whereas it is normal for students to divide their time between projects and other demands of a course. From a student perspective, industry and college each have different reward systems — remuneration and grades. Universities cannot simulate the culture of a company which students would encounter on a corporate training program such as that described by [Dawson92]. Most importantly, "real-world" teams tend to be a mixture of junior and experienced staff, with a prescribed management structure; participants in student projects are peers who have to build their own organizations and whose members have no power of coercion over colleagues.

Despite these restrictions, it is possible in student projects to simulate many of the problems encountered by software engineers in industry. Group projects designed in this way have been used successfully in computing courses for at least 20 years [Horning77]. In our projects, student teams are required to interact with clients and supervisors, elicit requirements, produce technical and user documentation and give presentations and demonstrations, all of which are key characteristics of industrial training practices [Dawson92]. Students experience all phases of development and maintenance, in projects which are comparable in scale with small to medium commercial software developments, working with and relying on others. These are desirable attributes of student projects [Erlinger89]. Group projects heighten students' appreciation of the need for co-operation, communication, compromise and professionalism.

32.4   Assessment of the Interactions

32.4.1   Sources

Quotations are taken from students' individual reports and from project histories, editing of excerpts has been limited to the correction of typographical errors and the removal of material extraneous to the issue under discussion. Statements taken from the BCS Code of Practice [BCS93] appear in italics.

32.4.2   Client

BCS Code of Practice statements:

5.1 *Exercise impartiality when evaluating each project with respect to its technical, moral and economic benefits.* (The supporting explanation reminds the reader of the importance of appreciating the client's needs.)

5.4 *Specify the system objectives, completion date, cost and security requirements with the client and the necessary criteria for their achievement.*

5.5 *Ensure that the client can participate in all stages of problem analysis, system development and implementation.*

5.7 *Specify and conduct program tests and system tests to ensure that all system objectives are met to the satisfaction of the client.*

5.9 *Ensure that input and output are designed to obviate misunderstanding.*

This is, in many ways, the easiest interface to assess. A professional attitude towards the client is essential, something which students come to recognize — although it can take individuals some time to reach this conclusion:

"In Phase 1 we lacked the communication both within the team and between the team and the customer. This was the main area we needed to improve on ... We arranged a meeting with the customer at the earliest possible moment [in Phase 2] and when the proposal was drawn up we got it signed off. Once the new [system] was produced we arranged a demonstration with the customer, this was to make sure the system met his requirements and to keep the customer in touch with the project."

Three aspects of the team-client interaction can be distinguished.

Discussions about application scope

The initial statements of requirements given to students are brief; teams are expected to negotiate their own scope of work. Teams typically meet the client 4-6 times during each phase. In the later meetings the client's role is to comment on drafts of the requirements specification. Students' initial disbelief when the first version of the specification is not immediately signed by the client turns to frustration as Phase 1 proceeds with disagreement remaining about some detail. Students come to appreciate that clients are interested in the presentation as much as in the content of requirements specifications. A sensible approach, adopted so far by only one team, was to produce a set of costed change proposals and ask the client to prioritize these changes, this process continuing until the team and client mutually agreed that a satisfactory application could be produced with the effort available.

" ... it was a good group decision in prioritizing the various customer requirements so we could deliver the more important requirements and if time existed then implement the minor changes."

Test and demonstration

Last year most of the teams offered the client a demonstration at the end of Phase 1; by the end of Phase 2, all the teams realized the importance of this to the client. Teams also receive satisfaction and reassurance if they are given at least an indication that their products are acceptable.

In contrast, the previous year demonstrations were mandatory at the end of Phase 1. On that occasion, student reaction to defects being discovered during these demonstrations ranged from calm acceptance and discussion of the work-around, through disbelief, to an argument about ambiguity in the requirements which culminated in one team member demonstrating true professionalism in persuading her dissident colleague that withdrawal from the conflict was the correct option.

System testing is the team's responsibility. On this subject one student noted:

"Originally I believed [the production of the test plan] to be a simple case of producing a few common possible errors and testing them at the end. Two main points were gained from this experience. The test plan needed to cover every conceivable input from the user, and thus took much effort to produce. Also designers don't always follow the specification, meaning that it still contained some ambiguity or they had not read it properly."

Assessment of product and user documentation

Each client tests the product and reviews the user documentation for functionality, usability, resilience and compatibility. Teams are provided with a list of product defects at the end of Phase 1. Teams rarely dispute this assessment, but occasionally find difficulty replicating a problem.

In such cases, teams have — professionally — enlisted the assistance of the client in recreating the error conditions. One team, whose system had more than its fair share of obscure defects, initially abandoned this process when some of the reported defects could be not reproduced but eventually tracked down the problems during an intensive testing session.

It is not easy to write useful user documentation. Pertinent examples are hard to find, and students need to produce documentation appropriate to their application. For instance, in the case of one project, a syntax checker, the error messages had to be explicit and remedial action clear — examples were highly desirable. In another project, concerned with a diagnostic system, teams took some time to realize that there were actually two systems — a diagnostic program and a diagnostic system builder — with two classes of user, so that two distinct user manuals were required.

32.4.3   Supervisor

BCS Code of Practice statements:

2.3 *Establish and maintain channels of communication from and to seniors, equals and subordinates.*

5.2 *Effectively plan, monitor, adjust and report on all developments, acquisition or replacement projects.*

Teams meet their supervisor weekly for about 20 minutes to report progress, highlight problems and discuss updates to plans. They are required to submit written progress reports and time sheets. Progress reporting has consistently been one of the weakest aspects of student performance on group projects. Students are unwilling to admit in writing that they are slipping against their schedules, although they demonstrate in discussions that they know what progress has been made and are aware of the implications. (In the author's experience, this attitude is no different from the majority of software developers in industry.) The realization that plans can be useful comes, eventually, to some:

> "The project plan is a working document, not a 'token' deliverable . . . The absence of an up-to-date project plan made it difficult to assess our current position . . ."

Project plans, schedules and quality plans, together with records of configuration management and of reviews, are retained as evidence of management processes in action.

Teams are required to present their projects to the supervisor and client at the end of each phase. Such presentations are common in student projects; [Sullivan93] and

[Chapman93] describe other instances. Enthusiasm and pride in their work are evident in most of the presentations we see.

32.4.4 Colleagues

BCS Code of Practice statements:

2.2 *Ensure that any specified tasks are assigned to identified individuals according to their known ability and competence.*

2.2 *Be accountable for the quality, timeliness and use of resources in the work for which he is responsible.*

2.2 *Ensure that effective standard procedures and documentation are available and used.*

2.2 *Ensure that each task is completed to a defined level before the next dependent task is started.*

Student teams differ from industrial Software Engineering teams in one important aspect — there is no imposed team leader. Team dynamics determine team organization. Most (but not all) teams appoint nominal leaders who act as a spokesperson and, in some cases, as the progress monitor and conscience of the team — in which case the title "project manager" is bestowed. This is not a title everybody wants.

> "Being project manager is a difficult job. It can be made impossible by people who don't care about their work."

Lakhanpal [Lakhanpal93] has argued that software productivity is affected more by team cohesion than by the experience and relative capability of its members. In the majority of student teams, cohesion increases during the project.

> "At the beginning of Phase 1, it took us several weeks to learn to work together effectively as a group." [The student describes interpersonal problems between group members, culminating in a crisis meeting mid-way through the phase.] "The single hour spent resolving the fundamental interpersonal problems within the group paid for itself many times over."

> "Better communication and cohesion was immediately noticeable [at the beginning of Phase 2], and like trust, grew stronger as the phase went on. We were all determined to learn from our mistakes in Phase 1 and produce a much better product."

> "Lessons that have been learned from this project are that putting people together in a group does not make a team. Team working is something that has to be worked at by all members and does not come easy."

The discipline of regular team meetings is recognized.

"[Weekly] meetings proved to be valuable to the communication between [team members] because everyone knew what progress was made and what tasks were to be undertaken in the following week."

Students are learning to depend on others, as [Etlinger90] points out. For instance:

"Another lesson learned from this experience was the need for pragmatism within the group. In the previous phase, much time was wasted arguing about which way we were going to do things ... This problem was overcome by skilful project management in the allocation of work, and a greater sense of trust amongst the group."

The possibility that team composition may change in Phase 2 provides a powerful incentive for team members to develop a shared understanding of their product.

Common practice in these projects is for individuals to compare their perceived strengths and interests at the start and allocate work accordingly. Students find that in Phase 2 they have an increased awareness of the true capabilities of their peers and can adapt individual working practices accordingly.

"Scheduling for Phase 2 was easier. I was able to draw on the experiences of Phase 1 and prepare more realistic plans. It was evident to which areas individuals strengths were, and how we could capitalize on them."

Students learn the benefits of configuration management — sometimes the hard way.

"If there was one main weakness in Phase 1 of the project it had to be configuration management. For example there were two different versions of the requirements document in circulation during Phase 1, and we had great difficulty retrieving some source code after an accidental deletion."

Technical reviews are an instance of team interaction. Those students who have not experienced having their work reviewed — and it appears that formal reviews are not common practice on many industrial placements — can find peer reviews intimidating but ultimately recognize the advantages.

"The reviews proved successful for the following reasons: they produced better documents; they gave other members an insight into what their colleagues were doing; they allowed all the other members to input their ideas into the document. Each document ... became a group effort."

Sometimes, though, reviews are ineffective.

"The team effectiveness in Phase 1 was not too good, and I feel that we worked more as individuals than as a team. We all produced good work but no one really checked anyone else's work and subsequently the quality of the work we produced was low."

Students also come to accept that software development is inevitably iterative, whatever the good intentions of Statement 5.6 in the BCS Code of Practice.

> "...the requirements specification took a long time to get signed off. This was not due to lack of functionality but mainly presentation and small detail. So the project developed in more of an incremental way, as opposed to a traditional waterfall model. By this I mean that the design started before the specification was fully completed, as the basis of the functionality was in place, and only fine details had to be resolved."

32.4.5 Successors

BCS Code of Practice statement:

5.8 *Ensure that systems are designed and sufficiently documented to facilitate subsequent audit, maintenance and enhancement and accurate comprehension by users.*

While there may be debate about the exact proportion, there is no doubt that more Software Engineering effort is expended on modifying existing software than on creating new software artefacts. Students are aware of this, although the vast majority aspire to work on new systems rather than to modify old ones. All project students experience the problems posed by enhancements in that Phase 2 involves changing the Phase 1 product, to incorporate new features as well as to correct defects.

Some teams experience maintenance from the start; the diagnostic system last year was based on an existing implementation. Students working on that project were faced with the choice of modifying the product or re-engineering the code. They had to recover the design, as the documentation they inherited was of unsatisfactory quality. In so doing, they learned to exercise judgement about the extent to which legacy code needs to be reverse engineered.

Students are encouraged to consider carefully the problem of maintainability and to produce appropriate documentation. Last year (1994/95), the second phase of the project was preceded by a critical review of all the technical documentation and source code produced by a team who tackled a different application in Phase 1. The reviewers were advised to treat this review as if they were about to assume ownership for the product. Students are expected to demonstrate professionalism by

1. Wording comments concisely and constructively, and giving praise where the quality of the work reviewed deserves it.

2. Acceptance or reasoned rejection of comments received, and taking action during Phase 2 to clear agreed deficiencies.

3. Appreciating that the types of defects that they have noted in others' work is quite likely to be found in their own.

Students rarely disappoint us in this respect:

"The key lesson that we have learned from the first phase, is that there is a difference between documentation needed to build a software product and that required for others to maintain it."

The task brought home to students the importance of critical reviews as a means of improving total product quality. They came to appreciate that maintainers are customers too. It sharpened their critical faculties and led to a marked improvement in their Phase 2 reviews.

"One of the problems which was highlighted by the examination of [another group's] technical documentation was that of traceability between the specification and design, etc ...we should be able to improve our Phase 2 product by creating a technical manual ..... [which will] probably consist of an overview of our system and the algorithms it uses."

32.4.6 Experts

BCS Code of Practice statement:

1.3 *Accept only such work as he believes he is competent to perform and not hesitate to obtain additional expertise from appropriately qualified individuals where advisable.*

Nobody is expected to be expert in everything. A mark of true professionals is that they understand their limitations and seek advice from accredited sources where necessary. Throughout the course, and particularly during their final year, students are encouraged to seek additional expertise. Opportunities exist to use tutors expertise — for instance, to request the informal review of deliverables — and to ask other students in the cohort, particularly those tackling other applications, for advice.

"... the transformation between system and detail design [in Phase 1] was unclear." [They describe a consultation with the lecturer who had taught this topic.] "From this meeting it was decided that we would include a duplicate system design to show the transition between the high level and low level designs by grouping processes and data stores together to produce modules."

One example arose in the last cohort, in one of the teams developing a syntax checking tool. Teams had been advised at the outset to use Lex and Yacc for this project. In the event, two teams deemed the learning curve excessive and developed the tool in C; the remaining team, one member of which had some understanding of these UNIX utilities, taught themselves to use Lex and Yacc effectively, despite being hampered by the shortage of appropriate texts in the library. When, late on in the first phase, they encountered a major problem, they successfully obtained advice through an Internet user group. The team could easily have admitted defeat, but were driven by a desire to solve the problem and in so doing proved to themselves that there is a wealth of knowledge available to be tapped if engineers look beyond their immediate confines.

32.4.7   Organization

Projects do not just produce products; they are also a vehicle for enhancing organizational capability and for improving the collective understanding of best practice. The latter effect can only be achieved if lessons are communicated. This involves reflection and analysis.

Lessons learned from projects, in the form of project histories or post mortem summaries [Tsui92] are the exception rather than the rule in industry. In contrast post mortems are quite common on student projects [Sullivan93]. In our group projects, teams are encouraged to reflect on the effectiveness of their engineering and management processes, on the methods and tools used, on the problems encountered and how these were overcome, as well as summarize their achievements. Some common lessons learned concern the quality system, technical reviews, technology selection and customer interaction.

The quality system must be appropriate

The need for quality in engineering is emphasized throughout the course. Students develop and use a quality system on an assignment during year 2 of the course. In the final year group project, they have the opportunity to pitch their systems at the level they find useful rather than that which they believe tutors expect to see.

> "Experience of a previous project had taught us that defining very detailed procedures carries a large overhead, with little benefit. We therefore made sure that the procedures were practical and relevant to the project . . ."

> "The main problem that we had during the first phase was of over-engineered quality and configuration plans which led to procedures that were impossible to implement within the restricted timescales that we had."

The outcome is not always successful:

> "Sometimes, however, it was felt that a disproportionate amount of time was spent on ensuring that the appearance of a form, for example, was perfect, rather than concentrating on the contents or indeed the real purpose behind the form."

Take technical reviews seriously

This is a specific example of the quality system in practice. Some teams, in Phase 1 of the project, paid lip service to reviews as a form of quality control — forms were duly completed and boxes ticked, but no serious attempt took place to seek out defects. In the second phase, these teams wake up to the usefulness of reviews. For the last cohort, we attribute this change to the success of the critical review at the start of Phase 2.

> "With the benefit of hindsight, the team realized that the quality procedures for the first phase were inadequate and more importantly not carried out

effectively. To this end a lot of time was spent developing a practical but effective review procedure."

" ... The review procedures were very useful in detecting document errors but it also helped the team to gain an understanding of the proposed system as it was being developed."

This is moving towards Weinberg's ideal of egoless programming [Weinberg71]. But there can be drawbacks if that ideal is not reached.

"I noticed that, as a result of the reviewing process, authors gradually took less and less responsibility for their documents. Often the documents were not spell-checked, and contained gross errors ...

In retrospect, I should have insisted on some minimum standards that must be reached by a document before it is even accepted for review."

Use appropriate technology

Another sign of professionalism is the choice of the right process, methods and tools for the job. There are no constraints on design techniques in the project. Pragmatism is expected.

"Although we had a choice of languages, it became obvious very quickly that C would be the wisest choice as both [X] and I had used it extensively throughout our placement years, and [Y] also had a good level of understanding. Although the OO approach meant that C++ would have been a preferable choice ... [Y] did not know it ... [and] we were reluctant to rely on only two coders."

Customer interaction

The problems with getting requirements approved have already been discussed. Many project histories dwell on this topic, although none come up with a universal remedy. In recognizing that the customer is invariably right, they are developing a "close to the customer" attitude [Peters82] which we hope future cohorts will follow.

"The requirements specification proved to be a troublesome document, it was not signed until very near the end of the project. This did not become a major problem because we had agreed verbally on the bulk of the functionally at an early stage, the hard part being writing the requirements in a way that was acceptable to everyone."

32.4.8   Self

BCS Code of Practice statement:

2.1 *Plan, establish and review objectives, tasks and organizational structures for himself, and subordinates, to help meet overall objectives.*

It is difficult to be self-critical. Let the students speak for themselves.

> "The biggest problem I found was making my ideas understood, both in written and verbal form. This I put down to a couple of factors: firstly, the complexity of some of the more technical details of the product ... Secondly I sometimes assumed (incorrectly) that some things were 'obvious' and so brushed over technical details."

> "One problem for myself was to understand that it is not possible for me to do everything, not only does this attitude offend other people by questioning their abilities but its just not possible in the time available."

> "I personally did not like the way some members of the team reviewed my documents ... I am too sensitive when documents are reviewed. This may be a failing on my part and something I will have to overcome ... "

> "The biggest problem that future historians will find with my code is the lack of comments and a rather suspect jump between the design and the code. In future I would hope that I will remember this and look towards producing a more comprehensive and complete set of maintenance documentation."

> "The second lesson I have taken to heart is not to become attached to any solution that I may have suggested. The designs and algorithms that I as Phase 1 design manager put forward just did not fit the bill in terms of actually programming them in Ada."

What clearer sign of professionalism could there be than the ability to constructively criticize ones own performance? We are a learning society. Perhaps there is a need for the BCS Code of Practice to include a statement on the importance of self-appraisal.

32.5 Summary

Group projects at undergraduate level provide tutors with the opportunity to help students studying Software Engineering and related subjects to develop professional attitudes. In a project environment, students experience the frustrations of client interaction, come to appreciate that a system consists of documentation as well as code, and see the importance of developing maintainable systems. The two-phase structure of our project enables students to reflect on performance between phases and to instigate improvements.

There are limitations to such projects. There is minimal opportunity for a student both to manage others or to be managed. The completion date is not negotiable, so the only project trade-offs that students can make concern effort and project scope. The issues of privacy and security, which are discussed in the BCS Code of Practice, are not addressed in the project; nor is the hand-over to live operation. Students are made aware of these issues in Software Engineering by other means.

The students' attitude to the thorny issue of quality is pleasing, particularly the success of technical reviews and the realization that quality systems must be workable. Although it is arguable that, in industrial projects, teams are more likely to have quality systems imposed on them than developed by them, at least the students come to appreciate that quality is a necessary investment.

The major benefit of group projects is that students experience cooperative development, with all that entails. Generally, what starts as a group of individuals becomes an effective team. Occasionally, interpersonal problems dominate and tutors have to take steps to rebalance the teams. At the other extreme is the project which goes too well. As one student remarked:

> "I have been lucky in the team that I worked with. I have not had to deal with any motivational or quality of work issues, so I am not sure how I would deal with these situations even now."

Several students have commented that the project required more of them than did the "real world" they experienced in their placement. In parts of that "real world", there are neither design documents nor test plans, and specifications are not expected to be up to date. It is hoped that the experiences gained on group projects, at Bournemouth University and at other institutions, will help to promote better practices as students take their understanding of professionalism into industry and commerce.

Chapter 33

Converting Computer Science Graduates into Professionals

33.1 Introduction

It is the experience of the GPT company (formerly Plessey Networks and Office Systems) that computer science graduates tend to come into the industrial world full of theory but without the awareness of the real world that is needed to apply their knowledge as effective professionals [Leventhal87] and [Dawson92] (upon which this chapter is based). The following quote about graduates, by an industrialist outside GPT, shows that other companies have similar views:

> "Very knowledgeable - but not a lot of use!"

The GPT company at Nottingham has for the past twelve years been running two week, full time project courses for Software Engineering graduate entrants to the company. These courses were devised at the request of managers to "knock the new graduates into shape" by giving them an experience of industrial working methods and practices. The courses are based on practical work with each graduate spending up to 90% of the time working on a programming project. This project work is undertaken in groups as an important part of the course requirement is to give experience of working effectively within a team.

Since the course was first implemented, the company has noticed a marked improvement in graduates in their awareness and preparation for the real world as more and more degree courses have introduced group projects, some working in the manner of a small software house sometimes referred to as the "Software Hut" [Horning77], [MacCallum85], [Wasserman76], some from as early as the first year [Mace87], [Roper88]. Nevertheless, GPT have still found that graduates will learn a lot from the GPT course even though some undergraduates will have already experienced group project work at their university. This chapter examines the GPT course and suggests why it is more successful than undergraduate courses in giving an experience of Software Engineering principles and practice in the "real" world.

33.2 The Course Format

Each of the GPT Software Engineering training courses is two weeks in length and is given to graduates working in software departments within the first couple of months of joining the company. In recent years a need has also been found for hardware engineers to have an appreciation of the principles of Software Engineering, and so many hardware department managers have sent their graduates on the Software Engineering course.

During the course the participants are divided into groups with each team working on the same project in competition with each other. The size of the groups has varied between a minimum of three people [Wortman87] and a maximum of five. Whenever possible a group size of four has been used, this size being found to be the optimum to ensure that all members "pulled their weight" without any one member becoming too dominant. Two or three such groups make up the total numbers for a single course.

The project work usually involves programming in a high level language such as Pascal, Coral or C though occasionally the project has required the use of an assembler language. Often the course follows an earlier GPT course in the same language so the graduates are familiar with both the language and the equipment provided at the GPT training centre. The training centre staff also get to know the graduates before the course which enables the teams to be picked with each group having a range of abilities and with every group having an equal chance of producing the best project.

33.3   Choice of Project

A number of different projects have been used for this course. In each case the project is chosen such that it would be possible to produce some usable software in the time available. However, there is always scope for any team to attempt to take on more than they can handle, and there is little margin for inefficiency and error in the development schedule.

Where possible a "real" project is used [Burns87], such as development of an administration system for the GPT Training Centre's own needs. There is no doubt that the thought that the best project would be actually used gives a little bit of extra motivation. Motivation has never been a problem, however, as each participant has to be present for the contractual company hours, and graduates are normally very keen to get on and do something positive within their new company environment. Successful courses have been run using simple computer games as the target product. Indeed, any project seems to be successful providing the participants can find some interest in the product they are developing.

33.4   Project Supervision

Supervision of the course is full time with at least one member of staff overseeing the two or three project groups involved. During the course the course leader will take on specific roles relating to the project. At any one time the course leader can play the part of:

- The lecturer or technical consultant — giving technical advice regarding the computer hardware and software, and any Software Engineering problems. Advice over problems encountered is often provided in the form of a help-desk where the advice is limited to a response to the symptoms presented. This means that if the graduates do not fully investigate the problem before seeking advice the consultant will give the most "likely" cause for the symptoms described, even though in reality the course leader may know there is some other underlying cause.

- The customers — who may have some overall technical knowledge but cannot follow, in detail, how any proposed system will work. As with all "real" customers, they can be vague about requirements, can change their mind, and can say things they didn't really mean!

- The manager — who may ask for project plans, progress reports and technical details, from time to time. Managers can apply additional requirements or constraints on the project teams working methods. They may also apply pressure when the project gets behind schedule.

- The quality auditor — who reinforces the manager role with quality checks and inspections of documentation and code throughout the project.

These roles are for the most part kept quite distinct. Course leaders will make it clear which role they are taking at any one time and will refuse to answer questions unsuitable for their current role, with comments such as "Only the customer would know that". Advice is also limited to the current role, so that, for example, as "the customer" course leaders will happily agree to product suggestions even though they know, as "technical consultants" the suggestions would be difficult, or impossible to put into practice.

33.5   Course Introduction — The First Day

The course starts with a half day of lectures giving an introduction to the industry working methods and practices and explaining some of the problems of working in groups. Although the amount the graduates take in at this stage is limited, and many graduates of computer science will have covered the same theory in their degree course, it is useful to refer back to these lectures as problems arise and at the end of the course. Indeed, it is possible to make quite accurate predictions of where problems will arise in the project knowing full well that most of the problems will still occur despite the warnings. This element of "I told you so" helps to drive home the message as the remainder of the course unfolds.

By lunch time of the first day the course participants are given the problem they are to undertake. The specification is deliberately vague, incomplete, and in places ambiguous. The course participants are then assigned to their groups where the first task is to pool their ideas and prepare a list of questions for the customer.

During the afternoon of the first day, each group has the opportunity to interview the "customer" (or "customers" if there is more than one staff member participating). During the interview, the customers are rather naive about their own requirements. However, a considerable amount of additional information is given, depending on the skill of the interviewing groups in choosing the right questions. Some of the extra information may actually contradict the initial specification, so it is up to the groups to determine what the customers really want.

Following the interview the "manager" will ask for an initial project schedule for the remainder of the time available. The groups are given until the end of the first day to produce their schedule. Without exception every group has so far produced a plan to develop their product in a single step referred to as the "waterfall" approach by Boehm [Boehm81]. Although warnings of the dangers of this method are given during the morning's session, no attempt is made to suggest any alternative once the actual problem is revealed. It would appear that while some graduates have learned of alternatives on their undergraduate course, none have so far had any ability to put these ideas into practice. The groups are allowed to follow the "waterfall" route in order that they experience the usual problems, and can appreciate the lessons learned when discussed at the wind up session on the last afternoon of the course.

33.6   Project Documentation Activities

As the project progresses the groups are asked by their "manager" to produce several documents. The documents required and the format of the documents has varied over the years as the course has been developed. In general, a customer requirements specification, a system design specification, a detailed design specification and a project development plan are usually required in the first week of the project, and a user manual, including any installation instructions, and maintenance manual are required by the project completion time. The scope and detail of each document depends on the project undertaken and the discretion of the course leader.

Attempts are made to ensure that the groups do not get bogged down in the documentation. The customer requirements may be required in the form of a short presentation to the customer and the rest of the class. Prompt sheets are usually supplied for the system and detailed design specifications and it is stressed that hand written documents with as many crossings out as required are perfectly acceptable providing they can still be read. Sometimes a group may, despite discouragement, make persistent demands for word processing facilities. In this case, to make a point, the course leader may provide what they desire. The result is always the same, the group spends too much time making their documents look pretty while their competitors are getting on with the project.

To save time the groups may be asked to present some documents verbally to the "manager" who will take notes during the presentation. The notes are sufficient for future reference when, for example, cross checking the code against design. Questions by the "manager" can make the verbal presentation interactive — a useful way of showing the group concerned how inadequately thought out their designs and plans may be.

33.7   Quality Audits

Quality checks are made whenever a course leader is shown any document or computer listing. Regardless of which hat that may be worn at the time the course leader will refuse to examine any document or code unless it is properly identified with name, version number and time of issue. As well as stressing the need for proper release control, this frequently saves the course leader's time, for example, when asked as a technical consultant to help debug code from out-of-date listings!

At any time a group may be asked to produce documents and code listings for inspection by the "quality auditor". General checks are made for structure and style and also that the code corresponds to the design. It is not difficult to catch a group out by finding differences between the code and the design, usually as a result of inadequate initial designs leading to participants performing retrospective design with much "hacking" at the terminal.

33.8   The Course Conclusion — The Last Afternoon

The deadline for completing the project work is the lunch time of the final day. During the last afternoon the groups each give a demonstration of their product and a short presentation where each group describes not only what they have done, but also how well they have performed as a team. As well as the "customer" in the person of the course leader, other members of the training centre staff and often the participants own managers will attend the final demonstrations and presentations. All those attending, including the competitor groups, may ask questions and pass comments on each team's performance. The knowledge that their managers may attend the final presentations gives a useful added incentive for all participants to produce a respectable performance during the course.

Following the presentations the course leader holds a "wash up" session reviewing the progress made and emphasising the lessons to be learned. It is usually possible to make useful comparisons at this stage, each group having encountered different problems through their projects. It is often possible to show the penalty paid by a group for a mistake by drawing on the experience of a competitor group who has not done things in quite the same way. The groups are encouraged to make their own comments and observations in this session, as a point is more forcibly made if it comes from the course participants rather than a member of the training centre staff.

33.9   Project Progress

The normal progress pattern for the project courses is for all to appear to go well in the first week. Half way through the week the groups will have what they consider to be a well thought out specification, and a realistic plan to produce the goods in the time available, usually they even allow a little leeway for things to go wrong. Neither the specification nor the plan will be flawless with an experienced course leader having little difficulty in finding a few holes in their proposals. Nevertheless after a bit of patching the participants are able to get under way, and indeed, during the remainder of the first week, and perhaps the first day of the second, the groups usually manage to keep within, if not ahead of their schedule.

The first signs of trouble usually come in the early part of the second week when the "quality auditor" points out differences between code and design. The initial design is usually inadequate or flawed and corrections have invariably been made at the terminal, directly to the code. The dangers of this action are often not fully appreciated at this stage as graduates appear to regard this method of working as normal even if they admit it is undesirable.

By about the second day of the second week the groups begin to see the first problems appear as they attempt significant integrations of different members' work. By half way through the second week there are signs of concern, if not alarm, that the deadline of the end of the week may not be met. The remainder of the week becomes a mad scramble to get something ready in time. The pressures of the second week often begin to show on the course participants who have been known to fall out with each other as recriminations fly over why a delay has occurred. The demonstrations at the end of the week are more often than not accompanied by a series of excuses as the products fail to live up to the specifications and are found to be full of errors.

33.10   Natural Disasters and "Dirty Tricks"

During the second week significant disasters seem to occur to hold up progress, an unknown fault will be found in the compiler, a team member will be off sick for a day, or the computer response will fall to an unacceptable level. Despite warnings, few participants make adequate backups of their work and configuration control is often haphazard. Some of these disasters will occur naturally as they would in any real working environment. However, within the space of two weeks, if left to their own devices groups can be either lucky or unlucky as to how many and how serious are the disasters. Here the course leader plays a significant role by making it certain that all sorts of real world problems occur. With a little "help" the computer or network will crash at the most inconvenient times and urgent errands are found that involve taking key team members away from the project at critical moments. A particularly mean "dirty trick" that has been used is to take a copy of one or more groups work over a lunch time, and then, half a day later, to replace their current systems by the out of date copy. The time taken to recover from such mishaps can be very revealing of each group's organization and control, and can be the subject of much discussion in the course wash up session.

Many of the tricks are played in the roles of the customer, manager or technical consultant. The course leader normally plays the customer as someone who does not know what is really needed or even wanted, then as the project progresses, the customer's ideas develop in quite different directions to those of the development teams. The requirements are constantly changed and often, when groups do not document their work adequately, it is then denied that the requirements had been anything different in the first place. The manager too will make changes, altering internal deliverable deadlines, working procedures and sometimes even providing new versions of the development software, with the usual promised but not actual "backward compatibility". The technical consultant compounds the dirty tricks by ensuring that the graduates have to deduce the real cause of the problems themselves, so for example, it will be suggested that as the help desk test of the server shows it is working there cannot possibly be a system fault when in fact it is the network that has been disabled.

If a second member of staff is available, both will take the role of customer, acting as different directors of a client company. In these circumstances the customers are deliberately given different personalities, and different ideas about what they expect from the product. For example, one customer (a "Mr. Nice") may be enthusiastic jumping at every suggestion a team may make no matter how impractical, the other (a "Mr. Nasty") may have a very authoritarian "you must do it my way" attitude, putting a dampener on any suggestion that differs from his original ideas regardless of how good the suggestion is. Although many students have been told customers may differ in this way, few are prepared for the difficulties and contradictions encountered. For most graduates, it is the first time they have met this type of problem.

33.11   Assessment

There is no formal assessment of the individuals or groups on the GPT project course. Only if a course participant performs either exceptionally well or exceptionally badly will a manager be notified of an individual's performance. As managers continue to be keen to send their newly recruited graduates (and sometimes other employees) on the course it can be deduced that they are pleased with the knowledge and experience the course gives. Only on a couple of occasions has a participant performed badly and refused to learn from the course. The two individuals concerned have both since left the company having found their outlook incompatible with the company's environment.

The attitude of the participants are surveyed both informally at the final wash up session, and more formally by question sheets at the end of the course. These attitudes have on the whole given a very positive assessment of the course with participants feeling they have gained a useful insight into software development in the "real world". The course is always subject to further development, however, so constructive criticisms are welcomed and have often lead to minor changes in the way the course is run.

33.12   Lessons Learned

The lessons learned on the course are many:

- For those that have never worked within a group before the experience of sharing and coordinating the work load is invaluable. This is perhaps the most important lesson of all for those who have never worked in a team before.

- The necessity of getting the design right from beginning if the "waterfall" development model is followed is emphasized, along with the difficulties encountered if the design is changed in the coding phase. Most groups realize that the time they spent on design was inadequate when seen in retrospect.

- It is also emphasized that if the waterfall development model is to be followed then detailed intermediate documentation is necessary. For example, a design document must have considerable detail if it is to be unambiguous enough for the coding to be generated from it.

- The difficulty of getting the requirements and design correct from the beginning when dealing with "real" customers is also illustrated. At the end of the course the course leader will point out where advantage could have been gained following development strategies other than the waterfall such as prototyping [Lichter94] or evolutionary delivery [Gilb88].

- The problems of integration are emphasized, underlining the importance of defining interfaces, unit testing, and of planning, and allowing enough time for the integration process itself.

- The need for personal skills is appreciated. The students find that communication and presentation skills are required at all levels. Ideas need to be communicated to both technically minded "consultants" and non technical "customers", both formally in the form of meetings and documentation and informally between team members. It will be pointed out that a very high proportion of the problems encountered can be attributed to failures to convey or understand needs and ideas.

- The participants become more realistic in their expectations when they learn that disasters are not exceptional. Often they will complain about the inadequacies of the computer and its software, or that too much was expected from them in the time available. In each case it is pointed out that they were responsible for negotiating their own targets with the customer with a full knowledge of the development equipment before the project was started. They learn that they cannot expect to live in an ideal world.

- Finally the graduates learn about their own limitations. One of the principal problems of graduates' lack of real world awareness is that they don't realize how much they don't know. This greater realization is a healthy development with the graduates becoming much less likely to make assumptions and much more likely to learn from the day to day experiences when they start work on real projects in their own department.

In each case some or all of these lessons could be said to have been gained from the participants' university courses. The difference is in how well the lessons have been learned. The graduates will often know the theory of the points made, but they do not fully appreciate the implications when it comes to their own work. There is no doubt that software managers appreciate their new graduate entrants being brought "down to earth'! This extra realism and awareness allows the graduates to slot into an existing team more easily and increases their effectiveness by reducing mistakes made through inexperience.

33.13   The Advantages of the GPT Course

Many universities have course modules in Software Engineering and the principles are well covered in standard text books [Pressman94], [Sommerville96]. Of these courses, many contain components that appear similar to the GPT course. Although usually spread over a longer period, in parallel to their other studies, most computer science students and those on some other courses undertake group software development projects as part of a study of Software Engineering. The project sizes are often similar, with similar sized teams, and with similar documentation requirements, quality audits or role play of the supervisor [Chapman93], [Jones87], [King87], [McKeeman87], [Weiss87], [Winder87]. Why is it, therefore, that the GPT course seems more successful in getting the points across? Examination of the course in detail reveals a number of differences:

- The course participants are kept strictly to company hours while on the GPT course. No extra work is allowed even over the lunch period. Students, on the other hand, are well used to doing their work at the last minute. Many have been experiencing a last minute rush to hand in work since their early school days. It is not unusual to find students working through the night to meet a coursework hand in date. It comes as no great surprise, therefore, to find themselves in a last minute rush to finish an undergraduate project though the problem may be more severe than usual. The extra hours required at the end of a project are subconsciously planned from the start. This is not the case on the GPT course where the graduates are aware of exactly how much time they have to complete a project. Consequently they are very surprised and quite alarmed to find out how far their planning can go wrong. The strict company hours of the GPT courses play a major part in "bringing home" the lessons of scheduling and timing.

- The role play by the course leader and other members of the GPT training centre staff is significant. Although some role play is enacted by some undergraduate project supervisors the roles are not usually as formally defined and the contact hours are often limited. This role play, particularly when playing customers that do not know what they really want, who change their minds regularly and who cannot agree among themselves is a valuable insight for the graduates. Very few graduates had met more than one customer presenting different ideas and opinions in their undergraduate projects.

- The close contact and observation of the groups by the course leader allows the emphasizing of points in the "wash up" session at the end of the course by relating to events experienced by the groups during the course. Furthermore, as the groups have all been working side by side for the same set hours, each group has been able to observe the experiences of others, and, as they are all working to the same project specification, each group can see where they have been outperformed by other groups. The course leader can draw attention to these differences during the wash up session to stress the conclusions that are made.

- As undergraduate courses are normally assessed as part of the degree, university project supervisors usually try to be totally fair to the participating students. This tends to reduce the inclination to try any "dirty tricks" such as deliberately disrupting the project work. This unfortunately leaves the students with too much of an expectation of an ideal environment. The dirty tricks, although seeming a little mean at times, educate the course participants on how to cope with the inevitable occurrences of the real life environment they will later experience.

Collectively, these points mean the GPT course gives a better insight into the working methods and practices of the industrial or commercial environment. The set company hours, the role play by the course leader and even the dirty tricks help to produce the right atmosphere to facilitate typical industrial working practices, and at the same time, an experience of the "real world" is given in relatively informal way. The GPT managers appreciate their new graduates having an idea of what to expect when they start work.

There is no doubt that the GPT course has significant advantages over the undergraduate equivalent. However, this has been gained by the use of considerably greater resources of time, effort and equipment. One member of staff is able to give full time attention to a maximum of a dozen students for two weeks with another member of staff often making part time contributions throughout each course. This must seem like luxury to many university lecturers. There is no doubt that most university lecturers will feel that given this level of interaction that it would be possible to increase the effectiveness of any undergraduate course. The computer equipment provided has varied and has not necessarily been either powerful or sophisticated, but it has been of a level that each team has had all day access to either their own PCs or to terminals connected to a multi-user computer capable of giving a full and immediate service. Sometimes the groups have been restricted to the use of fewer machines than team members, but this has been as a result of a policy to try and train the participants to plan the use of their time rather than a lack of available equipment.

33.14 Improvements Made in Undergraduate Courses

Since the company first introduced their course for graduates in 1983 the course leaders have been able to observe a steady improvement in graduates awareness of real world issues. Many undergraduate courses (though by no means all) have a component devoted to this issue. On many courses it comes under a heading of "Software Engineering" but the extent that the real world experience is given to students varies widely from one course to the next. One reason for this variation is that the term "Software Engineering" covers a wide subject [Boehm76] and a module with this title can equally be applied to, say, a course on formal methods without any project work at all. Nevertheless, without going as far as using the level of resources used on the GPT course, there are now features found in many courses which, in the experience of GPT, has greatly improved the preparation of graduates for the workplace.

Most university computer science courses involve a substantial project work element and nearly all have at least one group project. Where an improvement has been seen is that more courses involve some form of real world simulation in the group project. It is now relatively common to have a project with a vague, incomplete specification with role play to provide customers from which the real requirements must be determined. Some of these courses also involve requirements that change during the project. Less common, but present in a few courses is for other changes, such as to the working procedures or the development software to be introduced into the project.

Another very positive aspect noticed in graduates in more recent years is that their courses have put increasing emphasis on the personal skills of teamwork, time management, communication and presentation. In the experience of the company these skills can make a considerable difference in the graduates effectiveness when they integrate into the real world environment.

33.15   Improvements Still to be Made in Undergraduate Courses

The improvements in the undergraduate courses are regarded by GPT to be a very positive step in the right direction but there is still little prospect of GPT's own course becoming unnecessary. For the most part the reasons lie in the extent that the GPT course covers features of the real world compared with university courses. For example, changes in customers requirements and priorities or in working conditions and practices are comparatively few in the undergraduate courses compared with the GPT course. Role play varies from one university course to another but rarely is the level used at GPT encountered, and the students are very unlikely to have met the uncertainty of customers that do not know what they want or the conflict of customers that differ among themselves.

The company is not aware of any university course that submits its students to quite the same number of "dirty tricks' as the GPT course. This is perhaps one of the more controversial aspects of the company's course. Obviously the graduates find these tricks a little annoying and care has to be taken not to go so far as disillusion the participants, but each of these tricks simulate events which are not uncommon in the everyday working environment. Once it is explained that such disasters are not exceptional and the whole point is to get them used coping with these situations, graduates will normally accept the good intentions and learn from the experience. It is the belief of the authors that undergraduate students would also take these dirty tricks in the right light if the reasons were properly explained beforehand and so universities should not shy away from this type of real world simulation to avoid any adverse student feedback.

An important advantage of the GPT course highlighted by the authors' previous research [Dawson92] was the fact that all project work was strictly limited to standard company hours. This meant that graduates couldn't compensate for poor planning estimates by putting in extra hours towards the end of a project and they could certainly not work throughout the night before a deadline as they often do while at university. It was suggested in the previous article that universities set project work with access to the computers restricted to set times to help develop better estimating and planning skills. To date the company knows of no university course where this is done although it is planned at Loughborough University for the 1995-96 session.

A further improvement the company would like to see in most undergraduate courses is to see the real world issues addressed in more than a single module where it may constitute only one thirtieth or less of the whole course. Further modules need not be in the same format giving a full simulation of the real world, but could cover certain aspects such as changing specifications, quality audits, or limited role play. Theory modules could, perhaps, devote lectures to the reasons behind the "software crisis' of late deliveries, over run budgets and unusable software [Genuchten91]. Case studies of successes and failures of software systems could make a useful contribution in this respect.

Treating real world issues in isolation in a single module can have the effect of undermining the lessons of that module. There is no point, for example, in showing the students the importance of checking with the customer the ambiguities and interpretations of the specification if in other projects in other modules supervisors will automatically accept any solution that seems to satisfy the original specification no matter how vague it may have been, and will reward students with extra marks for including extra, unasked for bells and whistles to enhance their programs. The authors are not suggesting that innovation should be stifled in other modules but that the general ethos of checking with the "customer' before going your own way should be continued.

The final judgement of whether the GPT course will remain necessary in the future will lie with the software managers who send their new graduates on the course. The indications are that within the company the managers are still not satisfied that university graduates have sufficient awareness of real world issues and so the company's course will continue to be necessary.

33.16   Conclusion

For a graduate to become a professional software engineer it is necessary to have an awareness of the problems and conditions of the real world. The GPT Software Engineering group project course provides a valuable education for new graduates entering the company, helping to give an insight into the industrial working practices and experiences of the "real world". While there is an obvious expense for such a course the enthusiasm of GPT software managers to continue sending their new graduates is a strong indication that the benefits outweigh the costs. Many universities have group projects within the Software Engineering components of their courses and these have improved the standard of awareness real world issues over recent years, but these courses do not cover the issues to the same extent and still leave the graduates short of many experiences the company feels are necessary.

There is every indication that company managers will continue to want to send their new graduates on the GPT course in the future. It must be concluded, therefore, that other companies should find the GPT course a useful model to include in their own training programmes for Software Engineering graduate recruits.

Chapter 34
Stereotypes, Young People and Computing

34.1 Introduction

This investigation was designed to discover how far stereotypes of computer folk influenced users, particularly potential entrants to the profession. The target population reported in this chapter is a group of highly-able male and female sixth-formers. The hypothesis was that target groups would be affected significantly by stereotypes, with negative attitudes being stronger among female than male students.

The results did not bear out the hypothesis, for they indicated strongly that hardly any of the group were close enough to the world of computing to be influenced either by stereotypes or any other forms of information from that domain. In fact, few young people were considering computing as a profession at all. However, the results did give rise to other questions: first and foremost, whether the findings could be replicated elsewhere (in which case the computing profession may lack highly able recruits in the future) and secondly, if sixth-formers such as the group surveyed will not be joining the profession, then what sort of people *are* filling Computer Science courses all over the country?

It is hoped that clues towards an answer to the second question may be forthcoming from work on Computer Science students in progress but, regrettably, not ready for publication here. The initial investigation is presented, in the hope that it will encourage others to conduct similar surveys, so that we have some idea of the national picture. If the findings reported here are valid nationally, then something should be done. The remainder of this chapter presents a summary of results, with a brief commentary.

34.2 Survey Information

A questionnaire was given to 155 students, all in the first week of the second year of their A level courses. There were 89 females and 66 males. 153 people were seventeen years old, one was 16 and one 18. Respondents came from three institutions: almost all the second-year sixth form (68) of an independent girls' grammar school; a similar group (42) from a boys' grammar school on the same basis, plus groups of 21 female and 24 male students from a local sixth form college. Groups one and two covered the entire spectrum of A level subjects, group three was over-represented in the biological sciences.

Groups one and two were drawn from selective schools with distinguished academic records. Both schools are within the top thirty in the "league table" of British Advanced Level national examination results. The sixth form college students include former pupils of these schools who chose to transfer at age sixteen, together with many others drawn from comprehensive and independent schools in the region. The college is one of two in the immediate area, both with exceptionally good results. Broadly speaking, the two schools and the college draw from the same pool, within which the social and academic differences between intakes to independent and state schools and colleges are less than can be found elsewhere. This is partly because the catchment area contains a high proportion of parents who having themselves experienced higher education, are determined to ensure that their children follow a similar road. Many such parents send their children to state schools, either through political conviction or because they can't afford independent school fees.

It was therefore unsurprising that significant differences could not be found as between institutions, which made it possible to pool results. Furthermore, analysis of the results showed — surprisingly perhaps — that academic orientation was not significant in any of the areas being investigated; i.e. that it was impossible to predict how far a respondent would know and use computers, or attitudes to computer stereotypes and the computing profession, on the basis of A level subject combination and career aspiration. Therefore results are given for females, males and the whole group only.

34.3   Academic Orientation and Career Intentions

	Science		Arts		Mixed	
	Number	%	Number	%	Number	%
Males	43	65	16	24	07	11
Females	42	48	34	38	13	16

Table 34.1 A Level choice areas (n = 155)

Career group	Number	%
Armed services	1	0.6
Architecture	2	1.3
Art and Design	4	2.6
Applied Sciences	7	4.5
Business, Finance, Accountancy	16	10.3
Civil Service, Politics	4	2.6
Computing (as "fall-back')	1	0.6
Doctor, Dentist, Vet	19	12.2
Engineering (all branches)	10	6.5
Farming	1	0.6
Law	7	4.5
Leisure industries, sport	3	1.9
Paramedical	10	6.5
Scientific Research	5	3.2
Teaching, Lecturing	4	2.6
Writing, Journalism, Media	8	5.2
Uncertain	53	34.2

Table 34.2 Summary career intentions (n = 155)

All students were doing three or more A or A/S levels. Their choices can be grouped into science-based, arts-based and mixed (e.g. Biology, Geography, English). Neither the schools nor the college offered A Level Computer Science. About two-thirds of respondents also indicated a career intention.

It will be seen at once that computing is hardly over-represented. A follow-up question offered an indication of the relative status of computing as opposed to other occupations. A range of 20 high-status occupations was offered, spanning the main professions, the media and other well-regarded areas, including Chartered Software Engineer and Computer Consultant. Respondents were asked to select the top three under each of the headings, "Social Status", "Pay" and "Interest". One person put "Computer Consultant" as second under "Pay". There were no other references.

A further question suggested the most likely reason for such reticence. Only a handful of the students had a clear idea of what software engineers and computer scientists actually did, and one is hardly likely to specify an occupation of which one has no knowledge. Respondents were asked to give brief job descriptions for "software engineer" and for "computer scientist". Of 155 respondents 46 (30%) attempted an answer to the first question, split roughly 50:50 between females and males. Six responses showed that the respondents had no idea of the answer, and 37 of the remaining 40 were vague, although all centred on the idea of programming. The key concept "design" appeared in sixteen meaningful answers, although only three answers constituted an accurate and informative summary of the job. There were but 22 (14%) attempts to define the work of a computer scientist, all of which were from respondents who also attempted to define "software engineer". Only three people gave reasonably accurate answers to both questions.

In short, most respondents had no idea what either job entailed and a large percentage of those who even attempted an answer thought that "software engineer" was equivalent to "programmer". It is hardly surprising, therefore, that hardly anyone opted for an occupation which appeared so limited in scope. A "computer scientist", by the way, was thought by most people to be a scientist who used a computer as an aid to research.

A commentator on an early draft of this chapter questioned how far one might reasonably expect a group of seventeen year old students to be able to distinguish between "computer scientist" and "software engineer", especially as there are no universally agreed definitions even within the industry. This would have been a strong objection if one had expected precise definitions and distinctions. However, the questions aimed to do no more than discover if there was even an elementary understanding about the work of either of the two professional groups, and to that extent they were successful.

34.4 Computing Experience

What factors are in play which apparently cause teenagers such as these not to consider computing as a career?

A first step was to see if the respondents had too little practical experience of computing to understand the potential interest and possibilities of a career.

The answer to that question is a firm "No". All students reported that they could operate a computer. Almost all had first encountered computers between the ages of 6 and 11, the number of newcomers tailing off steeply after that age. Respondents were asked what was the most important source of their learning. The sources were as might be expected, but with one striking difference: 34 females (38% of all females) reported "school subject" as their most important source of learning, against 4 (6%) of males, whereas 31 males (47% of males) said they were self taught against 20 (22%) of females. Numbers taught by close family members or friends were roughly equal between genders.

All respondents have access to a computer at home or at school, or both. Table 34.3 summarizes responses to the (alternative) questions "Do you own a computer?" or "Is a computer available to you at home?"

	Males (n = 66)		Females (n = 89)		All (n = 155)	
	Number	%	Number	%	Number	%
Available	11	17	28	31	39	25
Owned	48	73	44	49	92	59
Total	59	89	72	81	131	84

Table 34.3 Computer availability

The students were asked how many hours they spent on any computer during term, under the headings "School or college work", "Private work, e.g. Word processing", "Games', "Programming and computer related work". 139 respondents (90%) used a computer for some purpose or another for at least one hour during the week. 11% of males and 12% of females estimated use at three hours per week, and 20% of males and 14% of females claimed to use the computer for more than three hours a week. A total of eight people (5 males 3 females) used a machine for games only. Thus the remainder made constructive use of the machines for educational and other purposes.

The conclusions here are that one or more machines are available for respondents to use if they wish, and that many do wish. This view was supported by responses to a question on the use of computer-aided sources of information. Full figures are not relevant here, but it is interesting to note that 111 respondents (72%) had used an information bearing CD ROM, such as Microsoft *Encarta*. There is also evidence of Internet use, not necessarily recent, by up to 20% of respondents. Males formed a clear but not overwhelming majority. Intensive personal use of the Internet now is probably about 2%, all male, with up to a further 8% of occasional use by both sexes.

The evidence taken as a whole suggests that respondents have accepted computers as a tool for work and leisure, to be used or set aside like any other tool. The evidence is against technophobia, ignorance or operational inexperience as factors in dissuading respondents from participating in computer-related activities.

34.5 Technical Knowledge and Computing Interest

The use of a tool does not, of course, indicate any special interest in tool making. I'm unlikely to be alone in just wanting the car to go when I turn the key, and leaving everything else to that group of benevolent public servants known collectively as the motor trade. The same is true of computing. Nevertheless, one wished to see if evidence of technical interest could be found, since such interest might be a prelude to a career commitment. Three questions were asked which would be easily answered by anyone who had considered, for example, whether a given machine would be suitable for purchase, or possessed even a superficial technical interest. 61% of respondents were unable to give a positive answer to all the questions; namely; "does the computer run Windows?", "Does the computer have more than 8 Mbytes of RAM?" "Does the computer possess a modem for talking to other computers?" The remainder could manage some or all of the questions.

Programming is rightly seen as one of the activities which differentiates what might be called a "computer-participant" from a "computer-user", and in some areas, notably games, the industry recruits a significant number of young programmers, who sometimes become entrepreneurs and computer professionals in their own right. Thirteen males claimed to do programming work, 9 for up to two hours per week, 3 for up to five hours, and one "hero" for more than ten hours a week. Only two females claimed to program, each for not more than one hour per week. It was noted that most of the total of 15 (10%) also gave acceptable job definitions for software engineer, which suggests that they were relatively knowledgeable. However, in two cases at most was programming activity linked to a possible career in computing.

The conclusion is straightforward enough: that a large majority of respondents have a computer, or access to one, and use it as they wish, but that somewhere between two thirds and three-quarters are indeed turnkey drivers, with no interest in what is happening under the bonnet.

34.6   Stereotypes

At first sight these findings are surprising, particularly for males. Who reads all those magazines? Whoever such people may be, respondents to the questionnaire are not a part of them. Yet if such people were not frightened of computers and had practical experience of their value, why did so few go further?

One suspects that several factors are at work. Inadequate careers advice, the social background of most entrants to the profession ('blue collar?') and patterns of recruitment within the industry all come to mind. Yet the question remains as to why gifted people, blessed with curiosity, with access to careers information and many other sources of knowledge, apparently do not investigate further. Putting it colloquially, why aren't more of them hooked? Could it be due to the effects of stereotypical views of computing professionals, and thus the profession to which they belong?

The absence — perhaps surprising — of a standard theoretical work on the origins and development of cultural or occupational stereotypes and their influence, requires one, for want of a better authority, to offer some suggestions myself.

Obviously, the subject must first experience the stereotype, through the media or via peer group or family, for it to have any effect. But the strength and influence of that experience is likely to vary, as may the degree to which the stereotype itself is recognized by a person as an influence on his or her thinking.

A stereotype may well be referred to, or quoted or adapted by other media, and not necessarily within the same cultural matrix as the original, so that it is both uttered and heard in a different context, where its influence may be less. Thus it is possible for a particular stereotype to be so well-known in one context, that *afficionados* assume it is known universally with the same force, whereas it is barely remarked or adopted but superficially elsewhere. To anticipate part of my conclusion, this is what has happened insofar as stereotypes of computing enthusiasts are found among the group under discussion. Stereotypical influence is present, and not without effect, but is often indirect and unperceived by the subjects, who are getting a reduced dose, so to speak, rather than the full fix which addicts.

Those within the computing profession may well take it for granted that many cultural stereotypes circulated via the media are universally known and potent when they are neither. Had that been the case, such an environment would have favoured and initiated recruitment through emulation. One thought that young males, including those of superior ability, would be familiar with that cultural environment, which they would individually either accept or reject. Equally, such is the power of stereotypical thinking itself, one assumed that young females would also be aware of the stereotypes (though perhaps to a lesser extent) but that such stereotypes themselves, because many of them are derogatory in nature, would dissuade young women even more than young men from considering the profession.

Sources from which respondents were likely to absorb stereotypes were checked one by one. Space forbids more than a summary of conclusions here. Essentially, most respondents saw a "serious" daily or Sunday newspaper not less than three times a week and a smaller number one of the "popular" national newspapers. Very few read specialist computing, general scientific or other magazines. Therefore they had no contact with the fevered world of *Byte* or *Personal Computer World*, or even *Computer Shopper*. The point is highly significant, because those magazines are inspiration and opinion-formers for many computer users and some industry professionals.

Nor did the group derive many ideas from scientific films or television programmes, for they saw but few of either. Furthermore, when asked if a headline suggesting that the story which followed was about computers made them more or less willing to read on, a substantial number replied "less", although the majority said it made no difference. The actual criteria for choosing whether or not to go on were unclear.

Science fiction was a significant reported category of reading. Since this genre includes material about computers, it is possible that it has contributed some stereotypes, either of the of the machines themselves or the eccentric nature of their operators. However, most respondents were unable to supply magazine, book or programme titles and descriptions relating to computers. The minority who replied mentioned only current productions, such as *The X Files* or the *Alien* series. The only computer specifically mentioned was "Hal", the computer which behaved badly in the film *2001*.

The conclusion is that our respondents, in common with the rest of the population, were exposed to some degree to the mainly derogatory stereotypes of computer people to be found in the mass media; that such general impressions, rather than hard information about computers or the computing profession, were probably the main sources of such stereotyped thinking as they displayed, but that the effects were little more than superficial.

Next we tried to find out whether the group recognized common stereotypical terms. The first set of questions asked whether respondents were able to define commonly-found stereotypical terms, as listed in Table 34.4.

Term	Suggested Definition	Correct Identification %		
		Males	Females	All
Boffin	scientific expert	70	73	71
Hackerl	very talented programmer	5	2	3
Hacker2	breaks into computer systems	85	93	90
Tekkie1	medium/low grade service engineer	38	25	30
Tekkie2	has deep technical knowledge	14	4	9
Nerd	socially hopeless	71	79	75
Suit	patronizing senior business person, often without technical knowledge	23	9	19
Anorak	person devoted to low status recreation, e.g. train-spotting	68	73	71

Table 34.4 Definition of stereotypical terms

The significance here is that those terms most often found in the media in general, "Boffin", "Nerd" and "Anorak", were well known to the group. A number of respondents selected other definitions for Nerd and Anorak which associated those derogatory terms with computer people. The percentage selecting the second, more acceptable, definition of "Tekkie" (having deep technical knowledge) is lower than its alternative, a point made even more forcefully with regard to "Hacker", where the mass-media pre-emption of the word has been preferred by the group, to the chagrin of specialists. Clearly, most of the group know most of the terms, but not within an informed cultural environment of personal computing. Consequently, they are potentially open to influence by the stereotype and denied the corrective knowledge which membership of a specialist computer sub-culture would bring. These findings are consistent with the general proposition that the group's perspective is of the outsider, looking in.

Further questions asked respondents how far they agreed with statements expressing stereotypical characteristics sometimes attributed to those interested in computers, particularly stereotypes which might lead a youngster to conclude that computing was not for him or her. The results are in Table 34.5.

"People seriously interested in computers are often . . ."	% Agree or strongly agree	% No view	% Disagree or strongly disagree
Intelligent but boring	59	17	24
Uninterested in sport	51	18	31
Obsessive, take their interest too far	47	29	22

Table 34.5 Percentage agreeing with selected statements on computing (n = 155)

Twenty individuals (13%) agreed or strongly agreed with all three propositions while ten (6%) disagreed or strongly disagreed with all three. Six (4%) had no view on any of these questions. The remaining 119 differed between questions. In all cases males were more "anti" than females, the percentages agreeing or strongly agreeing with each proposition being 62m 58f, 63m 42f & 53m 42f. The "no views" were about the same percentages of males and females for each question. The figures suggest that a derogatory stereotype is held, but not strongly, by a majority of respondents.

A further series of questions tested attitudes to the computing profession itself. Respondents were asked to state how far they agreed with the following statements:

Statement	Strongly agree or agree (%)	No view	Strongly disagree or disagree (%)
An aptitude for maths is essential in computing	50	15	35
A career in computing has little human interest	33	24	43
Computing requires exceptionally logical people	43	35	21

Table 34.6 Percentage agreeing with selected statements on computing (n = 155)

There is a persistent stereotype that a computer person must have something of the characteristics of the machine he or she controls; precise, numerate, logical and cold. Clearly, respondents were inclined to that view. This is a damaging characteristic so far as recruitment is concerned, since many people are frightened of mathematics and will anyway rarely characterize themselves as "exceptionally logical". 53% of young women held the view that exceptional logical abilities were needed, against 33% of young men. By a slimmer margin (54% to 45%) more young women than young men also thought that one had to be mathematical to succeed in computing. Nevertheless, this view too is not deeply held. 70% of young men and 66% of young women agreed with the statement that "Anyone reasonably intelligent can become a computer professional".

The statement that computer people are "much the same as any other scientifically-minded person" did not command the same unanimity, since 54% of young women and only 33% of young men were in agreement. It may be that young men consider they have a clearer picture of what constitutes a "computer person" than do young women, and are prepared to be more dogmatic.

Once again one detects a relatively shallow, but not trivial, bias against considering the profession as compared to others. After all, if one is "exceptionally logical" and has "an aptitude for maths" then, if other things are not equal — and they are not — then a whole variety of careers might beckon. If the influence of stereotypes causes high-ability leavers to see computing as less attractive than other careers, no matter what the truth may be, then the profession will lose a proportion of capable people who might otherwise have joined. If true, this would be regrettable, and there is no guarantee that a supply of equally capable people will be found from other sources. The danger of stereotypes is that they blind people to the truth; in this case the opportunities for job satisfaction and high earnings available in the profession.

34.7 Women and Computing

This section has been partly shaped by the work of others, particularly Gillian Love-grove, at Staffordshire University [Lovegrove95]. She lists ten factors relating to poor recruitment. We looked at five of these: role models; equal access; the perceptions that computing is a career for men, is just programming, lacks fulfilment and human interest.

Female respondents were asked if they knew personally any woman who held a technical job in computing, or lectured in computing at a University. Twenty-one out of eighty-nine (24%) answered "Yes". Since women hold around 10% of senior jobs in IT the figure appears to be encouraging, and not inherently improbable from students living in a high-tech area. However, only six respondents could specify what jobs the women cited actually did; namely: two programmers, two technical support personnel, one software designer and one IT consultant to a housing authority. This is hardly an inspiring group when compared with the substantial group of distinguished women in the region, which includes academics, a high-profile Member of Parliament and other public figures, plus a number of successful businesswomen. In any event, as no female student expressed any interest in computing, such role models as were available had not inspired emulation.

Equal access has been discussed above. The evidence shows, as far as this group is concerned, that no member of the group is denied access to a computer, or has had no experience of computers as a child. The quality of that experience is a different matter not explored here, but even if it was adverse for girls, figures for usage reported here suggest that they have overcome earlier indifference or inhibitions (if they ever existed) and now use computers as they see fit. Indeed, the implied link between early experience and current intention in the statement "Women get very little time on computers when young. As a result they rarely consider computing as a career." was rejected by 47% of female respondents, although 33% agreed.

Another possibility is that women may be dissuaded from what appears to be a profession short of human interest. This was rejected; 47% of females disagreeing with the statement that "a career in computing has little human interest." (Only 37% of males took that view.) Few of the group had any time for the statement "Computers are toys for the boys, and should be left to them." (63% of males and 89% of females disagreed.) The view that "The culture of computing is too male-oriented for women to feel comfortable", "split the vote", as it were, with 37% of females agreeing, 34% disagreeing and 29% having no view. Since none of the young women had had the opportunity to experience the culture of computing, however that phrase is to be interpreted, it is encouraging that about one third of them were prepared to reject the stereotype and another third to suspend judgement.

A bread-and-butter question asked for views on the statement that "Computing does not offer as good pay and working conditions as most other professions available to able women". Again, lack of information clearly prompted respondents to withhold judgement: 52% of females were not prepared to accept the proposition, 37% had no view and only 11% implied that they would be prepared to reject a career in computing. The figures for males were 21% agreed with the statement, 41% had no view and 33% felt that computing could offer women as materially worthwhile career as any other.

Two related questions tested certain other stereotypes relating to women's psychology and preferences. The first question read in full: "Women's intelligence differs from that of men. Men are better at writing computer programs and analysing systems, women better at many other equally worthwhile occupations." As might perhaps be expected from a sophisticated and confident group, the presumption behind the question was rejected by 72% of the young women; 19% expressed no view and only 10% were prepared to agree. Only one female respondent "strongly agreed" with the proposition. The figures for young men were 37% agreeing, 24% having no view and 33% disagreeing.

The second question substituted the word "interests" for "intelligence", and in this case the results were more diffuse. One third of the young women respondents agreed with this view, 43% rejected it and 25% expressed no view. The figures for the young men were similar at 36%, 33% and 24%.

The overall picture gained by this part of the investigation is that it would not take too much effort to shift young women's perspectives of computing as a profession. Most of the figures suggest a prudent reserve, stemming from knowing that one has insufficient knowledge of the matter to be heavily committed. There is no evidence that a large number of young women are for some mysterious psychological or social reason "put off" by computing. Significantly, the attitudes of male respondents to the same set of questions are not dissimilar in many respects. The evidence is against the propositions that young women actively rule out computing because it is "for" men, or because they feel that they will be odd-people-out in a "man's" profession. Whether young women from less supportive and sophisticated backgrounds do have that feeling is for others to investigate.

34.8 Conclusions

There is a perceptible but apparently not deep-rooted feeling among the group, something between indifference and mild aversion perhaps, to computing as a profession. It is relatively more strongly marked in young women but also distinctly present in their male counterparts.

This attitude does not stem from ignorance of computers or lack of experience in computing. Nor does it arise from adverse experiences of the profession itself, because contacts between group and members of the profession are few and superficial. Therefore it may be ascribed, at least in part, to the effects of cultural and occupational stereotyping offered repeatedly in the mass media and sufficiently potent to help form attitudes, though not strong enough to promote a wholesale aversion.

The positive counter-influence of a sub-culture of computing, centred on specialist magazines and books (which are themselves notable sources for stereotypes) is not brought to bear because hardly any respondents encounter such literature. The books, films and television programs consumed by this group of young people rarely transcend the traditional stereotypes of what computers and their operators do to describe intellectually challenging issues in computing or engaging and remunerative professional activities.

The results of the survey are not encouraging. There is a strong flow of recruits into computing, some of whom are of high quality, but one must question how many nationally are top flight, when a group such as that surveyed, whose background suggests that it is less likely to be ignorant of the power and interest of Software Engineering and Computer Science than any other, contributes almost no-one to that flow.

Granted that there are several routes of entry into the profession for capable people; for example, conversion MSc courses, or direct entry by graduates in a variety of subjects, to Software Engineering and other enterprises. But what we need most is a far greater supply of really able people with straight Computer Science as a first degree, and I wonder if we are getting enough of them. If we are not, who — if anyone — has the duty of changing the situation by making the nature and benefits of the profession clearly apparent to all potential university entrants of both sexes?

Finally, one is conscious that the research on which this chapter is based is limited and by no means methodologically impeccable. I would welcome further studies, as well as enough time to dig a good deal deeper myself. But the results have a measure of consistency and substance, and their implications are challenging.

Bibliography

[Abbott88]   Abbott A. *The System of Professions: An Essay on the Division of Expert Labour* University of Chicago Press 1988

[Abrahams75]   Abrahams P. *Structured Programming Considered Harmful* SIGPLAN Notices, April 1975, pp 23

[Acey95]   Acey M. *Bill to Promote Women in IT* Computer Weekly, 16 March 1995

[ACM/IEEE91]   ACM/IEEE-CS Joint Curriculum Task Force *Computing Curricula 1991* ACM Press and IEEE-CS Press, 1991

[ACM91]   *ACM Code of Professional Conduct* in [Kling95], pp 693-697

[ACM92]   *ACM Code of Ethics and Professional Conduct* ACM, 1992

[Aiken71]   Aiken M & Hage J. *The organic organization and innovation* Sociology, vol 5, 1971, pp 63-82

[Aldrich86]   Aldrich H & Auster R. *Even dwarfs started small: liabilities of age and size and their strategic implications* in Staw B & Cummings L (eds) *Research in Organizational Behavior* vol 8, JAI Press, 1986 pp 65-198

[Andersen94]   Andersen R et al. *Project Courses at the NTH: 20 Years of Experience* in [Diaz94] pp 177-188

[Anderson93]   Anderson R et al. *Using the New ACM Code of Ethics in Decision Making* CACM (36) 1, 1993

[Anderson94]   Anderson R. *The ACM Code of Ethics: History, Process, and Implications* in Huff C & Finholt T (eds) *Social Issues in Computing: Putting Computing in its Place* McGraw-Hill, 1994

[Ashridge91]   Ashridge College *A Profile of the Nineties Manager* Information Technology Environments, WiT, 1991

[Balkin88]   Balkin DB & Logan JW. *Reward policies that support entrepreneurship* Compensation and Benefits Review, (20) 1, 1988 pp 18-25

[Barby94]   Barby S & Strohmeier A. *The problematics of testing object-oriented software* SQM'94 Proceedings, vol 2, 1994, pp 411-426

[Bate94]   Bate R et al. *A systems engineering capability maturity model, version 1.0* Software Engineering Institute, 1994

[Bayles81]   Bayles M. *Professional Ethics* Wadsworth, 1981

[BCS90a]   British Computer Society *TickIT making a better job of software. Guide to Software Quality Management System Construction and Certification using EN29001* DTI, 1990

[BCS90b]   British Computer Society *Future Impact Of Information Technology* BCS, 1990

[BCS90c]   British Computer Society *From Potential to Reality* BCS, 1990

[BCS92]   *British Computer Society Code of Conduct* BCS, 1992

[BCS93]   *British Computer Society Code of Practice* BCS, 1993

[BCS95]   *British Computer Society Review and Directory* BCS, 1995

[BCSPR92]   British Computer Society *Notes for Membership Panel Assessors* distributed by BCS Membership Committee to their Professional Review panel assessors, 1992

[Beckett95]   Beckett A. *Revenge of the Town Planners* Independent on Sunday, 22 January 1995 pp 8-9

[Bentley92]   Bentley C. *Introducing PRINCE: The Structured Project Management Method* NCC Blackwell, 1992

[Berleur94]   Berleur J & d'Udekem-Gevers M. *Codes of Ethics, or of Conduct, within IFIP and in other Computer Societies* 13th World Computer Congress 1994 pp 340-348

[Betts92]   Betts A. *Euromethod: The Rationale, Conference Systems Development Methods in Europe: 1992 and All That* April 8-9, BCS, University of Bristol, 1992

[Beynon95a]   Beynon-Davies P. *Information Systems Failure and Risk Assessment: the case of the London Ambulance Service Computer Aided Despatch System* Proc. ECIS'95 Athens, June 1995

[Beynon95b]   Beynon-Davies P. *Information System Work: Professionalism and Professionalisation* Working Paper, Department of Computer Studies, University of Glamorgan, 1995

[Bierce11]   Bierce A. *The Devil's Dictionary* Originally published 1991, Enlarged Edition, Penguin, 1967

[Billington83]   Billington DP. *The Tower and the Bridge: The New Art of Structural Engineering* Basic Books, 1983

[Bissett95]   Bissett AK & Siddiqi JIA. *How will the CMM fare in Europe?* in [Ross95], pp 171-182

[Black92]   Black G. *Small is beautiful – and cheap* Software Management 32, 1992

[Bodker91]   Bodker S & Gronbaek K. *Design in Action: from prototyping by demonstration to cooperative prototyping* in Greenbaum J & Kyng M (eds) *Design at Work: Cooperative Design of Computer Systems* Erlbaum, 1991

[Boehm76]   Boehm BW. *Software Engineering* IEEE Trans (C-25) 12, 1976, pp 1226-1241

[Boehm81]   Boehm BW. *Software Engineering Economics* Prentice-Hall, 1981

[Boehm88a]   Boehm BW & Ross R. *Theory W Software Project Management: principles and examples* in Boehm BW (ed) *Software Risk Management* IEEE Press, 1988

[Boehm88b]   Boehm BW. *A spiral model of software development and enhancement* IEEE Computer, May 1988, pp 61-72

[Borking95]   Borking J & Cavoukian A *Privacy Enhancing Technologies: The Path to Anonymity* Information and Privacy Commissioner, Canada & Registratiekamer, The Netherlands, 1995

[Bott95]   Bott MF et al. *Professional Issues in Software Engineering* (2nd edition) UCL Press, 1995

[Brackhane85]   Brackhane R. *Zur Einordnung der beruflichen Rehabilitation in ein umfassendes psychologisches Concept*, Die Rehabilitation Heft 2, 1985

[Brahams89]   Brahams D & Wyatt J. *Decision-aids and the Law* Lancet ii, 1989 pp 632-634

[Bratchell82]   Bratchell GE. *Letter* The Structural Engineer, October 1982, pp 334

[Bray90]   Bray I, Jones O & Webster S. *Software product design: an organising concept for Software Engineering education* Journal of Information Technology 5, 1990 pp 37-40

[Broadman94]   Broadman JG & Johnson DL. *What small organisations say about the CMM* Proceedings 16th International Conference Software Engineering, IEEE Computer Society, 1994

[Brooks87a]   Brooks F. *No Silver Bullet: Essence and Accidents of Software Engineering* IEEE Computer (20) 4, 1987, pp 10-19

[Brooks87b]   Brooks F. *People Are Our Most Important Product* in [Gibbs87], pp 1-15

[Brooks95]   Brooks F. *The Mythical Man-Month* (2nd edition) Addison-Wesley, 1995

[Bucciarelli94]   Bucciarelli LL. *Designing Engineers* MIT Press, 1994

[Burgelman88]   Burgelman R & Sayles L. *Epilogue: A new organizational revolution in the making* in Burgelman R & Maidique A (eds) *Strategic Management of Technology and Innovation* Irwin, 1988

[Burns87]   Burns JE & Robertson EL. *Two complimentary course sequences on the design and implementation of software products* IEEE Trans Soft Eng (SE-13) 11, 1987, pp 1170-1175

[Carey92]   Carey T et al. *Half a loaf is better than waiting for the bread truck: a computerised mini-medical record for outpatient care* Archives of Internal Medicine 152, 1992, pp 1845-1849

[Cassell93]   Cassell C & Walsh S. *Being seen but not heard: Barriers to women's equality in the workplace* The Psychologist 6, 1993, pp 110-114

[CCTA90a]   CCTA *SSADM Version 4 Reference Manual* NCC Blackwell, 1990

[CCTA90b]   *SSADM Version 4: An Introduction* CCTA and the Central Office of Information, 1990, pp 30

[Chalmers95]   Chalmers D. *The Puzzle of Conscious Experience* Scientific American, December 1995

[Chapman93]   Chapman N et al. *"Slick systems" and "happy hackers": experience with group projects at UCL* Soft Eng Journal (8) 3, 1993 pp 132-136

[Checkland81]   Checkland P. *Systems Thinking Systems Practice* Wiley, 1981

[Checkland90]   Checkland P & Scholes J. *An Application of Soft Systems Methodology in the NHS* in *Soft Systems Methodology in Action* Wiley, 1990

[Church96]   Church J (ed). *Social Trends* Central Statistics Office, 1996

[Cockburn93]   Cockburn C & Ormrod S. *Gender and Technology in the Making* Sage, 1993

[Coe92]   Coe T. *The Key to the Men's Club* Institute of Management, 1992

[Cohen80]   Cohen S. *Folk Devils and Moral Panics: the creation of the mods and rockers* Martin Robertson, 1990

[Comer89]   Comer JR, Nute T & Rodjak DJ. *Some Observations on Teaching a Software Project Course* in [Fairley89], pp 215-229

[Computing92]   *Labour calls for inquiry into ambulance system* Computing 24 September 1992, pp 5

[Computing95]   *Join the NV Queue* Computing, 25 May 1995

[Constantine93]   Constantine LL. *Work organization: Paradigms for project management and organization* CACM (36) 10, 1993, pp 35-43

[Constantine95]   Constantine LL. *Constantine on peopleware* Yourdon Press, 1995

[Couger90]   Couger JD. *Motivating analysts and programmers* Computerworld, 15 January 1990, pp 73-76

[Couger95]   Couger JD & Ishikawa A. *Comparing motivation of Japanese computer personnel versus those of the United States* Proceedings 28th Annual Hawaii

International Conference on System Sciences, IEEE Press 1995 pp 1012-1019

[Council85]   Council Directive 85/374 of 25 July 1985 *on the Approximation of the Laws, Regulations and Administrative Provisions of the Member States Concerning Liability for Defective Products*

[Council89a]   Council Directive 89/336 of 3 May 1989 *on the Approximation of the Laws of Member States relating to Electromagnetic Compatibility*

[Council89b]   Council Directive 89/392 of 14 June 1989 *on the Approximation of the Laws of the Member States relating to Machinery*

[Council89c]   Council Directive 89/655 of 30 November 1989 *Concerning the Minimum Safety and Health Requirements for the Use of Work Equipment by Workers at Work (Second Individual Directive Within the Meaning of Article 16(1) of Directive 89/391* [OJ 1989, L393/13]. Enacted in Great Britain by the Provision and Use of Work Equipment Regulations 1992

[Council89d]   Council Directive 89/686 of 21 December 1989 *on the Approximation of the Laws of the Member States Relating to Personal Protective Equipment* [OJ 1989. L399/18]. Enacted in Great Britain by the Personal Protective Equipment at Work Regulations 1992

[Council90]   Council Directive 90/270 of 29 May 1990 *on the Minimum Safety and Health Requirements for Work with Display Screen Equipment* Commonly referred to as the "VDU Directive"

[Council91]   Council Directive 91/263 of 29 April 1991 *on the Approximation of the Laws of the Member States Concerning Telecommunications Terminal Equipment, Including the Mutual Recognition of their Conformity*

[Council92a]   Council Directive 92/59 of 29 June 1992 *on General Product Safety* [OJ 1992, L 228/24] (Enacted in the United Kingdom by the General Product Safety Regulations 1994)

[Council92b]   Council Directive 92/31 of 28 April 1992 *Amending Directive 89/336 on the Approximation of the Laws of the Member States Relating to Electromagnetic Compatibility*

[Council92c]   Council Directive 92/91 of 3 November 1992 *Concerning the Minimum Requirements for Improving the Safety and Health Protection of Workers in the Mineral-Extracting Industries Through Drilling (Eleventh Individual Directive Within the Meaning of Article 16(1) of Directive 89/391)*

[Council93a]   Council Directive 93/68 of 22 July 1993 *Amending ... Directive 89/336 (Electromagnetic Compatibility) ...*

[Council93b]   Council Directive 93/97 of 29 October 1993 *Supplementing Directive 91/263 in Respect of Satellite Earth Station Equipment*

[Cowling94]   Cowling AJ. *A Framework for Developing the Software Engineering Curriculum* Proc. ACM/IEEE International Workshop on Software Engineering Education, Sorrento, 1994, pp 111-118

[Crewe83]   Crewe NM & Zola IK. *Independent Living for Physically Disabled People* Jossey Bass Books, 1983

[Cronin92]   Cronin C & Kelly M. *Gender differences in technology: A way forward for women in Computing in Teaching Computing: Content and Methods* WiC National Conference, 1992

[Curtis88]   Curtis B, Krasner H & Iscoe N. *A Field Study of the Software Design Process for Large Systems* CACM 31 (11), 1988 pp 1268-1287

[Curtis90]   *Empirical Studies of the Software Design Process* in Diaper D et al (eds)
                Human-Computer Interaction – INTERACT '90 Elsevier, 1990, pp 35-40

[Curtis93]   Curtis B & Paulk M. *Creating a software process improvement program* Inf
                and Soft Tech (35) 6, 1993, pp 381-386

[Curtis95]   Curtis B, Hefley WE & Miller S. *People Capability Maturity Model draft
                version 0.3* Software Engineering Institute, 1995

[CW92]   *BCS President blames training for 999 failure* Computer Weekly, 19 Novem-
                ber 1992

[Dahlbom93]   Dahlbom B & Mathiassen L. *Computers in Context: The Philosophy and
                Practice of Systems Design* NCC Blackwell, 1993

[Dain88]   Dain J. *Getting Women into Computing* University Computing 10, 1988

[Davidson92]   Davidson M & Cooper C. *Shattering the Glass Ceiling* Paul Chapman, 1992

[Davis92]   Davis CJ et al. *Current practice in software quality and the impact of certi-
                fication schemes* Software Quality Journal 2, 1992 pp 145-161

[Dawson92]   Dawson RJ, Newsham RW & Kerridge RS. *Introducing new Software Engi-
                neering graduates to the "real world" at the GPT company* Soft Eng Journal,
                (7), 3, 1992 pp 171-176

[DeMarco87]   De Marco T & Lister T *Peopleware* Dorset House Publishing, 1987

[Deming86]   Deming WE. *Out of the Crisis* Cambridge University Press, 1986

[Dennet91]   Dennet D. *Consciousness Explained* Allen Lane, 1991

[Dennis91]   Dennis M. *TickIT: The DTI Involvement, Management and Design Division
                Colloquium on TickIT Certification Initiative: Objectives and Practice* IEE,
                1991

[Diaz94]   Diaz-Herrera JL (ed). *Software Engineering Education* Proc. 7th SEI CSEE
                Conf., San Antonio, LNCS 750, Springer, 1994

[Dion93]   Dion R. (1993) *Process Improvement and the Corporate Balance Sheet* IEEE
                Software, 10, 4. 1993 pp 28-35

[Downey68]   Downey WG. *Report of the Steering Group on Development Cost Estimating*
                HMSO, 1968 (the Steering Group reported in 1966 but its report was not
                published until 1968).

[DTI89a]   Department of Trade and Industry *The STARTS Guide* (2nd edition) NCC,
                1989

[DTI89b]   Department of Trade and Industry *The STARTS Purchasers' Handbook* (2nd
                edition) NCC, 1989

[DTI92]   *TickIT programme: Launch of 1993 Awards* JFIT News No 39, 1993

[DTI95]   Department of Trade and Industry *Schools Online to Internet* Tim Eggar
                Press Notice, 21 March 1995 pp 1-2

[Dunlop91]   Dunlop C & Kling R. *Social Controversies about Computerisation* in
                [Kling95]

[Earl89]   Earl MJ. *Management Strategies for Information Technology* Oxford Uni-
                versity Press, 1989

[Edwards89a]   Edwards HM, Thompson JB & Smith P. *Results of a Survey of the Use of
                SSADM in Commercial and Government Sectors in UK* Inf and Soft Tech
                (31) 1, 1989 pp 21-28

[Edwards89b]   Edwards HM, Thompson JB & Smith P. *Experiences in the Use of SSADM:
                A Series of Case-Studies. Part 1: First Time Users* Inf and Soft Tech (31) 8,
                1989 pp 411-419

[Edwards89c]   Edwards HM, Thompson JB & Smith P. *Experiences in the Use of SSADM: A Series of Case-Studies. Part 2: Experienced Users.* Inf and Soft Tech (3) 8, 1989 pp 420-428

[Ehn89]   Ehn P. *The Art and Science of Designing Computer Artefacts* Scandinavian Journal of Information Systems 1(1), 1989 pp 21-42

[Elliot72]   Elliot P. *The Sociology of the Professions* Macmillan, 1972

[Erlinger89]   Erlinger MA & Tam WC *An Academic Environment for Undergraduate Software Engineering Projects* in [Fairley89], pp 286-296

[Ermann90]   Ermann MD, Williams MB & Gutierrez C (eds). *Computers, Ethics and Society* Oxford University Press, 1990

[Etlinger90]   Etlinger HA. *A Retrospective on an Early Software Projects Course* ACM SIGCSE Bulletin 22 (1), 1990 pp 72-77

[Etzioni69]   Etzioni A. *The Semi-Professions and their organisation: teachers, nurses and social workers* Free Press, 1969

[Fairley89]   Fairley R & Freeman P (eds). *Issues in Software Engineering Education* Springer, 1989

[Ferguson92]   Ferguson ES. *Engineering and the Mind's Eye* MIT Press, 1992

[Finniston84]   Finniston M. *Overview of Issues in Engineering Education* in Goodlad S (ed) *Education for the Professions* Society for Research into Higher Education, 1984, pp 56-73

[Fletcher95]   Fletcher S. *seminar on "the Accreditation practises within ABET"* HKIE, 18 November 1995

[Forsythe93]   Forsythe DE. *Using ethnography to build a working system: Rethinking basic design assumptions Proceeding of the Sixteenth Annual Symposium on Computer Application in Medical Care* McGraw-Hill, 1993, pp 505-9

[Fox93]   Fox J. *Decision-support systems as safety-critical components: towards a safety culture for medical informatics* Methods of Information in Medicine 32, 1993, pp 345-8

[Frankfort92]   Frankfort-Nachmiais C & Nachmiais D. *Research Methods in the Social Science* (4th edition) Edward Arnold, 1992

[Freeman95]   Freeman E & Hupfer S. *TAP: Tapping Internet resource for women in Computer Science* CACM (38) 1, 1995

[Frey91]   Frey J & Finan W. *Engineering Education in Japan: A Career-long Process* Engineering-Education (81) 5, 1991, pp 466-72

[Friedman94]   Friedman B & Kahn P. *Educating Computer Scientists: Linking the Social and the Technical* CACM 37 (1), 1994, pp 65-70

[Frost95]   Frost R. *Behind the Hardware* Times Educational Supplement, 10 March 1995

[FT92a]   Financial Times *Staff revert to trusted radio and telephones* 30 October 1992, pp 4

[FT92b]   Financial Times *Dire effects of a failure to communicate: what caused the London Ambulance Service computer system to crash?* 30 October 1992, pp 1

[Galliers R92]   Galliers R. *Information Systems Research: issues, methods and practical guidelines* Blackwells, 1990

[Garfinkel67]   Garfinkel H. *Studies in Ethnomethodology* Prentice-Hall, 1967

[Genuchten91]	van Genuchten M. *Why is Software Late? An empirical study of reasons for delay in software development* IEEE Trans Soft Eng, (SE-17) 6, 1991, pp 582-590
[Gibbs87]	Gibbs N & Fairley R (eds). *Software Engineering Education: The Educational Needs of the Software Community* Springer, 1987
[Gibbs94]	Gibbs WW. *Software's Chronic Crisis* Scientific American, September 1994, pp 72-81
[Gilb88]	Gilb T. *Principles of Software Engineering Management* Addison-Wesley, 1988
[Gladden83]	Gladden GR. *Stop the Life-Cycle, I Want to Get Off* Software Engineering Notes 7 (2), 1983, pp 35-39
[Goffman90]	Goffman E. *Stigma: notes on the management of spoiled identity* Penguin, 1990
[Gotel94]	Gotel O & Finkelstein A. *An Analysis of the Requirements Traceability Problem* Proceedings of the First IEEE International Conference on Requirements Engineering, Colorado Springs, 18-22 April 1994, pp 94-101
[Gotterbarn91]	Gotterbarn D. *Computer Ethics: Responsibility Regained* National Forum: The Phi Kappa Phi Journal (LXXI) 3, 1991
[Goyal95]	Goyal A. *Mentoring Resources and programs for Women* CACM (38) 1, 1995
[Gregg93]	Gregg P & Machin S. *Is the Glass Ceiling cracking?* Paper 50, National Institute for Economic Research, 1993
[Guardian92]	Guardian *Ambulance Chief Resigns* 29 November 1992, pp 1-2
[Gürer95]	Gürer DW. *Pioneering Women in Computer Science* CACM (38) 1, 1995
[Hall94]	Hall T & Fenton N. *Implementing software metrics – the critical success factors* Software Quality Journal 3, 1994, pp 195-208
[Hall95a]	Hall T. *What do developers really think about software quality?* in [Ross95], pp 359-368
[Hall95b]	Hall T & Fenton N. *Software practitioners and software quality improvement* ACM International Conference on Software Quality, 1995
[Halstead77]	Halstead MH. *Elements of Software Science* North-Holland, 1977
[Hammer93]	Hammer M & Champy J. *Reengineering the Corporation* Harper Collins, 1993
[Hampden94]	Hampden-Turner C. *Corporate Culture* Piatkus, 1994, pp 11
[Hansard95]	Hansard *Women and Information Technology Bill* House of Commons, 7 March 1995, pp 147-150
[Hardy95a]	Hardy C, Thompson JB & Edwards HM. *A Survey of SSADM Usage in the UK, Occasional Paper 95-3* School of Computing and Information Systems, University of Sunderland, 1995
[Hardy95b]	Hardy C et al. *A Comparison of the Results of Two Surveys on Software Development and the Role of CASE in the UK* CASE95, Toronto, Canada, July 1995
[Hardy95c]	Hardy C, Thompson JB & Edwards HM. *The Use, Limitations and Customisation of Structured Systems Development Methods in the United Kingdom* Inf and Soft Tech, September 1995
[Harel80]	Harel D. *On Folk Theorems* CACM 23 (7), 1980, pp 379-389

[Heathfield93]   Heathfield HA & Wyatt J. *Medical Informatics: Hiding our Light under a Bushel, or the Emperor's New Clothes?* Methods of Information in Medicine 32, 1993, pp 181-182

[HEA95]   Health Education Authority *Expectations for the Future* 27 April 1995, pp 1-11

[Heathfield94]   Heathfield HA et al. *The PEN&PAD medical record model: A report of its use in the development of a clinical record system for hospital-based care of the elderly* Methods of Information in Medicine 33, 1994, pp 464-72

[Heathfield95]   Heathfield HA. *Decision Support Systems Synopsis* in IMIA Year Book of Medical Informatics, Schattauer, 1995

[Helle88]   Helle KM. *Voice Control equipment for the severely Disabled* Work Research Institute, 1988

[Helle90]   Helle KM & Tiller H. *Ny Teknologi og Yrkesmessig Attføåring* Work Research Institute, 1990

[Hemenway95]   Hemenway K. *Human Nature and the Glass Ceiling in Industry* CACM (38) 1, 1995

[Henlis91]   Henlis F. *Young Women and the Culture of Software Engineering* in Lovegrove G & Segal B (eds) *Women into Computing Selected papers 1988-1990* Springer, 1991

[Henwood93]   Henwood F. *Establishing Gender Perspectives on Information Technology: problems. Issues and Opportunities* in Green E, Owen J & Pain D (eds) *Gendered by Design* Taylor and Francis, 1993

[Hiles75]   Hiles J. *1975 National Computer Conference – Report on Selected Sessions* IEEE Computer, June 1975, pp 14

[Hirsh89]   Hirsh W & Jackson C. *Women into Management – Issues Influencing entry of women into Managerial jobs* Institute of Manpower Studies Paper 158, University of Sussex, 1989

[Holbrook94]   Holbrook D. *Technical Advance and the Organization of R&D: The Cases of Shockley Semiconductor Laboratories and Fairchild Semiconductor Corporation* paper at the annual meeting of the Society for the History of Technology, Lowell, Massachusetts, 1994

[Horning77]   Horning JJ & Wortman DB. *Software Hut: a computer program engineering project in the form of a game* IEEE Trans Soft Eng (SE-3) 4, 1977, pp 325-330

[Hounshell84]   Hounshell DA. *From the American System to Mass Production, 1800-1932* Johns Hopkins University Press, 1984

[HMSO71]   *Government Organisation for Defence Procurement and Civil Aerospace, Cmnd 4641*. HMSO, 1971

[HMSO93]   HMSO *Wessex Regional Health Authority Regional Information Systems Plan* 63rd Report of the Committee of Public Accounts, 1993

[Huax94]   Haux R & Leven FJ. *Twenty years medical informatics education at Heidelberg/Heilbronn: Evolution of a specialised curriculum* IMIA Year Book of Medical Informatics, Schattauer, 1994, pp 111-116

[Hull82]   Hull F & Hage J. *Organizing for innovation: Beyond Burns and Stalker's organic type* Sociology vol 16, 1982, pp 563-577

[Humphrey91a]   Humphrey WS. *Software and the Factory Paradigm* Soft Eng Journal (6) 5, 1991, pp 370-376

[Humphrey91b]   Humphrey WS, Snyder TR & Willis RR. *Software Process Improvement at Hughes Aircraft* IEEE Software (8) 4, 1991, pp 11-23

[IEEE75]   *Editorial* IEEE Trans on Soft Eng, March 1975, pp 1

[IM94]   *Management Development to the Millennium, the Cannon and Taylor Working Party Reports*, Institute of Management Research Report, July 1994

[Ince95]   Ince D. *Clockwork Factories* Times Higher Education Supplement, 10 March 1995

[ISM91]   British Computer Society *Industry Structure Model, Release 2* BCS, 1991

[ISO87]   *ISO 9000/1/2/3/4 Standards for Quality Management Systems* ISO, 1987

[Jackson70]   Jackson JA (ed). *Professions and Professionalisation* Cambridge University Press, 1970

[James79]   James P. *Introduction to English Law* Butterworths, 1979

[Johansen91]   Johansen R. *Longum Park etter et åšrs drif* Work Research Institute, 1991

[Johansson94]   Johansson C, Ohlsson L & Molin P. *Teaching Object-Orientation: from Semi-Colons to Frameworks* in King G et al (eds) *Software Engineering in Higher Education* Computational Mechanics Publications, 1994, pp 367-374

[Johne84]   Johne FA. *How experienced product innovators organize* Journal of Product Innovation Management vol 1, 1984, pp 210-233

[Johnson82]   Johnson TJ. *Professions and Power* Macmillan, 1982

[Johnson90]   Johnson B. *Going live at Penguin* in People and Technology: *How to make your IT investment work for you* Economist Conference Proceedings, 1990

[Johnson94]   Johnson DG. *Computer Ethics* (2nd edition) Prentice-Hall, 1994

[Johnston94]   Johnston L & Dart P. *Building on Experience: An Undergraduate Course with Two Year-Long Projects* in [Diaz94], pp 345-357

[Jones87]   Jones A & Birtle M. *An individual assessment technique for group projects in Software Engineering* Soft Eng Journal (2) 4, 1987, pp 226-232

[Jordan87]   Jordan G, Lee I & Cawsey G. *Learning from Experience: A Report on the Arrangements for Managing Major Projects in the Procurement Executive* Ministry of Defence, 1987

[Jorgensen95]   Jorgensen A. *Survey Shows Policies on Ethical Issues Still Lacking Enforcement Mechanisms* Professional Ethics Report (VIII) 1, 1995

[Joyce87]   Joyce E. *Software bugs: a matter of life and liability* Datamation 33, 5 May 1987, pp 88-92

[Kanter77]   Kanter RM. *Men and Women of the Corporation* Basic Books, 1977

[Kaplan94]   Kaplan B & Maxwell JA. *Qualitative Research Methods for Evaluating Computer Information Systems* in Anderson JG, Aydin CE & Jay SJ (eds) *Evaluating Health Care Information Systems* SAGE Publications, 1994

[Kassirer78]   Kassirer J & Gorry G. *Clinical decision analysis* Annals of Internal Medicine 89, 1978, pp 245-55

[Kidder81]   Kidder T. *The Soul of a New Machine* Little Brown, 1981

[Kim93]   Kim KK & Umanath NS. *Structure and perceived effectiveness of software development subunits: A task contingency analysis* Journal of Management Information Systems (9) 3, 1993, pp 157-181

[King87]   King PJB. *Experiences with group projects in Software Engineering* Soft Eng Journal (2) 4, 1987, pp 221-225

[Klawe95]   Klawe M & Levensen N. *Women in Computing - Where are we Now?* CACM (38) 1, 1995

[Klein87]   Klein HK & Hirschheim RA. *A Comparative Framework of Data Modelling Paradigms and Approaches* Computer Journal 30 (1), 1987, pp 8-14

[Kling95]   Kling R & Dunlop C (eds). *Computerization and Controversy: Value Conflicts and Social Choices* Academic Press, 1995

[Kolodny80]   Kolodny HF. *Matrix organization designs and new product success* Research Management vol 23, 1980, pp 29-33

[Kraft79]   Kraft P & Biggar L. *Women suffer at the bottom of the DP line* Computing, 19 July 1979

[Kraut95]   Kraut RE & Streeter LA. *Coordination in software development* CACM (38) 3, 1995, pp 69-81

[Kumar92]   Kumar A. *Women in IT* BSc project, School of Informatics, City University, 1992

[Lakhanpal93]   Lakhanpal B. *Understanding the factors influencing the performance of software development groups: an exploratory group-level analysis* Inf and Soft Tech 35, 1993, pp 468-473

[Lancet90]   *Medical Informatics* (editorial). Lancet 335, 1990, pp 824-825

[Land76]   Land F. *Evaluation of Systems Goals in Determining a Design Strategy for a Computer-Based Information System* Computer Journal 19 (4), 1976, pp 290-294

[Langford95]   Langford D. *Practical Computer Ethics* McGraw-Hill, 1995

[Larson77]   Larson MS. *The Rise of Professionalism: A Sociological Analysis* Univ of California Press, 1977

[Leavitt92]   Leavitt R & Wall A. *The Reorganised National Health Service* (4th edition) Chapman and Hall, 1992

[Leeming93]   Leeming A. *Breaking through the glass ceiling; Women and management education* Working paper, London City University Business School, 1993

[Leeming94]   Leeming A. *Letting down the Ladder Women developing management education* Working paper, BAM Conference Lancaster University, 1994

[Leeming95a]   Leeming A. *Acquiring Critical Competencies in IT and Management* Forum 95/1, 1995

[Leeming95b]   Leeming A & Olaitan A. *How to improve Marketing in the UK Software and Computing Services Industry* Report to the Worshipful Company of Information Technologists, 1995

[Leventhal87]   Leventhal LM & Mynatt BT. *Components of typical undergraduate Software Engineering courses: Results from a survey* IEEE Trans Soft Eng (SE-13) 11, 1987, pp 1193-1198

[Leveson95]   Leveson NG. *Safeware: System Safety and Computers* Addison Wesley, 1995

[Levy94]   Levy S. *Hackers* Penguin, 1994, (especially pp. 226-231)

[Lichter94]   Lichter H, Schneider-Hufschmidt M & Zullighoven H. *Prototyping in industrial software – Bridging the gap between theory and practice* IEEE Tran Soft Eng (SE-20) 11, 1994, pp 825-832

[Lie95]   Lie M. *Technology and Masculinity* European Journal of Women's Studies (2) 3, 1995

[Lloyd85]   Lloyd A & Newell L. *Women and Computers* in Arnold E & Faulkner W (eds) *Smothered by Invention* Pluto Press, 1985

[Logica88]   Logica Consultancy *Quality Management Standard for Software. A review for the Department of Trade and Industry* Logica, 1988

[Lovegrove87]   Lovegrove G & Hall W. *Where have all the girls gone?* University Computing 9, 1987

[Lovegrove94a] Lovegrove G et al. *Staffordshire IT EQUATE: Project and Plans* IFIP Conference on Women, Work and Computerization, Manchester UK, 1994, pp 511-518

[Lovegrove94b] Lovegrove G, Whitehouse C & Williams S. Women and Computing: IT EQUATE, Staffordshire University and Schools International Conference on The Development and Role of Women in Technology, Beijing, China, 1994, pp 189-195

[Lovegrove94c] Lovegrove G. *Report on the presentation of Women in Computing* Conference of Professors and Heads of Computing, Staffordshire University, 1994

[Lovegrove95]   Lovegrove G. *Women in Computing* in [Myers95], pp 110-133

[Lyytinen87]   Lyytinen K & Hirschheim R. *Information Systems Failures: a survey and classification of the empirical literature* Oxford Surveys in Information Technology vol 4 1987, pp 257-309

[MacCallum85]   MacCallum SL. *The Software Hut* Computer Bulletin (1) 1, 1985, pp 8-9

[MacKenzie90]   MacKenzie D. *Inventing Accuracy: A Historical Sociology of Nuclear Missile Guidance* MIT Press, 1990

[Mace87]   Mace BM. *Software Engineering within the context of a Computer Science degree programme* Soft Eng Journal (2) 4, 1987, pp 200-202

[Mackie77]   Mackie J. *Ethics* Penguin, 1977

[Madsen95]   Madsen J. *The Reptilian World of Software Teams* in [Myers95], pp 91-109

[Marciniak90]   Marciniak JJ & Reifer DJ. *Software Acquisition Management* Wiley, 1990

[Marr94]   Marr PB et al. *Bedside terminal and quality of nursing documentation* 1994 Yearbook of Medical Informatics, Schattauer, 1994, pp 241-247

[Marshall84]   Marshall J. *Women – Travellers in a male world* Wiley, 1984

[Martin90]   Martin CD & Martin DH. *Professional Codes of Conduct and Computer Ethics Education* Computers and Society (20) 1, 1990

[McCabe76]   McCabe TJ. *A complexity measure* IEEE Trans Soft Eng SE-2, 1976, pp 308-320

[McDermid91]   McDermid JA (ed). *Software Engineers Reference Book* Butterworth-Heinemann, 1991

[McDermid93]   McDermid JA. *Requirements Analysis: Orthodoxy, Fundamentalism and Heresy* in Bickerton M & Jirotka M (eds) *Requirements Engineering* Academic Press, 1993

[McFarlan84]   McFarlan FW. *Information Technology changes the way you compete* Harvard Business Review, May-June 1994

[McGuire96]   McGuire EG. *Initial effects of software process improvement on an experienced software development team* Proceedings of the 29th Hawaii International Conference on System Sciences, vol I, IEEE Computer Society Press, 1996, pp 713-721

[McIntyre92]   McIntyre SC. *Overcoming ad hoc development: Enabling / Disabling factors in software quality maturation* Proceedings of the 25th Hawaii International Conference on System Sciences, vol IV, IEEE Computer Society Press, 1992 pp 624-633

[McIntyre94]   McIntyre SC. *Organizational issues underlie software quality* Proceedings
                of the 27th Annual Hawaii International Conference on System Sciences,
                IEEE Computer Society Press, 1994, pp 820-821

[McKeeman87]   McKeeman WM. *Experience with a Software Engineering project course*
                IEEE Trans Soft Eng (SE-13) 11, 1987, pp 1182-1192

[McMahon84]   McMahon MA. *The Making of a Profession: A Century of Electrical Engi-
                neering in America* IEEE Press, 1984

[Mead95]   Mead G. *BSc Honours Degree in Computer Studies: Quality Enhancement
                Project* Graham Mead Associates, City University of Hong Kong, September
                1995

[Melford95]   Melford R. *If We Don't License Ourselves, Who Will?* IEEE Software (12)
                3, 1995

[Meyer91]   Meyer JW & Rowan B. *Institutionalized Organizations: Formal Structure
                as Myth and Ceremony* in Powell W & DiMaggio P (eds) *The New Institu-
                tionalism in Organizational Analysis* University of Chicago Press, 1991

[Miller82]   Miller RA, Pople HE & Myers JD. *INTERNIST-1, an experimental
                computer-based diagnostic consultant for general internal medicine* New
                England Journal of Medicine 307, 1982, pp 468-76

[Miller83]   Miller D. *The correlates of entrepreneurship in the three types of firms*
                Management Science (29) 7, 1983, pp 770-791

[Mintzberg79]   Mintzberg H. *The Structuring of organisations* Prentice-Hall, 1979

[Mishkin95]   Mishkin B. *Enforcing Codes of Conduct Through Professional Associations*
                Professional Ethics Report (VIII) 2, 1995

[Mohammed95]   Mohammed WEA & Siakas KV. *Assessing quality management maturity* in
                [Ross95], pp 325-336

[Moore87]   Moore WL. *New product development practices of industrial marketers*
                Journal of Product Innovation Management vol 4, 1987, pp 6-19

[Moore94]   Moore M & Potts C. *Learning by Doing: Goals and Experiences of Two
                Software Engineering Project Courses* in [Diaz94], pp 151-164

[Murray91]   Murray F. *Technical Rationality and the IS Specialist: Power, discourse and
                identity* Critical Perspectives on Accounting 2, 1991, pp 59-81

[Musen92]   Musen MA et al. *T-HELPER: Automated support for community-based
                clinical research* in Frisse ME (ed) *Proceedings of the Sixteenth Annual
                Symposium on Computer Applications in Medical Care* MacGraw Hill,
                1992, pp 719-723

[Museum95]   Science Museum London. *Destination Cyberspace? Bridging the Gender
                Gap on the Information Superhighway* 21 June 1995

[Myers95]   Myers C (ed). *Professional Awareness in Software Engineering* McGraw-
                Hill, 1995

[NAO94]   National Audit Office *Ministry of Defence: Defence Procurement in the
                1990s* HMSO, 1994

[Naur69]   Naur P & Randell B (eds). *Software Engineering: Report on a Conference
                Sponsored by the NATO Science Committee (Garmisch, Germany October
                7-11, 1968)* Scientific Affairs Division, NATO, Brussels, 1969

[NCET92a]   *Gender and the New Technologies, A reading list* Management of IT and
                Cross-curricular Issues, Directory of Information vol 3 MAN 6.3, August
                1992

[NCET92b]   *Gender Issues in Education with regard to Information Technology/Computing: evidence from research studies and statistical publications* Management of IT and Cross-curricular Issues, Directory of Information vol 3 MAN 6.2, October 1992,

[Neumann85]   Neumann PG. *What is Software Engineering?, Revisited* Software Engineering Notes, July 1985, pp 4

[NewSci92]   New Scientist *Did ambulance chiefs specify "safety" software?* 7 November 1992, pp 5

[Newton91]   Newton P. *Computing an ideal occupation for a woman?* in Firth-Cozens & West (eds) *Women at Work* Open University Press, 1991

[Nicholson95]   Nicholson IA et al. *Motivation of quality practitioners* in [Ross95], pp 350-357

[Nieswiadomy93]   Nieswiadomy RM. *Foundations of Nursing Research* (2nd edition) Appleton and Lange, 1993

[Nygren92]   Nygren E & Henriksson P. *Reading the medical record* Computer Methods and Programs in Biomedicine (I) 39, 1992 pp 1-12

[O'Connell94]   O'Connell F. *How to run successful projects* Prentice-Hall, 1994

[O'Neil80]   O'Neil D. *Interview* Comics Feature, (1) 4, July-August 1980

[Oppenheim92]   Oppenheim AN. *Questionnaire Design, Interviewing and Attitude Measurement* (2nd edition) Pinter, 1992

[Oz94a]   Oz E. *Ethics for the Information Age* Business and Educational Technologies, 1994

[Oz94b]   Oz E. *When Professional Standards are Lax: the Confirm failure and its lessons* CACM 37 (10), 1994, pp 29-36

[Page93]   Page D, Williams P & Boyd D. *Report of the public inquiry into the London ambulance service* South West Regional Health Authority, 1993

[Palmer90]   Palmer C. *Hybrids – A Growing Initiative* Computer Bulletin (2) 6, 1990

[Parker90]   Parker D, Swope S & Baker B. *Ethical Conflicts in Information and Computer Science, Technology and Business* QED Information Sciences, 1990

[Parnas86]   Parnas DL & Clements PC. *A Rational Design Process: How and Why to Fake It* IEEE Trans on Soft Eng (12) 2, 1986, pp 251-257

[Paulk93]   Paulk M et al. *Capability Maturity Model, Version 1.1* IEEE Software, July 1993, pp 18-27

[Pearl95]   Pearl A. *Editorial* CACM (38) 1, 1995

[Peel94]   Peel VJ *Management-focused health informatics research and education at the University of Manchester* Methods of Information in Medicine 33, 1994, pp 273-277

[Penrose94]   Penrose L. *Shadows of the Mind* Oxford University Press, 1994

[Peters82]   Peters TJ & Waterman RH. *In Search of Excellence* Harper Collins, 1982

[Petroski85]   Petroski H. *To Engineer is Human: The Role of Failure in Successful Design* St Martin's Press, 1985

[Petroski94]   Petroski H. *Design Paradigms: Case Histories of Error and Judgment in Engineering* Cambridge University Press, 1994

[Pitt95]   Pitt D. *Implications of the Data Protection Act* in [Myers95], pp 28-47

[Pressman94]   Pressman RS. *Software Engineering – A Practitioner's Approach* McGraw-Hill, 1994

[Pressman95]   Pressman RS. *A people-centered approach to software process improvement*
                  Software Process Improvement Forum (2) 2, 1995, pp 8-12

[PriceW88]   *Software Quality Standards: The Costs and Benefits* Price Waterhouse, 1988

[PriceW89]   *Information Technology Review* Price Waterhouse, 1989–1995

[Priestley95]   Priestley M. *Discipline or Punish: The cruelty of Not Teaching Software
                  Engineering* in [Myers95], pp 176-194

[ProMan94]   *Today's Male Managers Face Extinction* Professional Manager magazine,
                  September 1994

[Quintas94]   Quintas P. *Programmed Innovation? Trajectories of Change in Software
                  Development* Information Technology & People 1, 1994, pp 25-47

[Race91]   Race J. *Computer-encouraged Pilot Error* Man-Machine Interface Seminar,
                  IME, October 1991

[Radcliffe80]   Radcliffe Richards J. *The Sceptical Feminist* Penguin, 1980

[Rasch92]   Rasch RA & Tosi HL. *Factors affecting software developers' performance:
                  An integrated approach* MIS Quarterly, September 1992, pp 395-409

[Rector93]   Rector AL et al. *A framework for modelling the electronic patient record*
                  Methods of Information in Medicine 32, 1993, pp 109-119

[Rettig93]   Rettig M & Simons G. *A project planning and development process for small
                  teams* CACM (36) 10, 1993, pp 45-55

[Reynolds86]   Reynolds TS. *Defining Professional Boundaries: Chemical Engineering in
                  the Early 20th Century* Technology and Culture, October 1986, pp 694-716

[Riddle85]   Riddle WE. *Letter from the Chairman* Software Engineering Notes, April
                  1985, pp 2-3

[Roberts95]   Roberts E. *Women in Computer Science: Barriers to Academic Success* Jing
                  Lyman lecture series Institute of Research on Women and Gender, Stanford
                  University, 1995

[Robillard89]   Robillard PN. *A Project -Based Software Course: The Myth of the "Real-
                  World"* in [Fairley89], pp 297-308

[Robinson91]   Robinson M & Bannon L. Questioning Representations. in Bannon L, Robin-
                  son M & Schmidt K (eds) *Proceedings of the Second European Conference
                  on Computer-Supported Co-operative Work* (ECSCW-91), Amsterdam, The
                  Netherlands, 25-27 September 1991, pp 219-233

[Rogerson95]   Rogerson S & Bynum T. *Identifying the ethical dimension of decision making
                  in the complex domain of IS/IT* ETHICOMP95 Conference, 1995

[Roper88]   Roper BM. *Training first year undergraduates to produce quality software*
                  University Computing 10, 1988, pp 9-12

[Rosener90]   Rosener JB. *Ways Women Lead* Harvard Business Review, 1990

[Ross95]   Ross M et al. *Software Quality Management III, vol 1* Computational Me-
                  chanics, 1995

[Rowe87]   Rowe PG. *Design Thinking* MIT Press, 1987

[Royce70]   Royce WW. *Managing the development of large software systems: Concepts
                  and techniques* Proceedings of WESTCON, California, 1970

[Rugg93]   Rugg D. *Using a Capability Evaluation to Select a Contractor* IEEE Software
                  (10) 4, 1993, pp 36-45

[Ruse93]   Ruse M. *The significance of evolution* in [Singer93], pp 500-510 (with an
                  excellent list of references)

[Ryle49]   Ryle G. *Concept of Mind* Hutchinson, 1949

[Saleh87]   Saleh SD. *Relational orientation and organizational functioning: A cross-cultural perspective* Canadian Journal of Administrative Sciences (4) 3, 1987, pp 276-293

[Sauer93]   Sauer C. *Why Information Systems Fail: A Case Study Approach* Alfred Waller, 1993

[Scase89]   Scase R & Goffee R. *Women in Management – towards a Research Agenda* British Academy of Management Conference, 1989

[Schwartz70]   Schwartz WB. *Medicine and the Computer: The Promise and Problems of Change* New England Journal of Medicine 283, 1970, pp 1257-1264

[Schwartz75]   Schwartz JT. *What Constitutes Progress in Programming?* CACM, November 1975, pp 663-664

[Sears92]   Sears T. *Using Team Building on Computer Courses in Higher Education* in *Women into Computing, Annual Conference*, Keele University, 1992

[Sears92]   Sears-Williams L. *Microchip vs Stethoscopes: Calgary Hospital MDs face off over controversial computer system* Canadian Medical Association Journal (147) 10, 1992 pp 1534-1547

[SEJ89]   *Editorial* Soft Eng Journal, July 1989, pp 174

[Shapero85]   Shapero A. *Managing Professional People* Free Press 1985

[Shapiro92]   Shapiro S. *Its Own Worst Enemy: How Software Engineering Has Fallen Victim to Engineering Mythology* CRICT Discussion Paper 25, Brunel University, 1992

[Shapiro94a]   Shapiro S. *Boundaries and Quandaries: Establishing a Professional Context for IT* Information Technology & People 1, 1994, pp 48-68

[Shapiro94b]   Shapiro S. *Degrees of Freedom: Standards and the Shaping of Engineering Judgment* CRICT Discussion Paper 47, Brunel University, 1994

[Shaw90]   Shaw M. *Prospects for an Engineering Discipline of Software* IEEE Software, November 1990, pp 15-24

[Shaw91]   Shaw M & Tomayko JE. *Models for Undergraduate Project Courses in Software Engineering* in Tomayko JE (ed) *Software Engineering Education Proc. SEI Conference Pittsburgh* LNCS 536, Springer 1991, pp 33-71

[Sheppard81a]   Sheppard SB & Kruesi E. *The effects of symbology and spatial arrangement of software specifications in a coding task* Proc Trends and Applications: Advances in Software Technology, NBS, Gaithersburg, MD, available from IEEE, 1981, pp 7-13

[Sheppard81b]   Sheppard SB, Kruesi E & Curtis B. *The effect of symbology and spatial arrangement on the comprehension of software specifications* Proc 5th Int Conf on Soft Eng, San Diego, CA, available from IEEE, 1981, pp 207-214

[Shneiderman82]   Shneiderman B. *Control Flow and Data Flow Structures Documentation: Two Experiments* in Ledgard H (ed) *Technical Notes: Human Aspects of Computing* CACM 25 (1), 1982, pp 55-63

[Shortliffe75]   Shortliffe EH. *MYCIN: Computer-based Medical Consultations* Elsevier, 1975

[Shortliffe90]   Shortliffe E et al. *Medical Informatics. Computer Applications in Health Care* Addison-Wesley, 1990

[Siddiqi95]   Siddiqi JIA & Bissett AK. *Quality in the software world* in Kanji GK (ed) *Total Quality Management: Proceedings of First World Congress* Chapman & Hall, 1995, pp 367-370

[Sills68]   Sills D (ed). International Encyclopedia of the Social Sciences, Macmillan Company and The Free Press, 1968

[Simon72]   Simon H. *The Sciences of the Artificial* MIT Press, 1972

[Singer93]   Singer P (ed). *A Companion to Ethics* Blackwell, 1993

[Singer94]   Singer P (ed). *Ethics* Oxford University Press, 1994

[Skidmore92]   Skidmore S, Farmer R & Mills G. *SSADM Version 4 Models and Methods* NCC Blackwell, 1992

[Smith76]   Smith A. *The Wealth of Nations* i. 10. pt.2, 1776

[Smith92]   Smith AP. *How to do it: Design an information system* British Medical Journal 305, 1992, pp 415-417

[Solomon93]   Solomon RC. *Business ethics* in [Singer94], pp 360-361

[Sommerville96]   Sommerville I. *Software Engineering* (5th edition) Addison Wesley, 1996

[Souder87]   Souder WE. *Managing New Product Innovation* DC Heath, 1987

[Spector86]   Spector A & Gifford D. *A Computer Science Perspective on Bridge Design* CACM, April 1986, pp 268-283

[Stallman85]   Stallman R. *The GNU Manifesto* Available by anonymous ftp from: labrea.stanford.edu in the directory /pub/gnu/GNUinfo

[Stats95]   Statistical Bulletin. *Survey of Information Technology in Schools* Dept of Education, 1995

[Statz94]   Statz JA. *Training effective project managers* American Programmer (7) 6, 1994

[Stealers72]   Stealers Wheel *Stealers Wheel* (Album Cover) A&M Records, 1972

[Sternberg95]   Sternberg E. *Just Business* Warner, 1995, pp 52

[Stobart91]   Stobart SC, Thompson JB & Smith P. *Use, problems, benefits and future direction of computer-aided Software Engineering in United Kingdom* Info and Soft Tech (33) 9, 1991, pp 629-636

[Stranks94a]   Stranks MB. *Training and CPD – a partnership essential to the health of an industry which is short of professionals?* Conference on Engineering Management, Institution of Engineers, Melbourne, Australia, April 1994, pp 285-290

[Stranks94b]   Stranks MB. *Training Software Engineering Professionals in Hong Kong, and the Approach of 1997* Proceedings of Software Education Conference, November 1994 University of Otago, Dunedin, New Zealand, IEEE PR5870, pp 186-190

[Sullivan93]   Sullivan SL. *A Software Project Management Course Role-Play Team-Project Approach Emphasizing Written and Oral Communication Skills* ACM SIGCSE Bulletin (25) 1, 1993, pp 283-287

[Tannen92]   Tannen D. *You just don't understand* Virago, 1992

[Tanton94]   Tanton M. *Developing Women's presence* in Tanton M (ed) *Women in Management* Routledge, 1994

[Taylor11]   Taylor FW. *The Principles of Scientific Management* Harper and Row, 1911

[Taylor90]   Taylor W. *The business of innovation: An interview with Paul Cook* Harvard Business Review (90) 2, 1990, pp 97-106

[Thamhain90]   Thamhain HJ. *Managing technologically innovative team efforts towards new product success* Journal of Product Innovation Management vol 7, 1990, pp 5-18

[Thompson90]   Thompson JB. *A Software Tool and User's Reactions to it* Computer, Man and Organisation II, Nivelles, Belgium, May 1990

[Thompson93a]   Thompson JB. Discussion following presentation of paper by Davis et al *Current approaches to software quality assurance within the United Kingdom* at Software Quality Management Conference, Southampton, England, March 1993

[Thompson93b]   Thompson K & McParland P. *Software process maturity (SPM) and the information systems developer* Inf and Soft Tech (35) 6, 1993, pp 331-338

[Tsui92]   Tsui F, Hofmann SC & Goldstrohm WJ. *A software development post-mortem summary* Soft Eng Journal 7, 1992, pp 277-284

[Turkle94]   Turkle T. quoted in *Toys and Tools* Newsweek, 16 May 1994

[Tversky74]   Tversky A & Kahneman D. *Judgment under uncertainty: Heuristics and biases* Science 185, 1974, pp 1124

[US79]   US Government Accounting Office *Report FGMSD-80-4, 1979* reported in ACM Sigsoft Soft Eng Notes 10 (5), 1985

[VanDerLei91]   van der Lei J & Musen MA. *A model for critiquing based on automated medical records* Computers in Biomedical Research, 24, 1991 pp 344-378

[vanLuijk94]   van Luijk H. *Business ethics: the field and its importance* in B. Harvey (editor) *Business Ethics: A European Approach* Prentice-Hall, 1994

[vanTyle94]   van Tyle S. *The drive to streamline software development* Electronic Design (42) 1, 1994, pp 89-92

[VTC95]   *Manpower survey of requirements in the Computing and IT industries in Hong Kong, 1994* Vocational Training Council of Hong Kong, 1995

[Vehvilainen94]   Vehvilainen M. *Women defining their Information Technology* EJWS (1) 1, 1994

[Velasquez92]   Velasquez M. *Business ethics – concepts and cases* (3rd edition) Prentice-Hall, 1992

[Veradaguer93]   Veradaguer A et al. *Validation of the medical expert system PNEUMON-1A* 1993 Yearbook of Medical Informatics, Schattauer, 1993, pp 446-461

[Vincenti90]   Vincenti WG. *What Engineers Know and How They Know It: Analytical Studies from Aeronautical History* Johns Hopkins University Press, 1990

[Virgo92]   Virgo P. *Report to PITCOM* WiT, 1992

[Virgo94]   Virgo P *The Gathering Storm* (referenced by the Parliamentary Bill introduced by Judith Church), 1994

[Walz93]   Walz D, Elam J & Curtis B. *Inside a software design team: Knowledge acquisition, sharing, and integration* CACM 36 (10), 1993, pp 63-77

[Wareham94]   Wareham E. *ISO9000 and the very small firm* IEE Review (40) 5, 1994, pp 207-209

[Wasserman76]   Wasserman AI & Freeman P (eds). *Software Engineering Education: Needs and Objectives* Springer, 1976

[Waters93]   Waters R. *The Plan that Fell to Earth* Financial Times, 12 March 1993

[Webster83]   Webster's Ninth New Collegiate Dictionary, Merriam Webster, 1983

[Webster95]   Webster J. *What do we know about gender and Information technology at Work?* EJWS (2) 3, 1995

[Weinberg71]   Weinberg GM. *The Psychology of Computer Programming* Van Nostrand Reinhold, 1971

[Weiss87]	Weiss DM. *Teaching a software design methodology* IEEE Trans Soft Eng (SE-13) 11, 1987, pp 1156-1163
[WiT92]	*The Nightmare Scenario* IT Skill Trends Report, WiT Foundation, 1992
[WiT93]	*The Nightmare unfolds* IT Skill Trends Report, WiT Foundation, 1993
[Wilson95a]	Wilson DN, Petocz P & Roiter K. *Motivation for software quality assurance in practice* (paper supplied by the authors), 1995
[Wilson95b]	Wilson DN, Petocz P & Roiter K. *A study in software quality assurance in practice* [Ross95], pp 159-169
[Winder87]	Winder R, Cole R & Easteal C. *Software Engineering in a first degree* Soft Eng Journal (2) 4, 1987, pp 133-139
[Wortman87]	Wortman DB. *Software projects in an academic environment* IEEE Trans Soft Eng (SE-13) 11, 1987, pp 1176-1181
[Wright95]	Wright S et al. *Procurement of software-rich systems* British Telecommunications Engineering (14) 2, 1995, pp 156-166
[Wyatt90]	Wyatt J & Spiegelhalter D. *Evaluating Medical Expert Systems: what to test and how* Methods of Information in Medicine, 15, 1990, pp 205-217
[Wyatt91]	Wyatt J. *Computer-based Knowledge Systems* Lancet 338, 1991, pp 1431-36
[Wyatt94a]	Wyatt J. *Use of medical knowledge systems: lessons from computerised ECG interpreters* in Barahona P & Christensen J (eds) *Knowledge and Decisions in Health Telematics* IOS Press, 1994, pp 73-80
[Wyatt94b]	Wyatt J. *Clinical data systems, PartIII: Developing and evaluating clinical data systems* Lancet 344, 1994, pp 1682-88
[Yeung95]	Yeung Kwok-keung *reported in the Campus Post Section* South China Morning Post, 8 June 1995
[Yourdon92]	Yourdon E. *Decline and Fall of the American Programmer* Prentice-Hall, 1992
[Zahniser93]	Zahniser RA. *Design by walking around* CACM (36) 10, 1993, pp 115-123
[Zultner93]	Zultner RE. *TQM for technical teams* CACM (36) 10, 1993, pp 79-91